D0936520

GEOGRAPHICAL INTERPRETATIONS OF
HISTORICAL SOURCES

STUDIES IN HISTORICAL GEOGRAPHY

General Editors: Alan R.H. Baker
                  J.B. Harley

In Preparation

CELTS, SAXONS AND VIKINGS:
STUDIES IN SETTLEMENT CONTINUITY   Glanville R. Jones

HISTORICAL GEOGRAPHY: AN INTRODUCTION   Alan R.H. Baker

ENGLISH MARKET TOWNS BEFORE
THE INDUSTRIAL REVOLUTION   J.H.C. Patten

MEDIEVAL REGIONS AND THEIR CITIES   J.C. Russell

PROGRESS IN HISTORICAL GEOGRAPHY   Alan R.H. Baker
                                                          (editor)

HISTORICAL GEOGRAPHY OF RURAL
SETTLEMENT IN BRITAIN   Brian K. Roberts

Associated volume: GEOGRAPHICAL INTERPRETATIONS OF
HISTORICAL SOURCES

Geographical Interpretations of Historical Sources

Readings in Historical Geography

Edited by

Alan R.H. Baker
University of Cambridge

John D. Hamshere
University of Manchester

John Langton
University of Cambridge

BARNES & NOBLE, Inc.
NEW YORK
PUBLISHERS & BOOKSELLERS SINCE 1873

First published in the United States of America in 1970
by Barnes & Noble, Inc.

SBN 389 04036 3

Printed in Great Britain

Contents

Preface   9

Acknowledgements   11

Geographical Interpretations of Historical Sources: Introduction   13
Alan R.H. Baker, John D. Hamshere and John Langton

Domesday Woodland   29
H.C. Darby
Reprinted from *Economic History Review*, III (1950-1), 21-43

Population Trends and Agricultural Developments from the Warwick-   55
shire Hundred Rolls of 1279
J.B. Harley
Reprinted from *Economic History Review*, XI (1958-9), 8-18

The Distribution of Wealth in East Anglia in the Early Fourteenth   71
Century
R.E. Glasscock
Reprinted from *Transactions and Papers of the Institute of British
Geographers*, 32 (1963), 113-23

Evidence in the 'Nonarum Inquisitiones' of Contracting Arable Lands   85
in England during the Early Fourteenth Century
A.R.H. Baker
Reprinted from *Economic History Review*, XIX (1966), 518-32

The Market Area of Preston in the Sixteenth and Seventeenth   103
Centuries
H.B. Rodgers
Reprinted from *Geographical Studies*, 3 (1956), 46-55

The Combination and Rotation of Crops in East Worcestershire,   117
1540-1660
J.A. Yelling
Reprinted from *Agricultural History Review*, 17 (1969), 24-43

Family Limitation in Pre-Industrial England   141
E.A. Wrigley
Reprinted from *Economic History Review*, XIX (1966), 82-109

The Foley Partnerships: The Iron Industry at the End of the   173
Charcoal Era
B.L.C. Johnson
Reprinted from *Economic History Review*, IV (1951-2), 322-40

Some Statistical Maps of Defoe's England   195
J.H. Andrews
Reprinted from *Geographical Studies*, 3 (1956), 33-45

Agricultural Changes in the Welsh Borderland. A Cultural Diffusion at   211
the Turn of the Eighteenth Century
D. Thomas
Reprinted from *Transactions of the Honourable Society of Cymmrod-orion*, Part I (1961), 101-14

Changing Regional Values during the Agricultural Revolution in   227
South Lincolnshire
D.B. Grigg
Reprinted from *Transactions and Papers of the Institute of British Geographers*, 30 (1962), 91-103

Locational Change in the Kentish Hop Industry and the Analysis of   243
Land Use Patterns
D.W. Harvey
Reprinted from *Transactions and Papers of the Institute of British Geographers*, 33 (1963), 123-44

The Urban Hierarchy and Historical Geography: A Consideration with   269
Reference to North-East Wales
H. Carter
Reprinted from *Geographical Studies*, 3 (1956), 85-101

Boroughs in England and Wales of the 1830s   291
T.W. Freeman
Reprinted from R.P. Beckinsale and J.A. Houston (eds), *Urbanization and its Problems: Essays in Honour of E.W. Gilbert* (1968), 70-91

The Pre-Urban Cadaster and the Urban Pattern of Leeds   317
D. Ward
Reprinted from *Annals of the Association of American Geographers* 52 (1962), 150-66

Contents

The Lancashire Cotton Industry in 1840   337
H.B. Rodgers
Reprinted from *Transactions and Papers of the Institute of British Geographers*, 28 (1960), 135-53

The British Hosiery Industry at the Middle of the Nineteenth Century: 359
An Historical Study in Economic Geography
D.M. Smith
Reprinted from *Transactions and Papers of the Institute of British Geographers*, 32 (1963), 125-42

The Population of Liverpool in the Mid-Nineteenth Century   381
R. Lawton
Reprinted from *Transactions of the Historic Society of Lancashire and Cheshire*, 107(1955), 89-120

Agricultural Changes in the Chilterns 1875-1900   419
J.T. Coppock
Reprinted from *Agricultural History Review*, 9 (1961), 1-16

Moated Settlements in England   439
F.V. Emery
Reprinted from *Geography*, 47 (1962), 378-88

Index   455

Preface

Historical studies have figured prominently in geographical teaching and research since the inception of the subject as an academic discipline, yet the number of published works devoted solely to topics in historical geography is relatively small. Perhaps more commonly than most of their academic colleagues, historical geographers tend to publish the results of their research as learned articles rather than books, and the absence of a journal devoted specifically to historical geography exacerbates the relative inaccessibility of its literature.

This collection of essays is intended to provide more convenient access to part of that literature. It is neither a random nor a representative sample, but is organised around the theme of source materials and their interpretation. The primary criteria used in making the selection were that the essays should illustrate the range of historical source materials that exists, the types of problems that these data present to geographical analysis, and some of the methods that have been employed to overcome these problems. Most of the essays focus on one major source or a number of similar sources because such essays best illustrate this theme, although most work in historical geography utilises material gathered from diverse sources to attack a particular problem. All the authors whose work is included are professional geographers. The editors fully realise that the semantics of academic appellation are often meaningless, and that much work done by economic historians and demographers in particular is of considerable geographical interest and relevance. Nevertheless, the work of specialist geographers is usually more apposite to the specific requirements of this volume, and the recognition of disciplinary boundaries, meaningless though they often are, provided one way of simplifying the task of selecting so few essays from the wealth that is available. The collection is also limited to works on English and Welsh topics, but this gives some unity to a group of essays which must perforce address widely differing geographical problems and utilise sources which vary greatly in type and in date.

The essays have been arranged according to the date of their principal source or group of sources rather than with reference to the historical period which they study. Thus, Emery's paper on moated settlements appears last because the Ordnance Survey maps which provided the author's basic information were compiled in the twentieth century, though the features analysed date mainly from the twelfth, thirteenth and fourteenth centuries. This method of arrangement is least satisfactory in the case of through-time studies like those of Wrigley, Johnson, Grigg, Harvey and Carter. Any method of organisation would present problems and give rise to some eccentricities of arrangement: the editors considered that their use of the date of the source employed involves the least.

Suitable essays far exceeded the number that could be included despite the limitations imposed upon selection, and the subjective whims of the editors loomed large in the final stages of selection, as in arrangement. Fortunately purely editorial shortcomings cannot detract in any way from the intrinsic merits of the essays.

Once the choice was made all the authors were invited, if they wished, to add a short note to their articles which could draw attention to more recent contributions to the same subject or to changes in the author's own views. The note of each author who accepted this invitation is published here at the end of the essay concerned.

Alan R.H. Baker
John D. Hamshere

Cambridge and Manchester, August 1969
John Langton

Acknowledgements

The editors are grateful to the following authors for permission to reprint their articles:-

H.C. Darby, J.B. Harley, R.E. Glasscock, A.R.H. Baker, H.B. Rodgers, J.A. Yelling, E.A. Wrigley, B.L.C. Johnson, J.H. Andrews, D. Thomas, D.B. Grigg, D.W. Harvey, H. Carter, T.W. Freeman, D. Ward, D.M. Smith, R. Lawton, J.T. Coppock, F.V. Emery.

We also thank the following societies for permission to reprint from their journals:-

The Economic History Society for articles by H.C. Darby, J.B. Harley, A.R.H. Baker, E.A. Wrigley, B.L.C. Johnson.
The Institute of British Geographers for articles by R.E. Glasscock, D.B. Grigg, H.B. Rodgers, D.W. Harvey, D.M. Smith.
The Geographical Association for the article by F.V. Emery.
The Honourable Society of Cymmrodorion for the article by D. Thomas.
The Association of American Geographers for the article by D. Ward.
The Historic Society of Lancashire and Cheshire for the article by R. Lawton.
The Agricultural History Society for the articles by J.A. Yelling and J.T. Coppock.

Our thanks are also due to Basil Blackwell Ltd for permission to reprint the chapter by T.W. Freeman, to Dr J.K. St Joseph for permission to reprint the air photographs used in the articles by F.V. Emery, and to the Ordnance Survey for permission to reprint the maps used in the articles by F.V. Emery and D. Ward.

Introduction

Both the purposes and the methods of historical geography have, like those of geography itself, changed over the years. As H.C. Prince pointed out in a recent review of progress in historical geography, the body of works published under the title of historical geography includes gazetteers of the ancient world, accounts of the influence of geography upon history, reconstructions of past geographies, studies in sequent occupance, chronicles of change through time, retrogressive narratives, investigations of relict features, critical appreciations of the perception of the past and essays in theory.[1]

In a methodological survey of the subject, H.C. Darby grouped his discussion under four headings - geographies of the past, changing landscapes, the past in the present and geographical history - and stressed the modern relevance of the first two.[2] It was not the purpose of the essays reprinted in this present volume to illustrate all or any of these approaches to the subject, for each was chosen for its treatment of a particular source or group of source materials. Nevertheless, it is interesting to discover in retrospect how closely this collection of articles reflects the methodological ethos of English historical geography over the last twenty years.

Only one of the articles, that on moated settlements by F.V. Emery (pages 439-53), is specifically concerned with relict features, with the past in the present. The rest are more or less equally divided between articles whose concern is to reconstruct some of the aspects of the geography of a past period and those whose concern is the study of geographical changes through time. The line between these two basic approaches in historical geography is, nonetheless, an artifical one. While some of the cross-sections relate to a single year, others are concerned with a much wider span of time during which some changes were inevitably happening. Furthermore, period reconstructions focussed on a single year or a narrow span of time frequently raise more questions than they answer: the geography reconstructed and described needs to be analysed and explained, a task that is only possible by going beyond the time period of the cross-section itself. Period reconstructions amply illustrate how solutions to one set of problems immediately raise new questions demanding further research. The artificiality of the distinction is also exemplified in those studies of changes through time which achieve their aim by comparing two or more static cross-sections rather than by examining change as a continuous process.

These articles also emphasise the traditionally empirical approach in historical geography while at the same time making it clear that theory has not been entirely eschewed. As D.W. Harvey points out in the supplementary note to his own article, historical geography can only progress through a careful integration of theory and empiricism (page 265). A basic problem confronting historical geographers today is how to integrate traditionally empirical techniques which must eventually reach out for a theoretical framework and the theoretical analysis which must in turn reach out to embrace the complexities of the real world. Some of the difficulties lie in the characteristics of the source materials available to an historical geographer and some lie in the nature of the theories which have so far been developed. A fuller understanding of each of these sets of difficulties is a *sine qua non* to the consummation of the marriage between the empirical and theoretical approaches in historical geography.

In the essays collected together in this volume the range of source materials used varies widely both in date and form, yet one problem remains common to their interpretation. In most cases the original sources were prepared for such purposes as taxation, valuation or administration and are thus not explicitly geographical. This provides the historical geographer with his main problem of interpretation — to build from and into his source material the necessary spatial dimension. In order to do so, the historical geographer must be aware of the exact nature of his source material, its original purposes, its limitations, and its context, for he is doubly removed from the spatial patterns he is reconstructing and analysing. He has not the advantage of geographers working in the present of being able to check in the landscape the pattern he is studying, instead he must rely upon his own interpretation of others' perception of the spatial pattern. This fundamentally involves the historical geographer in scholarship, because he must understand not only the specific source he is analysing, but also the motivation, background and perception of the people who constructed the documents with which he is working.[3]

Intimately connected with this understanding of the nature of the documents is the need for an awareness of the extent to which the sample being studied can be considered to be representative. In the case of historical geography this exists in two dimensions, the temporal and spatial. In the former case the problem concerns the timing of the observations upon which the spatial descriptions are being based, for as Harvey illustrates in his study of the Kentish hop industry (pages 243-65), large scale annual variations can be virtually obscured by consideration of the decennial census alone.[4] The problems of spatial samples are common throughout geography, but are particularly accentuated in historical geography due to the chance nature of document construction and survival. Throughout the middle ages it was predominantly the large ecclesiastical authorities who possessed both the means and the necessity of constructing and preserving records of estate management. Thus, much of our knowledge of land use and economy during the middle ages can hardly be said to be representative of the country as a whole. Similar problems in the eighteenth century are illustrated by Johnson's study of the Foley partnerships (pages 173-91), where the charcoal iron industry of England is studied through the Foley papers, which, of course, deal predominantly with the family concerns. Thus, areas where Foley interests were relatively weak, such as the Weald or south-west Yorkshire, are not represented by the documents with correct relative weight *vis-a-vis* the West Midlands or the Forest of Dean.

The problems concerned with the analysis of specific documents are inextricably linked with the previous points, but vary with the nature and period of the documentation. In many aspects documentary interpretation requires some degree of historical training, although skills such as palaeography can only be taught to a limited extent, most being learned from practice with the documents concerned.[5] Fortunately, much evidence now appears in transcribed or translated form due to the work of local record societies and the Record Commissioners.[6] Problems connected with palaeography are not limited, as might be expected, to medieval times for in many respects handwriting of the eighteenth and nineteenth centuries poses as many problems in illegibility as does that of earlier periods and does not have the conventions of style and language of earlier 'Court Hands'.[7]

In order to understand fully the limitations imposed by a particular source material it is imperative that the historical geographer is aware of the manner in which and the purpose for which his material was originally compiled. Considerable inaccuracies can result in the extraction of figures from documents if the worker is unaware of the constraints imposed by the type of source being exploited, as even negative areas in the resultant spatial pattern may well be explicable in terms of the manner and organisation under which the source was originally constructed.[8] This applies even to the use of material as ostensibly spatially representative as early maps, where some knowledge of the methods of the surveyors and the purpose of the map are necessary for their correct interpretation. For example, because a particular feature was not marked on an early map it does not necessarily mean that it was not in existence at that date, it simply may not have been considered important for the purpose of the compiler.[9] It is thus essential to read as widely as possible about the source to be exploited, concerning the administration of the collection of the data and the purpose for which it was intended.

As the geographer is essentially concerned with spatial patterns and relationships, one of the main problems facing the historical geographer is the location and size of the areal units to which his data is applicable. Much of the work concerns periods before detailed maps were in existence and the documents themselves may well be based on areal units that have long since disappeared. Old Hundred boundaries and the locations of early mines and factories often cannot be reconstructed without considerable supplementary work in the field and extensive researches through much additional source material. This even applies to much of the early census material, as the data collection was based on units now often obsolete and difficult to reconstruct. Considerable errors can result from incorrect location and transference of data. based on archaic areal units, to modern administrative areas.[10]

Similar problems occur in dealing with weights and measures during the period before standardisation. This is exemplified by the problems faced by Darby in the mapping of Domesday woodland (pages 29-51), for not only are the measurements of woodland in the survey given in five distinct ways, but the nature of even the linear measurement is not fully understood. Estimates of the modern equivalent of the Domesday league vary from one-and-a-half miles down to half a mile making it impossible to approach any degree of standardisation for the whole country. The weights of industrial and agricultural produce were often recorded in 'baskets' or 'cartloads', the content of which varied considerably within small areas let alone on a national scale.[11] Even such a familiar land measurement as the acre varied in size within single counties and the size of the widely used hide remains obscure. Such

quantitative variety and imprecision does, of course, provide the historical geographer with extremely difficult problems, particularly when
they are combined with methods of accounting peculiar to each source.
In dealing with annual production figures it is imperative to understand
the basis of the accounting procedures used in the documents, particularly when comparison of output from more than one point is being
considered. The accounting year, items brought forward or held in
abeyance, and the calculation of profit are likely to have varied from
one output point to another. Even in relatively standardised accounts,
such as medieval manorial accounts, discrepancies can occur, for the
accounting year ran from Michaelmas to Michaelmas, that is 29 September to 28 September. When converting figures to calendar years
some authors have used the calendar year of the opening Michaelmas
account whilst others have used that of the closing Michaelmas account.
This gives apparently wide discrepancies in production figures for
single years based on the same estate.[12] This problem continued into
the nineteenth century, for, despite the attention drawn by economic
historians to the emergence of double entry book-keeping, the accounting processes of many businesses in the early part of that century are
often difficult to comprehend.[13]

Problems of this nature are associated with all types of source materials used by historical geographers and are far too numerous to be
individually itemised. The point to be emphasised is that no geographer
can approach historical source material *de novo* and immediately extract data to be mapped and analysed. An immense amount of scholarship and time must be spent in understanding the nature of the source
material before a start can be made in analysis. At the same time, it is
obvious from the evidence provided by the essays reprinted below that
much remains to be learned from historical source materials, either
through a larger scale geographical analysis of sources which have to
date been studied only for relatively small areas, or through a search of
neglected aspects of sources of which a portion only has so far been
exploited.[14]

Indeed, the sheer weight of the detailed information that they contain is probably the major reason why sources such as tax records,
census enumerators' books, crop returns, parish records, wills, and
government statistics have been scrutinised for subnational areas when
a fully national coverage is extant, or for single or sample years when
longer and denser chronological runs are available. Thorough examina-

tion, collation and analysis of sources such as these on their full geographical and temporal scales is often not within the scope of the individual researcher. Team research projects, using the vast capacity for data storage, collation and analysis provided by the computer, would seem to be the only means of attempting to realise the full potential of sources such as these.[15]

Statistical analysis of a less comprehensive nature than such fully computerised projects is, of course, providing many new insights in the social sciences as a whole. Mathematical indices of spatial distribution patterns, rigorously formulated sampling designs, variance and regression analysis, significance tests and various types of numerical taxonomy, particularly factor analysis, are now relatively common in most branches of human and physical geography,[16] and they are becoming so in economic history.[17]

It would thus seem that both the methods and the data of historical geography are amenable to statistical treatment. However, mathematical techniques will probably never be so widely used in historical geography as they are in other branches of geography. The empiricism of its practitioners should obviate the employment of statistical techniques as an end in itself, rather than as a means to the end of meaningful geographical analysis,[18] and furthermore, many historical data will not accommodate such a treatment. The description and comparison of distribution patterns through statistically derived indices of centrality or clustering, for instance, must be an exercise of dubious value, when, as the following essays show must sometimes be the case, the maps from which they are derived comprise samples of unknown, possibly different, sizes, when all points cannot be located with the same degree of accuracy, and when comparable measures of magnitude are available for only a part of the mapped population. Similarly, the use of parametric techniques, which require normally distributed data and accurate measures of central tendency and dispersion, is not appropriate to many historical data because much of this is not normally distributed and does not represent a random sample. However, much more could be learned from a judicious use of these powerful tools of description and analysis. Linear regression has been used to good effect by, for example, Thomas;[19] variance analysis has proved useful in the analysis of parish registers (pages 141-70); numerical taxonomic techniques, which are generically similar to those used by Yelling (pages 117-37) and Thomas (pages 211-24) to ascertain crop combinations, have been used with great success to analyse the massive data of nineteenth-century trade directories[20] and censuses,[21] and non-parametric rank analysis has helped to draw significant conclusions about the changing geographical distribution of wealth from medieval taxation assessments.[22] This list could be greatly extended, but the point has been sufficiently laboured that certain historical sources can yield much more than hitherto by the application of techniques which are commonly used in other branches of geography. The possibility of using statistical methods to overcome problems that are inherent in the source materials, rather than in spite of them, holds much promise. These range from the use of simple time-series regression to extract the temporal trend from data which refer to different places within an area at different times over a span of years, thus allowing 'timeless' comparison in geographical space, to more complex non-standard procedures like that employed by Friedlander and Roshier to derive migration flow paths from nineteenth-century census returns, which provide information only on places of birth and current residence.[23]

Empirical analysis has always been overwhelmingly prevalent in English historical geography, and there is no reason to believe that this will not continue to be the case. But empiricism does not necessarily equate with antiquarianism, and though the production of deductive theory is precluded by this approach, the logical conclusion of empirical analysis is the inductive derivation of theoretical principles. One of the major current objectives of human geography is the formulation and testing of formal hypotheses,[24] the anticipated culmination of which is the establishment of dynamic theories of location.[25] The contribution of historical geography to this end is potentially massive, especially if, as seems likely, the systems concept is to provide a framework for the analysis of dynamism. Within such a scheme, study of the complex reciprocating processes through which systems equilibria are achieved, dynamised, disturbed, retarded or confounded over the long and short term will assume great importance.

Theory must, of course, be given formal statement; hypotheses and the assumptions from which they are derived must be explicitly formulated, and the logical connections between them must be rigorously crystallised. As much current geographical work testifies, the construction of models of the assumptions, the hypotheses and the logic that connects them is one of the most convenient and meaningful methods of achieving this: 'to think in terms of the model is ... frequently the most convenient way of thinking about the structure of the theory'.[26] Furthermore, an expression of the model in mathematical terms is usually the most rigorous and unambiguous method of formulation. Two problems are immediately apparent in the suggestion to conduct analysis in historical geography through this statistico-theoretical model approach. The first, which is common to all academic enquiry, is that any large-scale model of the operation of complex cause and effect processes through time is fraught with fundamental difficulties. As Desai has pointed out,[27] the only situation in which this type of analysis is appropriate is where 'the large phenomenon .. [is] made up of many separable and small though interconnected parts. If these parts are ordered in a hierarchical chain of causation so that the first small part influences the rest of the parts but is independent of them, and the second part is dependent only on the first but independent of the others, and so on, then this structural characteristic makes it easier ... to study large problems'.[28] Intuitively, it would be concluded that this kind of causal system is rare in geography, where complex reciprocal patterns rather than one-way causal chains seem to be normal. However, analysis of even complex processes over shorter time-spans can readily utilise model structures based on theoretical principles, and the problems of feedback, which bedevil the analysis of long-term changes, can be overcome by the use of model sequences, comprising connected submodels which individually incorporate only short spans of time.[29] The second obvious problem involved in the construction of statistico-theoretical models of complex processes in historical geography is both directly apposite to, and amply illustrated by, the essays collected together in this volume. It will probably rarely occur that data pertaining to all the parameters and variables that are relevant to such process models can be quantified. Recent attempts to build models of eighteenth and nineteenth-century American economic processes have been severely criticised because of the flimsiness of their data on crucial parameters.[30] It thus seems probable that, however beguiling the prospect, it will usually not be possible to construct statistico-theoretical models of the long-term evolution of such complex phenomena as central place systems,[31] technological diffusion patterns,[32] urban formal and functional structures, agrarian systems, or the geometry and impact of successive transportation networks.[33]

Although it will not usually be possible to achieve mathematically formulated studies of such complex systems as these, statistico-theoretical studies of less widely ramified phenomena can produce excellent results,[34] and, more generally, all historical studies can, even in the total absence of quantifiable data, aim explicitly at the induction of theoretical principles. As Golledge and Amadeo have recently pointed out 'presenting research results in a rigorous manner and examining the possibility that a form of lawfulness may have been discovered is as good a way as any to start developing a meaningful and sound philosophical base in the discipline'.[35] Work of a predominantly fact-finding nature will continue to serve the pressing need to discover and explore features of past landscapes that are at present completely or partially unknown, but a wider geographical relevance can be gained by overtly considering theoretical principles. The essays of Carter, Harvey, Thomas and Wrigley in particular amply illustrate that this is possible despite the sometimes severe limitations that are imposed by the quantity and the quality of the available source material. 'The unfortunate gap', recognised by Harvey,[36] 'between the scholarly studies of the specialist historical geographers ... and the analytical techniques of human geographers concerned with contemporary distributions' must be closed if historical studies are to make their full contribution to geography, and if specialist historical geographers are to understand fully the significance of the phenomena which they examine.

What is advocated is not the indiscriminate application of principles and techniques derived from studies in contemporary geography to historical situations;[37] nor is it suggested that the search for theory should become more important than the ordered portrayal and attempted explanation of the reality which the theory is meant to illuminate. 'Theory should not be thought of as a panacea which will solve all the problems of historical explanation in geography. It is, rather, the means we use for sorting and sifting through our own expectations (about reality) and of determining the sometimes quite complex implications of those expectations'.[38] A full grasp of current thinking in other branches of human geography should be allied with an intimate working knowledge of the potentialities and problems of historical source materials. Because of the rapidity with which the concepts and methods of human geography are evolving, further specialisation is necessary, and the existence of, for example, 'historical social geography' and historical industrial geography' needs not only *de facto* but also *de jure* recognition, at least in university courses.[39] Whether or not such recognition is granted, we can be sure that the profoundest insights will only be gained by assiduously searching for generalisations about the geographical processes of the past using the most rigorous analytical techniques and theoretical frameworks available. This search will be most fruitful if technical ability and a full grasp of the conceptual problems and achievements of modern human geography are combined with an appreciation of the historical context of source materials and the expertise necessary to use them properly.

Alan R.H. Baker
John D. Hamshere
John Langton

References

1   Prince, H.C. 'Progress in historical geography', being pp 110-22 of Cooke, R.U. and Johnson, J.H. (eds), *Trends in Geography: An Introductory Survey* (London, 1969)

2   Darby, H.C. 'Historical geography', being pp 127-56 of Finberg, H.P.R. (ed), *Approaches to History. A Symposium* (London, 1962)

3   See Clark, G. Kitson *The Critical Historian* (London. 1967) for a discussion of perception and problems of historical interpretation. Also Kerlinger, F.K. *Foundations of Behavioural Research* (New York, 1964) pp 698-700

4   See also Harvey, D.W. 'Models of the evolution of spatial patterns in human geography' being pp 549-608 of Chorley, R.J. and Haggett, P. (eds), *Models in Geography* (London, 1967)

5   Many aids to the handling of documents now exist which are of use to the historical geographer. For example, Gooder, E.A. *Latin for Local Histians. An Introduction* (London, 1961)

6   See Baker, A.R.H. *infra,* pp 85-100, for use of the *Nonarum Inquisitiones* transcribed by the Record Commission in 1807

7   Useful introductions to palaeography can be gained from Hector, L.C. *The Handwriting of English Documents,* 2nd edn (London, 1966) and Grieve, H.E. 'Examples of English handwriting 1150-1750' *Essex Record Office Publication,* 21 (1959)

8   See Grigg, D. *infra* pp 227-39, and Glasscock, R.E. *infra* pp 71-81, who emphasise the necessity for a complete understanding of the nature of taxation records in order to account for the limitations imposed on any interpretation of the geographical distributions of wealth derived from them

9   For example see Yates, William *A Map of the County of Lancashire, 1786.* Reprinted in facsimile by the Historic Society of Lancashire and Cheshire, (1968), with an Introduction by Harley, J.B. who in considering Yates' map as evidence for coal mining in Lancashire pointed out that, due to the method and scale of construction of the map and the nature of the industry at that time, there was necessarily an under enumeration of coalpits, with considerable spatial variation in accuracy

10   Even where the collection unit is known, difficulty can be experienced in map construction, for example see Coppock, J.T. 'The relationship of farm and parish boundaries: a study in the use of agricultural statistics', *Geographical Studies*, 2 (1955) pp. 12-26; also Coppock, J.T. 'The parish as a geographical statistical unit', *Tijdschrift voor economische en social Geografie*, 51 (1960) pp 317-26

11   This problem is further discussed by Langton, J. in 'Measures of weight and volume used in the South West Lancashire coal industry during the seventeenth and eighteenth centuries' forthcoming in *Trans Lancs and Cheshire Antiquarian Soc* in 1970. More general references can be found in Nef, J.U. *The Rise of the British Coal Industry* Vol II (London, 1935) pp 374-7 and Rees, W. *Industry before the Industrial Revolution* (Cardiff, 1968) pp 129-132

12   Titow, J.Z. *English Rural Society, 1200-1350* (London, 1969) pp 23-33 discusses the accounting process used in the drawing up of Manorial Account Rolls

13   See Pollard, S. 'Capital accounting in the Industrial Revolution' *Yorkshire Bulletin of Economic and Social Research*, 15 (1963) pp 75-91

14   For instance, though Grigg has used the agricultural data in the Land Tax Assessment Returns there is no equivalent analysis of the industrial data which they provide

15   The work on parish registers of the Cambridge Group for the History of Population and Social Structure, of which Dr E.A. Wrigley is a co-founder, is salutory in this respect. For an introductory examination of the potential value of the computer in the analysis of census data in general, and a report on its use in a research project on the households of Camberwell as described in the census enumerators' books of 1841-1901, see Dyos, H.J. and Baker, A.B.M. 'The possibilities of computerising census data', being pp 87-112 of Dyos, H.J. (ed), *The Study of Urban History* (London, 1968)

16   For a collection of essays which employ techniques of this type see Berry, B.J.L. and Marble, D.F. (eds), *Spatial Analysis: A Reader in Statistical Geography*, (Englewood Cliffs, New Jersey, 1968)

17   The recent literature is vast, but see, for example, Redlich, F. ' "New" and traditional approaches to economic history and their interdependence', *Journal of Economic History*, 25 (1965) pp 480-95; Fogel, R.W. 'The new economic history; its findings and methods', *Economic History Review*, 2nd Ser, 19 (1966) pp 642-56; David, L. 'Professor Fogel and the new economic history', *Econ Hist Rev*, 2nd Ser, 19 (1966) pp 657-63; and Desai, M. 'Some issues in econometric history', *Econ Hist Rev*, 2nd Ser, 21 (1968) pp 1-16

18   See G. Olsson's review of Berry, B.J.L. and Marble, D.F. op cit, in *Journal of Regional Science*, 8 (1968) pp 253-5 for a spirited criticism of the use of statistical analysis for purely descriptive purposes and of the idea that geography can be equated with applied geometry

19   Thomas, D. 'Climate and cropping in the early nineteenth century in Wales' in Taylor, J.A. (ed), *Weather and Agriculture* (Oxford, 1967) pp 210-12

20   Caroe, L. 'A multivariate grouping scheme: "association analysis" of East Anglian towns', being pp 253-69 of Bowen, E.G., Carter, H. and Taylor, J.A. (eds), *Geography at Aberystwyth* (Cardiff, 1968)

21   Taylor, P.J. 'The location variable in taxonomy' *Geographical Analysis* 1 (1969) pp 181-95

22   Buckatzsch, E.J. 'The geographical distribution of wealth in England, 1086-1843', *Econ Hist Rev*, 2nd Ser, 3 (1950) pp 180-202 and Schofield, R.S. 'The geographical distribution of wealth in England, 1334-1649', *Econ Hist Rev*, 2nd Ser, 18 (1965) pp 483-510

23   Friedlander, D. and Roshier, R.J. 'A study of internal migration in England and Wales, Part I: geographical patterns of internal migration 1851-1951', *Population Studies*, 19 (1965-6) pp 239-79

24   See Golledge, R. and Amadeo, D. 'On laws in geography', *Annals of the Association of American Geographers*, 58 (1968) pp 760-74

25   Haggett, P. 'Changing concepts in economic geography', in Chorley, R.J. and Haggett, P. *Frontiers in Geographical Teaching* (London, 1965) pp 107-9; King, L.J. 'Approaches to locational analysis; an overview', *East Lakes Geographer*, 3 (1966) pp 15-16; and Pred, A.R. *The Spatial Dynamics of US Urban-Industrial Growth, 1800-1914* (Cambridge, Mass, 1966) p 3

26   Braithwaite, R.B. *Scientific Explanation: A Study of the Function of Theory, Probability and Law in Science* (Cambridge, 1968) p 92

27   Desai, M. op cit p 16

28   Blalock, H.M. *Causal Inferences in Non-experimental Research* (Chapel Hill, North Carolina, 1961) pp 52-60 contains a lucid exposition of the manner in which such 'recursive systems' can be expressed and evaluated mathematically

29   Desai, M. op cit, *passim*; much the same conclusions are reached, though through a different line of reasoning, in Harvey (1967), op cit, p 570. One great empirical benefit of such models is that they can readily accommodate the cyclical reality of change through time, which is much neglected in current geographical process models

30   McClelland, P.D. 'Railoads, American growth and the new economic history: a critique', *J econ hist*, 28 (1968) pp 102-23. Desai, op cit also comprises a review of a number of these works

31   A remarkable attempt was made by Morrill to simulate the development of the central place system of Småland in Sweden between 1860 and 1960 by means of a sequence of Monte-Carlo probability models, though Pred considers that the grossness of some of the assumptions and approximations used means that 'we gain absolutely no additional comprehension of the processes involved', Morrill, R.L. 'The development of spatial distributions of towns in Sweden: an historical-predictive approach', *Ann Ass Am Geogr*, 53 (1963) pp 1-14; and Pred, A.R. 'Postscript' in Hägerstrand, T. (trans. A.R. Pred) *Innovation Diffusion as a Spatial Process* (Chicago, 1967) pp 317-9

32   Because of the complexity of the variables which determine the cost of innovating a manufacturing technique, the possibility of being able to afford innovation, which varies through time, and the geographical distribution of adopters, who constitute a very small and constantly varying proportion of the total population of an area, this process is far less amenable to this type of analysis than the less economically significant diffusions which have been successfully analysed through such models. For a discussion of the complexity of just one of the cost factors involved, see Frankel, M. 'Obsolescence and technical change in a maturing economy', *American Economic Review*, 45(i) (1955) pp 296-319

33 Lachene, E., 'Networks and the location of economic activity', *Papers of the Regional Science Association,* Ghent Meeting, (1965) pp 183-96, contains an interesting theoretical treatment of this problem

34 See, for example, Harvey, D. *infra,* pp 243-65; Thomas, D. (1969) op cit; and Lindberg, O. 'An economic geographical study of the localisation of the Swedish paper industry', *Geografiska Annaler,* 35 (1953) pp 28-40

35 Golledge and Amadeo, op cit p 774. Of particular relevance to historical geographers are their remarks on 'historical' and 'developmental' laws

36 Harvey, D.W. (1967) op cit p 550

37 See, for example, the use made of certain aspects of central place theory in Clarke, J.D. *Analytical Archaeology* (London, 1968) pp 507-9, and Russell, J.C. 'The metropolitan city region of the middle ages', *J reg Sci,* Vol 2, No 1 (1960) pp 63-4

38 Harvey, D.W. personal communication

39 A similar plea was recently made for the recognition of such sub-specialisms in urban history, and 'urban historical geography' was one of them. See Schnore, L.F. 'Problems in the quantitative study of urban history', being pp 189-208 of Dyos, H.J. op cit

Domesday Woodland
H.C. Darby
Reprinted from *Economic History Review,* III (1950-1),
21-43

DOMESDAY WOODLAND

By H. C. DARBY

ONE of the most important factors in the evolution of the English landscape has been the clearing of the wood which once covered the greater part of the countryside. A ready means of reconstructing the vegetation of prehistoric times is by inference from the surface geology. The heavier impervious clays presumably carried great stretches of oakwood mixed with other trees. Recent work has shown that even the lighter soils were not devoid of wood when farming first began, and that so-called 'natural heath' had its origin in the clearing of its wood by Neolithic farmers. In spite of the activity of successive prehistoric peoples, it seems clear that when the Romans invaded Britain in A.D. 43, the main centres of population were still upon the lighter soils: the real attack on the claylands had scarce begun. Four centuries of Roman civilization left their mark. The Romans needed to clear not only for agriculture but also for other purposes, and iron-smelting in the Weald and in the Forest of Dean, for example, must have consumed substantial quantities of wood. But the total effect of this clearing seems to have been relatively small. There was certainly no wholesale occupation of the claylands, and when the Romans left Britain, it was still very largely a wooded country. We are told that on the second edition of the Ordnance Survey Map of Roman Britain (1931) 'regions of natural woodland (dense or open) are marked and have been restored upon a geological basis'. In detail, this map has been criticized, and Professor Tansley has declared that there was probably a good deal more wood than is shown.[1] Still, it does serve to show something of the order of magnitude involved when we speak of the woodland of Roman Britain.

By the time of the Domesday Inquest in 1086, much of this woodland still remained, but it is clear that the countryside was already becoming the open land we know to-day. Between the fifth and the eleventh centuries, the attack on the woodlands had begun in earnest. Much of the clayland had become arable, and was tilled by the sturdy plough-teams of oxen that feature so prominently in the entries of the Domesday Book. This achievement was the work of the Anglo-Saxons, and also, in the north and east, of the Scandinavians. It is perhaps not an exaggeration to describe their work as 'the making of England'. Over this span of centuries we can obtain some idea of the distribution of the disappearing woodland from the evidence of place-names: names ending in 'leah', 'hurst', 'holt' and the like indicate either woodland or clearings in woodland. At the end of the period, with the coming of the Normans, the statistics of the Domesday Book enable us to write another chapter in the history of the clearing.

[1] A. G. Tansley, *The British Islands and their Vegetation* (Cambridge, 1939), p. 173.

1. THE DOMESDAY ENTRIES

The effects of the Anglo-Saxon and Scandinavian invasions upon the landscape of England were summed up in the Domesday Inquest of 1086. The inquest has many imperfections, but it also has the great advantage of covering the greater part of England. No earlier record is as comprehensive, nor any later record for a very long time. The Domesday Book has long been regarded as a unique source of information about legal and economic matters, but its bearing upon the reconstruction of the geography of England during the early middle ages has remained comparatively neglected. The extraction of this information is not always as simple as it might appear to be from a casual inspection of the Domesday folios. Not only are there general problems of interpretation, but almost every county has its own peculiar difficulties. The original survey was made in terms of counties, hundreds and villages, but the Norman clerks reassembled the information for each county under the headings of the different landholders. The first task, therefore, is to undo their work, and rearrange the survey once more upon a geographical basis. It is only after this has been done that we can start to plot the information upon a map.

One of the questions put by the Domesday Commissioners was 'How much wood?' The form of the answers varied. The usual term used to describe wood was 'silva', but, as we shall see, there were variants. Occasionally, we encounter such phrases as 'silva infructuosa', 'silva inutilis', 'silva nil reddens', indicating useless wood, but these are rare. Normally, woodland formed an important item in the economy of a medieval village, and that is why we know as much about it as we do. Almost every page of the Domesday Book shows that eight hundred years ago there was more wood in England than at any subsequent time. Broadly speaking, the answers to the question fall into five groups. Sometimes they state that there was enough wood to support a given number of swine. A variant of this is a statement not of total swine but of the number returned as rent from the wood. A third type of answer gives the length and breadth of the wood in terms of leagues and furlongs and, maybe, perches. A fourth type states the size of a wood in terms of acres. The fifth category of answers is a miscellaneous one that includes a number of variants and idiosyncrasies occasionally encountered in the text.

Normally, each county is characterized by one type of entry, and the distribution of these types is shown on Fig. 1. In most counties, however, the dominant type of entry is accompanied by some subsidiary entries of a different character. Thus, the wood of most Leicestershire villages is measured mainly in terms of its length and breadth, but there are a few Leicestershire villages for which it is measured in terms of acres. Norfolk likewise contains a few villages for which acres of wood are entered, but the wood of the great majority of Norfolk villages is measured in terms of swine. These variations between county and county, and within each county, throw some light upon the process of the survey. Separate bodies of commissioners visited different groups of counties, and the returns of their respective circuits seem to be marked by general differences of phraseology. But in reconstructing these different circuits, the evidence of the wood entries has to be considered in relation to other differences between county and county.

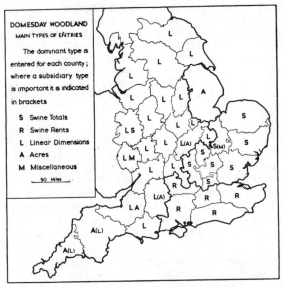

Fig. 1. England: Distribution of types of wood entries.

II. SWINE TOTALS

Wood formed an important item in the economy of the eleventh century because its acorns and beech-mast provided food for swine. Some indication of this importance may be seen from the prominence given to mast-bearing woods in the laws of Ine (*c.* A.D. 694) and in other Anglo-Saxon documents. In post-Domesday times, document after document also bears witness to this importance. In the Domesday Book itself different phrases are used to indicate the number of swine. The normal formula is 'wood for *x* swine'—*silva ad* x *porcos, silva de* x *porcis* or just *silva* x *porcos*. In the Shropshire swine entries, the usual formula is 'wood for fattening (*incrassandis*) *x* swine', and there are many other variations. The number of swine thus recorded ranges from just a few (one, two or three) up to many hundreds, and occasionally to over a thousand: there were even some villages with wood for over 2000 swine. The large entries are given in round numbers that may indicate estimates rather than definite numbers, but, on the other hand, the many instances of detailed figures (1, 3, 19, 47) suggest exactness. Occasionally the precision is carried to great lengths: at Strincham in Norfolk there were two sokemen who had 'wood for 18 swine and two-thirds of another'.

It is interesting to note that one of the earliest attempts to map the data of the Domesday Book seems to be J. H. Round's attempt to plot the swine entries of Essex in 1903. It is true that he did not print a map, but he certainly had one in mind.

The only way [he wrote] in which to gauge the distribution of woodland at the time of King Edward's death is to mark down on a map of the county the amount, reckoned in swine, as given for each parish. The results of this tedious process are of interest if treated with that caution which is always so essential in dealing with Domesday figures. When one finds such estimates as 100, 500, 1000 frequently made, it is obvious that the estimate can only be accepted as a very rude one. Moreover the number of swine has to be compared with the acreage, a most laborious task. Certain general conclusions are therefore the most that one can hope for.[1]

But any attempt, along these lines, to calculate densities in terms of the acreages of each parish raises many difficulties. Thus the modern parish of Brentwood was not mentioned in the Domesday Book, and it formed part of the old parish of South Weald. In this, and the many other similar cases, adjustments to the acreages must be made. But it is sometimes impossible to make such adjustments with even the roughest accuracy. In the Essex hundred of Becontree there is a group of five modern parishes not mentioned in the Domesday Book—Dagenham, Romford Rural and Urban, Hornchurch and Noak Hill. The woods, like the other resources of this area, were presumably entered with those of surrounding parishes, but it is quite impossible to apportion the amounts. The principle upon which Fig. 2 has been constructed avoids such difficulties. While not without local uncertainties, it gives a better general picture than could any density map. But even so, Round's analysis must always be interesting as an early experiment in Domesday cartography. It is a pity that the map he had in mind was never published.

Whatever cartographical method be adopted it is obvious, as Fig. 2 shows, that Essex was a very wooded country, and it is interesting to compare this map with Dr P. H. Reaney's maps showing the distribution of place-names ending in 'leah', 'haeg', 'ryden' and the like.[2] The wood was widely spread over both Boulder Clay and London Clay alike, but the greatest concentration was in the west of the county.[3] Here were many villages with wood for over 1000 swine, and some with sufficient even for 2000. Miss E. M. J. Campbell's as yet unpublished maps of Hertfordshire and Middlesex show how the dense Essex woodland was continued westwards. The eastern hundreds of Essex, on the other hand, were less wooded, and a feature of Fig. 2 is the number of places with but small quantities of wood in the hundreds of Tendring and Rochford.

Bedfordshire was another county for which wood was entered in terms of swine. Like Essex, it occupies an interesting place in the history of

[1] J. H. Round in *V.C.H. Essex* (1903), I, 375.
[2] P. H. Reaney, *The Place-Names of Essex*, maps in pocket (Cambridge, 1935).
[3] See also H. C. Darby, 'Domesday Woodland in East Anglia', *Antiquity* (Gloucester, 1934), XIV, 211–14.

Domesday mapping, because a number of Domesday maps of the county were drawn by G. H. Fowler in 1922. One of these showed woodland, but, like that of Round, it is not above reproach. In the first place, Fowler converted the measurements of swine into modern acreages at the rate of $1\frac{1}{2}$ statute acres for each head of swine, although he was careful to point out

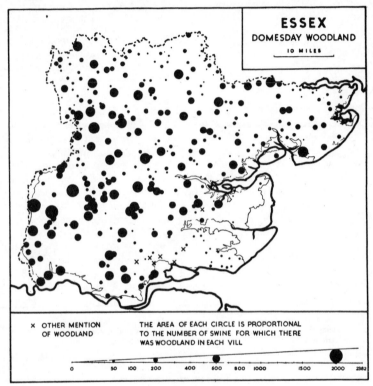

Fig. 2. Domesday woodland of Essex.
(The edge of the alluvium is marked.)

the 'difficulties and dangers of the method'.[1] In view of the inevitable doubts associated with such conversions it would have been better to plot the Domesday units directly on to the map. In the second place, the percentage of land occupied by wood was calculated on the basis of each parish. In view of the fact that the acreages of many parishes have changed, it would have been better to use a method that by-passed this problem. In spite of these criticisms, Fowler's maps marked a very distinct advance, and will always remain a most interesting experiment.

[1] G. H. Fowler, *Bedfordshire in 1086* (Bedfordshire Historical Record Society, 1922), p. 107.

Norfolk was yet another county for which wood was reckoned in terms of swine, but it was a much less heavily wooded county than either Essex or Bedfordshire. The most notable feature of Fig. 3 is the concentration of wood on the medium soils of mid-Norfolk where there were many villages each with wood sufficient to feed several hundred swine, some with enough

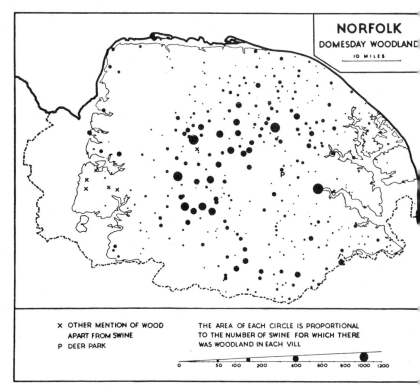

Fig. 3. Domesday woodland of Norfolk.
(The edge of the affluvium is marked.)

even for a thousand. These medium soils continue south-eastwards in a belt to the southern boundary of the county, and we might, perhaps, expect the wood cover in this southern area to have been more dense than it apparently was. The Domesday population and plough-team maps, however, show that the district to the south of Norwich was a closely settled arable area, and the absence of dense wood is therefore all the more understandable.[1] In the north-east of the county, in the loam region, there was a moderate amount of wood, but nothing to compare with that of mid-Norfolk. The

[1] H. C. Darby, 'The Domesday Geography of Norfolk and Suffolk', *Geog. Jour.* (1935), LXXXV, 438.

closely-settled Flegg hundreds, for example, were particularly devoid of wood. Finally, the light soils of the north-west of the county, and the even lighter soils of the Breckland to the south, formed very open country, and this in spite of the fact that the western area was not densely peopled. It is interesting to see how the comparatively dense woodland of mid-Norfolk thinned out along the margins of this western area. There were, it is true, some local patches of wood here and there, but, on the other hand, so were there patches of heavier soils.

One feature of the wood entries of the three eastern counties of Norfolk, Suffolk and Essex is the contrast that is sometimes drawn between conditions in 1066 and 1086. Thus, on a holding at Blickling in Norfolk, we are told: 'Then wood for 200 swine, now for 100.' Decreases are recorded for thirty-three places in Norfolk, thirty-seven in Suffolk and forty-two in Essex. The Domesday text gives no indication of the purpose of this cutting, but Mr Reginald Lennard has recently demonstrated that it was not accompanied by any extension of the arable.[1] Many of the holdings from which wood had disappeared show not an increased number of plough-teams, as one might perhaps expect, but a smaller number in 1086 than in 1066. He concludes that the evidence points not to assarting but to wasting: 'The tall trees had gone and with them the acorns and beech mast on which the pigs of the peasantry had fed. But the tree stumps, one suspects, remained and they must have been a serious obstacle to cultivation, while thickets of scrub must have taken the place of the standing timber.' In Essex there are a few entries that specifically tell of wasting. Wasted wood (*silva vastata*) is entered for Bowers Gifford, Fanton and Wheatley. The general picture that emerges for these 112 places is one of robber economy and not of agricultural development. Similar wasting must, presumably, have gone on in other counties, but the Domesday text is silent about it.

III. Swine rents

In some south-eastern counties the number of swine entered for a holding implies not a total but an annual rent paid to the lord in return for pannage in his wood. The form of the entry varies. Thus at Lewisham in Kent we are told 'from the wood 50 pigs for pannage'; while the corresponding entry for Kennington in the same county reads: 'as much wood as renders for pannage 40 pigs or 54½d.' There are many other variations in phrasing. What was the relation of these renders to total numbers? It is difficult to give a satisfactory answer to this question. At Leominster, in Herefordshire, we are told, in an unusually long account of the wood, that each villein having ten pigs gave one 'de pasnagio'. There is, apparently, no other Domesday entry which clearly states the ratio of render to total for mast swine, but there are some references for Sussex and Surrey which give ratios for grass swine—'de herbagio' or 'pro pastura'. Every villein at Patcham in Sussex had to render one out of seven pigs 'de herbagio', and

---

[1] Reginald Lennard, 'The Destruction of Woodland in the Eastern Counties under William the Conqueror', *Economic History Review* (1945), xv, 36.

a marginal note adds: 'likewise throughout the whole of Sussex'. The same ratio is specifically mentioned in entries relating to Ferring, Elstead and Woolavington. At Aldingbourne, however, the ratio seems to have been one out of six, and at Bishopstone one out of three, but it is possible that both the *vi* and the *iii* are mistakes for *vii*. The ratio of one in seven is also mentioned in the Surrey entries for Malden and Titsey, but at Battersea and Streatham in the same county it was the tenth pig that seems to have been due. Whether similar proportions characterized the use of wood we cannot say and, in any case, we cannot assume that the swine rent provides a constant index of the woodland of different places. Where, however, there were a number of adjacent villages all rendering swine, we may safely conclude that they were situated in or near a wooded district, and the figures enable us to make an intelligent guess at the order of magnitude of the wood in relation to that of other areas.

Kent, Surrey and Sussex are three of the counties characterized by swine renders, and they present problems of particular interest because each includes a part of the Weald. The presence of very ancient English names in the Weald suggests that, in Anglo-Saxon as in Roman times, it was far from being an impenetrable and trackless waste. But although the repellent nature of the Weald has often been overstressed, it is obvious that it was not an ideal area for close settlement in early times, and the implications of any map showing the distribution of Domesday names in south-eastern England are clear. The settlements in the Weald were small, and many of them escaped mention because they were attached to parent-centres elsewhere, and because their wood and other resources were recorded under the name of the main centre. Many of the villages around the Weald must thus be visualized as each having a hinterland in the Weald, or, at any rate, having an outlier in it. Fig. 4, constructed by Dr S. H. King, and showing the distribution of woodland recorded under the Domesday names of Sussex, thus has inherent limitations. Its symbols do not represent the actual location of the wood on the ground. They must be 'spread out', so to speak, by eye over the adjacent Weald.

The Domesday Book is disappointingly silent over the colonization that must have proceeded from the parent centres into the Weald. The folios for Kent, however, enable us to glimpse something of what was taking place. Pre-Domesday charters show the intercommoning of Kentish villages on a large scale. A village, in addition to rights of common in nearby waste or wood, often had denns, denes or swine-pastures in the Weald, sometimes at considerable distances away. These were connected to their parent villages by drove-ways. 'Along these droveways were driven the swine for whose pasture the denns were originally occupied, the oaks and beech of the weald affording excellent mast. Other additional uses of the woodlands, however, were common even in early times. The charters show them as sources of supply for wood for burning and building and salt-making.'[1] The total number of denes mentioned in the Domesday

[1] N. Neilson, *The Cartulary and Terrier of the Priory of Bilsington, Kent* (British Academy, 1928), p. 5.

account of Kent is forty-eight, together with three half-denes.[1] Distinction is made between large denes and small denes, and, also (obviously cutting across the other division) between *denes de silva* defined, maybe, by swine

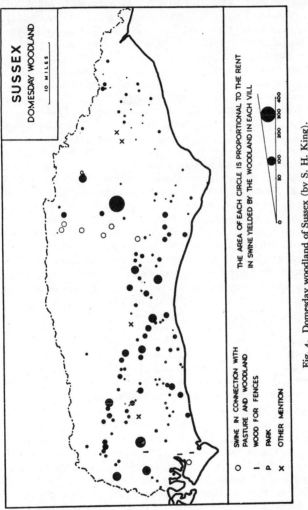

Fig. 4. Domesday woodland of Sussex (by S. H. King).

rents, and other denes which had progressed beyond the wooded state and which were cultivated by villeins and bordars, and measured by the ordinary measures of arable land. Thus Peckham had three denes where there were four villeins, and Bircholt had a dene with two villeins and half

[1] N. Neilson in *V.C.H. Kent* (1932), III, 182.

a plough. Some places once rated as denes had grown to be ordinary villages and were entered in the usual manner, e.g. Benenden and Newenden. But we do not know enough about the conditions under which the swarming-off from established villages was begun and conducted, and we cannot speculate with any certainty. Kentish surveys of the thirteenth and fourteenth centuries show that denes still played an important part in the economic life of the county. Putting the evidence of these and of the Saxon charters together, it is evident that the Domesday list of denes is by no means complete. Those mentioned were probably inserted because of some particular circumstances, while many more were silently included in the entries of the villages to which they were attached.

The Domesday Book records no denes for Sussex and only one (at Ewell) for Surrey, although other evidence shows that there must have been many, especially in Sussex. There is, however, one piece of circumstantial evidence that may indicate colonization of the Sussex Weald, and Mr L. F. Salzman has interpreted it to show what probably happened. In the northern, or Wealden, half of the rape of Hastings, four localities are named in the Domesday Book, but there are also about twenty unnamed estates which are said to belong to one or other of a group of places lying outside the Weald in the neighbouring rape of Pevensey. This group lies in the triangle formed by Eastbourne, Laughton, and Firle, an area which was early settled and well developed by 1086. The northern portion of Hastings rape, on the other hand, 'was pretty certainly uncleared backwoods. It seems to me,' writes Mr Salzman, 'quite probable that, at some uncertain date, claims in the Hastings backwoods were allotted to such of the lords of the Pevensey triangle as would take them up and that this forest district was deliberately colonized.'[1] The date of the colonization was not long after 1011, the year in which the Danes, according to the Anglo-Saxon Chronicle, overran 'Sussex and Kent and Hastings'. As Mr Salzman is careful to point out, this hypothesis is based only on circumstantial evidence, but it does explain the curious association of the North Hastings estates with Pevensey. Presumably some such colonization was also proceeding elsewhere, but the Domesday Book is silent about it.

IV. LINEAR DIMENSIONS

As Fig. 1 shows, the woodland of the majority of counties was measured in terms of its length and breadth.[2] The normal entry reads wood (*silva*) or wood for pannage (*silva pastilis*) '*x* leagues in length and *y* leagues in breadth'. The length of a Domesday league (*leuca*, *leuga* or *leuua*) has been a matter for much discussion. The twelfth-century Register of Battle Abbey in Sussex stated that a league comprised 12 *quarentenae* or furlongs and that a *quarentena* comprised 40 perches. This would make a league equivalent to

[1] L. F. Salzman, 'The Rapes of Sussex', *Sussex Archaeological Collections* (Cambridge, 1931), LXXII, 23. See also *V.C.H. Sussex* (1905), I, 357–8.
[2] Numerous examples of this type of measurement are discussed in F. W. Morgan, 'Domesday Woodland in Southwest England', *Antiquity* (Gloucester, 1936), XVI, 306–24.

$1\frac{1}{2}$ miles, but it must be remembered that the number of feet in a perch is obscure, and that the whole subject is complicated by local usage and by the existence of local or 'customary', as distinct from standard, units.[1] Furthermore, in his study of Domesday Worcestershire, J. H. Round thought that a league might well have comprised only 4 furlongs (i.e. about half a mile) because there he never found a figure higher than 3 furlongs below the league.[2] Our knowledge of the measures characterizing different districts is far too slight to allow us to speak with confidence on these matters. All we can do for each county is to regard the figures as indicating conventional units by which relative density may be gauged.

Quite apart from the problem of the size of the units, there are other difficulties: the exact significance of this type of entry is not clear. Is it giving extreme diameters of irregularly-shaped woods, or is it making rough estimates of mean diameters, or is it attempting to convey some other notion? We cannot tell, but we certainly cannot assume that a definite geometrical figure was in the minds of the Domesday commissioners. Nor can we hope to convert these lineal measurements into acres by any arithmetical process, and it would be rash to make any assumptions about the superficial extent of woodland measured in this way. All we can safely do is to regard the dimensions as conventional units and to plot them diagrammatically as intersecting straight lines. This objective method will, at any rate, give us some idea of its general distribution over the face of a county. Sometimes, however, these diagrams raise difficulties. On the assumption that a league is roughly equivalent to $1\frac{1}{2}$ miles, the limits of the wood on a Domesday holding occasionally extend beyond those of the modern parish where presumably it lay. This may be explained by the non-coincidence of manor and parish, or by changing boundaries, or, indeed, by the fact that the length of a league may have varied in different parts of the country. But for the most part, the dimensions of the wood on a holding lie well within the limits of the corresponding parish of to-day. In some entries, only one dimension is given, and we are merely told, for example, that there is, say, a league of wood. Whether such an entry is intentional or whether it is the result of scribal error, we cannot say.[3] Its frequency in Shropshire and Worcestershire seems, however, to rule out the possibility of error as far as those counties are concerned. Another curious type of entry that occasionally occurs is that which involves a mixture of linear dimensions and acres. Thus at Upton by Chester there was wood '1 league long and 2 acres broad', and at Hampton in the same county there was another wood '5 acres long and 2 broad'.[4] Whatever notions the commissioners had in mind, it is clear that they were sometimes trying to be very

[1] F. W. Maitland, *Domesday Book and Beyond* (Cambridge, 1897), pp. 371–6 and 432. For earlier discussions see (1) Henry Ellis, *A General Introduction to Domesday Book* (1833), I, 157–60; (2) R. W. Eyton, *A Key to Domesday: the Dorset Survey* (1878), pp. 24–8.

[2] J. H. Round in *V.C.H. Worcestershire* (1901), I, 271–2. See also Round's discussion in *V.C.H. Northamptonshire* (1902), I, 279–81.

[3] For 'areal leagues', see R. W. Eyton, op. cit. pp. 31–5.

[4] For 'linear acres', see O. J. Reichel in *V.C.H. Devon* (1906), I, 387.

accurate. At any rate, a number of entries suggest precision. At Folks-worth in Huntingdonshire, for example, there was a wood '6 furlongs in length and 2 furlongs and 6 perches in breadth'. There are many similar instances of detailed figures. Intermixed with these, however, are many figures that suggest estimates rather than exact measurements. A wood recorded as being two leagues by one in size may well have been measured by eye rather than by hand.

It sometimes looks as if these Domesday lengths and breadths represent in some way a sum total of separate tracts of woodland, but if this is so, it is difficult to imagine the arithmetical process that lay behind the result. There was a wood 5 by 1½ furlongs entered for Keyston in Huntingdonshire, but the dimensions are preceded by the words *silva pastilis per loca* which seem to imply a scattered distribution. The same phrase *per loca* is also found in connexion with some Lincolnshire entries, but this wood is measured in acres. A similar impression of a total is given by a number of entries for what is now Lancashire. The Domesday information relating to this area is in a very summarized and unsatisfactory form, but this summary nature may at any rate throw a little light upon the nature of the linear dimensions used to measure the wood. The settlements of the hundred of Newton, for example, are surveyed in a single composite entry covering the main locality itself together with fifteen berewicks. The total wood is recorded as being 10 leagues in length and 6 leagues 2 furlongs in breadth: presumably this represents the sum of the different stretches of woodland in all sixteen places. Other Lancashire hundreds have two entries for wood, one relating to that of the main locality, and the other to that of the out-lying places. Thus in Salford hundred, Salford itself had wood (*foresta*) 3 leagues by 3 leagues, while that of its twenty-one berewicks measured 9½ leagues in length by 5 leagues 1 furlong in breadth. Obviously it is impossible for us to resolve these composite measurements into their components.

Cheshire was another county for which wood was measured mainly in terms of linear dimensions. Mr I. B. Terrett has shown that it was a relatively sparsely settled county, and that its expanses of Boulder Clay carried much wood in Domesday times (Fig. 5).[1] A number of areas, however, seem to have been devoid of wood. One was the infertile and villageless Pennine area; any wood here was presumably entered under the names of the adjoining villages, which certainly have large amounts of wood entered for them. Another area without record of wood was the sandy upland of Delamere; but there may have been unrecorded wood here in the forest. The third area with but little record of wood was the peninsula of Wirral; the absence of wood here is not surprising in view of the fact that this was the most arable and densely peopled part of the county. Whatever be the exact significance of the linear dimensions of the Cheshire folios, there can be no doubt about the heavily wooded character of much of the Cheshire plain in the eleventh century.

[1] I. B. Terrett, 'Domesday Woodland in Cheshire', *Trans. Historic Society of Lancashire and Cheshire* (Liverpool, 1948), c, 1–7.

The Gloucestershire woodland was likewise measured lineally, but it was far less in amount than that of Cheshire. Fig. 6 shows how it was disposed either in the Severn plain or along the edge of the Cotswolds. The Cotswolds themselves formed for the most part open country. The Domesday Book makes no specific mention of the Forest of Dean, but there are a few

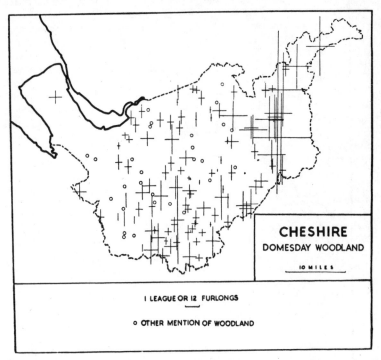

CHESHIRE
DOMESDAY WOODLAND

10 MILES

I LEAGUE OR 12 FURLONGS

o OTHER MENTION OF WOODLAND

Fig. 5. Domesday woodland of Cheshire (by I. B. Te rett).

casual references that indicate its existence and its considerable size. Fig. 6 may be compared with the map of Domesday woodland prepared by G. B. Grundy in 1936.[1] Grundy attempted to convert Domesday measurements into modern acres and so obtain a quantitative estimate of the wood cover in 1086. He then interpreted this partly in terms of geological formations a: d partly in terms of the distribution of place-names indicating the progress of the Saxon settlement. As an early attempt at plotting Domesday data his map is a most interesting experiment, and the outline of his wooded area is shown on Fig. 7. In general, Fig. 6 agrees with it, bearing in mind that Grundy made allowance for the unrecorded wood of the Forest of

[1] G. B. Grundy, 'The Ancient Woodland of Gloucestershire', *Trans. Bristol and Gloucs. Arch. Soc.* (Gloucester, 1936), LVIII, 56–155.

Dean. The differences lie mainly in the absence of wood from the Vale of Berkeley, but the Domesday entries for Thornbury, and a number of other villages certainly mention wood.

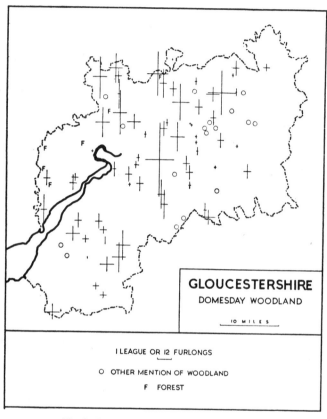

Fig. 6. Domesday woodland of Gloucestershire.

V. MEASUREMENT IN ACRES

As Fig. 1 shows, Lincolnshire is the only county which has its wood (and underwood) measured almost exclusively in terms of acres. The precise form of the expression varies, but the most frequent formula is '*x* acres of wood for pannage' (x *acrae silvae pastilis*). The mention of pannage is sometimes omitted, but, on the other hand, the phrase 'throughout the territory' (*per loca*) is occasionally added, and this, as we have seen, may imply a scattered distribution. The quantities vary from one acre to many hundreds and, in one entry, to over a thousand. The detail of many of the entries (e.g. 3, 63, 117) suggests that they were intended to be exact figures rather than estimates. No attempt has been made on Fig. 8 to equate these Domesday 'acres' with those of the present day; they have been plotted merely as arbitrary units that give an idea only of relative distribution throughout the county.[1]

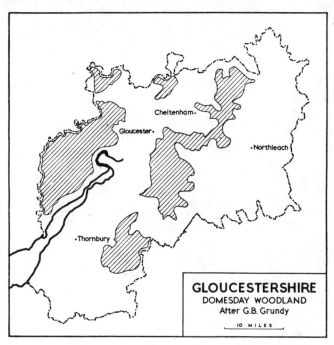

Fig. 7. Domesday woodland of Gloucestershire according to G. B. Grundy.

A few Lincolnshire woods are measured lineally in leagues and furlongs. Sometimes the woodlands of different holdings within the same village are recorded differently; that is so, for example, at Bourne where the wood on one holding was measured in acres, and that on another two holdings in terms of linear dimensions. There are even examples of both types of measurement occurring within a single entry. At Irnham, we are told, 'there is wood for pannage 1 league in length and 10 furlongs in breadth. Besides this there are 200 acres of wood for pannage throughout the territory.' Can we assume that the first entry refers to a solid mass of woodland, and that the second entry denotes scattered parcels of wood?

When plotted on a map, the Lincolnshire wood entries are seen to lie disposed in three main groups. One is on the clay country to the south-east of Louth, extending to the margins of the Wolds. A second and more

[1] H. C. Darby, 'Domesday Woodland in Lincolnshire', *The Lincolnshire Historian* (Lincoln, 1948), 1, 55–9.

43

densely wooded area is that stretching southwards from Market Rasen to the northern borders of the Witham Fens as far as Tattershall. The greater part of this area lies in the Clay Vale of Lindsey; the rest extends eastward

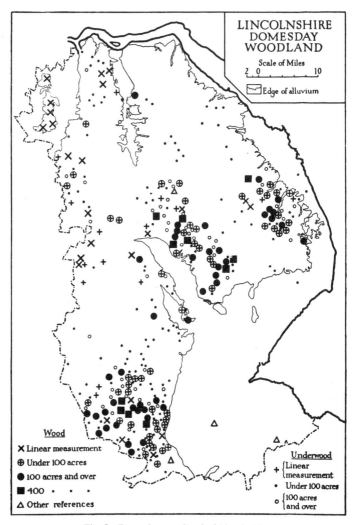

Fig. 8. Domesday woodland of Lincolnshire.

on to the Clay Wolds and southward on to the sands and gravels around Tattershall, near the edge of the Fenland. The third area of wood is on the clays of southern Kesteven, to the south-east of Grantham: this was the most extensive and most densely wooded area. Kesteven is spelt 'Chetseven' in the Domesday Book, and the first element 'Chet' is probably derived from the British 'cēto' which is cognate with the modern Welsh 'coed' meaning wood.

In all three areas the bulk of the wood entries were in terms of acres. Apart from these, there were isolated parcels of woodland, more particularly on the western border of the county, in Lindsey, and these, as Fig. 8 shows, have the peculiarity of being recorded for the most part in terms of linear dimensions; the woods of the Isle of Axholme were entirely entered in this way. All three main areas, and also the western borders of Lindsey, had some underwood, and there were in addition a number of isolated localities with underwood. In general, the underwood was more widely and sporadically scattered than the woodland itself. Beyond and around the main woodlands stretched the open areas of Lincolnshire—on the Wolds, along the oolite belt that runs north of Grantham past Lincoln to the Humber, and in the Fenland.

While Lincolnshire is the only county with woodland measured almost entirely in acres, this unit also plays an important role among the wood entries of many other counties, e.g. Cornwall, Devon, Somerset, Nottinghamshire, Northamptonshire. In a tract of wood along the eastern border of Leicestershire, for example, acre measurements are intermingled with linear ones; but they are virtually absent from the remainder of the Leicestershire woodlands, which are measured in a linear fashion. In these counties it would seem that the smaller woods are measured in acres and the larger ones by their lengths and breadths. Acres are also found in the woodland entries of other counties, but only rarely and sporadically; thus a few acre measurements are mingled with the swine entries of Norfolk and Suffolk. Whether the 'acres' of all these various counties denoted the same unit, and whether that unit was identical with the 'acre' of the Lincolnshire folios are matters that lie deep in the obscurity that surrounds the history of English measures.

VI. MISCELLANEOUS ENTRIES

As we have seen, the dominant type of wood entry in a county was usually accompanied by a number of other entries of a different character; thus the wood of the Essex villages was almost exclusively indicated in terms of swine, but the wood on a few holdings in the county was measured in acres and even in hides. These subsidiary entries that appear in most counties are very miscellaneous in character. Outside the four main categories, the Domesday references to wood exhibit the greatest variety. Occasionally, the term 'nemus' is used in contrast with the more general 'silva', and in some places at any rate they appear to be interchangeable. 'Silva minuta' or 'silva modica' denote underwood or coppice; it is a feature of the Lincolnshire folios, but it also occurs sporadically elsewhere. There is also occasional mention of 'broca' (brushwood); of 'grava' (grove); and of 'spinetum' (spinney or, perhaps, thorny ground); and there are many variants. Individual species of trees are rarely named, but we do find rare mention of oaks, alders, osiers and ash-trees. Sometimes, we are told of 'customs' or of money payments or of renders of honey due from some woods. Other stretches of woodland provided cartloads of fuel for the saltworks of Cheshire and Worcestershire; thus, in the latter county, 300 cartloads were yielded annually from the wood of Bromsgrove for the saltworks at Droitwich. Or again, 'hays' in the wood (enclosures for catching deer) form a frequent stem in some counties.

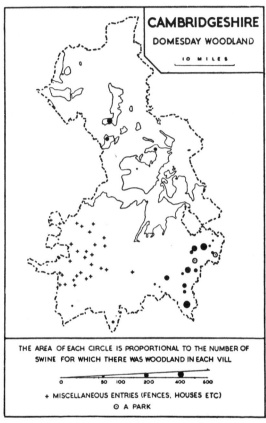

Fig. 9. Domesday woodland of Cambridgeshire.
(The edge of the affluvium and peat is marked.)

For most counties these subsidiary references are scattered sporadically amongst the more usual entries. In Cambridgeshire, however, there is a group of miscellaneous references that call for special comment. They indicate the presence of sufficient wood 'for making the fences' or 'for the houses' or, in one entry, 'for fuel'. When plotted on a map, they are seen to lie closely together on the western claylands of the county, and stand in contrast to the swine entries of the eastern claylands (Fig. 9). The difference in the method of recording was certainly not due to the absence of swine in the west for we know from the parallel record of the *Inquisitio Comitatus Cantabrigiensis* that there were many swine in the western hundreds.[1] But, apparently, the woodland of this area was not dense enough to provide pasture for them, although it was sufficient for the miscellaneous needs of the inhabitants; there were only a few western villages with small amounts of wood for swine. The contrast between east and west is striking. Similar miscellaneous references to wood 'for the fences' or 'for the houses' are to be found in other counties, but they are few in number and scattered in location.

Among the miscellaneous entries must be included those that refer to the clearing of woodland. In the eastern counties of Norfolk, Suffolk and Essex, as we have seen, wood was certainly cut down in 112 villages between 1066 and 1086. The circumstantial evidence of the Wealden arrangements also indicate clearing. The cartloads of wood that fed the salt industry point to the toll that the industrial demands of the time were levying upon the woodlands. Iron works must have consumed more, but we are told nothing about this demand. Indeed we shall be disappointed if we expect to find many references to clearing throughout the Domesday Book in general. It is certain, however, that clearings for cultivation were already known as 'assarts', a word derived from the French *essarter* meaning to grub up or clear land of bushes and trees, and so make it fit for tillage. But Hereford is the only county for which they are mentioned. At Much Marcle there were 58 acres 'reclaimed from the wood', and the word 'assart' is written above 'reclaimed'; at Leominster the profits of the assarts in the wood were 17s. 4d.; while both at Fernhill and at Weobley, land for one plough had been reclaimed. Four solitary references are not much, but there is no reason to believe that what happened in Herefordshire did not happen in other counties. The general form of the Domesday entries has concealed the activity which is accidentally revealed here.

But although clearing was taking place generally, the reverse process was going on in some localities. Land devastated by raiding, or by the march of armies, would soon become overgrown with thicket and wood if allowed to remain unattended. For Herefordshire again the Domesday Book records plough-lands in Hezetre hundred which had been wasted and were overgrown with wood; and elsewhere in the county there was other land which had 'all been converted into woodland'. Similar growth must have taken place on some of the wasted lands of other counties, though the Domesday Book tells us nothing of it. In any case, such regeneration of woodland was exceptional to the main trend of the time.

VII. The compilation of woodland maps

The Domesday information for a county gains greatly in interest when set against that of neighbouring counties. There are many differences in phraseology between individual counties and between groups of counties.

[1] H. C. Darby, 'The Domesday Geography of Cambridgeshire', *Trans. Cambs. Antiq. Soc.* (Cambridge, 1936), xxxvi, 46.

Some of these differences arose from varying economic and social conditions. Others may reflect nothing more than the language and ideas of different sets of commissioners. The distribution of Domesday woodland in the eastern counties illustrates in a clear way both the limitations and the advantages of Domesday mapping (Fig. 10). For Norfolk, Suffolk, Essex and eastern Cambridgeshire, woodland is recorded mainly in terms of the number of swine that could feed upon its acorns or beech-mast. In Huntingdonshire, it is measured in terms of its length and breadth. In Lincolnshire, it is measured in terms of acres, both of wood and of under-wood. There are also miscellaneous methods of recording the presence of wood; these are found sporadically in all counties, but are especially characteristic of western Cambridgeshire. The difficulty that arises from this variety of information can be simply stated. It is impossible satis-factorily to equate swine, acres and linear dimensions, and so reduce them to a common denominator. Any map of Domesday woodland must suffer from this restriction. Thus, on Fig. 10, we cannot be sure that the visual impression as between one set of symbols and another is correct; Kesteven appears to be about as thickly wooded as central Norfolk, but there is no way of being sure that this similarity is a true reflection of actual conditions on the ground.

It is possible to make assumptions about the relation of acres to swine, but such assumptions must always be full of uncertainty. The relation of both acres and swine to linear dimensions raises even greater difficulties for, as we have seen, the implications of this system of measurement are far from clear. It is true that a few Domesday entries tantalize us by suggesting possible equations. Thus at Ashby-de-la-Zouch in Leicestershire, there was 'woodland one league in length and four furlongs in breadth, sufficient for (*ad*) 100 swine'. On the other hand, at Crowle in Worcestershire, there was half a league of wood also sufficient for (*ad*) 100 swine. Even if it were possible to equate these two entries, we could not be sure that the relation between swine and dimensions was constant over a county, to say nothing of over all England.

Despite these limitations, much can be gained from Fig. 10. With all its problems, it does not leave us in doubt about the main features of the dis-tribution of wood over the eastern counties in the eleventh century. As far as Norfolk, Suffolk, Essex and eastern Cambridgeshire are concerned, there is no uncertainty; and in this area, the dense woodlands of Essex stand out prominently. Elsewhere it is clear that the claylands of Huntingdonshire, of Kesteven and of Lindsey also carried substantial amounts of wood. All this takes us some way, at any rate, towards visualizing the face of the countryside in 1086.

VIII. Forests

In addition to woodland itself there was also forest land about which the Domesday Book says little. 'Forest' is neither a botanical nor a geogra-phical term, but a legal one. The origin of the word has been disputed but one view is that it implied an area outside (*foris*) the common law and subject to a special law that safeguarded the king's hunting. Forest and woodland were thus not synonymous terms, for the forested areas included land that was neither wooded nor waste. Whole counties were sometimes placed under

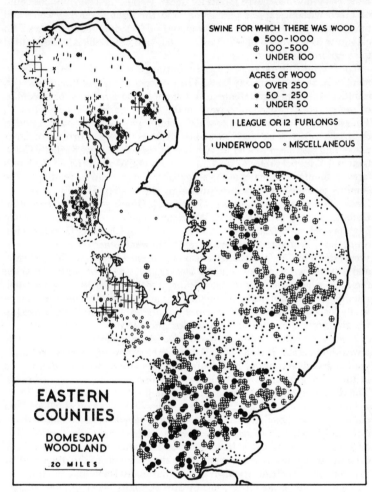

SWINE FOR WHICH THERE WAS WOOD
- ● 500 - 1000
- ⊕ 100 - 500
- · UNDER 100

ACRES OF WOOD
- ◑ OVER 250
- ⊗ 50 - 250
- × UNDER 50

1 LEAGUE OR 12 FURLONGS

ι UNDERWOOD   ○ MISCELLANEOUS

EASTERN
COUNTIES

DOMESDAY
WOODLAND

20 MILES

Fig. 10. Domesday woodland of the eastern counties.
(The boundary of the Fenland is marked.)

forest law. But still, a forested area usually contained a nucleus of wood, and sometimes large tracts of wooded territory. The existence and extent of these forests before 1066 is an obscure matter, but it is certain that after the Norman Conquest the forest law and forest courts of Normandy were introduced into England on a large scale. There was a rapid and violent extension of forest land. The Norman kings had a passionate love of the chase, and the Anglo-Saxon chronicler wrote under the year 1087 that King William 'made large forests for deer'. Within these, no animals could be taken without express permission, and the right of cutting wood and making assarts was severely restricted and subjected to fines and dues. An elaborate organization of wardens, foresters and other officials was created to safeguard the forested areas.

These forests, being royal property outside the normal order, are rarely mentioned in the Domesday Book. The existence of some of them, however, is indicated by various statements to the effect that a holding, or part of it, or sometimes its wood only, was 'in the forest' or 'in the king's forest'. Thus at Windsor, in addition to wood yielding fifty swine for pannage dues, there was other wood (*alia silva*) placed in enclosure. Portions of other places had also been placed in Windsor Forest: the entries for both Cookham and Winkfield refer to land 'in the Forest of Windsor' or 'in the king's forest'. Similar references to forests occur in various entries relating to the counties of Berkshire, Cheshire (including the modern Flintshire), Dorset, Essex, Gloucester, Hampshire, Hereford, Huntingdon, Northampton, Oxford, Sussex, Wiltshire and Worcester. There are also references to hays, or enclosures (*haiae*) for catching animals, in Cheshire, Herefordshire, Shropshire, Worcester, and, more rarely, in some other counties. Thus at Weaverham in Cheshire there was wood '2 leagues long and 1 league wide, and 2 hays for taking roedeer' (*ii haiae capreolorum*). The duty of making these deer-hays was known as *stabilitio*, and it is frequently mentioned. Finally, a number of parks are mentioned; and sometimes these were specifically for wild beasts (*parcus bestiarum silvaticarum*). A number belonged to the king; others to various lay or ecclesiastical lords.

There is one forest, and only one, about which the Domesday Book gives a wealth of detail. It is the New Forest, and it occupied a special section in the Domesday account of Hampshire. The amount of destruction involved in the making of the New Forest has long been a matter for controversy. The chronicles of the twelfth century declared that the Conqueror reduced a flourishing district to a waste by the wholesale destruction of villages and churches. Some modern historians have developed this theme of destruction, and Freeman's *History of the Norman Conquest* made much of it. But, on the other hand, many have declared this tale of destruction to be a calumny that is not borne out either by the poor soils of the district or by the Domesday evidence itself. It is true that many Domesday holdings are said to be 'now in the forest', but by distinguishing between those villages wholly afforested and those only partially so, the late F. H. Baring showed in 1901 what probably happened. Roughly speaking, William found about 75,000 acres of waste land comprising for the most part infertile sands and gravels.[1] He enlarged this by taking in some twenty villages and a dozen

[1] F. H. Baring, 'The making of the New Forest', *Eng. Hist. Rev.* (1901), xvi, 427.

hamlets amounting to between 20,000 and 25,000 acres. This constituted the Forest proper, and around this, portions of other villages were taken in to protect the deer; these additions were mainly woodland and amounted to between 10,000 and 20,000 acres. To-day, the outer boundary of the Forest includes about 92,000 acres.

University College, London

**Population Trends and Agricultural Developments from
the Warwickshire Hundred Rolls of 1279**
J.B. Harley
Reprinted from *Economic History Review*, XI (1958-9),
8-18

POPULATION TRENDS AND AGRICULTURAL DEVELOPMENTS FROM THE WARWICKSHIRE HUNDRED ROLLS OF 1279

By J. B. HARLEY

THE significance of the Hundred Rolls of 1279 has been appreciated since the end of the nineteenth century by those historians concerned with the social and economic evolution of England in the early middle ages. The latest, most comprehensive and authoritative treatment of this source is by E. A. Kosminsky;[1] his chief preoccupation, however, is with the correction of a previously over-simplified or idealized concept of manorial structure, and consequently much of his book is devoted to this central theme, together with the allied topics of peasant tenure and rent, the evolution of social and economic differences within the peasantry, and the function of the small landowner in medieval England.

These studies are based mainly on categories of information which the 1279 Hundred Rolls afford in reasonable detail and accuracy,[2] although variably for each manor. Essentially these are:

1. A survey of the demesne: arable land, and sometimes meadow, woodland, mills and other appurtenances.

2. A survey of the land in peasant tenure and of the scattered possessions of the larger landlords, which includes a list of the tenants by name, the size of their holdings and the nature of their rent. These lists are sub-grouped in the folios for land in free tenure, in villeinage, and that held by cottagers.

The contention of this paper is that problems outside the scope of Kosminsky's work can be clarified through a regional and comparative analysis of the Hundred Rolls. Accordingly from the unpublished Warwickshire folios [3] two groups of statistics have been abstracted: first, the number of the total landholding population; and secondly, the total of recorded arable land, given in both cases for the manorial unit. It is proposed to employ this information to assess:

1. The regional pattern of population change by direct comparison with Domesday figures.

2. The relationship of these changes to agricultural development, specifically as expressed by the amount of arable land recorded in the manor.

I

The evolution of any aspect of society or economy cannot be divorced from the physical qualities of the landscape in which it is rooted, or the historical

[1] E. A. Kosminsky, *Studies in the Agrarian History of England in the Thirteenth Century* (Oxford, 1956).
[2] For a discussion of the validity of the Hundred Rolls see E. A. Kosminsky, *op. cit.* pp. 26–35.
[3] P.R.O. Exch. K.R. Misc. Books No. 15.
I am indebted to the following: to Miss June Wray, former research student in the School of History, University of Birmingham, for a transcript of these folios; to Dr R. H. Hilton for help in checking this with the MSS. on micro-film; and also to Dr Hilton and Dr H. Thorpe of the Geography Department, University of Birmingham, for advice about the presentation of this paper.

development which pre-dates this evolution. Stoneleigh and Kineton, the hundreds embraced by the Warwickshire folios, lie athwart the river Avon and its tributaries, and extend from Coventry in the north, southward for a distance of over 30 miles, to the point at which Kineton abuts on the Oxfordshire border. By way of contrast, from east to west the two hundreds seldom exceed 8–10 miles in width. Though arbitrarily defined by a quirk of documentary survival, this peculiarly elongated transect of Warwickshire embodies marked contrasts in both its physical character, historical evolution and social and economic development at the time of Domesday Book. These contrasts reach their maximum development in the area of Stoneleigh north of the river Avon, and that part of Kineton which lies south of the Foss Way, respectively. Physically these two areas have distinctive associations of relief, geology, soils [1] and vegetation, in part natural and in part man-induced. In particular, the survival of large tracts of uncleared woodland in Stoneleigh north of the Avon was of great social and economic significance, and had given the landscape a special individuality. This region stood in contrast to Kineton hundred, where the forest had largely disappeared through the activity of the cultivator by 1086. The nature of these contrasts is indicated more precisely in Table 1, a summary of Domesday statistics,[2] for a selected group of twelve parishes chosen from the two hundreds, in relation to position (see Figure 1b) and to the size of the settlement.

Table 1. *Domesday statistics for parishes whose location is shown on figure 1b*

STONELEIGH PARISHES	Acreage (1899)	Recorded Population	Landholding Population per 1000 acres of parish	Plough Teams	Woodland
Stoneleigh	9968	76	7.61	36	4L by 2L
Kenilworth	5899	27	4.58	3	½L by 4F
Walsgrave on Sowe	2675	18	6.72	7½	4½L by 4F
Brandon	1968	11	5.9	3	2F by 2F
Ashow	1059	31	29.3	7	½L by 3F
Coundon	1049	13	12.4	—	3F by 3F
KINETON PARISHES					
Burton Dassett	4469	75	15	27	- - - - -
Honington	2460	53	21·5	13	- - - - -
Wormleighton	2425	50	20·7	23	- - - - -
Oxhill	1844	42	22·7	10	- - - - -
Ratley and Upton	1723	31	18	9	- - - - -
Priors Hardwick	1523	49	32·1	15	- - - - -

L = League   F = Furlong

In these and subsequent tables the parish has been used as the administrative unit for statistical analysis. The method used is to group data together for manors whose location in 1086 and 1279 is accurately known, and can there-

[1] The relief of Stoneleigh hundred is dominated by the shallow valleys of the river Avon and its north-bank tributaries; that of Kineton, by two well-marked scarps, the northwestern followed in part by the Foss Way, the southern and best-known rising to 700 feet in the Edgehill fringe of south Warwickshire. The geological and soil complexes show marked regional variations too, and range from fertile Upper Coal Measure soils in the north west of Stoneleigh, through the light gravels of the valley terraces, to heavy clays and then sands and marlstones on the Liassic formations in south Kineton. Such differences present local variations of great significance in the economy of a primarily agricultural society, but their consideration lies outside the scope of this paper.

[2] Based on the translation of the Warwickshire Domesday folios in *Victoria County History*, Warwickshire, Vol. 1.

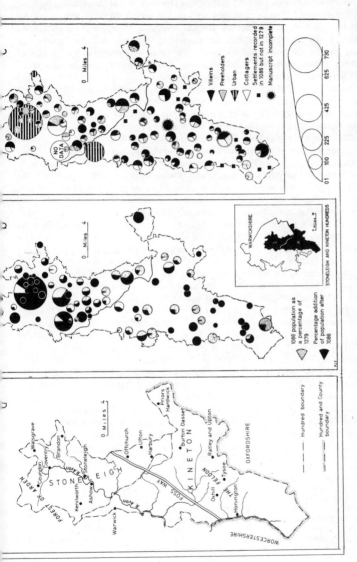

FIGURE I. Stoneleigh and Kineton Hundreds of Warwickshire. Areas of circles are proportional to recorded population in 1279 on the scale shown.

    a. Stoneleigh and Kineton Hundreds: parishes referred to in the text.
    b. Population growth, 1086–1279.
    c. Population structure, 1279.

In the case of Coventry and Warwick population shown as 'urban' is based on number of dwelling-places.
    Figures b. and c. are reprinted by permission of the Institute of British Geographers from J. B. Harley, 'The Settlement Geography of Early Medieval Warwickshire', *Transactions and Papers of the Institute of British Geographers*, 34, 1964, pp. 115–30.

57

fore be placed within, or excluded from, the area of the 1899 parishes. There is strong evidence in Warwickshire for an antiquity and subsequent fixity of parish boundaries [1] which would justify this method. In the population figures, totals of recorded landholding population are given in all cases, and no attempt has been made to employ the conventional multipliers to obtain an appraisal of absolute population, because it is felt that relative figures are adequate for the temporal and regional comparisons envisaged. The device of calculating population per 1,000 acres of parish eliminates the factor of variable acreage in relation to density of population.

The main contrast between Stoneleigh and Kineton which emerges from these Domesday statistics is summarized in the last three columns of Table I. Stoneleigh, excluding those parishes south of the Foss Way which really belong to south Warwickshire in character,[2] stands out as an area of relatively low prosperity, with generally a small number of ploughteams per settlement, a low density of population of the order of five to ten landholders per thousand acres, and of large blocks of woodland still uncleared.[3] It is an area identifiable with the south-east margins of the medieval Warwickshire forest of Arden.[4] As such it is a region, with some exceptions passed by and peripheral to the waves of early Anglo-Saxon settlement which had reached the south of the county by both Severn-Avon and Trent valley routes.[5] It was, therefore, occupied relatively late by man, whose settlement was often manifested by scattered hamlets and homesteads, with inclosure and holding in severalty a feature of the associated field-system.[6] A statistical summary of Domesday Book data for the 25 Stoneleigh parishes lying north of the Foss, reveals that six were of insufficient importance to be mentioned at all in the survey,[7] and of the remaining 19, 11 have a population density of under ten landholders per thousand acres of parish, while 14 contain substantial blocks of woodland.

The antithesis of Stoneleigh in 1086 lay in the hundred of Kineton,[8] whose territory rose from the fertile and easily-worked terraces of the river Avon in the north-west to the Edgehill scarp. It was in this southern part of the county that the centre of gravity of economic development, prosperity and population lay. Here was an intensively-cultivated landscape, with many ploughteams associated with large and valuable manors. Population densities were accordingly high, averaging 15–20 recorded landholders per thousand acres of parish, while this intensity of land utilization had its corollary in an absence of large woodland tracts. Anglo-Saxon penetration and settlement had come early to the region, giving rise to strongly nucleated villages and a related system of communal agriculture. By 1086 in many cases the economic and

[1] See *The Place Names of Warwickshire*, ed. A. Mawer & F. M. Stenton (Cambridge, 1936), Introduction xvi–xvii, for a discussion of the antiquity of certain parish boundaries in Stoneleigh and Kineton.

[2] Namely Offchurch, Ufton, Harbury and Bishops Itchington.

[3] For an amplification of this theme see R. H. Kinvig, in *The Domesday Geography of Midland England*, ed. H. C. Darby and I. B. Terrett (Cambridge, 1954), Chapter VI.

[4] In this context it is interesting that in the thirteenth-century Stoneleigh Abbey Leger Book, Stoneleigh parish is referred to as Stoneleigh in Arden.

[5] See H. Thorpe in *Birmingham and its Regional Setting*, British Association Handbook (1950), pp. 87–113 for a description of the pattern and progress of Anglo-Saxon settlement in this area from archaeological and place-name evidence.

[6] The peculiarities of the North Warwickshire Field System are discussed by R. H. Hilton in *Social Structure of Rural Warwickshire in the Middle Ages*, Dugdale Society Occasional Papers No. 9 (Oxford, 1950), appendix pp. 22–25.

[7] For example, Allesley is first mentioned in 1176, Keresley in 1144 and Bretford in 1199.

[8] Kineton is a post-Domesday, pre-thirteenth-century amalgamation of contiguous parts of the Domesday Hundreds of Tremelau, Honesberie, Fexhole and Barcheston.

social framework of the area conformed well to the classical conception of manor and open field. At this time out of a total of 40 parishes [1] in Kineton for which data are available, only five are still to be documented, and of the remaining 35, ten have a landholding population of 15–20 per thousand acres, another 17 over 20, while only six carry any record of woodland. This was the countryside well known to the sixteenth-century topographers as the Feldon or open country, in contrast to that part of Warwickshire known as the Arden or woodland country. [2]

II

It is generally recognised that the years between Domesday and the time of the Hundred Rolls in 1279 witnessed striking changes in the English countryside. Physically the landscape was being transformed by the destruction of its woodland and waste, [3] a process theoretically counterweighted by an expansion of the total area under cultivation. The upward population trends [4] were reflected in increasing densities and the emergence of new settlements. Economic organization was being modified through the influence of expanding boroughs, markets [5] and a money economy. Within the property structure of the landed estate, the process of subinfeudation was partly offset by the territorial acquisitions of the new monastic orders. While it is known that such complex and varied forces interacted at large to evolve new regional patterns, the detail of the local scene is often incomplete or obscure, according to the quality of the sources. It is partially to bridge such gaps in, and to reinforce narrowly-based generalisations about, the processes of social and economic change in the early middle ages, that Domesday Book and the Hundred Rolls of 1279 can be used, in comparison, and individually. Within the limits of the statistics that they afford, a more precise estimation can be made of population trends and agricultural developments, both temporally and regionally.

Table 2 shows population change 1086–1279, and population density for 1279 for the same groups of parishes in Stoneleigh and Kineton as in Table 1.[6] The analysis of population changes between 1086 and 1279 reveals no general picture of an increase of population. In Table 2, parishes within the two most contrasting areas in 1086, north of the Avon and south of the Foss respectively, have markedly different population histories; they were reacting differently to the forces of social and economic change. South Warwickshire, the older

[1] Including those four Stoneleigh parishes south of the Foss Way.
[2] For example, this distinction between the two major regions in the county is well brought out by Leland. See *The Itinerary of John Leland*, ed. L. Toulmin-Smith (1906–10), pp. 47–51, 155–6.
[3] See H. C. Darby, *An Historical Geography of England before 1800* (Cambridge, 1936), pp. 166–189 for a discussion of this process on a national scale.
[4] See the conclusions of J. C. Russell in *British Medieval Population*, (Albuquerque 1948), pp. 246–260.
[5] Within the Hundreds of Stoneleigh and Kineton alone, 12 market charters were granted between Domesday and the end of the thirteenth century.
[6] The population data of the Hundred Rolls is fairly full, and landholders are subgrouped according to tenurial status as Table 2 indicates. The chief problem in analysis is that a duplication of the same tenants holding different lands often occurs, which confuses enumeration. Especially in Kineton Hundred, too, there are deficiencies and illegibilities in the manuscripts. These are not sufficiently large, however, to affect the overall picture and the parishes in Table 2, for example, are well documented.

settled area and region of maximum population density in 1086 shows only small increases in population, or had remained stationary by 1279. Indeed, in seven parishes out of the forty in Kineton which were analysed, a small decrease was noticeable.[1] Apparently in this area, closely farmed and occupied in Domesday times, some equilibrium or point of saturation had then been reached between economic resources and population capacity at the local medieval level of technical initiative and skill, and was apparently maintained during the next two centuries.[2]

Table 2. *Changes in recorded Landholding Population 1086–1279,*
and Densities in 1279

STONELEIGH PARISHES	Landholding Population 1279				Population Change + = % increase D = % decrease	Density per 1000 acres
	Vill.	Free	Cott.	Total		
Stoneleigh	22	70	159	251	230+	25·2
Kenilworth	– – – no data – – –			232	759+	39·4
Walsgrave on Sowe	10	31	2	43	139+	16·05
Brandon	44	3	12	59	264+	30·0
Ashow	—	16	17	33	67·8+	17·0
Coundon	—	16	3	19	46·1+	18·1
KINETON PARISHES						
Burton Dassett	69	24	—	93	24+	18·7
Honington	24	9	30	63	15·9+	25·5
Wormleighton	30	14	—	44	D	18·2
Oxhill	19	8	16	43	2·38+	23·25
Ratley & Upton	25	8	7	40	12·9+	20·3
Priors Hardwick	29	10	3	42	D	27·5

By contrast the lands lying north of the river Avon are shown in 1279 to be outstanding as areas of population increase, almost without exception. The Stoneleigh parishes in Table 2 illustrate this, and overall figures for the Hundred show five parishes with an increase of 100–200%, another seven with over 200% while eight settlements recorded for the first time between 1086 and 1279 are carrying by the latter date population densities comparable with the older places.

Column 3 in Table 2, gives the density of total recorded land-holding population per thousand acres from the Hundred Rolls. Its purpose is to indicate how the changes discussed above had affected the general patterns of regional population density by 1279. From it one observes a fairly even distribution of population over both Hundreds. Where the range of density in 1086 (Table 1) was 4·58–32·1 per thousand acres, in 1279 it was 16–39, and, moreover, one should stress that the last high figure of 39 was for Kenilworth which lies in Stoneleigh Hundred. In 1279, out of 66 parishes analysed, 34 fall within the range 20–30 landholders per thousand acres and another 12 approximate closely to these figures. In Stoneleigh, with its more dynamic population trends, the process of change had gone even further, for several high figures (e.g. 38 at Leek Wootton and 39 at Kenilworth), indicate a re-location of the chief centres of population away from the south. This regional

[1] The decreases of population which occur in some of the southern parishes are an interesting presage of the many depopulations which are recorded as occurring in this area in the later middle ages, attributable to the spread of pasture farming.

[2] In this period there were no major successions of plagues as in the mid-fourteenth century to disrupt this inertia.

re-adjustment of population densities, must have been characterized at one stage by a time of more general uniformity, but the movements were culminating in 1279 with, if anything, a tendency towards the ascendancy of the north, noticeable in certain cases.

A complicating factor is that behind this facade of two regions with compatible population densities in 1279, wide contrasts can be discerned in the social composition of the population,[1] reflecting the different historical evolution of the areas north and south of the Avon. These are relevant to the ensuing correlation between population trends and agricultural development. They are illustrated in Table 2, by figures of free, villein and cottager elements in the population, and the basic differences thus reflected in social structure between the two Hundreds have already been summarized in statistics quoted by Hilton.[2] In Stoneleigh Hundred, 50 per cent of the landholding population were free tenants, 27 per cent were villeins or serfs and 23 per cent were smallholders of the cottager class. On the other hand the figures for Kineton Hundred, show that the free tenants comprised 30 per cent of the population, the villeins or serfs 46 per cent, and the small holders of various categories, 24 per cent. The basic difference then, lies in the higher proportion of freeholders in the region north of the Avon, compared with a much greater incidence (nearly 20 per cent more) of servility in the older-settled, more heavily-manorialised area of south Warwickshire.

III

In seeking to account for these changes and contrasts, a first proposition might be that north of the Avon intensive and vigorous colonization, with consequent increase of arable cultivation, occurred in the previously scantily-populated Hundred of Stoneleigh, whose forest soils were, moreover, potentially fertile.[3] It may be argued that such an expanding economic framework in turn provided greater opportunities for individual peasant enterprise, and in the process of supplementing their agricultural resources in forest and waste, the small-holders of Stoneleigh Hundred were emancipated from the servile tenurial incidences of the south. However, in evoking such reasoning it is not at all axiomatic that population expansion in the north was accompanied by a proportionate increase of the cultivated area. A comparative analysis of the acreages of arable land associated with population densities in the two major regions offers some rather anomalous conclusions on this point, as Table 3 indicates.

Arable [4] is the only comprehensive land-use figure given for manors described

---

[1] See R. H. Hilton, *Social Structure of Rural Warwickshire in the Middle Ages, op. cit.* for a detailed treatment of this problem. Also Kosminsky, *op. cit.* Chapter IV. The population was differently grouped, too. As in 1086, in the south the characteristic unit of settlement was the nucleated village, while in the north hamlets and scattered homesteads predominated.

[2] R. H. Hilton, *op. cit.* pp. 15–16.

[3] The soils in this area are of a uniformly high quality according to recent soil surveys. See A. W. McPherson, *The Land of Britain,* part 62, Warwickshire (London, 1946), pp. 688–698 for an appraisal of soil conditions in this area. It is of interest that the northern, later-settled area had soils much superior to the heavy Lower Liassic clays occupying much of the Feldon, one of the areas first chosen for cultivation by the Anglo-Saxons as their farms expanded from primary settlements along the scarp-foot zone into this region.

[4] It is often implicit that the arable virgate and other measures included a fixed area of meadow or pasture appurtenant to them, although this was not necessarily detailed in the surveys. Such land would, of course, be essential to support the plough beasts of any cultivating region.

in the Warwickshire Hundred Rolls. As the major basis of local subsistence in the early middle ages, its correlation with population density and composition is an important index of prosperity. Column 6 in Table 3 shows the recorded arable land for each parish expressed as a percentage of its total area. The significant fact emerging is that Kineton Hundred has retained the pre-eminence as an area of arable farming which it held in 1086. The highest percentages of total parish area under arable occur here. For example, even on a conservative basis of a virgate of 20 acres, five parishes are recorded with over 65 per cent of their total area under arable, while another 17 fall in the 50–65 per cent group. As one passes north into the Avon valley the figures are more intermediate, and the range is from 30–60 per cent. By way of contrast, north of the river there are uniformly low percentages limited to 25–30 per cent in most cases, but falling to ten per cent in three places. Yet, as we have seen, the regions both north and south of the Avon were carrying similiar population densities.

Table 3. *Population Density and Arable Land*

STONELEIGH PARISHES	Population density per 1000 parish acres in 1279	Arable land 1279 [1]				Arable Acreage as % of parish area	Recorded Population per 1000 acres arable land
		D.	F.	V & C	Tot.		
Stoneleigh	25·2	960	1757	499	3216	32	79·6
Kenilworth	39·4	- - - - - - - - - no data - - - - - - - - - -					
Walsgrave on Sowe	16·05	240	335	100	675	24·9	64·6
Brandon	30·0	160	250	36	446	22·7	131·0
Ashow	17·	55	158	—	213	20·0	232·0
Coundon	18·1	20	60	—	80	7·5	240
KINETON PARISHES							
Burton Dassett	18·7	800	570	930	2300	46·1	40·4
Honington	25·5	*	401	680	1081	43·9	58·1
Wormleighton	18·2	320	86	310	716	29·5	61·3
Oxhill	23·25	470	422	360	1252	67	37
Ratley & Upton	20·3	480	192	240	912	53	38·3
Priors Hardwick	27·5	400	71	340	811	57·9	47·6

Arable Land: D = Demesne F = Freehold V & C = Villein and Cottager
* = Manuscript illegible

Column 7 attempts to define this anomaly between an agricultural population and their means of subsistence in another way. It records the number of landholding peasants per thousand acres (or 50 virgates) of recorded arable land. The advantages of this presentation are that the variables both of acreages and non-arable land are eliminated, so that a direct comparison exists between people and arable land. The smallest groups of landowners in proportion to arable are found in Kineton Hundred, where in 28 parishes there were merely 20–60 recorded peasants per thousand acres of arable land,

[1] The areal units of land measurement in the Warwickshire Hundred Rolls are carucates for land held in demesne and virgates for peasant land. It is often conventionally assumed that a virgate is 30 acres and a carucate is four virgates, i.e. averaging 120 acres. While in the Warwickshire folios there is no direct evidence to contradict these assumptions, other sources show that while there were four virgates to a carucate, the size of the virgate varied from manor to manor, being 10, 16, 30, or even 40 acres in different places but revealing no significant regional pattern. In view of this inconsistency, a figure of a virgate equalling 20 acres has been adopted for statistical analysis, which represents the average of the definite evidence.

and only in four places does one find a figure in excess of 60. In Stoneleigh, however, ten parishes carry 95 landholders, or over, per thousand acres of arable, and only in one case is there a figure of under 50. In other words, though the areas have similiar population densities, in the north in some cases the same amount of arable land was supporting four times as many people as in the southern parishes. The conclusion of a comparative deficiency of arable land north of the Avon, in contrast to more abundant arable per capita in south Warwickshire at the end of the thirteenth century, is accordingly emphasized.

But against these conclusions the limitations of both the documents and the method must be counter-weighed. There is some evidence that the size of the virgate may have been larger in Stoneleigh—about 30 acres,[1]—and thus we may be under-estimating the amount of arable which existed north of the Avon by using an average of 20 in calculations. Another factor is that the well-developed manorial economy of the south probably employed a number of pure wage labourers or famuli,[2] which, as non-landholders, would go un-recorded in the extents but may have been a significant element both in the population and as consumers of arable produce. Indeed, a cursory examination of the total burden of labour services on the Kineton manors, suggests that they would be inadequate to maintain the economy of the large demesnes. Such deficiency as existed could be met partly by the famuli, and partly by the casual or seasonal wage labour of the cottagers, a group poorly endowed with arable land. Another line of reasoning is that the fertile, recently re-claimed lands of the north may have been more productive in terms of area yield, than the anciently-worked farmlands of the south, with their extensive open-fields of intractable clays. Though such arguments can be adduced to partially explain the different relationships which have evolved between man and land in these two regions of medieval Warwickshire, the main impression that one gains from the Hundred Rolls is of a different agricultural economy and regime north and south of the river Avon.

The most important evidence which the Hundred Rolls afford of these regional differences in agrarian economy is the data they give indirectly of the size of the units of agricultural production. These can be defined as the amount[3] of arable land cultivated by a particular landholder or entrepreneur, within the manor. Initially there is a major distinction between the units of landlord production, the demesnes, and the smaller holdings of the peasant farmers.

When the total amount of land held in demesne is expressed as a percentage of the total arable recorded in the parish, the contrasts north and south of the Avon are not remarkable, though the highest figures generally occur in Kineton Hundred. When, however, the absolute size of the demesne is examined, the area of the Feldon south of the Avon emerges as the region of the large

[1] The man who wrote the Stoneleigh Register in 1392 definitely considered it to be 30 acres. 'Summa totalis acrarum terre quas prior tenet in Stonle ut prefertur preter terram de Cloude, et Fynburghe xii et xvii virgate terre et dimidia et 11 acre quia xxx acre faciunt virgatum terre in Stonle,' Stoneleigh Abbey Leger Book, folio, 85 v. This reference is from an edition of the Leger Book edited by Dr R. H. Hilton, shortly to be published by the Dugdale society.

[2] M. M. Postan, *The Famulus. The Estate Labourer in the Twelfth and the Thirteenth Centuries, Economic History Review*, Supplement No. 2 cites detailed evidence for the existence of such a group on the Estates of the Bishop of Worcester some of which lie close to the south-west of Kineton Hundred.

[3] Thus size is the only available criterion for these units. Many other factors are of course significant, such as regional differences in fertility, perhaps technical efficiency, and a large range of other social and economic factors which may have influenced farming regimes in thirteenth-century Warwickshire.

demesne *par excellence*; and the demesne at this period is known to have been often a highly-organized agricultural unit, actively engaging in market production. Large demesnes are exemplified by the Kineton parishes in Table 3, and a survey of the Hundred reveals 18 parishes with a domanial area in excess of four carucates in 1279. Four, five or six carucates represent an average, but figures of seven and even ten are recorded, obviously associated with large-scale units of agricultural production. Peasant holdings in this area tend to be substantial too, and one or even two virgates were not uncommon. Tysoe, for example, had 27 villein holdings of virgate size, one of two virgates, and only four of half a virgate;[1] Honington had one villein holding of three virgates, eight of two, and fifteen of one.[2] One should emphasize that these were servile holdings, but in the same manors there were also free holdings, equally, if not more substantial in many cases. Thus, south of the river Avon, both the large demesnes and the larger peasant holdings were agricultural units conceivably producing a market surplus[3] over the needs of manorial and family subsistence. Moreover, it is in the light of this economic framework that the analysis of population figures is intelligible. Here was a primarily arable region, capable of supporting an average density of 20–30 recorded persons per thousand acres. The concentration of the means of production in large landlord demesnes, and the existence of a peasantry with substantial land-holdings, helps to account for the high per capita ratio of arable land, despite the existence of a fairly numerous small-holding class (24 per cent). Finally, the bias in the social composition of the population towards a servile peasantry (46 per cent) is related to the demands of the same large-scale demesne enterprise in this region.

It is more difficult to reach conclusions concerning the agrarian economy of Stoneleigh Hundred, lying North of the Avon and on the fringe of the forest of Arden. Certainly the average size of the demesne was much smaller. In four parishes no demesne is recorded at all, and in three instances only does it exceed two carucates, one of these being the eight carucates scattered within the large parish of Stoneleigh (9968 acres). Peasant holdings were much smaller too. The ten *servos* of Walsgrave on Sowe held only half a virgate each,[4] while at Ashow, the 14 free tenants and 14 cottagers possessed only 220 acres between them,[5] the size perhaps of a small demesne south of the Avon. As an area of arable farming then, Stoneleigh hundred was relatively insignificant, and apparently any expansion of the cultivated area undertaken between 1086 and 1279 had lagged considerably behind the well-marked increases of population. A number of interesting questions spring to mind about the economic development of this region. Was its smaller-scale agriculture near to the margins of subsistence, the wealth of the area being correspondingly diminished?[6] Or did alternative means of livelihood, pastoral[7] or

[1] P.R.O. Exch. K.R. Misc. Books no. 15, fol. 95B.
[2] P.R.O. Exch. K.R. Misc. Books no. 15, fol. 105A.
[3] Evidence for the growth of market centres has already been cited. Another indication of a well-developed money economy at the end of the thirteenth century is the fact that many of the peasant rents detailed in the Hundred Rolls, while containing elements of labour services, often involve a pure money rent as well, a due only obtainable by market activity.
[4] P.R.O. Exch. K.R. Misc. Books no. 15, fol. 42B.
[5] P.R.O. Exch. K.R. Misc. Books no. 15, fol. 31B.
[6] That this may have been so is suggested by the low assessments of the settlements north of the Avon for the 1/15 of the 1332 Lay Subsidy, 53 years later. At this time, the centre of economic wealth, if not of population, lay in the Feldon south of the Foss Way.
[7] An important factor in the population increases of the area north of the river Avon was the important monastic foundations which had arisen there in the early middle ages. The

industrial, exist? [1] Or, in view of its arable deficiencies in relation to population, was it the market for the surplus grains of the Feldon? But such problems would require the investigation of other sources and are beyond the scope of this paper. The writer has tried to show that the evidence of the Hundred Rolls demonstrates clearly that quantitatively regional growth of population in the early middle ages was a very uneven process. Those areas with much forest or waste in 1086, typified in Warwickshire by the Arden region, were the scene in the next two centuries of as vigorous a population expansion as one might expect. Alternatively, in more anciently-settled regions, such as the Feldon of south Warwickshire, by the time of Domesday, population numbers were already fixed in a more stable relationship with the resources of the land and changed only slowly in the next two centuries. The impression is also confirmed that in areas of expanding population, different social and economic systems developed and the traditional unit of agricultural organization, the manor, was often radically modified. The failure of cultivation to keep abreast of population increases indicates that the emphasis on arable farming of earlier developed regions was not necessarily emulated. Further investigations in other areas with similiar contrasts in their physical and human environments, are necessary before one can establish whether these basic differences in population history and agrarian development are more widely applicable.[2]

University of Birmingham

Benedictine Priory of Coventry founded in 1043 was already richly endowed by the time of Domesday; in 1122 the Augustinian Priory of Kenilworth was established, while the Cistercian houses of Stoneleigh and Combe were founded in 1154 and 1140 respectively. The relevant fact in the present argument is that it is known that by the end of the thirteenth century these houses were engaging in pastoral activities. It has been calculated that at this time four Cistercian houses in this district (Stoneleigh, Combe, Merevale and Bordesley), kept about 20,000 sheep between them. This estimate is probably a minimum as it is based on Pegalotti's list which did not necessarily include all the sheep, some of the fleeces of which might be sold elsewhere.

[1] The growth and industrialization of Coventry, well advanced by the end of the thirteenth century, may well have helped to modify the economic structure of this region considerably.

[2] Work is at present proceeding in other areas covered by the Hundred Rolls to see whether compatible trends emerge.

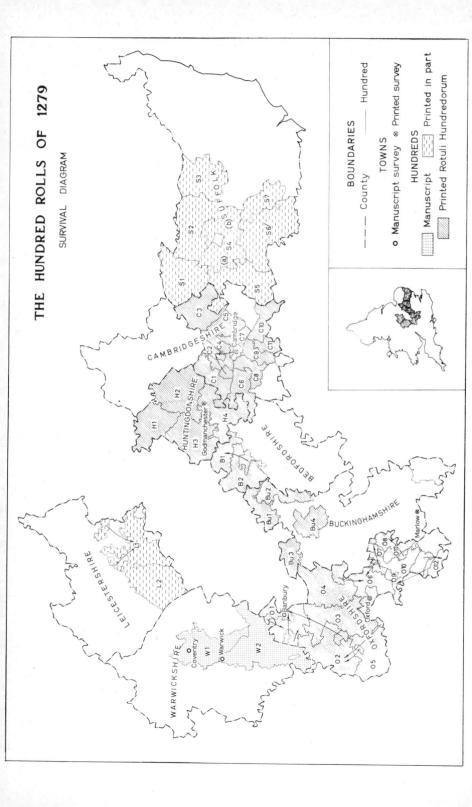

THE HUNDRED ROLLS OF 1279

SURVIVAL DIAGRAM

BOUNDARIES
– – – County
——— Hundred

TOWNS
○ Manuscript survey ⊗ Printed survey

HUNDREDS
Manuscript
Printed Rotuli Hundredorum
Printed in part

LEICESTERSHIRE

WARWICKSHIRE
○ Coventry
○ Warwick
W1
W2

OXFORDSHIRE
⊗ Banbury
⊗ Oxford
Marlow ⊗
O1
O2
O3
O4
O5
O6
O7
O8
O9
O10
O11
O12

BUCKINGHAMSHIRE
Bu1
Bu2
Bu3
Bu4

BEDFORDSHIRE
B1
B2

HUNTINGDONSHIRE
Godmanchester ⊗
H1
H2
H3
H4

CAMBRIDGESHIRE
⊗ Cambridge
C1
C2
C3
C4
C5
C6
C7
C8
C9
C10
C11

SUFFOLK
S1
S2
S3
S4 (a)
(b)
S5
S6
S7

Supplementary Note

In retrospect both greater caution and different techniques could have been used in the analysis of statistics of population and arable land derived from the Warwickshire Hundred Rolls of 1279. M.M. Postan has discussed some of the pitfalls which must temper our use of such data and his observations on the 'lure of aggregates' are especially pertinent to the manipulation of the evidence for medieval population change.[1] Villein holdings might be mere tenurial units and the existence of under-settles (unrecorded in tenant lists) may lead us simultaneously to underestimate population yet to overestimate the size of peasant farms. The gradient of regional contrast described in the paper may accordingly be less sharp than appears at face value. The potential misinterpretations may also be reduced by abandoning the calculation of parish density figures (although this remains worthwhile where medieval boundaries can be reconstructed) and by analysing all data without such additional assumptions. A more recent study is argued from this premise, and a map from this article has been added to the simple location map in the 1958 paper to elaborate the selected statistics in Tables 1-3 (Figure 1).[2]

Key to figure opposite

Bedfordshire	B1	= Stodden	B2 = Willey
Buckinghamshire	BU1	= Bunsty	BU2 = Mousloe
	BU3	= Stotfold	BU4 = Mursley
Cambridgeshire	C1	= Papworth	C2 = Chesterton (3 detached portions)
	C3	= Staploe	C4 = North Stowe
	C5	= Staine	C6 = Longstowe
	C7	= Flendish	C8 = Wetherley
	C9	= Thriplow	C10 = Chilford
	C11	= Whittlesford	
Huntingdonshire	H1	= Normancross	H2 = Hurstingstone
	H3	= Leightonstone	H4 = Toseland
Leicestershire	L1	= Gartree	L2 = Guthlaxton
Oxfordshire	O1	= Banbury	O2 = Chadlington
	O3	= Wootton	O4 = Ploughley
	O5	= Bampton	O6 = Bullingdon
	O7	= Thame	O8 = Lewknor
	O9	= Dorchester	O10 = Ewelme
	O11	= Pyrton	O12 = Langtree
Suffolk	S1	= Lackford	S2 = Blackbourne
	S3	= Hartismere	S4 = (a) Thingoe (b) Thedwastre
	S5	= Risbridge	S6 = Basbergh
	S7	= Cosford	

Space prohibits the inclusion of a post-1958 bibliography (students can consult the annual bibliographies in the *Economic History Review*) but recent research convinces the writer (albeit a truism) that such geographical contrasts as are revealed by the Hundred Rolls can only be evaluated and understood when used collaterally with a wide range of other manorial and public documents. To do otherwise may relegate geographical interpretation to prolegomena: in Warwickshire, for instance, charter evidence (to cite but one supplementary source) as analysed by B.K. Roberts is critical to the study of the aspects of social and economic change measured by the Hundred Rolls.[3] The Hundred Rolls for other counties await a full locational analysis. both by traditional and newer techniques. An availability diagram (Figure 2) is reprinted from J.B. Harley, 'The Hundred Rolls of 1279', *The Amateur Historian,* 5 (1961) to point to a task in historical geography which would enhance our understanding of a seminal period.

1   Postan, M.M. 'Medieval agarian society in its prime. 7. England' being pp 548-632 of Postan M.M. (ed), *The Cambridge Economic History of Europe,* 1, 2nd ed (London 1966). See especially pp 561-3

2   Harley, J.B. 'The settlement geography of early medieval Warwickshire', *Transactions of the Institute of British Geographers,* 34 (1964) pp 115-30

3   Roberts, B.K. 'A study of medieval colonization in the Forest of Arden Warwickshire', *The Agricultural History Review,* 16 (1968) pp 101-13

J.B. HARLEY   August 1969

**The Distribution of Wealth in East Anglia in the Early
Fourteenth Century**
R.E. Glasscock
Reprinted from *Transactions and Papers of the Institute of
British Geographers,* 32 (1963), 113-23

THE DISTRIBUTION OF WEALTH IN EAST ANGLIA IN THE EARLY FOURTEENTH CENTURY

R. E. GLASSCOCK, B.A., PH.D.

ALTHOUGH there is a wealth of material to be drawn from many different sources for the historical geography of medieval England, no single source gives such a comprehensive picture of the country for any one year as the Domesday Book of 1086. Among the mass of records of medieval taxation, there is, however, one source, the Lay Subsidy of 1334, from which a similar but less detailed cross-section may be constructed. This is possible because the amounts of taxation agreed upon in that year were standardized after 1336 and continued to be the bases for subsequent taxations until 1623.[1] This means that the gaps caused by the fragmentary survival of the rolls of 1334 can be filled from information contained in later documents. In this way data are obtainable for the whole of England, with the exception of Cumberland, Westmorland and Northumberland, which were excused the 1334 tax because of damage done by invading Scots, and the palatinates of Chester and Durham which were not liable. This coverage makes the 1334 subsidy unique among the taxes on movable goods. Moreover the date is a most significant one, coming as it does just before the Black Death and before the full impact of the recession of the later Middle Ages, and it is the aim of this short paper to show that, despite drawbacks, the information afforded by this subsidy may be used as a basis upon which to consider the economies of different regions at this critical period.

The 1334 Subsidy

On a number of occasions in the early fourteenth century taxation took the form of a grant, made by Parliament to the Crown, of a proportion of the value of a man's movable goods (principally crops and stock) as distinct from his fixed possessions (land and dwelling).[2] Such a tax was the 'Fifteenth and Tenth' of 1334, so called because a fifteenth was asked from those in rural areas and a tenth from those in boroughs and ancient demesnes. The year was one of innovation in medieval taxation: the old method of direct assessment of the value of individual possessions was replaced by that of agreement by negotiation on the sum that each community was to pay. This move was reflected in the new format of the county rolls, for the lists of personal names that had characterized the rolls before 1334 were replaced by comparatively brief statements showing only the quotas agreed upon for each township or borough.

It is important to emphasize that this change, among others, was introduced to remedy corruption and therefore the 1334 quotas, which are usually slightly higher than those of 1332, might be expected to be nearer the truth than their predecessors. It is, however, an inescapable fact that every tax roll, medieval or modern, conceals the malpractices of both taxers and taxed. There is no evidence to suggest that particular localities were more dishonest than others but that attempts were made to conceal the truth must be accepted as a limita-

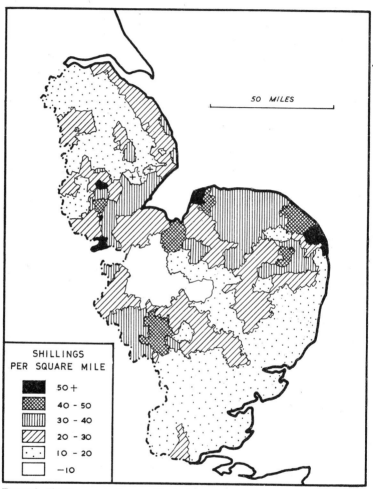

FIGURE 1—The assessment of lay movables in six eastern counties in 1334. The quotas of the boroughs are excluded. Areas marked + are new Fenland townships of the early nineteenth century whose areas are excluded from the calculations.

tion of this particular kind of source material. By standardizing the 'Fifteenth and Tenth', the Crown was assured of a fixed sum of money (that is, the same total income as in 1334) that would neither decline for economic reasons nor as a result of corrupt practices. Whereas the standardization robs the subsequent taxes of much of the interest that they might have possessed had there been a fresh assessment of wealth at every grant, it makes possible the supplementation of the few 1334 survivals by later rolls.

In addition to providing lists of medieval settlements, the 1334 rolls may be used to show how prosperity differed from one area to another, assuming that the tax paid bore some relation to the ability of an area to pay. Maps of the 1334 data showing the average number of shillings per thousand acres have already been produced for five counties, Devon by F. W. Morgan, Dorset by B. Reynolds, Leicestershire by C. T. Smith, Norfolk by H. C. Darby, and Oxfordshire by W. G. Hoskins and E. M. Jope; and numerous local studies have included lists of 1334 quotas.[3] The maps produced are clearly not unrealistic, but as always are not without anomalies. As detailed analysis cannot be attempted without the study of other contemporaneous source materials, the interpretation has of necessity been tentative rather than conclusive. Most of the authors have shown an awareness, some more than others, of the two greatest drawbacks in the source material. First, that the assessments are clearly not on total wealth; the best that we can hope for is that they are a useful guide to relative wealth. Secondly, that as J. F. Willard has shown,[4] most of the movable wealth of the Church was excluded from the Lay Subsidies, although this is offset to some extent by the inclusion of the goods of the villeins of the clergy. Nevertheless a county with much clerical property would tend to appear less wealthy relative to others than it would have done had a complete assessment been carried out.

The Eastern Counties

With these drawbacks in mind, the 1334 quotas, expressed as the average number of shillings per square mile, have been plotted for six counties of eastern England: Lincolnshire, Norfolk, Suffolk, Essex, Cambridgeshire and Huntingdonshire (Fig. 1).[5] These form a convenient unit and contain a wide range of values. With a view to comparing results the areal units used for each county in this mapping correspond with those used by Darby in the work on the Domesday geography.[6] In order to avoid undue distortion of rural distributions, the quotas of the thirteen taxation boroughs and of three other places are omitted.[7] Elsewhere quotas at a tenth have been converted to a fifteenth for mapping purposes. There is little reason to suspect a lack of standardization between the assessors of each county, for the average figures on both sides of county boundaries show no alarming inconsistencies.

By far the largest area was assessed at between ten and twenty shillings per square mile, the value of almost the whole of Essex, much of Suffolk including the Sandlings, part of south-west Norfolk, and much of the western clayland of Lincolnshire. The only area with a lower average, under ten shillings per square mile, was the peat fen of Cambridgeshire and Huntingdonshire. A number of areas were assessed at between twenty and thirty shillings per square mile, the largest of which were in Lincolnshire (the eastern clays and silts, parts of the western lowlands, and Elloe wapentake in the Fenland) and in the boulder-clay area of north Suffolk and south Norfolk. Averages of between thirty and forty shillings per square mile were characteristic of north and south-east Norfolk, much of the Lincolnshire fen and west Cambridgeshire. The highest averages, in fact among the highest in England, were those of central Cambridgeshire, parts of west and north-east Norfolk and some small pockets on the clays of Kesteven.

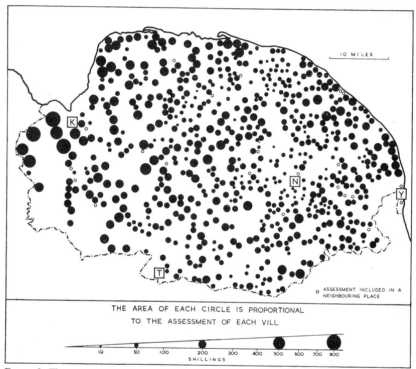

FIGURE 2—The assessment of lay movables in Norfolk in 1334. The quotas of the four boroughs are excluded.

Whilst this is the broad picture, the distribution of lay wealth within individual counties demands closer attention. Both in Suffolk and Essex the uniform spread of lay wealth was striking, for most of the two counties was assessed at between ten and twenty shillings per square mile, an average only exceeded on some of the boulder-clay areas of Suffolk, and even then, never above thirty shillings. This uniformity may be misleading, and should not be taken as indicating similar sources of wealth. For example, it is most unlikely that in Essex the economy on the London Clay and alluvium in the south was the same as that on the more tractable soils in the north of the county. That this uniformity conceals differences in agricultural economies is undoubtedly true.

In contrast to this apparent uniformity of wealth in Suffolk and Essex, the two counties with substantial areas of peat fen, namely Cambridgeshire and Huntingdonshire, showed startling contrasts in values. This is best seen in Cambridgeshire where the poverty of the peat fen is emphasized by the great wealth of the near-by central uplands.

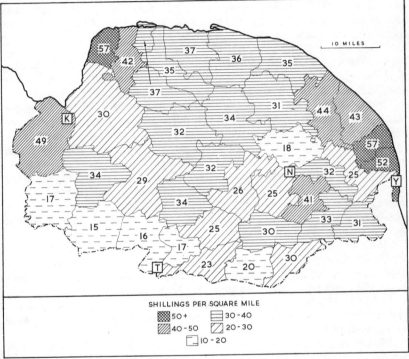

FIGURE 3—The assessment of lay movables in Norfolk in 1334. The quotas of the four boroughs are excluded.

As might be expected Norfolk and Lincolnshire, the counties with the greatest variations in topography and soils, show the most complex patterns and the greatest range of lay wealth, and for this reason these two counties are selected for more detailed study.

Norfolk

Norfolk (Fig. 2) has 650 quotas of which the largest are those for the fen townships to the west of King's Lynn, and those around the northern rim of the county. In the south settlements were more numerous but their quotas less substantial. As many of the large quotas represent movable wealth on large land areas, a better idea of the distribution of lay wealth may be seen from a choropleth map (Fig. 3).

As the 1334 quotas for Norfolk have already been published[8] they have been used by geographers in studies of various parts of the county. Smith used the high amount of lay wealth in the Broadland as a possible indicator of a high density of population in the fourteenth century.[9] By compiling a map of the assessment in 1334 as average number of shillings per thousand acres, Darby was able to show the richness of the silt fen of west Norfolk,[10] and Miss J. B. Mitchell has emphasized the great wealth that was to be gained from this region before the extensive drainage schemes of later years.[11] From studies of the customs accounts of King's Lynn she has suggested that the sources of wealth in the area were the hides and skins of cattle fed on rich pastures and the corn crops of the drier land, rather than wealth accruing from the wool of marshland sheep.

Most of mid- and south-east Norfolk and the loams of the north-east had movable wealth assessed at between thirty and forty shillings per square mile, whilst part of the Good Sand region of the north-west averaged above forty shillings. Exactly why this north-western tip of the county was so rich both in 1086 and 1334 is as yet unexplained. Although Arthur Young's term 'Good Sand' served to distinguish north-west Norfolk from the very light sands of the Breckland it seems clear that the light soils of the north were carrying considerable agricultural wealth in the fourteenth century, presumably stemming from a husbandry based on sheep and corn, similar to that described by K. J. Allison for the sixteenth century.[12]

Although the figures for the light sands of the Breckland were low compared with the rest of Norfolk, they were comparable with those for almost the whole of Essex and much of Suffolk. The little wealth there was probably came from sheep. Another area where there was little wealth was that immediately to the north of Norwich, today characterized by much heath and rough pasture. The poverty of this region in contrast to the surrounding area is a striking feature both in 1086 and 1334.

Taken as a whole, the Norfolk map substantiates the belief that Norfolk was one of the richest counties in medieval England, and the distribution of lay wealth clearly bears some relation to the potentialities of the various distinctive parts of the county.

Lincolnshire and the Fenland

Lincolnshire (Fig. 4) displays characteristics similar to those of Norfolk, for of the 700 rural quotas the largest were those of the fen townships, the western fen margins and the long coastal strip, all areas containing extensive low-lying marsh. Regions already devised for the mapping of Domesday statistics have been used as a base upon which to calculate the average 1334 assessments

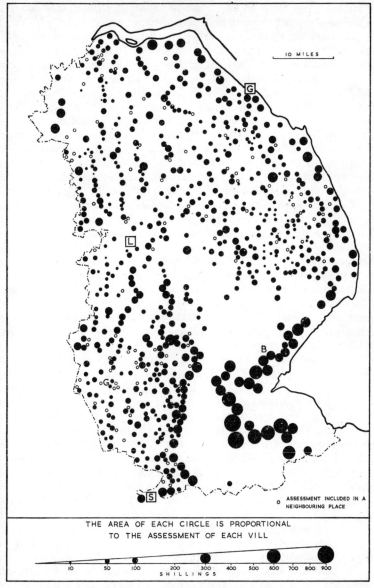

FIGURE 4—The assessment of lay movables in Lincolnshire in 1334. The quotas of the three boroughs, plus Grantham and Boston are excluded.

per square mile (Fig. 5). While such regions are largely artificial they do serve as a background against which to discuss the data.

Despite considerable variations in topography and soils most of the north-west and parts of the south-west of the county had an average assessment of between ten and twenty shillings per square mile. This includes the distinct units of the Isle of Axholme, the sands and clays of Lindsey, the middle Witham fens and the chalk Wolds, areas which like the Good Sand of Norfolk owe much of their later prosperity to the agricultural improvers. Yet it seems likely that the light soils of Lincolnshire were carrying far less agricultural wealth in 1334 than their Norfolk counterparts, and their average assessments were more closely paralleled in both the Breckland and the claylands of Essex and Suffolk. The poverty of the chalk Wolds contrasted with the higher assessments on the neighbouring heavier soils, particularly the distinctive south-western part of the Wolds covered with chalky boulder-clay, and to the east, the long coastal strip of clays and silts. Some of the highest assessments in the county occurred on the fen and it is to this area that attention must now be turned.

A feature of the Fenland in the fourteenth century was the striking differ-ence between the amounts of movable wealth on the silt and the peat (Fig. 6). The average assessment of the peat fen of Cambridgeshire and Huntingdonshire was the lowest figure in the six counties and showed barely one-quarter of the movable wealth of the more fertile silt. The only exception to the greater wealth of the silt was the low figure for the wapentake of Elloe in south Lincolnshire; it has been suggested that this was due to the small amount of movable wealth on the badly drained silt between the Nene and the Wash.[13] In recent papers, H. E. Hallam,[14] working from the late thirteenth-century censuses of Spalding Priory, has demonstrated the tremendous increase in population in the Lincoln-shire fen between 1086 and 1287, and has shown that this was accompanied by the reclamation of over one hundred square miles of land in Elloe alone during the period. The same process must have been at work elsewhere on the silt fen to account for the fact that it was carrying almost twice as much movable wealth as some of the surrounding uplands. The Fenland is one of the few areas where we can be fairly certain of the nature of movable wealth; Hallam's work on the Spalding toll-list of 1336 has shown that the fen products included much cheese and butter, horses and cattle, hides and skins, turves and wood. These products also appear on the customs accounts of King's Lynn.

It is only where such contemporary documents have been studied that the pattern produced by the 1334 figures can be interpreted and brought to life, for the quotas give no clues to the nature of the movable wealth. The mapping has shown that quite different amounts of wealth were to be found on areas of similar physical conditions, and, on the other hand, similar amounts were to be found on contrasting areas. For example, an average lay wealth between thirty and forty shillings per square mile is indicated for the silts of the Lincoln-shire fen, the clays of west Cambridgeshire, the heavy soils of south-east Norfolk, and the light soils of north Norfolk. It is therefore clear that while topography

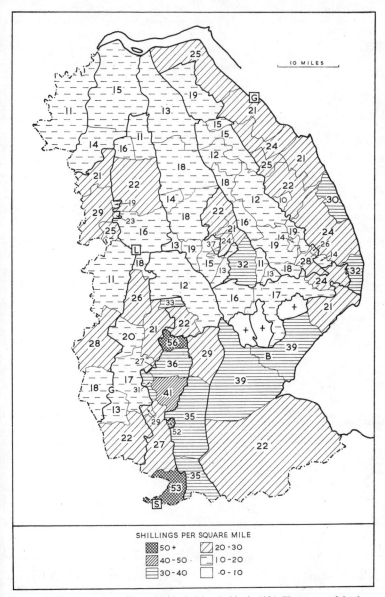

FIGURE 5—The assessment of lay movables in Lincolnshire in 1334. The quotas of the three boroughs, plus Grantham and Boston are excluded. Areas marked + are new fenland townships of the early nineteenth century whose areas are excluded from the calculations.

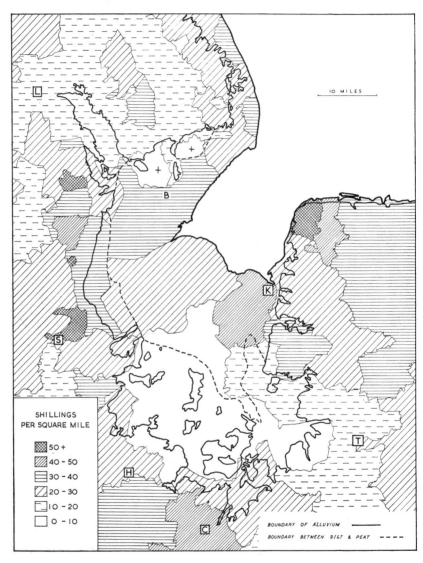

FIGURE 6—The assessment of lay movables in the fenland in 1334. The quotas of the boroughs and Boston are excluded. Areas marked + are new townships of the early nineteenth century whose areas are excluded from the calculations.

and soils exert broad controls over agricultural practice, the complex distribution of wealth can only be explained by examination of the economic and social conditions of particular areas. While the broad pattern outlined above may be modified by subsequent knowledge of the distribution of ecclesiastical wealth, the 1334 evidence does provide a framework into which the mass of local evidence from other sources may be placed in an effort to determine the nature of local agrarian economies at this transitional period.

ACKNOWLEDGMENT

The author wishes to acknowledge a grant from The Queen's University of Belfast to cover the cost of the illustrations.

NOTES

[1] For a convenient summary of taxation in this period see M. W. BERESFORD, 'The Lay Subsidies', *The Amateur Historian*, 3 (1958), 325–8, and 4 (1959), 101–9.

[2] The standard work is J. F. WILLARD, *Parliamentary taxes on personal property, 1290 to 1334* (Cambridge, Mass., 1934).

[3] F. W. MORGAN, 'The Domesday geography of Devon', *Transactions of the Devonshire Association*, 72 (1940), 321; B. REYNOLDS, 'Late medieval Dorset: three essays in historical geography', unpublished M.A. thesis, University of London, 1958; C. T. SMITH in *Victoria County History, Leicestershire*, 3 (1955), 134; H. C. DARBY, *The medieval Fenland* (1940), 134–5; W. G. HOSKINS and E. M. JOPE in A. F. MARTIN and R. W. STEEL (eds.), *The Oxford Region* (1954), 109. For examples of local studies see W. G. HOSKINS and H. P. R. FINBERG, *Devonshire studies* (1952); M. W. BERESFORD in *Victoria County History, Essex*, 4 (1956), 296–302, and in *Victoria County History, Wiltshire*, 4 (1959), 294–303.

[4] J. F. WILLARD, op. cit., 102–9.

[5] This forms part of a general survey of the 1334 subsidy for England, in progress.

[6] H. C. DARBY, *The Domesday geography of eastern England* (1952).

[7] The boroughs are Lincoln, Stamford, Grimsby: Norwich, King's Lynn, Thetford, Great Yarmouth: Dunwich, Ipswich, Orford: Colchester: Cambridge: and Huntingdon. The three other places, excluded because of their large quotas, are Boston, Grantham and Bury St. Edmunds.

[8] W. HUDSON, 'The assessment of the townships of the county of Norfolk', *Norfolk Archaeology*, 12 (1895), 243–97.

[9] C. T. SMITH in J. M. LAMBERT and others, *The making of the Broads*, Royal Geographical Society, Research Series, 3 (1960), 82.

[10] H. C. DARBY, op. cit. (1940), 134. The data has been remapped to show average number of shillings per square mile to make the Norfolk map uniform with those of the other counties.

[11] J. B. MITCHELL, *Historical geography* (1954), 191–4.

[12] K. J. ALLISON, 'The sheep-corn husbandry of Norfolk in the sixteenth and seventeenth centuries', *The Agricultural History Review*, 5 (1957), 12–30.

[13] H. C. DARBY, op. cit. (1940), 137.

[14] H. E. HALLAM, 'Some thirteenth-century censuses', and 'Population density in medieval Fenland', *Economic History Review*, second series, 10 (1958), 340–61, and 14 (1961), 71–81.

Evidence in the 'Nonarum Inquisitiones' of Contracting Arable Lands in England during the Early Fourteenth Century
A.R.H. Baker

Reprinted from *Economic History Review,* XIX (1966), 518-32

Evidence in the 'Nonarum Inquisitiones' of Contracting Arable Lands in England during the Early Fourteenth Century

By ALAN R. H. BAKER

During the early decades of the fourteenth century, the high tide of medieval land colonization in England was on the turn. The arable acreage, which had been expanding for centuries, now began to contract. Attempts to explain this retrenchment have invoked soil exhaustion and climatic changes as well as an easing of the pressure of population upon land resources. Whatever the causes, it is invariably suggested that marginal land, what M. W. Beresford has called 'half-wanted land', was the first to be abandoned.[1] A revealing insight into this reversion of arable land is provided for much of England by the *Nonarum Inquisitiones* of 1342. This present paper, based upon the published returns of this inquiry,[2] investigates regional variations in the abandonment of arable land in the early fourteenth century, first within England as a whole and secondly within three counties in particular.

I

The *Nonarum Inquisitiones* relate to a grant by Parliament to Edward III in 1342, to assist him in his wars, of one-ninth of the value of corn, wool and lambs produced in the realm. The value of these items was assessed, parish by parish, from the evidence given by groups of parishioners under oath. The inquiries were conducted in the early months of 1342 but related to agricultural production during 1341. Because the ninth was assessed after the tithe had been taken, it was in fact one-ninth of nine-tenths of the total value of lay agricultural production and therefore identical with the tithe of these three items (corn, wool and lambs). As a guide, therefore, the jurors who compiled the parish returns had before them an assessment of one-tenth of clerical incomes in 1291, the taxation of Pope Nicholas IV.[3] The jurors were required to explain the discrepancy between the old and new values. Discrepancy there inevitably was, for clerical incomes included more than the tithe of corn, wool and lambs; there was, in addition, the value of the glebe and monastic holdings, the revenue from the small tithes of cider, flax, hemp, geese and poultry, together with oblations, mortuary fees and other items. Other discrepancies, however, arose from changed agricultural conditions, most notably a contraction in the

---

[1] M. Beresford, *The Lost Villages of England* (1954), pp. 201–5.
[2] *Nonarum Inquisitiones in Curia Scaccaria*, ed. G. Vanderzee (Record Commissioners, 1807), pp. 1–450.
[3] *Taxatio Ecclesiastica Angliae et Walliae auctoritate Papae Nicholai IV circa 1291*, ed. J. Caley and S. Ayscough (Record Commissioners, 1802).

arable acreage between 1291 and 1341.[1] In many instances, jurors explained that the value of the ninth in 1341 was lower than that of the tithe of 1291 in part because *terre jacuerunt inculte et frisce* or because *terre jacuerunt frisce que arari et seminari solebant.*

Although the Record Commission published a transcription of the *Nonarum Inquisitiones* as long ago as 1807, this body of evidence has not been fully employed. It has, however, been distinctively used by R. A. Pelham and E. M. Yates. In 1931 Pelham produced a map showing the 1341 valuations of corn, wool and lambs in each Sussex settlement, which demonstrated the overwhelming predominance of corn-growing even among settlements in the Chalk zone, long regarded as primarily a sheep-raising region.[2] Pelham has also used the valuation of wool in the parishes of Sussex to estimate the number of sheep in each parish in 1341; he drew a map showing the distribution of sheep in the county in relation to its geology, demonstrating that there was a marked concentration of sheep on the South Downs, especially towards the east which was probably more open than the loam-covered area further west and that large numbers of sheep belonged to parishes on the rich arable area of the coastal plain around Chichester.[3] More recently Yates has shown that there was in western Sussex a positive relationship between the values of corn, wool and lambs in 1341 and soil fertility: the highest valuations were recorded in parishes on the most fertile soils, the lowest valuations in parishes on the least fertile soils.[4] In these studies, only incidental reference was made to the decline in values because of a contracting arable acreage. Much more emphasis on this aspect of the returns is to be found in E. Venable's study of the *Nonarum Inquisitiones* for Cambridgeshire. Venables, in a lecture to the Cambridge Antiquarian Society delivered in 1850, said: 'The first thing which strikes us as worthy of remark in examining these entries is the very large quantity of land lying untilled, and that not waste land merely, which had never been brought into cultivation, but land thrown out of cultivation from the poverty of tenants or other causes ... no less than 4,530 acres of land were lying fallow in 20 parishes of the county. ... In most of these parishes the cause assigned for the lands lying uncultivated is the poverty of the tenants, and their inability to find seed, while the complaints are bitter and frequent of the innumerable "taxes and tallages" by which they have been so impoverished.' [5] M. W. Beresford has pointed out that this contraction of the arable in England during the fourteenth century revealed itself 'not in a thin long high-water

[1] E. M. Yates, 'Medieval assessments in north-west Sussex', *Transactions and Papers of the Institute of British Geographers*, 20 (1954), 75–92; J. L. M. Gulley, 'The Wealden landscape in the early seventeenth century and its antecedents', unpublished Ph.D. thesis, University of London, 1960, pp. 504–7.
[2] R. A. Pelham, 'Studies in the historical geography of medieval Sussex', *Sussex Archaeological Collections*, LXXII (1931), 157–84.
[3] R. A. Pelham, 'The distribution of sheep in Sussex in the early fourteenth century', *Sussex Arch. Coll.* LXXV (1934), 128–35.
[4] E. M. Yates, *loc. cit.* pp. 83–92 and 'The Nonae Rolls and soil fertility', *Sussex Notes and Queries*, 15 (1958–62), 325–8.
[5] E. Venables, 'The results of an examination of the "Nonae Rolls", as they relate to Cambridgeshire', *Proceedings of the Cambridgeshire Antiquarian Society*, 1 (1859), 7–14.

mark, the whole length of a shore, but in many scattered pools'.[1] He observed that even a casual study of the extents among the *inquisitiones post mortem* of the early fourteenth century showed many examples of land lying uncultivated, although he seems to have overstated the case in saying that 'the *Nonarum Inquisitiones* of 1340 have many such entries in all counties'.[2] Beresford also noted that generally there was no positive correlation between villages having uncultivated lands recorded in the *Nonarum Inquisitiones* and villages which were later to be deserted: 'Many of the churches of our deserted villages appear in the 1340 list without any plea for consideration.'[3]

The *Nonarum Inquisitiones* have also been employed in a number of unpublished studies. B. Reynolds's study of late medieval Dorset, for example, included a map, based largely on these returns, showing the distribution of places with references to untilled lands in the early fourteenth century. Many of these places had a common location, in what Reynolds described as 'the depressed area south of Yetminster'. Here, he claimed, were the true marginal lands of Dorset, the lands first to go out of cultivation in a period of agricultural retrenchment. The soils of this area, formed mainly on the Cornbrash, Oxford Clay and Upper Greensand, are coarse and with a tendency to acidity; and the Upper Greensand soils here are more stony and less retentive of plant food than their kindred soil further north. It was this north-western position of Dorset whose arable acreage was first to be drastically reduced.[4] J. L. M. Gulley, in his study of the Weald, included a map showing changes in prosperity in the Kent and Sussex Weald between 1291 and 1341. In some instances (Hellingly, Ticehurst, Heathfield, Burwash), parishes which included uncultivated land in 1341 had declined in their tax-paying capacity during the previous fifty years. At Hooe and Ninfield not only had marshes been inundated but upland arable lay untilled because of the poverty of the parishioners and the total valuation of both parishes had fallen. In other parishes, the existence of untilled land was not always indicative of declining prosperity. At Itchingfield, where over 350 acres lay uncultivated in 1341, the valuation was higher than in 1291 and this was true also of Rudgwick, where over 300 acres lay untilled, and of four parishes (Brede, Icklesham, Pett and Fairlight) which had lost land to the sea. There was no significant change in prosperity 1291–1341 at Etchingham and Mayfield, which had lands untilled, nor at Salehurst, Udimore, Wartling and Guestling, where land lay submerged. On the other hand, parishes like Pulborough had declined in their valuation though their returns made no mention of land going out of cultivation. In the two parishes where land untilled was specifically attributed to poverty, the valuation had declined; but land went out of cultivation for other reasons, many less connected with general prosperity – hence the variable relation between untilled land and general prosperity. In at least five instances, land had been lost by imparking; in Burwash,

[1] M. Beresford, *op. cit.* p. 204.
[2] *Ibid.* p. 427.
[3] *Ibid.* pp. 313–14.
[4] B. Reynolds, 'Late medieval Dorset: three essays in historical geography', unpublished M.A. thesis, University of London, 1960, pp. 129–30, 166–8.

supplementary documentation shows that while some land reverted to waste, other was newly enclosed. Gulley concluded: 'It is thus hardly possible to regard the scattered instances of *terra frisca* in the 1341 returns as the first signs of a general decline; the period between 1291 and 1341, the early fourteenth century, was one of general stability in the condition of Wealden agriculture.' [1] Gulley's perceptive study thus serves as a warning against taking all of the un- tilled lands recorded in the *Nonarum Inquisitiones* as being indicative of declining prosperity.

II

Each of the above studies has been concerned with the *Nonarum Inquisitiones* for only a part of England. There has been no serious attempt to view the evidence for the country as a whole. A map has now been drawn showing the distribution of those vills in which uncultivated lands were recorded in 1341 (Fig. 1). Even the picture presented by this map is not complete. The published transcriptions of the *Nonarum Inquisitiones*, on which the map is based, relate to only 27 English counties and for two of these, Essex and Cornwall, the returns are too brief to be used as reliable guides to the existence or otherwise of abandoned arable land. So information has been plotted on the map for only 25 counties. As the inquiries were conducted on a parochial basis, one cannot be sure that they were carried out with any great degree of uniformity from one county to another or even from parish to parish within a single county. Some of the irregularity in the distribution of vills with uncultivated lands recorded in 1341 must be related more to this lack of standardization in the conduct of the inquiry than to any actual contrasts in the distribution of untilled land. This would seem to be the case in at least two instances: first, none of the Lincolnshire vills had uncultivated lands recorded in 1341 and yet it is known from other sources that land was being abandoned here, es- pecially on the Wolds [2]; secondly, although many vills in northern Bucking- hamshire and northern Bedfordshire recorded untilled lands, immediately across the adjacent county border, in Northamptonshire, no mention was made of the abandonment of arable lands in any of the vills. The absence of vills with uncultivated lands recorded in Lincolnshire and the sharp contrast along the boundary of Northamptonshire with Buckinghamshire and Bedfordshire together suggest that this map may only be interpreted in a positive, not in a negative, manner. Where vills have been plotted, formerly cultivated lands were certainly lying untilled; but an absence of vills from any particular area must not be interpreted as necessarily implying an absence of untilled arable in that area.

This map of some of the contracting arable lands of England in 1341 clearly

[1] J. L. M. Gulley, *op. cit.* pp. 345–8.
[2] M. Beresford, *op. cit.* pp. 164, 170–2, 202–4, 241. For a number of Lincolnshire vills, the 1341 returns state that the parishioners were not taxed *propter debilitatem*, but made no reference to abandoned lands. Such was the case at Farforth; *Nonarum Inquisitiones*, p. 261.

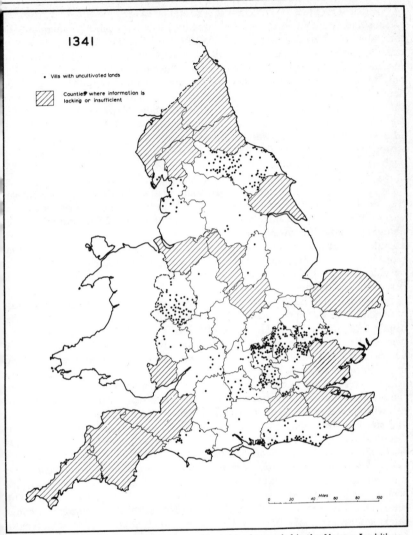

Fig. 1. England: distribution of vills with uncultivated lands recorded in the *Nonarum Inquisitiones*.

has serious limitations. Nevertheless, it does indicate at least four areas in which acreages of abandoned land were considerable.

(1) *The North Riding.* Land had gone out of cultivation here in at least 90 vills, many of which lay in the northern section of the Vale of York and in Pennine valleys.[1] The amount of untilled land is usually recorded in carucates

[1] *Nonarum Inquisitiones*, pp. 219–45.

or bovates, sometimes as a fraction of the total cultivated lands, and occasionally as a measurement in acres. Consequently, it is impossible to calculate the total amount of land recorded as lying untilled here. There is no sure way of relating the 40 carucates of untilled lands at Romaldkirk, for example, with the idle lands at Danby, where one-third of the cultivated area lay waste.[1] For only five vills is any reason given for the abandonment of land: at Alne 200 acres lay untilled, worth nothing, another 1,000 acres were not worth more than 2*d.* an acre *propter sterilitatem terre*; at Easingwold, 200 acres lay untilled *pro defectu vaniagii* (for lack of a plough team); and at Bowes, Brignall and Marske a total of 17 carucates lay waste, *distructe per Scotos* [2]. Raids and destructions by Scots were also called to account for abandoned arable lands in each of the 14 Lancashire vills in which such lands were recorded in 1341.[3]

(2) *Shropshire*. Land had gone out of cultivation here in more than 50 vills, most of which lay in the uplands to the south-west of the River Severn.[4] As was the case in the North Riding, the amount of untilled land was recorded in a variety of ways and no calculation may safely be made of the total amount of abandoned land. In over half of the vills concerned, arable land had been abandoned because of the poverty of parishioners: in many instances, growing crops had been destroyed by bad weather and sheep afflicted by murrain. In 17 vills the uncultivated lands were those of impoverished tenants who had deserted their holdings.

(3) *Sussex*. Land had gone out of cultivation here in more than 50 vills, most of which lay in southern Sussex.[5] The amount of untilled land in each vill was usually recorded in acres: in all, more than 5,600 formerly cultivated acres were said to be lying untilled and a further amount of more than 3,500 acres had been flooded by the sea. In addition, some uncultivated land was recorded in carucates or virgates, some was recorded in vague terms. Clearly, more than 10,000 acres of land in Sussex had been withdrawn from cultivation or lost to the sea during the half-century before 1341. The reasons stated by jurors for this withdrawal of land from cultivation included fear of attacks by the French and sterility of the soils, but most common was the poverty of the tenants: at Goring, 900 acres, including some of the demesne lay unsown *propter defectu hosebondrie et propter impotentiam tenentium (sic)*.[6]

(4) *A group of counties to the north and west of London*. The *Nonarum Inquisitiones* show clearly that much land was going out of cultivation in the early fourteenth century in and around the Chiltern Hills and the Oxford Clay Vale. The returns for three of the counties in this area (Bedfordshire, Cambridgeshire and Buckinghamshire) have been analysed more closely than those of the areas so far considered and the results of this more detailed analysis will now be presented separately.

[1] *Ibid.* pp. 233, 232.
[2] *Ibid.* pp. 233–4, 242–3.
[3] *Ibid.* pp. 35–41.
[4] *Ibid.* pp. 182–94.
[5] *Ibid.* pp. 350–403.
[6] *Ibid.* p. 389.

III

Study of the Bedfordshire returns has shown that in about two-fifths of the parishes of the county for which the returns have been published the value of corn, wool and lambs in 1341 was lower than it had been half a century earlier because some land had been abandoned since 1291.[1] Relatively more land was going out of cultivation in the upper than in the middle reaches of Bedfordshire's river valleys; relatively more land was going out of cultivation on light soils than on heavy and on intermediate soils; and the abandonment of arable lands was closely associated with reduced population pressure and with shortages of seed corn. Relatively more vills were contracting their arable areas in the higher parts of the north-west and south-west, and relatively fewer vills were contracting their arable areas in the lower parts of the east, in the Vale of Bedford along the lowlands of the Ouse and Ivel rivers. Particularly instructive evidence relates to lands in the extreme south of Redbornstoke hundred, located on the greatest extent of light soils in Bedfordshire, derived from the Lower Greensand. At Segenhoe, where more than 200 acres lay uncultivated, jurors noted that the reduced value of the ninth was due partly to the fact that land there was *zabulosa* (sandy, gravelly), *pro majori parte nec crescit nisi siligo*.[2] At Millbrook, in addition to more than two carucates of untilled demesne and 50 untilled acres of William of Stodden, *parochiani non seminaverunt hoc anno medietatem terrarum suarum pro debilitate terre quia zabulosa est nec crescit nisi siligo pro majori parte*.[3] At Flitwick, where one carucate lay vacant, *terra zabulosa est nec crescit nisi siligo pro majori parte*.[4] And at Maulden 24 acres *jacent frisce pro debilitate terrarum que debuerunt seminari et non fuerunt*.[5] In five other parishes soils were called to account for reduced values of the ninth.[6]

Rarely did the local jurors state whether the land had been abandoned in the years immediately preceding 1341 or some considerable time before. At Millbrook, it was said that lands had not been sown *hoc anno* but at Battlesden, in Manshead hundred, the lord of the manor was reported to have had 40 acres which had not been sown for 30 years.[7] In some parishes the changes already effected in the landscape by 1341 suggest that much land had been abandoned for some time: arable land had reverted to pasture and dwellings had tumbled into ruins. At Hockliffe, in Manshead hundred, it was said of 40 acres *solebant seminari et modo jacent ad pasturam*.[8] At Eversholt, in the same hundred, and at Caddington, in Flitt hundred, *multae mansiones extrepuntur ubi magnus numerus bidentium nutriabatur et . . . rediguntur in pasturam*.[9] Decayed dwellings resulted from punier populations. At Tottenhoe, in Manshead hundred, many

[1] A. R. H. Baker, 'The contracting arable lands of Bedfordshire in 1341', *Bedfordshire Historical Records* (forthcoming); *Nonarum Inquisitiones*, pp. 11–22.

[2] *Nonarum Inquisitiones*, p. 14.

[3] *Ibid.* p. 14.

[4] *Ibid.* p. 14.

[5] *Ibid.* p. 15.

[6] Chellington, Houghton Regis, Potton, Meppershall and Studham: *ibid.* pp. 11, 16, 17, 21.

[7] *Ibid.* pp. 12, 14.

[8] *Ibid.* p. 12.

[9] *Ibid.* p. 12.

messuages were *derelicta pro defectu inhabitantum*; at Stodham, in the same hundred, 60 messuages were *derelicta sine habitatoribus*; and at Luton *circa ducentes messuagia sunt derelicta sine habitatoribus*.[1] In all of these localities, as well as the Meppershall in Clifton hundred, and at Steppingly in Redbornstoke hundred, decayed dwellings were associated with abandoned arable lands.[2] The *Nonarum Inquisitiones* suggest, in fact, that the most common causes of abandoned arable lands in Bedfordshire were a shrinkage of village populations and a shortage of seed corn.

The published transcriptions of the *Nonarum Inquisitiones* provide returns for 139 parishes in Cambridgeshire and abandoned land is recorded in 36 of them.[3] Thus in a quarter (25·9 per cent) of the parishes, the value of corn, wool and lambs in 1341 was lower than it had been half a century earlier because arable land had gone out of cultivation in the intervening period. For many vills, the acreage of untilled land is recorded, but for some it is measured only in terms of carucates or virgates and for others only a vague statement is given of the proportion of the erstwhile arable lands lying uncultivated. At least 4,870 acres of arable land were recorded in 1341 as having gone out of cultivation since 1291. A map (Fig. 2), showing the location of both vills with untilled lands and those not having uncultivated lands recorded, may be used together with the generalized soil map and the statistics set out in Table 1 to investigate regional variations in the contraction of arable lands in Cambridgeshire and any relationship between this retrenchment and soil types.

Because of the very different numbers of vills involved within each hundred, the relative number of vills having uncultivated lands recorded is of greater significance than the absolute numbers of such vills. In each of the five hundreds of Longstow, Weatherley, Staines, Radfield and Chilford, the number of vills having untilled lands expressed as percentages of all such vills in the county was markedly greater than the total numbers of vills in each of these hundreds expressed as percentages of the total number of vills in the whole county. In other words, relatively more vills had uncultivated lands recorded in these hundreds than in the other hundreds of Cambridgeshire. In the three hundreds of Ely, North Stow and Whittlesford, on the other hand, the opposite was the case: in each of these hundreds the number of vills having uncultivated lands expressed as percentages of all such vills in the county was markedly less than the total numbers of vills in each of these hundreds expressed as percentages of the total number of vills in the whole county. In addition, none of the 18 vills for which returns are available in the three hundreds of Staploe, Chesterton and Cheveley had any untilled lands recorded in 1341.

The *Nonarum Inquisitiones* for Cambridgeshire suggest that in the early fourteenth century relatively more vills were witnessing contractions of their arable lands in the two upland clay areas in the south-west and south-east of the county and that relatively fewer vills were experiencing such contractions in the fenland and in the belt of chalk country with lighter soils which separates

[1] *Ibid.* pp. 11, 14.
[2] *Ibid.* pp. 17, 21.
[3] *Ibid.* pp. 201–18.

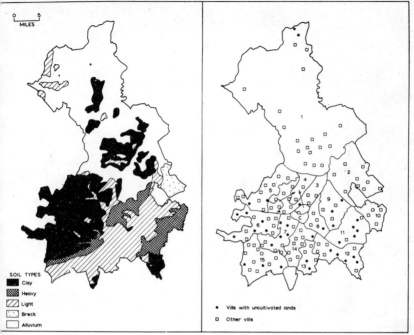

Fig. 2. Cambridgeshire: a generalized map of soil types and the distribution of vills in the 1341 returns.

Key to the hundreds:

1. Ely
2. Staploe
3. North Stow
4. Chesterton
5. Papworth
6. Long Stow
7. Weatherley
8. Flendish
9. Staines
10. Cheveley
11. Radfield
12. Chilford
13. Whittlesford
14. Thriplow
15. Armingford

the two clay areas. There was a broad correlation between the uplands and heavy soil areas on the one hand and a particularly marked contraction of arable lands on the other hand. A more exact relationship between soil types and diminishing arable lands cannot be established from a study of the *Nonarum Inquisitiones* alone: even within a single parish there often occurred considerable edaphic diversity but the returns are not sufficiently descriptive to allow the exact location of the uncultivated lands to be determined. In only three vills (Orwell in Weatherley hundred, and Balsham and Weston Colville in Radfield hundred) was sterility of the land called to account for the contracting arable, but it is interesting to note that all three lay in the Clay uplands.[1]

Of the 4,870 acres of untilled arable in Cambridgeshire in 1341, 1,220 acres

[1] *Ibid.* pp. 210, 212.

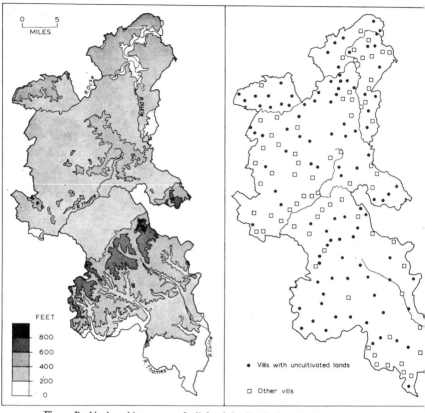

Fig. 3. Buckinghamshire: a map of relief and the distribution of vills in the 1341 returns.

lay in the fenland. At Tydd St Giles more than 400 acres had been inundated
and laid waste *per fadacionem turbarum* and at Newton 620 acres of arable land
had been flooded for the same reason.[1] At Impington in North Stow hundred,
200 acres of arable and 100 acres of pasture were recorded as having been laid
waste by flooding.[2] In all, some 1,420 acres of arable in Cambridgeshire lay
submerged in 1341. The remaining untilled lands – more than 3,450 acres –
had gone out of cultivation for other reasons, principally shortages of seed corn
and poverty of the tenants and because a great part of the Lent corn had
perished that year; at Bassingbourn, 400 acres lay untilled because of the
tenants' impoverishment and because the Lent corn had totally perished.[3]
Harvest failures, partial or total, meant that there was less seed for sowing in
the ensuing agricultural year and the arable acreage was consequently reduced.

[1] *Ibid.* p. 203.
[2] *Ibid.* p. 204.
[3] *Ibid.* pp. 205–6.

The poverty of the tenants was in some places, such as Kingston and Swaffham Prior, ascribed to the frequency of recent taxation.[1] Whatever the precise causes, much land which had once been cropped lay untilled and neglected. In at least one instance abandoned arable lands were associated with a shrinking population: at Long Stow, where a great part of the parish lay untilled, *plura messuagia existunt vacua*.[2]

The published transcriptions of the *Nonarum Inquisitiones* for Buckinghamshire provide returns for 176 identified parishes in Buckinghamshire and uncultivated land is recorded in 101 of them.[3] Thus in more than half (57·4 per cent) of the parishes, the value of corn, wool and lambs was lower in 1341 than it had been half a century earlier because land had been taken out of cultivation

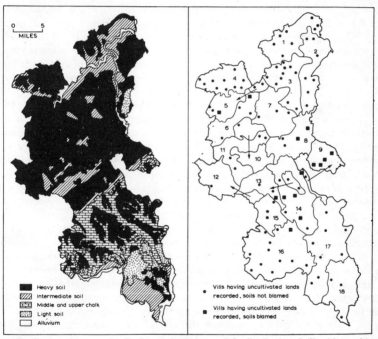

Fig. 4. Buckinghamshire: a generalized map of soil types and the distribution of vills with uncultivated lands recorded in 1341.

Key to the hundreds:

1. Bunsty	7. Mursley	13. Stone
2. Moulsoe	8. Cottesloe	14. Aylesbury
3. Seckloe	9. Yardley	15. Risborough
4. Stotfold	10. Waddesdon	16. Desborough
5. Rowley	11. Ashendon	17. Burnham
6. Lamua	12. Ixhill	18. Stoke

[1] *Ibid.* pp. 208, 211.
[2] *Ibid.* p. 208.
[3] *Ibid.* pp. 326–40.

in the intervening period. For many vills, the acreage of untilled land is recorded, but for some it is measured only in terms of carucates or virgates and for others only a vague statement is provided of the proportion of the erstwhile arable lands lying uncultivated. At least 5,539 acres were recorded in 1341 as having gone out of cultivation since 1291. A map (Fig. 3), showing the location of both vills with untilled lands and those not having uncultivated lands recorded, may be used together with a map of relief, a generalized soil map (Fig. 4) and the statistics set out in Table 2 to investigate regional variations in the contraction of arable lands in Buckinghamshire and any relationship between this retrenchment and soil types.

As in the Cambridgeshire analysis, the relative numbers of vills having uncultivated lands is of greater significance than the absolute numbers of such vills because of the very different numbers of vills involved within each hundred. In each of the three hundreds of Bunsty, Stotfold and Desborough the number of vills having uncultivated lands expressed as percentages of all such vills in the county was markedly greater than the total number of vills in each of these hundreds expressed as percentages of the total number of vills in the whole county. In the four hundreds of Moulsoe, Waddesdon, Ixhill and Stoke, on the other hand, the opposite was the case: in each of these hundreds the number of vills having uncultivated lands expressed as percentages of all such vills in the county was markedly less than the total numbers of vills in each of these hundreds expressed as percentages of the total number of vills in the whole county. The *Nonarum Inquisitiones* for Buckinghamshire suggest that in the early fourteenth century relatively more vills were witnessing contractions of their arable lands in the extreme northern and south-western parts of the county. No clear correlation between contracting arable lands and particular soil types is immediately discernible. The highest proportion of vills with uncultivated lands were located in Desborough hundred, in the Chilterns, on a variety of heavy, light and chalk-derived soils. Much of the woodland of the Chilterns was probably on the heavy soil derived from Clay-with-flints, so that much of the arable abandoned here must have been on the lighter and chalkier soils. In Desborough hundred mention is made of soil poverty as a factor contributing to the arable retrenchment in only one vill (Hughenden).[1] In northern Buckinghamshire, Bunsty and Stotfold hundreds were located on intermediate and heavy soils and perhaps much of the arable abandoned would have been on the heavier soils. In none of the the vills of these hundreds, however, was soil poverty called to account for the arable retrenchment. In Buckinghamshire as a whole, soil poverty was mentioned as a factor contributing to the declining acreage of arable in only 14 vills, the villages of eight of which lay on the loamy, fertile, easily-worked soils of the Lower Chalk bench below the escarpment of the Chilterns.[2] In these eight, land had been abandoned *propter debilitatem terre* and the untilled acres probably lay to the north in the clay vale

---

[1] *Ibid.* p. 334.
[2] Buckland, Edlesborough, Ellesborough, Great Missenden, Hughenden, Ivinghoe, Linslade, Little Kimble, Marsworth, Pitstone, Preston Bisset, Thronborough, Wendover and Wing: *ibid.* pp. 326–31, 334.

r to the south in the Chilterns: the return for Little Kimble, in Stone hundred, pecifically states that one-third of the arable had been abandoned because f its poverty and that the untilled acres lay above the Icknield Way.[1]

The principal reason given for the abandonment of arable lands in Buckinghamshire was not poverty of the soil but of the tenants. At Ivinghoe more than oo acres lay neglected partly because the parishioners were impoverished, having neither animals for ploughing nor seed for sowing; and at Great Missenden 200 acres lay in a similar condition and for a similar reason.[2] In some parishes, land lay untilled because impoverished parishioners *non habent unde terras suas colere possunt*: at Chetwode and Foxcote large parts of the erstwhile arable lay uncultivated for this reason, at Maids' Moreton 30 acres, at Burnham 300 acres and at Hitcham 50 acres.[3] In some places abandoned lands resulted from shrinking populations: at Saunderton many tenants had gone, leaving their lands untilled and their houses empty; at Hambleden 12 carucates lay neglected and nearly all of the tenants of these lands were reported to have left their messuages; and at Cublington, two carucates lay untilled and 13 dwellings stood empty, their tenants having gone away because of their poverty.[4]

IV

Any conclusions derived from this study must suffer from being based upon only a broad consideration of the national picture and somewhat more detailed yet till broad considerations of only three counties. Nevertheless, the evidence of the *Nonarum Inquisitiones* presented here does suggest that during the early fourteenth century arable land was being abandoned on a variety of soils. It seems that in Bedfordshire more land was going out of cultivation on light than on heavy soils, whereas in Cambridgeshire the reverse was the case and in Buckinghamshire no clear correlation between contracting arable lands and particular soil types in discernible. But in all three counties, the contraction of arable lands was more marked in the uplands than in the lowlands. The 'half wanted lands' embraced a variety of soils and were more abundant in the higher than in the lower parts of these three counties. The *Nonarum Inquisitiones* also suggest that the reversion of arable land and the dereliction of many messuages were closely associated with impoverished and shrinking populations and with shortages of seed corn. If local jurors are to be believed, this tendency towards reversion was in some places aided by soil exhaustion and abetted by climatic hazards. When a harvest failed wholly or partially, whatever the reason, there was less seed available for sowing in the following agricultural year and the arable acreage contracted. Again, when a harvest failed both peasants and livestock might die of hunger or at least have their effectiveness impaired by undernourishment, and with fewer and weaker beasts for ploughing and fewer and weaker hands to hold the plough and tend to the crops, the arable acreage

---

[1] *Ibid.* p. 328.
[2] *Ibid.* pp. 326, 328.
[3] *Ibid.* pp. 330–2.
[4] *Ibid.* pp. 327, 334, 335.

might have diminished still further. The general picture outlined in this paper needs to be brought into sharper focus by more detailed studies of narrower localities. Such studies would surely reveal the influence of individual personalities, of land tenure, of village size and of other parochial factors in addition to the regional edaphic and topographic factors considered here. It seems probable, for example, that proportionately more land would have remained in cultivation longer in parishes with relatively dense populations than in parishes with relatively sparse populations, for the *Nonarum Inquisitiones* suggest that the link between the cultivated area and the pressure of population was a strong one during the early fourteenth century.

Department of Geography, Cambridge

Acknowledgement

The author wishes to thank Mr G. R. Versey and Miss M. Lawson, of the Drawing Office, Department of Geography, University College London, the former for advice on the construction of the maps and the latter for drawing them.

Table 1

Hundred	A No. of vills involved in this study	B No. of vills with uncultivated lands	No. of vills with uncultivated lands as % of total no. of vills involved in a particular hundred	No. of vills in a particular hundred as % of the total no. of vills involved in the county	No. of vills in a particular hundred with uncultivated lands as % of total no. of vills in the county with uncultivated lands
			B as % of A	A as % of C	B as % of D
1. Ely	20	2	10·0	14·4	5·6
2. Staploe	9	0	—	6·5	—
3. North Stow	10	1	10·0	7·2	2·8
4. Chesterton	5	0	—	3·6	—
5. Papworth	11	2	18·2	7·9	5·6
6. Long Stow	13	6	46·2	9·4	16·7
7. Weatherley	12	5	41·7	8·6	13·9
8. Flendish	4	1	25·0	2·9	2·8
9. Staines	6	3	50·0	4·3	8·3
10. Cheveley	4	0	—	2·9	—
11. Radfield	7	5	71·4	5·0	13·9
12. Chilford	11	5	45·5	7·9	13·9
13. Whittlesford	5	2	40·0	3·6	5·6
14. Thriplow	9	1	11·1	6·5	2·8
15. Armingford	13	3	23·1	9·4	8·3
	139 (C)	36 (D)		100·1	100·2

Table 2

Hundred	A No. of vills involved in this study	B No. of vills with uncultivated lands	No. of vills with uncultivated lands as % of total no. of vills involved in a particular hundred	No. of vills in a particular hundred as % of the total no. of vills involved in the county	No. of vills in a particular hundred with uncultivated lands as % of total no. of vills in the county with uncultivated lands
			B as % of A	A as % of C	B as % of D
1. Bunsty	12	8	66·7	6·8	7·9
2. Moulsoe	16	7	43·8	9·1	6·9
3. Seckloe	17	11	64·7	9·7	10·9
4. Stotfold	12	10	83·3	6·8	9·9
5. Rowley	8	5	62·5	4·5	5·0
6. Lamue	8	4	50	4·5	4·0
7. Mursley	5	3	60	2·8	3·0
8. Cottesloe	6	4	66·7	3·4	4·0
9. Yardley	8	5	62·5	4·5	5·0
10. Waddesdon	7	1	14·3	4·0	1·0
11. Ashendon	9	4	44·5	5·1	4·0
12. Ixhill	8	1	12·5	4·5	1·0
13. Stone	8	5	62·5	4·5	5·0
14. Aylesbury	11	7	63·6	6·3	6·9
15. Risborough	5	3	60	2·8	3·0
16. Desborough	13	12	92·3	7·4	11·9
17. Burnham	14	8	57·2	8·0	7·9
18. Stoke	9	3	33·3	5·1	3·0
	176 (C)	101 (D)		99·8	100·3

Supplementary Note

In the same year as this article was first published, Barbara F. Harvey surveyed the demographic trends of the first half of the fourteenth century and concluded that land values and our present topographical studies do not support the thesis that the agricultural crises of the decade 1311-1320 inaugurated a continuous decline in population down to the Black Death. In particular, she argued that the crises of 1315-17 only brought about a levelling of the population trend, not a fall.[1] J.C. Russell has suggested that the proportion of the mortality of 1315-17 caused by epidemics rather than by starvation has been underrated.[2] One doubts whether such a distinction between starvation and disease is valid, for chronic malnutrition could well cause low resistance to disease.

Changes in English agrarian economies during the first half of the fourteenth century, as evidenced by such sources as the *Nonarum Inquisitiones,* are consistent with a halt in the growth in population, and perhaps with a slight decline. The *Nonarum Inquisitiones* demonstrate that during the early fourteenth century arable land was being abandoned in widely separated parts of England for a variety of reasons, among which impoverished and shrinking populations and shortages of seed corn were important. Some of the doubts about the changing nature of the national economy in this period stem from the already considerable variations in levels of prosperity from region to region[3] and from the fact that the pace and nature of change also varied regionally, making generalisation at a national level difficult. Only more detailed studies of particular localities will clarify the picture. The results of a closer analysis of the *Nonarum Inquisitiones* for Sussex have been published and for Bedfordshire are forthcoming.[4] But no further attempt has been made to compare precisely the changes in prosperity between 1291 and 1341 and this major research field awaits its cultivator.

1   Harvey, B.F. 'The population trend in England 1300 -1348', *Transactions of the Royal Historical Society,* 5th ser, 16 (1966) pp 23-42

2   Russell, J.C. 'The pre-plague population of England', *Journal of British Studies,* 5 (1966) pp 1-21

3   Glasscock, R.E. 'The distribution of wealth in East Anglia in the early fourteenth century', *Transactions of the Institute of British Geographers,* 32 (1963) pp 113-23, reprinted *infra* pp 71-81, 'The distribution of lay wealth in Kent, Surrey and Sussex, in the early fourteenth century', *Archaeologia Cantiana,* 80 (1965) pp 61-8

4   Baker, A.R.H. 'Some evidence of a reduction in the acreage of cultivated lands in Sussex during the early fourteenth century', *Sussex Archaeological Collections,* 104 (1966) pp 1-5; 'The contracting arable lands of Bedfordshire in 1341' *Bedfordshire Historical Records,* 49 (forthcoming)

ALAN R.H. BAKER   August 1969

**The Market Area of Preston in the Sixteenth and
Seventeenth Centuries**
H.B. Rodgers
Reprinted from *Geographical Studies,* 3 (1956), 45-55

THE MARKET AREA OF PRESTON IN THE SIXTEENTH AND SEVENTEENTH CENTURIES

By H. B. Rodgers

In recent years increasing attention has been paid, especially by geographers, to the associations between town and country. It is now fully recognized that every town, whatever its size and character, provides services not only for its own community but for the populations of surrounding rural areas and smaller urban centres. Dependence on the area so served, the urban field or hinterland, varies with the type of town. To many industrial towns the link with the countryside has become purely incidental, but the simplest type of market town still serves, for its size, a very large area, with which its economic life is closely linked.

Before the industrial revolution remodelled the English landscape and economy most towns were essentially market towns and were associated at least as intimately with the country as are modern representatives of the type. Indeed, town and country were then more closely interdependent, for to some extent market town and market area formed an economic unit. The former existed largely to provide the latter with commercial and social services and with the products of domestic industry in exchange for food and many types of raw material. The ability of the town to grow beyond the limits set by its own resources of agricultural land by specializing in trade and industry was thus governed by the extent, productivity and density of population of its market area. A reconstruction of the limits of a town's influence over the surrounding countryside in past centuries is thus a useful key to an understanding of its growth.

Unfortunately, the practical difficulty of assembling sufficient data to enable the former limits of market areas to be plotted is a serious one. Their accurate delimitation in the modern landscape is far from easy and invariably necessitates much first-hand inquiry, while for their past extent we are entirely dependent on documentary sources. Moreover, many of the records which would have been of most value in the solution of this problem, for example tradesmen's account-books and details of transactions in the market, were naturally considered to be of trivial importance by contemporaries and have rarely survived. Thus, in the majority of cases, the reconstruction of the town's zone of influence in past periods must depend on scraps of evidence preserved by chance in records of a variety of types. Exact delimitation can hardly be expected, but from the following discussion of Preston's market area in the late sixteenth and the seventeenth centuries it is hoped to show that even an approximate indication contributes something to an understanding of town growth.

In Lancashire a broad upland salient, divided by the valley of the Ribble into the Rossendale and Bowland Fells, extends westwards from the main mass of the Pennines towards the coast. Between the coast and the steep flanks of the fells the drift-covered Triassic plain—the ultimate extension of the English Lowlands—tapers northwards and is almost severed by the deep re-entrant of the Ribble estuary. Preston, at the head of the estuary, commanded the lowest fords and bridge, and was thus in a position of great importance, for the west-coast route to Scotland has no easier alternative than to cross the Ribble here. All lines of communication from Roman to modern times have been forced to pass through or close to the town. To the north-east of Preston the Ribble valley leads directly to one of the lowest of the Pennine passes and the Aire valley. This route also has been followed by Roman, medieval and modern communications. Preston thus stood at the junction of two nationally important routes and was invested by its position with a measure of strategical significance. But the town was never a military centre, for its site in no way assisted fortification. Lancaster, at another critically narrow point on the north-south route, eclipsed Preston strategically, for here the Lune crossing was commanded by the easily fortified Castle Hill. Preston thus grew slowly and naturally as a commercial centre, rather than with the artificial rapidity of a fortified town.

To Preston, therefore, the local aspects of its position were of greater significance than its strategical values. Much of Lancashire, through high altitude or poor drainage, remained unfit for agriculture and thinly settled at least until the eighteenth century. Preston, however, was centrally placed relative to some of the most productive and populous districts of the county. From the time of the Scandinavian settlements the undulating drift-plain of the Central Fylde seems to have been unusually densely peopled.[1] Certainly, Domesday vills were more closely spaced here than anywhere else in the county, and sixteenth-century records reveal remarkably low proportions of waste land.[2] On the well-drained peat-free soils of this boulder-clay upland, most land was in arable use and already the region almost deserved its eighteenth-century title 'the granary of Lancashire'. In great contrast, the mosses and marshes of the north and west of the Fylde were virtually empty of settlement, and here agriculture was necessarily pastoral in character. The mossland thus made a small but distinctive contribution to Preston's trade, especially in cattle.

In the Lancashire Plain south of Preston there were similarly sharp contrasts between the belt of undrained moss and marsh flanking the coast from the Ribble to the Alt and the higher, better-drained country inland. Here, too, settlement in the mosslands was confined to the few expanses of boulder-clay and sands, and the use of mosses and marshes as summer pasture promoted pastoral specialization. East of the Douglas, on drift-smeared Triassic platforms, arable farming was dominant and settlement as close as in the Fylde. Less than five miles from Preston the Bowland and Rossendale Uplands rise abruptly, to heights of almost 2000 feet. Like the mosslands of the plain these, too, were regions of thinly scattered population and pastoral farming. Indeed, the highest moorland was empty, and has remained so to the present day. But both regions turned their most favourable faces towards Preston. The Loud valley of the Bowland Fells and the Calder-

---

[1] F. T. Wainwright, 'The Scandinavians in Lancashire', *Transactions of the Lancashire and Cheshire Antiquarian Society*, vol. LVIII (1945-46), p. 77.
[2] H. B. Rodgers, 'Land Use in Tudor Lancashire' (*Transactions and Papers, 1955*, Institute of British Geographers, no. 21, pp. 79-98).

Darwin lowland of the Rossendales open out towards Preston and were easily accessible from the town. Of even greater significance to Preston was the broad trough of the Ribble valley, separating the two moorland blocks, where farming showed almost as great an emphasis on tillage as in any other part of Lancashire. In one respect Upland Lancashire was of greater consequence to Preston than the plain: in the Rossendale valleys domestic woollen manufacture was becoming rather more than a mere supplement to an unrewarding agriculture[1] and Preston was able to share in the brisk trade in yarn and cloth.

Relative to these contrasted regions of North and Central Lancashire Preston occupied a central and nodal position. On the threshold of three areas of intensive arable farming in the peat-free lowlands and the Ribble valley, it was also within easy reach of regions of pastoral specialization in the mosslands and fells. No town was better placed to benefit from the trade which inevitably sprang from these regional contrasts with their associated surpluses and deficits. Moreover, the town's positon between the granaries of the Lancashire Plain and the embryonic industrial areas of Rossendale and South-east Lancashire, already outgrowing their local food-supply, was becoming significant. But all these advantages of position must have remained sterile had not an effective system of highways linked the town with its hinterland. In fact, as Fig. 1 shows, Preston was one of the main foci of the county's road system. Almost all the highways shown on this map are known from contemporary sources to have been in use at this period or earlier, though to a few no reference earlier than Moll's map of 1724 has been discovered. The map demonstrates how closely the town was tied to its hinterland.

Almost every aspect of Preston's position thus encouraged its growth as a market centre and, later, as the county town in fact if not in name. Even in the Domesday survey it has a special significance, for it was the capital manor of the large Hundred of Amounderness. From 1199 rights to hold markets and a fair were granted by the Crown and the borough quickly became a major trade centre. By the seventeenth century the thrice-weekly market could no longer be accommodated in the market place and overflowed into the principal streets of the town. A full contemporary description[2] leaves no doubt of the very great volume and variety of the town's trade. Perhaps the most significant function of the market was that it was the clearing house not only for the agricultural surpluses but also for the textile manufactures which were being produced in increasing quantities in its market area. Wheat and wool, cattle, hides and dairy-stuffs all had their places in the square or adjacent streets, but in addition there was a weekly yarn market and a considerable trade in cloth. The market served also as an outlet for the products of Preston's own craftsmen. The Guild Rolls,[3] which serve almost as a trades' directory to the seventeenth-century town, show that most of the townsmen practised a craft, and their shoes and saddlery, cloth, guns and wheels added to the town's trade. Indeed, seventeenth-century Preston was essentially an industrial community: pure commerce gave employment to comparatively few, and the town's economy rested on

[1] G. H. Tupling, *Economic History of Rossendale*, 1927, p. 167.
[2] R. Kuerden, *A Brief Description of the Borough and Town of Preston c. 1682*, 1818.
[3] W. A. Abram (ed.), 'Preston Guild Rolls 1397-1682', *Record Society of Lancashire and Cheshire*, vol. IX (1884).

the supply of manufactured articles to the country people who thronged the town on market and fair days.

For an attempt at a reconstruction of the market area in the late sixteenth and seventeenth centuries four types of evidence are available. First, a very general indication of its limits is given by the contemporary distribution of adjacent markets, shown on Fig. 2.[1] It will be noted that the distribution of markets in Lancashire at this period was far from even. The two highland areas, the Rossendale and Bowland Fells, were poorly served. Most of their trade was handled in towns around their flanks, of which Preston was one. Except in the uplands the most marked discontinuity in the pattern of markets was that surrounding Preston and the nearby village of Walton-le-Dale. The latter was not the serious rival to Preston that the map suggests for it failed to grow and was quite over-shadowed by the larger town.

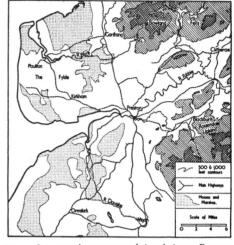

Fig. 1. Seventeenth-century roads in relation to Preston·

Its markets were held on days when there were none in Preston, to which it appears to have been commercially subservient. Apart from that at Walton no market was held within seven miles of Preston to the west and south and only one (at Blackburn) was less than twelve miles to the east or north. No claim can be made that Preston dominated the whole of the area within these arcs, for the series of smaller centres undoubtedly served parts of it. But there is evidence (cited below) to suggest that many of the markets in the surrounding towns were in decline, and that these were situated eccentrically in their market areas with little influence over the country towards Preston. Valuable though it is, however, the evidence contained in the map of contemporary markets has serious limitations. The map makes only an approximate suggestion of the extent of market areas; it gives no indication of the tendency of these to overlap nor does it hint at the ability of the larger towns to poach within the preserves of the smaller centres, thus capturing a proportion of their trade. Fortunately, evidence from other sources is available to counteract these weaknesses.

Direct evidence of the former extent of the market area is given by records of transactions in Preston in which the homes of the buyers or sellers are mentioned, though regrettably little of this material appears to have survived. Examination

[1] The markets plotted are listed in G. H. Tupling, 'An Alphabetical List of the Markets and Fairs of Lancashire', *Transactions of the Lancashire and Cheshire Antiquarian Society*, vol. LI (1936).

of the borough records, supplemented by a few chance discoveries in other documents, yielded only the cases plotted in Fig. 2. Slight as it is, this evidence is

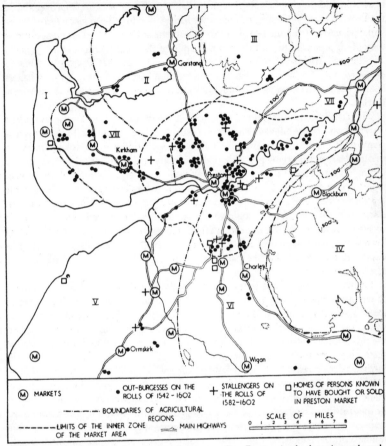

Fig. 2. Distribution of markets in the area surrounding Preston in the late sixteenth and seventeenth centuries. The Roman numerals in Fig. 2 refer to the contemporary agricultural regions. The West Fylde (I), the North Fylde and Over-Wyre (II), the Bowland Fells (III), the Rossendale Upland (IV) and the greater part of South-west Lancashire (V) were all regions of dominantly pastoral farming. In the plain this was primarily the consequence of poor drainage, in the fells of steep slopes, damp climate and poor soils. In the lowland of Central Lancashire (VI), in the Ribble Valley (VII) and Central Fylde (VIII), all of which were free from poor drainage and peat-mosses, a better-balanced system of agriculture with far greater emphasis on arable land was established (See H. B. Rodgers, op. cit.). From the map it is clear that Preston was centrally placed in relation to these districts of contrasted agriculture, and was therefore able to dominate the inter-regional trade in complementary surpluses and deficits.

suggestive. Most of the transactions involved men living less than seven miles from the town, within the area between it and the ring of competing centres. But one of the more distant symbols is of particular interest, for it represents the villagers of Marton, 13 miles west of Preston, who clearly made frequent use of the town's market in addition to their local centre, Kirkham. Their plea for improvement of the Preston road on the grounds that they had by flooding 'been many tymes in the winter debarred from the benefit of the Marquette at Preston[1]' leaves no doubt that they often preferred to visit the town in spite of the long journey, which actually lay through Kirkham. Thus it is unsafe to conclude that Preston's influence extended only to the circle of smaller centres. Where roads were good, villagers from a greater distance seem habitually to have visited it in addition to their local market.

The distribution of the homes of a class of Preston burgesses known as stallengers may also contribute evidence of the extent of the market area. The rights and status of the stallengers, many of whom were not resident in the town, are by no means clear, but it seems probable that originally their only privilege was that of setting up their stall in the market-place and selling on equal terms with the townsmen.[2] Later their status becomes obscure, but to the out-of-town stallenger the right to sell in the square must have remained important. Thus a map of the distribution of their homes should add to our knowledge of the range of Preston's commercial contacts. Again, the symbols representing stallengers on Fig. 2 fall mainly within seven miles of Preston. But a few lived at greater distances, strengthening the impression that the market drew part of its trade from districts up to fifteen miles away.

Finally, the rolls of out-burgesses, who were usually residents of surrounding towns and villages, may perhaps assist in the delimitation of Preston's market area. The out-burgesses had only limited privileges of citizenship: in a sense they were 'country members' of the urban community. Apart from their right to attend the proverbially infrequent Guild celebrations, they were entitled only to buy for themselves and their families and to sell foodstuffs, both with freedom from toll, in the town's market.[3] If this privilege — for which a substantial fee was paid — was habitually exercised, a map of their homes must give some indication of the market area. But gradually, especially in the seventeenth century, the character of the out-burgesses appears to have changed. By this time Preston was in most respects the real county town, and the out-burgesses, who had become far more numerous, seem to have valued the social privileges of citizenship more highly than its economic advantages. Thus only the earlier Guild Rolls are of any possible value in this context, and only those of the late sixteenth century have been used in the construction of Fig. 2. This evidence corroborates that from other sources. Almost three-quarters of the out-burgesses lived within seven miles of Preston, but a considerable minority had homes almost a score of miles away.

The map of the homes of stallengers and out-burgesses cannot be accepted without reserve as evidence of the extent of the market area, for the ill-defined

---

[1] A petition to the Quarter Sessions in 1655, quoted in R. Sharpe-France, 'The Highway from Preston into the Fylde', *Transactions of the Historic Society of Lancashire and Cheshire*, vol. XCVII (1945) p. 33.
[2] H. W. Clemeshay, *A History of Preston*, 1912, p. 85.
[3] Ibid., p. 84.

status of these two groups makes for great difficulty in interpretation. Certainly, no reconstruction could depend on this evidence alone, but it is significant that it closely corroborates evidence from other and safer sources. Indeed the fact that each of these four quite different approaches to the problem of setting limits to Preston's commercial influence leads to virtually the same conclusions increases the confidence with which Fig. 2 may be used and interpreted.

It is quite clear from Fig. 2 that the core of Preston's market area, within which it appears to have dominated all trade, occupied most of the country between it and the circle of smaller centres. These seem to have had little attraction for villagers living between them and their powerful rival. But Preston's influence was by no means limited to this district within a radius of some seven to twelve miles: it was clearly able to compete successfully with the smaller towns throughout their market areas. It was a town of higher rank than Kirkham, Chorley, Garstang and others of their type. Preston offered a wider range of goods and services than these and was visited — perhaps most frequently, though not exclusively, during its two annual fairs — by the populations of the smaller towns and their market areas. The townsmen of Kirkham, for example, are known to have bought their wine and other luxuries there.[1] Thus, beyond the area completely dominated by Preston lay another zone, whose trade the borough shared with local centres. To some of the smaller towns the effects of Preston's competition seem to have been disastrous. Leland found that Chorley had a 'wonderful poore or rather no market'.[2] The condition of Croston was similar and that of Garstang worse, for here the market had apparently ceased to function.

The limits of neither the inner nor the outer zone of Preston's market area were arranged symmetrically round the town. On both zones the influence of communications, themselves closely guided by physical factors, can be seen. The area which focused exclusively on Preston extended farthest from the town to the west, north and south. In all these directions communications were good and rivals weak. To the south-east and south-west the map suggests that Preston's influence declined more abruptly. The failure of the borough to attract much trade from the south-east was doubtless the result of competition from Blackburn, also growing quickly at this time. But the abrupt falling off in Preston's influence to the south-west was more apparent than real, for here was a group of thinly settled peat-mosses. Preston doubtless dominated what little trade there was from this area, but it was one of the least productive parts of the market area.

The limits of the outer zone of the market area, within which the town's influence was strong but not unchallenged, were even more irregular. The whole of the Fylde was closely associated with Preston. Here accessibility undoubtedly fostered the extension of commercial contacts, for the low expanse of boulder-clay which runs from Preston to the coast at Blackpool carries a road which dates in part from Roman times. Similarly, the Ribble valley was well served by roads from the town and, as far east as Clitheroe, was strongly under Preston's influence. But there is little sign that the borough attracted even occasional trade from the area

[1] R. C. Shaw, *Records of the Thirty Men of Kirkham*, 1930.
[2] L. Toulmin Smith (ed.), *Leland's Itineraries*, 1910, vol. 5, p. 44.

centred on Garstang. The Bowland Fells and the mosses north of the Wyre were almost empty of population, which may explain the absence of any evidence of their association with Preston. The mid-Wyre valley was more densely settled, but its villages appear to have looked to Lancaster as a regional centre. Southwards from Preston the outer zone of the market area extended much further than to the north. The two main highways to Chorley and Wigan passed through a closely settled region of intensive arable farming and made it possible for villages up to fifteen miles distant from the town to maintain easy contact with it. But Blackburn seems to have been strong enough to prevent the penetration of Preston's influence south-eastwards into the remoter Rossendale valleys. And to the south-west a physical obstacle, the Douglas valley, stood in the way of any extension of Preston's commercial links. Though three roads crossed the valley they were often impassable in winter through flooding and, beyond the river, Ormskirk was able to dominate the trade of the mosslands.

Though the market was by far the strongest of the bonds between the town and the countryside other aspects of Preston's life strengthened its position as a regional centre. Since the Conquest Preston has been hardly inferior to Lancaster as a legal centre, and in the seventeenth century six courts, of which three were of more than local importance, held their sittings in the town. Indeed they were so prominent in its life as to prompt from a contemporary observer the opinion that 'Preston lived largely by the quill'.[1] The evidence of the Guild Rolls is that few townsmen were employed directly in legal work, but there is no doubt that trade in the market and shops must have received a stimulus from the sessions of the more important courts. Of these the Chancery Court of the Duchy served the entire county, while the Quarter and Special Sessions heard cases from both the Hundreds of Amounderness and Blackburn. The courts thus strengthened the ties between the town and its market area and brought on occasional journeys potential customers from far beyond the normal limits of its commerce. The legal function thus made a considerable, though indirect, contribution to growth.

The last of the regional functions which Preston had acquired by the end of the seventeenth century is the most difficult to define though it was becoming progressively more significant. Preston was now the accepted centre of the social life of the greater part of the county, the county town in all but name. Some of the absentee squires who established their town houses here have left in their diaries[2] evidence of the importance of this side of the town's life. Certainly the craftsmen and traders must have derived great benefits from this influx of purchasing power. How far Preston's influence as a social centre extended is not easy to discover, but the rolls of out-burgesses of the seventeenth century probably — though by no means certainly — give some indication. It has already been noted that the out-burgess of this period appears to have sought this status for its social rather than commercial advantages. Indeed, membership of the Guild seems to have been

---

[1] Ralph Thoresby in his diary, quoted in H. Fishwick, *The History of the Parish of Preston*, 1900, p. 61.
[2] Extracts from one of these diaries, kept by Lawrence Rawstorne of Rawtenstall between 1683 and 1686, have been published in the *Preston Guardian* between January and March 1909.

something of a social symbol among the petty gentry. There can be little doubt that, having taken the trouble and expense to secure citizenship, they must have made frequent visits to Preston to take advantage of its widening range of shops and social amenities, which now included a theatre. If this is true a map of their

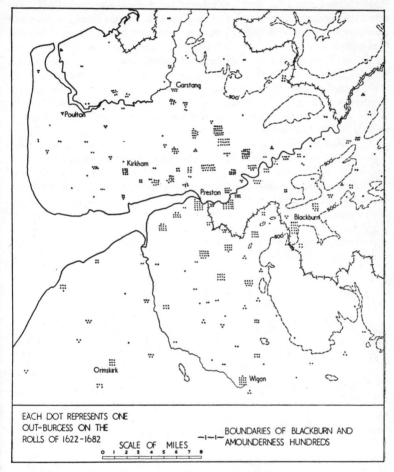

Fig. 3. Homes of Out-Burgesses of Preston 1622-82.

homes should give some indication of the area for which Preston was a social focus. As Fig. 3 shows, most of the towns and villages within fifteen miles of Preston and many as far as twenty miles away now had representatives on the rolls. Even the larger market town which, like Ormskirk and Blackburn, had been able to resist the spread of Preston's commercial influence were unable to rival it as a social centre and accordingly they too sent their contingents. Only Liverpool, Manchester and Lancaster, all on the borders of the county, were socially, as well as commercially, the equals of Preston.

Imperfect and tentative though this attempted reconstruction of the past extent of Preston's market area has been, a number of conclusions, some perhaps of more than local interest, may be drawn from it. It is clear that the essence of Preston's commercial strength lay in its status as an inter-regional market centre. Unlike its local rivals it was not associated exclusively with a single region—as Kirkham was with the Central Fylde or Clitheroe with the Ribble valley — but, thanks to its nodality, was able to dominate and regulate the reciprocal trade of contrasted areas. Thus it had tended to usurp the functions of the smaller nearby market centres, some of which were declining. Certainly the oft-quoted assertion that a market town at this period could draw trade only from the countryside within a day's return journey on foot, a distance variously estimated at from five to eight miles, did not apply to Preston. Given good roads villagers from as far as fifteen miles away made regular use of the town.[1] Finally, this study of Preston reveals what must have been a very common tendency for the larger market towns to acquire new regional functions and thus to strengthen their dominance of smaller centres. Preston's legal and social significance, additional testimony to its nodality, sprang from and in turn strengthened its commercial prominence. Indeed by the early eighteenth century, in many ways Preston's golden age, it had all the character of a major regional centre, a position it could not retain in the new Lancashire soon to be created by industrial growth.

---

[1] H. Thorpe found that Lichfield, another regional centre, also attracted trade from approximately a fifteen-mile radius. (H. Thorpe, 'Lichfield: a study of its growth and function', *Staffordshire Historical Collections*, 1950-51, p. 34, Fig. 6.) Thorpe also makes the point that the extent of market areas was as likely to depend on the limit of a day's return journey on horseback as on foot.

Supplementary Note

There seems to be a distinct tendency for the evolving methodology of historical geography to reflect the techniques and concepts being developed from time to time by geographers concerned with modern problems. For example, it would be surprising if the present interest, and growing competence, of geographers in the application of elaborate data-processing equipment to the solution of correlative and multi-variate problems did not lead to a re-working of much of the evidence of the Domesday Survey. In the early 1950s the relations of town and country were evoking a great deal of interest among urban and social geographers. Christaller's seminal study of the urban hierarchy in south Germany had been continued in Britain by R.E. Dickinson and A.E. Smailes, while F.H.W. Green had produced maps of the hinterlands of British towns using accessibility by bus as his guide.

It was clear that these concepts might be applied with profit to the study of the town at earlier stages in its development. The analysis of the market area of Preston during the sixteenth and seventeenth centuries began as an attempt to reconstruct an urban hierarchy for contemporary Lancashire, using the number and frequency of markets and fairs as the primary evidence. This quickly demonstrated that there were great rank-differences between market centres, and that these were related, primarily, to accessibility and the hinterland. Only for one town in the region, Preston, was it possible to assemble any credible information as to the extent of the market area, entirely because of the availability of the superb range of Guild documents.

It is impossible to read one's work of fifteen years ago except self-critically. One must confess that there is a dangerous degree of dependence on circumstantial rather than direct evidence, and therefore on inference rather than proof. Did the stallengers really make regular use of Preston market? Can one confidently infer that the out-burgesses felt, by reason of their status as 'country' members of the Guild, a close link with the town; and did Preston therefore serve them as a primary social centre, as the paper suggests? This seems very probable but it cannot be demonstrated with certainty. All that may be said in self-defence is that most of the evidence used to illuminate the town-hinterland relationship at the present day is also inferential and indirect; accessibility by bus or the extent of newspaper circulation areas have the same quality, as evidence, as the materials used in my paper. Even the 'shopping survey' conducted to establish the extent of the modern hinterland is a sampling operation, not in nature very different from the use of court-rolls to discover the homes of people known to have visited the town, centuries ago, on business.

H.B. RODGERS   August 1969

The Combination and Rotation of Crops in East Worcestershire, 1540-1660
J.A. Yelling
Reprinted from *Agricultural History Review,* 17 (1969), 24-43

The Combination and Rotation of Crops in East Worcestershire, 1540–1660

By JAMES YELLING

STUDIES of English agriculture in the early modern period have always been much concerned with the nature of common-field farming and the economic significance of enclosure. But the methods of approach have varied, and the last decade has seen a noticeable increase in local studies which utilize the existence of a close and well-defined pattern of farming regions. One purpose of such research is to define open field and enclosed territory more precisely so that each may be studied in some degree of isolation. It is also possible to examine the response of the various systems to specific physical and economic conditions. What might be termed 'the method of regional testing' will no doubt be even more widely employed now that Dr Thirsk's general survey of English agricultural regions has been completed.[1] In the present paper it is used to examine one particular aspect of farming, the production of tillage crops, under the contrasting conditions of champion and woodland country.

The area chosen for study is that of Worcestershire, east of the Severn.[2] This district was divided quite distinctly between two farming regions which were similar to the better-known Arden and Feldon of adjacent Warwickshire. One part, which will be called the 'South', was village territory lying principally in open field,[3] and most of its townships were eventually enclosed by Act. In the other part, the 'North and West', settlement was much more dispersed and common field was never as extensive. By 1540 it had already been subject to a considerable degree of piecemeal enclosure, especially in the north-east, and enclosures of open field by Act were of small importance.

The approximate boundary between these champion and woodland regions is indicated on Fig. I. The map also shows that East Worcestershire contains an interesting variety of physical conditions. The bulk of the area is a clay plain formed from Lower Lias and Keuper Marl, but terrace deposits give rise to soils of lighter character along the river valleys, especially those of the Severn and Avon. North of Worcester itself a more extensive area of light soils

[1] 'The Farming Regions of England' in J. Thirsk (ed.), *The Agrarian History of England and Wales*, IV, *1500–1640*, 1967, pp. 1–109.

[2] The modern county boundary is used except in the south where parishes formerly in Gloucester county and diocese are excluded. Few probate inventories survive for these parishes.

[3] Enclosure conditions in East Worcestershire are described more fully in J. A. Yelling, 'Open Field, Enclosure, and Farm Production in East Worcestershire', Ph.D. thesis, Birmingham, 1966.

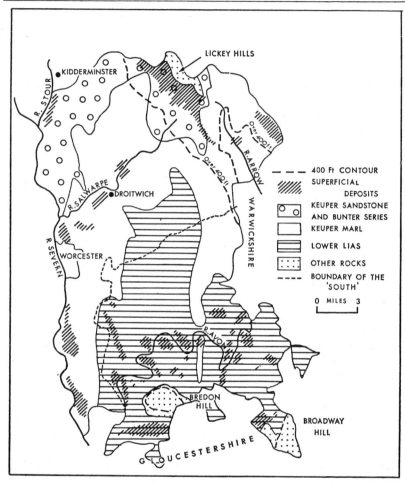

FIG. I

THE STUDY AREA

is based on the outcrop of Bunter and Keuper sandstones, whilst in the north-east higher land associated with the fringes of the Birmingham Plateau introduces a further complicating factor.

The study begins with an overall survey of crop distributions and combinations. This is obtained by statistical comparison of the acreage entries in probate inventories, aggregated by area and period in the manner successfully adopted by Thirsk, Long, and others.[1] Such a general view serves two main purposes: (i) it provides quantitative material for comparison with other periods and districts; (ii) it provides a framework for more detailed study and suggests themes for further investigation. These are then taken up in the second and main part of the paper (Sections II–V) which uses inventories in a more flexible manner in conjunction with material derived from surveys and terriers.

I

Probate inventories are now sufficiently well known as source material not to require any extended treatment from the methodological point of view. It may be remarked, however, that their use in regional statistical studies is subject to two sorts of error: (i) that arising from the small number of inventories which supply full quantitative information; and (ii) that arising from periodic and regional variations in farming types. These two factors have to be balanced against one another, but in practice nearly all studies have involved small numbers of inventories relating to relatively large areas of uniform physical character. In the present case, though the approach is similar, the emphasis is placed on the use of relatively small areas, and for this purpose the whole body of available inventories was searched.[2] East Worcestershire itself comprises only 226,000 acres[3]—less than the Lincolnshire Fens or Yorkshire Wolds—and this is divided into seven regions. The boundaries of the regions were determined by preliminary inspection of the inventories parish by parish.[4] Two periodic divisions are used, namely 1540–99, and 1600–60.

The inventory entries show that in East Worcestershire as a whole barley was the most important crop in the sixteenth century, occupying about 26 per cent of the total crop acreage.[5] It was closely rivalled by wheat (22 per cent), whilst pulses (19 per cent), rye (17 per cent), and oats (10–11 per cent) were the other major crops. Muncorn, vetches, and dredge were also mentioned, but only in small amounts. These overall totals, however, conceal the existence of strong contrasts in the pattern of crop production between one part of East

---

[1] J. Thirsk, *English Peasant Farming*, 1957; W. H. Long, 'Regional Farming in Seventeenth Century Yorkshire', A.H.R., VIII, 1960, pp. 103–14.

[2] The Worcester Diocesan inventories are housed in the Worcester County Record Office (=WRO).

[3] Excluding the former Gloucestershire parishes.

[4] Even so, some important local variations in cropping practice are bound to be concealed if quantitative data alone is used. These variations are described in the more detailed sections which follow.

[5] These figures have been adjusted by weighting the crop proportions found in each region according to its total crop acreage recorded in the 1867 Agricultural Returns. Whilst this is in many ways unsatisfactory, it does help to eliminate error caused by biased regional 'sampling', and produces trends in cropping practice which accord with those found within the individual regions. The crude figures are also given in Tables I and II.

Worcestershire and another—a feature emphasized by the virtual absence of each of the major crops from at least one of the regional divisions employed (Table I, Fig. II).

TABLE I

REGIONAL CROP STATISTICS, 1540–99

Wh=Wheat, *Mu*=Muncorn, *Ba*=Barley,
Pu=Pulse, *Dr*=Dredge, *Ve*=Vetches, *Ma*=Maltcorn

Area		Wh	Mu	Rye	Ba	Oats	Pu	Dr	Ve	Other	Total
ABE†	acres	5	—	35	3	35½	—	3½	—	8(Ma)	90
	%	6	—	39	3	39	—	4	—	9	
C	acres	—	—	31	27½	2	—	1	4		65½
	%	—	—	47	42	3	—	2	6		
DF†	acres	55	10½	5	23	10	77	1	—	15½(Ma)	197
	%	28	5	3	12	5	39	½	—	8	
GJ	acres	121½	2	—	122½	1	105½	—	—		352½
	%	34	½	—	35	½	30	—	—		
KL	acres	115½	7½	20	148	4	93	—	—		388
	%	30	2	5	38	1	24	—	—		
HO	acres	77½	16	79½	145½	2	90½	—	—		411
	%	19	4	19	35	½	22	—	—		
MN	acres	166	—	2	158	—	117	—	—		443
	%	37	—	½	36	—	26	—	—		
Total	acres	540½	36	172½	627	54½	483	5½	4	23½	1,947
	%	28	2	9	32	3	25	—	—	1	
*Adj. Totals** %											
N. and W.		12	2	30	19	18	13	2	1	3	
South		34	1	1	36	2	27				
Total		22	2	17	27	10	19	1	2	1	

* These totals are adjusted according to the total crop acreage recorded in each area in 1867.

† Without maltcorn the percentages were: ABE—wheat 6; rye 43; barley 4; oats 43; dredge 4; DF—wheat 30; muncorn 6; rye 3; barley 13; oats 5; pulse 42.

In the case of the winter crops a relatively simple pattern of substitution seems to have occurred. Wheat dominated the south, and rye the extreme north and west, whilst muncorn achieved some importance in the transitional

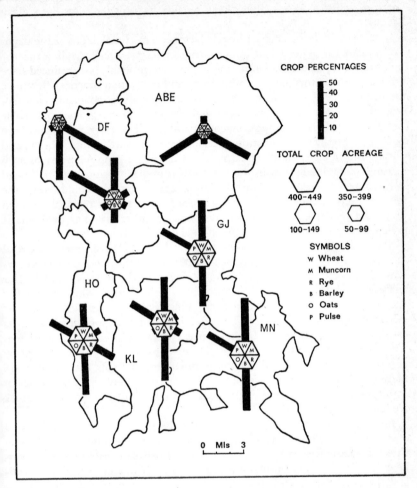

Fig. II
CROP DISTRIBUTIONS, 1540–1599

zone. There is the expected strong correlation between the use of rye and the
presence of light soils—on the sandstone outcrop and Severn terraces—
whilst the higher relief of the north-east seems also to have favoured this crop.
The most widespread of the spring crops was barley, which was important
everywhere except in the north-east, where it was largely replaced by oats.
Pulses were also virtually absent from this district and also from the sandstone

outcrop, whilst oats was little grown outside its stronghold on the plateau fringes.

Certain easily recognizable physical factors seem, therefore, to be the major determinants of all these distributions. Indeed, it is reasonable to allow that the significance of physical variations for land use has probably been reduced since the sixteenth century by improved crops and cultivation practices. Even so, there is much else to explain. The clear-cut regional distinctions in choice of crops are still surprising, and there is also within many regions a noticeable simplicity and balance in the crop combinations. This is especially true of the South, where the three constituent regions each favoured wheat, barley, and pulses, and in significantly equal proportions. The reason for many of such features undoubtedly lies in the mechanism by which crops and rotational systems were selected. Communal organization or tradition could reduce the range of crop combinations in local areas, and so accentuate regional variation by producing a 'step-like' distributional change rather than a gradual one. It is hoped to demonstrate this in the more detailed sections which follow.

The crop statistics for the second period (Table II) are similar in broad terms to those of the sixteenth century, and many of the minor changes represented no doubt arise through 'sampling error' in the material available for analysis. Stability is especially noticeable in the South, whilst the major changes which were to revolutionize cropping practice in the North and West were not yet fully under way. The beginnings of two important adjustments can, however, be discerned. In some areas rye was beginning to give place to wheat, although this trend was not yet very pronounced. Again, the spring crops were becoming relatively more important, and oats and pulses were more widely distributed. This was a reflection of the growing importance of arable in the economy, and of the increased use of tillage crops in livestock feeding.[1]

In spite of this, it is generally true to say that the period under review was one in which the market was biased towards pastoral products. It was under these circumstances that contrasts in farming between champion and woodland districts were most pronounced, and the study of crop statistics immediately helps to make it clear that this was not a simple matter of 'advanced' or 'backward' farming, but of two specialist systems. The champion region possessed a crop combination which was suitable to a mainly arable economy. Conversely, the choice of crops in the woodland district resulted not only from the relative absence of high-yielding arable soils, but also from the pre-

[1] The relative importance of livestock and crops in East Worcestershire at this time is described in J. A. Yelling, *op. cit.*, pp. 205–35. Spring crops were also becoming more important in Leicestershire during this period.—W. G. Hoskins, 'The Leicestershire Farmer in the Seventeenth Century', *Agric. Hist.*, 25, 1951, pp. 11–14.

dominant interest in livestock farming which reduced the incentive to improve crop rotations or to overcome physical deficiencies through beneficial cultivation practices.

II

Cropping systems are easiest to study in the South where communal organization was strongest. In consequence, survey evidence is of more value in this district, and may be used to supplement information derived from the inven-

TABLE II

REGIONAL CROP STATISTICS, 1600–60

Abbreviations as in Table I

Area		Wh	Mu	Rye	Ba	Oats	Pu	Dr	Ve	Other	Total
ABE	acres	14	1½	72	10	133	5½	—	—		236
	%	6	½	31	4	56	2	—	—		
C	acres	—	1	67½	29	17½	11½	4	1½		131
	%	—	1	52	22	13	9	3	1		
DF	acres	26½	20	—	23½	4	62½	—	—	7(Ma)	143½
	%	19	14	—	16	3	43	—	—	5	
GJ	acres	52	1½	1	60½	2	62½	—	2		181½
	%	29	1	½	33	1	35	—	—		
KL	acres	115½	7½	20	148	4	93	—	1		389
	%	30	2	5	38	1	24	—	—		
HO	acres	59	5	15	87	7	85½	—	—		258½
	%	23	2	6	34	3	33	—	—		
MN	acres	23½	—	7	24	—	29	—	—		83½
	%	28	—	9	29	—	35	—	—		
Total	acres	290½	36½	182½	382	167½	349	4	4½	7	1,423
	%	20	3	13	27	12	25				
Adj. Totals*	%										
N. and W.		11	4	25	16	28	18				
South		28	2	5	27	—	33				
Total		18	3	16	24	15	24	0·4	0·3	0·6	

* These totals are adjusted according to the total crop acreage recorded in each area in 1867.

tories. For 1584–5 there are sixteen terriers of glebe holdings[1] in the South which describe in some way the layout of common field arable, and, of these, eight mention the existence of four fields. Most are very simple in style; for example, at Flyford Flavell there was recorded, "One yardland containing by estimation 40 acres or thereabouts, lying in the four fields of Flyford Flavell aforesaid by eight or ten acres in every field." In addition, twenty terriers deal with common arable either for 1616 or for 1634–5, and, of these, eight again describe four fields. The existence of such four-field layouts clearly correlates with the crop combinations noted from the inventories, namely wheat, barley, and pulses in roughly equal proportions. To these three crops may now be added a fallow to make up the fourth shift in the rotation.

Large numbers of terriers, however, refer only to furlongs, or sometimes use a mixture of field and furlong names. The exact significance of this cannot be proved, but it is unlikely to mean that the four-course system was absent. Most of the townships involved are known from documentary sources to have possessed a four-field layout at some other time within the study period. But there is no clear pattern of historical development. Usually, an early terrier listing land only by furlongs is followed by a later example giving both fields and furlongs, but in some cases the sequence is reversed. The most important evidence, however, comes from inventories, examined parish by parish. For despite the small numbers of returns available, four-course cropping characteristics may be recognized for the vast majority of Southern townships.

Some examples of inventories for particular parishes are given in Table III. These returns, of course, highlight the differences which occurred between farms, but on the whole the regularity of their crop combinations is impressive. In most cases the irregularities which do occur are within the limits compatible with the normal layout of holdings, even in those parishes, such as Church Honeybourne, which were to be enclosed before the period of Parliamentary awards. In these examples the wheat and barley shifts were more or less equal; only slight differences are observable between their acreages, giving a bias sometimes to the one and sometimes to the other crop. The acreage in the pulse shift, however, was not infrequently out of line with that of the other two, and, unlike the minor irregularities just mentioned, this seems to have arisen from cropping practice, and not from the layout of holdings. Indeed, in these cases the acreage sown in the pulse field often represented about half the amounts in the other two fields, as at Bretforton in the two inventories for 1558 tabulated below. This feature was widespread in the South, and continued into the early eighteenth century, but only in a minority of the returns for any particular parish. It is probable that the land not sown with pulses

[1] These terriers are contained in WRO 2358 and 2735. They are described in more detail in J. A. Yelling, *op. cit.*, pp. 329–35.

was left uncropped, but it is just possible that grass seeds were sown with the preceding barley crop, producing a one-year ley which passed unrecorded in the inventories. If such grassland existed, however, it could not be correlated with the 'leys' mentioned in surveys which were of a much more permanent nature.

TABLE III

INVENTORIES FOR SOUTHERN PARISHES

L=Lands. Other abbreviations as in Table I.

Other figures in acres.

The symbols * and † mean that the acreages given apply to all the crop types indicated.

	Wh	Mu	Rye	Ba	Oats	Pu	Ve	Total
Bretforton								
1557/112‡	18			20		3		41
1558/442	10		2	10		6		28
1558/498	26			26		12		64
1598/61d	24*		*	32		26†	†	82
Church Honeybourne								
1557/109	13			11		11		35
1592/28	18			20		15		53
North Piddle								
1597/72	2L			1		1		
1618/383	2L			4L		3L		9L
1619/62	1			1		1		3
1623/5	20			20*	*	20		60
1640/195	29L			27L		27L*	*	83L
Bishampton								
1615/172	2			2		3		7
1616/263h	3			4		3		10
1619/35b	$2\frac{1}{4}$			$2\frac{1}{2}$		2		$6\frac{3}{4}$
1620/9	5*		*	7		$6\frac{1}{2}$		$18\frac{1}{2}$
1623/35	24*	*		18†	†	17		59
1642/50	10			7*	*	7		24

‡ The inventories are referenced by number within each year, i.e. 1560/1 denotes the first inventory in the collection for 1560.

These occasional shortfalls in the acreage under pulses may in fact be a lingering reflection of the manner in which the four-field system was originally introduced. It seems likely that it developed from the two-field system by 'hitching' part of the fallow field for pulses. Certainly, many townships in the

South possessed two-field systems in the thirteenth and fourteenth centuries; for example, Upton Snodsbury, which had four-course cropping by the end of the sixteenth century and four fields in 1771.[1] The glebe terrier of Naunton Beauchamp (1585) makes the derivation even more explicit. It mentions 24 acres of arable in North Field (46 lands) and South Field (41 lands) and continues "which said two fields are divided into four parts or fields according to the course of husbandry for three crops of corn to be had and taken thereof and for the fourth to lie yearly fallow." Two other townships—Bishampton and Peopleton—persisted in two-field nomenclature in their glebe terriers,[2] but from the inventories it seems most likely that they followed the four-course cropping pattern (Table III).

The transition from two fields to four fields in the South therefore seems to have been completed by about the middle of the sixteenth century. This means that it occurred rather earlier than the general dates given by Gray who remarked that "a four-field system making its appearance in the English Midlands in the sixteenth and early seventeenth centuries, was employed more and more in the course of the latter century and in the early eighteenth."[3] It also means that it must have occurred some time between 1350 and 1550, when elsewhere there was widespread conversion of arable to pasture, and when the desertion of villages was at its height. In the face of the same market pressures, it looks as though the villagers of the South chose instead to retain their arable system and to improve its efficiency.

III

In contrast to the uniformity of the champion district, the North and West possessed several distinct cropping systems, and these may be dealt with in turn. Conditions were most closely similar to those of the South around Droitwich (Area DF), and the major crops were the same, although grown in different proportions. Here, too, a considerable amount of common field was still present in the study period, especially in the southern part, and, although there were also many piecemeal closes, these were probably used mainly for pasture. Even in 1777, although only 49 per cent of the improved land in Himbleton lay in common, this included 78 per cent of the arable; similar figures are available for neighbouring Tibberton at the same date.[4] Two centuries earlier, when the proportion of closes was probably not so great, and the market less favourable to arable products, the correlation between enclosure and pasture would have been even more pronounced.

[1] Birmingham Reference Library, Calendar of Manuscripts relating to Worcestershire in the Shrewsbury (Talbot) Collection of the British Museum, Worcs. M16; WRO 1861.

[2] Glebe Terriers—Bishampton, 1616, 1670, 1714; Peopleton, 1585, 1616.

[3] H. L. Gray, *English Field Systems*, 1915, Reprint 1959, p. 136.

[4] WRO 1691/14; 1691/32.

The distribution of common arable was in itself, however, often complex. The surveys and terriers fall mainly into two groups. The first type, of which Himbleton, Salwarpe, and Rushock[1] provide examples, mentions a large number of small fields. The glebe at Himbleton, for instance, in 1616 included lands in six fields—Ladiaker (4), Inning (9), Mill (9), Stocking (3), Blackpit (8), and Hill (12 and 2 layes). It is known from later evidence that such a distribution was not peculiar to the glebe, that all the arable lay in one township, and that the fields were not always separated from each other by enclosures. Such features, however, may account for some of the irregularities in other terriers. In contrast, certain surveys seem to refer to a three-field allocation of land. Examples of this type relate to Hadsor, Bredicot, Westwood, and Huddington[2] where the fields were Shatherlong (36 acres), Badney or Windmill (20 acres), and Hill (30 acres). All these townships are small, but their field descriptions are of added significance in that they are the only ones in this district which might conceivably correspond with a regular rotation practice.

In view of the presence of piecemeal closes and some complex field divisions, the entries in the inventories appear surprisingly regular. In several parishes to the south of Droitwich, including Himbleton (Table IV), the acreage of pulses frequently equates with the acreage of winter cereals and barley combined. These same parishes also followed the practice, not found elsewhere, of grouping the winter cereal and barley acreages in many of the inventories. This cropping regularity was undoubtedly followed in the common fields, since in many parishes most of the arable lay open at this time, and the Oddingley inventory 1625/239 specifically mentions that both wheat and barley were growing in the common field there known as Old Field.[3] It may be added, too, that the rotation wheat or barley, pulses, fallow, was frequently found in Leicestershire common fields during this period.[4]

Another cropping regularity can be recognized in the parishes of Salwarpe, Elmley Lovett, and Rushock. There, the acreage under winter cereals was roughly equal to that of all the spring crops (Table IV). Again, this certainly reflects a common-field rotation. Indeed the Salwarpe inventory 1603/13 names the fields involved. In Copcote Field there were 5 acres of rye, in Postell Field 1 acre of barley, and 4 acres of oats, and in Little Field 6 kine and 3

<hr/>

[1] Himbleton, Glebe Terrier 1616, WRO 1691/14; Salwarpe, Glebe Terrier 1617; Elmley Lovett, Glebe Terriers 1585, 1635.
[2] Hadsor, Glebe Terrier 1585, Bredicot Glebe Terrier (no date); Parliamentary Survey—T. Cave and R. Wilson, *The Parliamentary Surveys of the Lands and Possessions of the Dean and Chapter of Worcester, c. 1649*, 1924, pp. 14–17; Westwood, PRO E 315/400; Huddington, PRO E 317, Worcs. 6.
[3] Old Field is mentioned as a common field in the Calendar of Shrewsbury (Talbot) MSS., *op. cit.*, Worcs. K 37 (1619).
[4] W. G. Hoskins, *op. cit.*, p. 11.

calves. In most cases, however, the chief crops continued to be wheat or rye, and pulses, as in the parishes mentioned in the last paragraph. Compared with these latter parishes there was simply a slight shift in production from pulses to winter cereals. This shift was, in fact, part of a general trend from spring to winter crops which was encountered in moving northwards in East Worcestershire to more pastoral districts with grass feeding. In the South winter cereals accounted for one-third of crop production. To the south and west of Droitwich this proportion rose probably to about 40 per cent, and further north-east to one-half.

TABLE IV

THE DROITWICH DISTRICT

Abbreviations as in Table I; symbols and references as in Table III.

	Hard Corn	Lent Corn	Wh	Mu	Rye	Ba	Oats	Pu	Other	Total
Himbleton										
1555/43			10*		*	4		15		29
1556/113			14		2	5		12½		33½
1557/156			4		3	2½	4*	8	*(Ma)	21½
1560/40			13	4		8		22*	*(Ve)	47
1561/92a			6			2		5		13
1563/93			8*			*		10		18
1570/317						1		1		2
1587/65a			13*			*		14		27
1623/186			4*		*	7		6		17
1628/139			1*			*		1		2
1633/175			10*			*		8		18
1634/121				3*		*		6		9
1643/37			1½			7		9		17½
1649/92			24*	*		*		21		45
Elmley Lovett										
1582/20c	5	5								10
1619/25	5	12								17
1622/68			13*		*	4	†	9†	†(Ve)	26
1630/154		8	9*		*					17
1639/15	12	12								24
Salwarpe									3½(Ma)	
1558/848	6							8*	*(Ve)	17½
1560/60	10	11								21
1594/84			14*	*	*	†	†	16†	†(Ve)	30
1601/181				2		3	*	4*	2(Ma)	11
1603/83					5	1	4*		*(Ve)	10

The main problem in dealing with common-field agriculture in this district lies, therefore, not so much with the pattern of production, which seems reasonably clear, but with the methods of field management in those townships where complex divisions were recorded. Collective management must have persisted in at least some spheres, since common pasture stints are recorded in glebe terriers, and one can only assume that most fields were grouped for rotation either on the basis of the entire township or in sectors. The other main problem is to assess the impact of piecemeal enclosure on production, and this is extremely difficult because one cannot be sure that any township lay wholly enclosed during this period, and there was certainly no sharp boundary beyond which farms with a large enclosed sector could be recognized from their crop combinations. It appears from later evidence,[1] however, that the general result of enclosure was to break down the pre-existing symmetry of production, and to emphasize spring crops to a greater extent. But no township can be said with certainty to have been dominated by this type of cropping pattern within the study period.

IV

The next district to be considered is the Severn Valley, beginning with the section north of Worcester where almost all the arable was located on light or very light soils. Here common field was still present in many parishes before 1660, but was of very varying importance. It was probably of greatest extent in Ombersley where piecemeal closes were relatively few in 1605, and mainly in the outer parts of the parish, whilst the central part definitely possessed a three-field system.[2] Three fields are also mentioned in a glebe terrier (1585) of Churchill near Kidderminster, which lay on sandstone soils immediately to the north of the present study region. Again, a court roll of Hartlebury (1649)[3] was concerned with regulating common pasture in the "campos siligenos" and "campos hordeos" of Charlton and Torton hamlets. In short, where large amounts of common field remained they were almost certainly cropped in a three-course pattern, and examination of individual inventories must be concerned to reveal the details of this practice, and to see if it dominated crop production as a whole.

The inventories of the two largest parishes, Chaddesley Corbett and Ombersley, have been selected for more detailed study (Table V). It is noticeable that during the study period the crop choice changed more radically in these parishes than in those previously encountered. In both cases, however, the sixteenth-century entries relate mainly to rye and barley, a feature which is equally true if one looks beyond the acreage statistics to the far larger number

[1] J. A. Yelling, *op. cit.*, p. 381. [2] WRO 3190/29.
[3] Court Roll, 5 April 1649, WRO 2636 (92373).

of inventories which recorded their crops in some other way. In Chaddesley pulses and wheat were not specifically mentioned in an inventory until 1627 but oats and pulses were quite common in the second quarter of the seven

TABLE V

THE SEVERN DISTRICT

L=Lands. Other abbreviations as in Table I; symbols and references as in Table III.

	Winter Crops	Spring Crops	Wh	Mu	Rye	Ba	Oats	Pu	Other	Total
Chaddesley Corbett										
1545/23					16	16				32
1598/53		6			8					14
1598/54		3½			3					6½
1601/47					5	1				6
1614/226					8	5	3			16
1624/24					3				4(Dr)	7
1627/25	4					3¾	½	1	1½(Ve)	10¾
1627/142				1			2			3
1644/90					3	*	4	7*		14
Ombersley										
1568/64					6	13*	*		*(Ve)	19
1593/31					8	9				17
1614/70					2	1			3L(Ve)	
1614/204	6	6								12
1619/16					10		2	3		
1620/70	3	3								6
1625/130	4					1	4			9
1625/198					23	13	4	3		43
1638/129			*		8*	6		6†	†(Ve)	20
1641/115					5		1	3		9
(1656) 794/33			16*		*	16†		†		32
Severn Stoke										
1565/51					8	5		1		14
1574/30					6	4				10
1574/73					7	5		3		15
1587/91	30				16	*		22*	*(Ve)	68
1589/52					7½	6½	1	1		16
1596/34			7*		*	2		10		19
1603/76					4	7		1½		12½
1614/10			4*		10*	5		8		27
1643/100				2		2		2		6
1643/103			7*		*	5	1	4		17

teenth century. At Ombersley, too, wheat was not recorded until 1626, but half the sixteenth-century inventories mentioned pulses, and these together with oats were normal crops after 1600.

A key feature in these returns is the presence or absence of balance between the acreages of spring and winter crops. During the sixteenth century, when rye and barley dominated, such a regularity does in fact occur in many inventories. Taken in conjunction with the survey evidence already recorded, including that relating to Ombersley itself, this strongly suggests that the current common-field rotation in this district was rye, barley, fallow. The next point to determine is what happened to this balance when oats and pulses became increasingly popular. Here, some contrast is noticeable, more especially after 1620, between Ombersley where regularity was preserved, and Chaddesley Corbett where it was not. The small number of inventories involved, however, make it necessary to go beyond the boundaries of the study period in order to reinforce this point.

INVENTORY CROP ACREAGES

	Chaddesley Corbett		Ombersley	
	winter	spring	winter	spring
Pre-1620	40	34½	32	35
1620–50	11	23¾	59	60
1660–99	59¾	133	65½	57½
1700–50	53	108	102	153½

It seems reasonable to suppose that the balance between winter and spring crops at Ombersley, found throughout the seventeenth century, was connected with the strong survival of common field in that parish. The degree of enclosure was small in 1605, and although piecemeal enclosure developed strongly after the Civil War, a substantial amount of open land was still present in 1695.[1] Only after this date did spring crops attain the ascendancy. This means that pulses and oats were introduced into the common fields in the barley shift, which is theoretically logical, and in accord with the evidence of individual inventories. In effect, it brought common field practice in Ombersley very close to that of adjacent Elmley Lovett and Salwarpe (Table IV). The change may well be connected with the introduction of horses as plough animals instead of the oxen which predominated in the sixteenth century.

At Chaddesley Corbett, the proportion of spring crops—no more than half before 1620—was never less than two-thirds thereafter. This parish was cer-

[1] PRO E 134, 5W. & M., Mich., 54.

tainly wholly enclosed in 1745,[1] and in 1635 the vicarage had "five fields of arable, all which contain three score and twelve acres." It is likely, therefore that the cropping practice observed after 1620 related mainly to enclosed arable; thus there was some contrast with the production in common fields in the same district. Whether common land was present in any quantity in Chaddesley Corbett before 1620 is a matter for speculation, but it seems a strong possibility.

Lastly, the crop region delimited to the south of Worcester on Fig. II can be shown by more detailed analysis to consist of two distinct parts. To the east most parishes followed the practice of the South, their arable being mainly open and cropped according to the four-course arrangement. Only the parishes actually bordering the Severn, where much of the arable was located on light terrace soils, followed a distinctive practice similar to that of the Severn district north of Worcester. Severn Stoke is an example (Table V). The crop choice appears similar to that further north except that pulses were more common and oats less so. From the reasoning of the last paragraph, most of the arable in the seventeenth century would seem to have been enclosed, because spring crops dominate. On the other hand, in the sixteenth century the arable even if enclosed, was cropped according to the prevailing common-field pattern.

V

The final region, the north-east, was the most enclosed part of East Worcestershire, and predominantly pastoral in character. Although subject to continuing piecemeal enclosure, some common field persisted around most of the main nucleations, but these lay far apart. Although collective management still continued in some cases, there is no evidence of any regular common-field divisions during the study period. One solitary piece of evidence points to the previous existence of a three-field system.[2] In any event, closes must soon have come to dominate the arable in most parishes as crop production rose from 1540 onwards.

The early inventories for Bromsgrove and Tardebigge (Table VI) show that rye and oats were the main crops in this district with barley playing a lesser role. At Bromsgrove rye remained virtually unchallenged by wheat before 1650, and the main change was the gradual adoption of pulses. The inventory record is not satisfactory before 1600, but after this date spring crops certainly predominated. Wheat was much more important at Tardebigge where the presence of common field in substantial quantities also seems more likely. There were certainly farms in the north-east during the sixteenth century where most of the arable lay in common field—the glebe at Belbroughton in

---

[1] WRO 844.   [2] At Shurnock (Feckenham) in 1237.—H. L. Gray, *op. cit.*, p. 504.

132

TABLE VI

THE NORTH-EAST

Fl=Flax, *de*=days earth (i.e. work). Other abbreviations as in Table I; symbols as in Table III.

	Winter	Spring	Wh	Rye	Ba	Oats	Pu	Other	Total
Tardebigge									
1560/85				3de	*	4de	*		7de
1563/35				4	1	5			10
1587/31				6		5			11
1591/74			9*	*	8	6			23
1603/113			2	11		19			32
1641/12			1		4*	2	*		7
1642/28			6			4		1(*Fl*)	11
Bromsgrove									
1552/95				1				1(*Dr*)	2
1552/98				1		1			2
1567/85				1de	1de				
1569/34				18		20		8(*Ma*)	46
1602/56				5		21			26
1603/44				14		42			56
1614/164				14	4				18
1616/17				2½	*	5½*		*(*Ve*)	8
1616/29				7	3	5			15
1617/1				2		3½	½		6
1625/103				5		4	2		11
1628/142	4				16				20
1642/63				2	3	5½*		*(*Ve*)	10½
1644/21					3	3	3		9
1646/83					½	3			3½
1648/40				6		6			12
Feckenham									
1592/80	10			2½	6	*	18*		36½
1632/20			9*	*	1½	7	7		24½
(1634) 821/3874			3		2	*	6*		11
1646/52					3	2½	1		6½
Stoke Prior									
1552/94	7de	2de							9de
1576/1	7				£1	*	6*		
1593/5d	12	6							18
1624/6					3	2	4		9
1638/162			16*	*	2	13†	†		31
Hanbury									
1579/304			29*	*	†		34†		63

133

1585 is one example. Although there is no proof, it may well be that the cropping pattern on such common land was similar to that suggested in the early inventories for Tardebigge, namely, one shift of rye, one of oats with a little barley, and a third fallow. Such an arrangement would be similar to that practised immediately to the west, except that oats was substituted for barley because of the higher altitude and wetter climate of the plateau region.

The inventories show that the parishes of Feckenham, Hanbury, and Stoke Prior possessed crop combinations which were rather distinct from those of the rest of the north-east. All those places lay off the plateau itself, just to the south, and grew less oats in favour of pulses, whilst wheat was also more prominent (Table VI). Unfortunately, there are not enough inventories to describe the pattern in more detail, but the three-course framework found elsewhere in the North and West is discernible. In many ways the choice of crops appears similar to that of the Droitwich district, but the entries show a greater degree of irregularity.

VI

The cropping arrangements revealed by these more detailed investigations are conveniently summarized in Fig. III. Perhaps the most surprising feature is the extent to which farms in many parts of the North and West followed regular cropping systems similar to those of their neighbours. In most cases these systems were the ones used in the common fields, and the regularity prevailed despite the frequent presence of piecemeal closes and complex field divisions. Especially in the early part of the study period, when pastoral products received most attention, the bulk of the arable in many parishes lay open, and in others farms with a mixture of open and enclosed land may have continued to use the normal rotation of the district in which they lay. This does not mean that cropping practice was inflexible. Indeed, it is clear that the communal system was capable of accommodating marked changes in crop combinations within limited areas where physical or economic conditions required these. If the probable rye–oats–fallow of the north-east is allowed, there were at least five different regional cropping systems in East Worcestershire's common fields.

There is also no reason to believe that common-field practice remained static for a very long time in the face of decisive economic trends. In the study period arable products were becoming more profitable, and in the North and West oxen were being replaced by horses. The economy of the South was already well-suited to take advantage of these new conditions. In the North and West, too, many districts used a wide variety of crops with some choice within the principal shifts. It was the two-crop districts of the mid-sixteenth century which underwent most alteration in cropping practice before 1650, including,

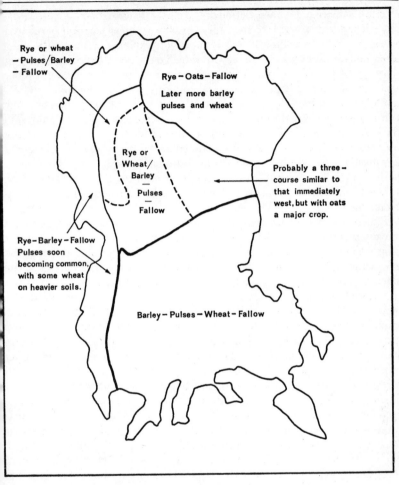

FIG. III

TENTATIVE MAP OF DOMINANT CROPPING TYPES

n common-field land, the introduction of a wider range of crops into the
Spring Field. It may be added that, since the economy of the medieval period
was by no means static, none of the rotations prevalent in the sixteenth century
can be regarded as necessarily of great antiquity.

A more stable element appears in the boundary between four-course and
three-course cropping, which more or less coincided with the edge of the

champion district. This association of the most intensive rotation with the area most dependent on arable seems logical, but it was almost certainly of relatively recent origin. The boundary itself is not easy to explain in purely physical and economic terms, except on the Severn side. To the north the coincidence with the edge of the Lias is only approximate and not very convincing. Modern accounts of soil and land use[1] give no emphasis to such a boundary, and it is not apparent in the crop and fallow distributions revealed by the early Agricultural Returns. On the other hand, this same line of division is significant in the enclosure history of the area and in the distribution of settlement types,[2] features which may have been shaped in character at a relatively early stage of colonization. In sum, there are strong reasons to suspect that this is an inherited boundary, but there can be no proof until the limits of the medieval two-field system and the date of origin of the Northern three-course are established.

Finally, there is the problem of enclosed arable in the woodland district. As already mentioned, this does not appear to have had much direct impact on cropping arrangements in the early part of the study period, but the indirect effect, through the creation of a more pastoral economy, may have been considerable. In any case, enclosed arable came into greater prominence as time progressed, both as the result of contemporary enclosure activity and the conversion of land previously under pasture. The relative flexibility of the communal system ensured that there was no dramatic contrast between the cropping of such enclosed land and that of neighbouring common field; for instance, the same crops were used on each. But there were recognizable differences, at least in the seventeenth century. In particular, the equivalence in the acreages of specific groups of crops, denoting a regular shift structure, was not characteristic of enclosed ground. Related to this was the dominance of spring crops, comprising two-thirds or more of the total output. In this respect, production became similar to that of the South, and, although there is no evidence, there may also have been some lengthening in the fallow interval. In any event, the main impact of enclosure was probably to upset the regional three-shift arrangements formerly characteristic of Northern cropping. This meant the rejection of an aspect of communal cropping which seems to owe more to historical inheritance than to current needs.

[1] For example K. M. Buchanan, *The Land of Britain, Part 68, Worcestershire*, 1944.
[2] J. A. Yelling, *op. cit.*, pp. 23–63.

Supplementary Note

From the geographical point of view studies of cropping patterns from probate inventories might be divided into three types according to the detail in which they specify the locality and farming conditions to which the returns refer. The preceding essay represents a combination of two of these types, whilst the third has, as far as I know, never been systematically attempted.

Regional studies These provide a simple statistical description of the distribution of the main crops, variations in regional combinations of crops and changes in cropping patterns from one period to another. Many studies of this nature are now available, but they vary considerably in method of approach, in the number of inventories used and in the size of the regions and periods involved. This partly results from the big differences in the number and chronological range of documents in inventory collections. Despite their variability all these studies may eventually be put together to provide a basic geography of crop distributions in England and Wales during the early modern period. But many areas for which inventories exist still await treatment even at this level.

Parish studies These use the parishes as a locational reference and attempt to discern similarities in their cropping patterns. At this scale the inventories can be studied together with other documents from which the settlement patterns and field system(s) of the parishes may be determined. This allows more elaborate study of crop combinations and rotations, particularly where the parish represents a township lying in common field and thus forms a real farming unit.

Farm studies Eventually even in common field parishes proper understanding of cropping arrangements will only be possible if the inventories can be related to specific farm units whose size and structure are known. It may be possible to do this in some places with good manorial records. It would be a laborious but possibly very rewarding task, especially where irregular field systems or enclosed fields existed.

J.A. YELLING   August 1969

Family Limitation in Pre-Industrial England
E.A. Wrigley
Reprinted from *Economic History Review*, XIX (1966),
82-109

Family Limitation in Pre-Industrial England

By E. A. WRIGLEY

M. Louis Henry of the *Institut National d'Etudes Démographiques* in Paris has, by his development of the technique of family reconstitution, placed a powerful new weapon in the hands of historical demographers in those countries fortunate enough to possess good parish registers. By this method any running series of births (baptisms), deaths (burials), and marriages can be exploited to provide a detailed picture of many aspects of the fertility, mortality and nuptiality of a community.

Family reconstitution is in principle a simple operation.[1] Information abstracted from the registers is transferred initially to slips, each event in each register being recorded on a separate slip. This in turn is collated on Family Reconstitution Forms (F.R.F.s) on each of which there is space to record the dates of baptism and burial of the two principals to the marriage, the date of the marriage itself, the names of the parents of the married couple, and, in the lower half of the form, the names and dates of baptism, marriage, and burial of all issue of the marriage. There is also space to record other information about residence, occupation, place of baptism and burial, and so on. Only a small proportion of families can be completely reconstituted in most parishes, but for many purposes partially reconstituted families can also be used. From the F.R.F.s a wide range of demographic measures can be calculated, including such things as age at first marriage, age-specific marital fertility, infant and child mortality, expectation of life (subject to some margin of error), birth intervals, and the percentage of pre-nuptial first pregnancies.

Only those registers in which there are few or no breaks are suitable for family reconstitution. Nor is it always the case that a register without any missing year is of use since for successful reconstitution the information given at each entry must normally be sufficient to allow the individual in question to be indentified with confidence. Many English registers fall short in this respect. Nevertheless by modifying French practice somewhat to take account of the idiosyncracies of English parish registers it is possible to apply Henry's family reconstitution methods to some English registers. As a result it is reasonable to hope that in time the demographic history of England during the period from the mid-sixteenth to the mid-nineteenth century will be seen much more fully and in much sharper focus.

---

[1] For a full description of the method and a discussion of the type of register to which it can be applied see E. A. Wrigley (ed.), *Introduction to English Historical Demography* (1966), chapter 4. This in turn is largely based upon the earlier French manual of M. Fleury and L. Henry, *Des registres paroissiaux à l'histoire de la population. Manuel de dépouillement et d'exploitation de l'état civil ancien*, I.N.E.D. (Paris, 1956). A new and expanded edition of this work has recently been published.

Although in general it may be true that French parish registers lend themselves more easily to family reconstitution than English because the French *curés* were in the habit of recording much more detail in their registers than the English vicars in theirs,[1] in one respect England is very fortunate. A few hundred English registers go right back to 1538 and a much larger number is still extant from the early seventeenth century, though of course it often happens that there are gaps, especially for the Civil War years.[2] In France in contrast the registers are seldom of use for family reconstitution purposes before the last quarter of the seventeenth century. The middle years of the seventeenth century both in England and on the Continent were often a turning-point in demographic history when a period of rapid population growth came to an end and a different pattern of slower growth, stagnation or decline set in. This occurred before most French registers are suitable for reconstitution, but some English parishes maintained good registers from a much earlier date. In them a complete cycle of demographic experience can be examined, beginning with a period of rapid growth in the sixteenth and early seventeenth centuries, followed by a check and decline, which in turn gave way to renewed growth during the eighteenth century.

I

The parish of Colyton in the Axe valley in east Devon possesses an exceptionally complete register. The record of baptisms, burials and marriages is uninterrupted from 1538 to 1837 (the date of the beginning of civil registration) and beyond. Moreover, the degree of detail given at each entry varies considerably in different periods of the register. These two characteristics in combination made the Colyton register particularly suitable for a pilot study of family reconstitution using English parish registers. The second is important because it makes it possible to determine the threshold level of information necessary for successful reconstitution below which the identification of the people named (especially in the burial register, the most sensitive of the three in this respect) becomes in many cases impossible.[3] In the event Colyton proved to be a parish of the greatest interest from a general, as well as a technical, point of view, for Colyton's population history was very varied during these three centuries. The changes in fertility which occurred are especially striking. The bulk of this article is devoted to this topic. Other aspects of the parish's demographic history are touched on only *en passant*.

Figure 1 shows the totals of baptisms, burials and marriages in Colyton plotted

---

[1] The second chapter of E. Gautier and L. Henry, *La Population de Crulai*, I.N.E.D. Cahier no. 33 (Paris, 1958), gives an account of the type of information to be found in a good French register. See also E. A. Wrigley, *Some Problems of Family Reconstitution using English Parish Register Material*, Proceedings of the Third International Economic History Conference, Munich, 1965.

[2] No good general inventory of parish registers exists, though the Society of Genealogists hopes shortly to publish a revised edition of the *National Index of Parish Registers* which will cover both originals and transcripts. The inventory which Rickman published in the 1831 Census is still the best starting point for work in many counties.

[3] This question is dealt with in Wrigley, *Some Problems of Family Reconstitution*.

Figure I

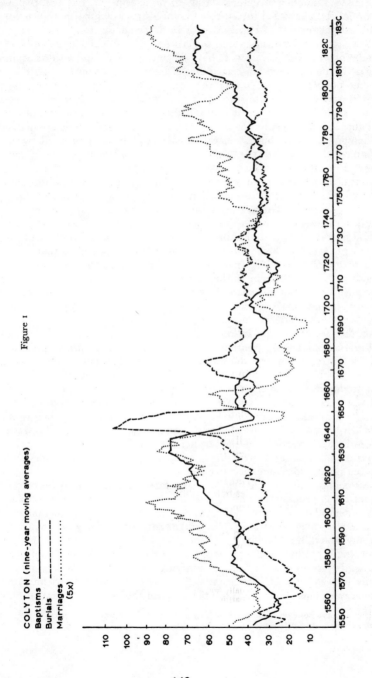

COLYTON (nine-year moving averages)
Baptisms ——————
Burials - - - - - -
Marriages ···········
   (5x)

as nine-year moving averages. From them it appears that the population history of the parish fell into three phases: a first in which there was usually a substantial surplus of baptisms over burials and the total population rose sharply; a second during which burials usually exceeded baptisms and the population as a whole appears to have fallen somewhat; and a third beginning only in the 1780's when large surpluses of baptisms over burials again appear and the population rose sharply once more. The second period may be sub-divided about 1730, since after that date there was near balance between baptisms and burials, whereas before it there was usually a surplus of burials. The abruptness of the division between the first and second periods is masked by the moving averages but is clearly revealed by annual figures. Between the beginning of November 1645 and the end of October 1646, 392 names are recorded in the Colyton burial register, in all probability as a result of a last and virulent outbreak of bubonic plague. This was perhaps a fifth of the total population. After this drastic mortality the number of baptisms stayed upon a much lower level. The average annual figure 1635–44 was 72·8, higher than in any subsequent period in the Colyton register. In the decade 1647–56 the annual average fell to 40·0. Apart from the first decade after the catastrophe the moving averages show that there were normally more burials than baptisms for two generations. The boundary between the second and third major periods is also quite sharp. In the decade 1776–85 the average annual surplus of baptisms over burials was only 0·5, a figure typical of the preceding half century. In the next ten years the average surplus rose to 7·8 and increased considerably thereafter.

Another feature of the moving averages is worth remarking. There was a well-marked inverse correlation between baptisms and burials until the end of the seventeenth century which can still be detected at times in the eighteenth. Periods which encouraged the formation of a large number of marriages and thus produced a rise in the number of baptisms were periods of low mortality and vice versa. This may seem a very natural correlation to appear, but it is interesting to note that there were parishes in which marriages, baptisms and burials were positively correlated in an equally marked fashion. This was true, for example, of Hartland on the northern coast of Devon. The further investigation of this issue may well throw much light on the question of the links between populations and their livelihood.[1]

The changes in the balance between births and deaths revealed in the annual totals of baptisms and burials show that great changes took place in Colyton in the three centuries between Thomas Cromwell's injunction and the inception of civil registration. But although the crude figures may arouse curiosity about the changes in fertility, mortality, nuptiality and migration which could produce such big swings in the relative numbers of baptisms and burials, they cannot go far towards satisfying that curiosity. To penetrate more deeply into the matter it is essential to dispose of more refined measures of demographic conditions. For example, a fall in the number of baptisms might

---

[1] Hartland also possesses an unusually fine register. Mrs J. V. Stewart is at present engaged upon a family reconstitution study of this parish.

the result of a rise in the average age at first marriage, or a rise in the average
interval between births (perhaps as a result of changes in suckling customs,
perhaps through the practice of abortion or the employment of a contraceptive
technique), or even in some communities a reduction in the number of ille-
gitimate births.[1] On the other hand, it might simply be the result of heavy
migration without any significant changes in general or marital fertility of the
type just mentioned. And still other changes, for example in the age and sex
structure of the population, might produce similar fluctuations in the relative
number of births and deaths. To be able to decide between the many possibilities and to measure the changes accurately family reconstitution is necessary.

II

It is convenient to begin the discussion of fertility changes at Colyton by
considering the fluctuations in age at first marriage of the two sexes. In societies in which there is little control of conception within marriage this is
one of the most important variables bearing upon reproduction rates. Indeed,
it is sometimes asserted that a lowering of the age of first marriage for women
largely accounted for the rapid rise of population in England in the second
half of the eighteenth century. The mean age at which women bore their last
child in European communities with little or no control of conception was
usually about 40,[2] and for some years before this their fecundity declined

Table 1. *Age at First Marriage*

Men	No.	Mean	Median	Mode [3]
1560–1646	258	27·2	25·8	23·0
1647–1719	109	27·7	26·4	23·8
1720–69	90	25·7	25·1	23·9
1770–1837	219	26·5	25·8	24·4
Women				
1560–1646	371	27·0	25·9	23·7
1647–1719	136	29·6	27·5	23·3
1720–69	104	26·8	25·7	23·5
1770–1837	275	25·1	24·0	21·8

Note. The total numbers of marriages in the four periods were 854, 379, 424 and 888 respectively.

rapidly. It is clear therefore that a mean age at first marriage of 22 in these
circumstances will give rise to twice as many births in completed families as a
mean age of, say, 29 or 30. Table 1 shows that in Colyton there were remarkable changes in the mean age at first marriage of women, though the mean age

[1] Registered bastard baptisms might reach quite a high percentage level even as early as the sixteenth century. For example, 135 out of the total of 876 children baptized at Prestbury in Cheshire
1581–1600 (16 per cent) were bastards. I am indebted to Dr Stella Davies for this information.
[2] See, for example, L. Henry, *Anciennes familles genevoises*, I.N.E.D. Cahier no. 26 (Paris, 1956),
p. 88; J. Ganiage, *Trois villages de l'Ile de France*, I.N.E.D. Cahier no. 40 (Paris, 1963), pp. 71–2;
Gautier and Henry, *La Population de Crulai*, p. 157.
[3] The mode was calculated here from the mean and median using Tippett's formula, Mean-Mode =
3(Mean-Median). See L. H. C. Tippett, *The Methods of Statistics*, 4th revised ed. (1952), p. 35.

of men did not greatly vary. The strangest period to modern eyes was the period 1647–1719.[1] Immediately after the terrible mortality of 1646 the average age at first marriage of women shot up to almost 30 and was maintained at this very advanced age for some 70 years.[2] During this period, moreover, the mean age of women at first marriage was two years higher than that of men. Table 2 shows the means for shorter periods. It is noteworthy that the new

Table 2. *Mean Age at First Marriage*

	Men		Women	
	No.	Mean	No.	Mean
1560–99	73	28·1	126	27·0
1600–29	124	27·4	162	27·3
1630–46	61	25·8	83	26·5
1647–59	38	26·9	48	30·0
1660–99	36	27·6	61	28·8
1700–19	35	28·1	27	30·7
1720–49	55	26·2	58	27·2
1750–69	35	25·0	·46	26·3
1770–99	93	27·6	107	26·4
1800–24	67	25·6	100	24·9
1825–37	59	25·9	68	23·3

pattern established itself very quickly after 1647 in Colyton. The change was abrupt and decisive. Before this middle period and again for a time after it the mean age for men and women differed very little, being in each case 26–27 while in the latest sub-period and possibly also in the earliest the more familiar pattern of men marrying women younger than themselves is found. By the period 1825–37 the mean age at first marriage for women had fallen to only 2 while that for men was 26, figures which appear to modern eyes much more 'normal'.

Changes in the median age at first marriage for women were much less violent than the changes in the mean while the modal age did not change at all until the end of the eighteenth century, being unaffected in the middle period, 1647–1719. The commonest age at first marriage at that time remained about 23, but there was a much longer 'tail' to the right of the distribution. The contrast between different periods is well brought out by a table showing the percentage of old and young brides at different periods of Colyton's history. By the last decade of the three centuries a quarter of the brides were teenagers in the period 1647–1719 only 4 per cent; while on the other hand 40 per cent

[1] The time divisions used here and in subsequent tables were chosen to maximize the difference between the main periods of Colyton's demographic history.
[2] The difference between the two means 1560–1646 and 1647–1719 is 2·61 years. The standard error of the difference is 0·69 years. The difference of the means is therefore 3·8 times the standard error of the difference, and we may properly conclude that women in the second period were really marrying later than in the first.
[3] See Wrigley, *Some Problems of Family Reconstitution*, for a full discussion of the accuracy of the figures of age at marriage. See K. M. Drake, *Marriage and Population Growth in Norway, 1735–1865*, unpublished Ph.D. thesis (Cambridge, 1964), esp. pp. 93–103, for a very interesting examination of the factors which might induce men to take brides older than themselves in Norway in the late eighteenth and early nineteenth centuries.

Table 3. *Women at First Marriage*

	-19		30+		40+	
	No.	%	No.	%	No.	%
1560–1646	24	6·5	95	25·6	18	4·9
1647–1719	6	4·4	54	39·7	14	10·3
1825–37	17	25·0	5	7·4	1	1·5

were above thirty when they married for the first time in the earlier period compared with only 7 per cent in the later.

The male mean, medians and modes were notably 'sticky'.[1] Men entered married life at much the same time for almost three hundred years (only in the last few decades was there a slight fall in the male mean), but they proved remarkably flexible in their judgment of what constituted an acceptable age in their brides. A higher proportion of men married women older than themselves in the period 1647–1719 than either before or later. In the period 1560–1646 in 48 per cent of the first marriages in which the age of both parties is known the man was older than the woman, in 47 per cent the woman was older than the man, and in 5 per cent their ages were equal. In the period 1647–1719 the percentages were 40, 55 and 5, while by the period 1800–37 the figures were 59, 29 and 12.

The figures of age at first marriage demonstrate immediately the great range of general fertility levels which might be found in pre-industrial communities. Other things being equal, the changes in mean age of marriage alone provided scope for a very wide range of rates of increase (or decrease) of population. In marriages not prematurely interrupted by death an average age at first marriage for women of, say, 24 might well produce two more children than marriages contracted at an average age of, say, 29. The most extreme female mean ages at first marriage found at Colyton (30·7 in 1700–1 and 23·3 in 1825–37) can easily result in average completed family sizes differing from each other by a factor of 2.

The details of age at first marriage in themselves go far towards explaining the changes in numbers of children baptized which are apparent in the moving averages of crude totals of baptisms. However, any changes on the fertility side of the population history of Colyton which arose from changes in the mean age of first marriage were considerably amplified by changes in fertility within marriage as Table 4 and Figure 2 will make clear.

In the first period 1560–1629 the age-specific marital fertility rates in Colyton were high, being distinctly higher than those found at Crulai in the late seventeenth and early eighteenth centuries.[2] There is a marked decline of

[1] This may well be a very common feature of European demography in many centuries. See, for example, *Report of the Royal Commission on Population*, Cmd. 7695, p. 249, para. 25, for England in recent decades. See also E. A. Wrigley, *Industrial Growth and Population Change* (Cambridge, 1962), pp. 155–7, for nineteenth-century France and Germany.

[2] The Crulai figures reveal in a very striking way the phenomenon of teenage subfecundity. This is absent in the Colyton figures, but its absence is not significant because a very high proportion of first births in Colyton were pre-nuptially conceived (about a third until the nineteenth century when the figure rose to about half). A large proportion of these in turn were born shortly after marriage (22 per cent of all first births were baptized within six months of marriage 1538–1799, 36 per cent 1800–37).

Table 4. *Age-specific marital fertility (children born per thousand woman-years lived* (In brackets the number of woman-years on which the rate is based)

Colyton

	15–19	20–4	25–9	30–4	35–9	40–4	45–9
1560–1629	412 (17·0)	467 (205·5)	403 (473·5)	369 (561·5)	302 (517·0)	174 (443·0)	18 (383·5)
1630–46	500 (4·0)	378 (63·5)	382 (120·5)	298 (107·5)	234 (55·5)	128 (23·5)	0 (16·0)
1647–1719	500 (4·0)	346 (52·0)	395 (187·5)	272 (253·5)	182 (258·5)	104 (249·5)	20 (200·5)
1720–69	462 (19·5)	362 (69·0)	342 (164·0)	292 (216·0)	227 (203·0)	160 (156·0)	0 (138·0)
1770–1837	500 (34·0)	441 (279·0)	361 (498·0)	347 (504·5)	270 (430·0)	152 (224·0)	22 (186·0)

Crulai

| 1674–1742 | 320 (65·5) | 419 (305·5) | 429 (599·0) | 355 (633·0) | 292 (588·5) | 142 (505·5) | 10 (205·5) |

Note. The Crulai figures are taken from Gautier and Henry, *La Population de Crulai*, pp. 102 and 105 and Table VII, pp. 249–54. The Colyton rates are derived from marriages formed during the year specified, except that marriages which bridge the period 1630–1646 to 1647–1719 are divided at the end of 1646, data from before that date being allocated to the earlier period, beyond it to 1647–1719. The reason for this appears in the text below, pp. 91–2.

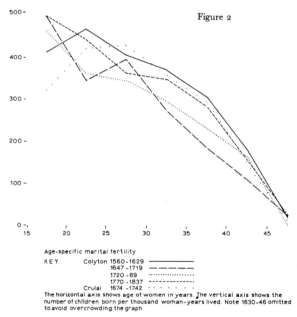

Figure 2

Age-specific marital fertility
KEY   Colyton 1560-1629 ──────
              1647 -1719 ── ── ── ──
              1720 - 69   ·················
              1770 -1837 ------------
        Crulai   1674 -1742 · · · · · ·
The horizontal axis shows age of women in years. The vertical axis shows the number of children born per thousand woman-years lived. Note 1630–46 omitted to avoid overcrowding the graph.

fertility in the last fifteen years before the plague of 1645–6 and this became more pronounced after 1646. Fertility remained low throughout the period marked also by an exceptionally high average age at first marriage for women.[1] During the period 1720–69 there was some recovery in the rates, while during

Teenage brides, like others, were often pregnant at marriage and since most births to teenage mothers were first births, the 15–19 rate is inflated as a result and no valid comparison with Crulai can be made. The same is true to a lesser degree of the age-group 20–4.

[1] It is unfortunately not possible to estimate what changes took place in the proportions of women ever married at, say, 45.

he final period 1770–1837 the rates were much higher though still not quite
at the level attained in the sixteenth and early seventeenth centuries. There
was therefore a cycle in marital fertility levels, passing from high through low
to high once more during the three centuries under review. Both the transition
from the initial high level to a lower level of marital fertility and the subsequent
recovery in fertility levels are of the greatest interest, but in this article I shall
concentrate chiefly on the change from high to low levels of fertility in the mid-
seventeenth century, though the rise in fertility during the eighteenth century is
a matter of equal fascination. Comparison of the periods 1560–1629 and
1647–1719 reveals the fact that the relative difference between the five-year
age-groups becomes more and more marked with rising age. With 1560–
1629 as 100 in each case the figures for 1647–1719 are 74, 98, 74, 61 and 60
for the age-groups 20–4, 25–9, 30–4, 35–9 and 40–4 respectively. The anomalous
figure for the 20–4 age-group may be explained perhaps by the small number
of years in marriage from which it was derived, but apart from this the progressively greater gap is well marked. When represented graphically the
curve of the period 1560–1629 is convex to the upper side, while the curve of
the later period is slightly concave to the upper side in the later years of the
fertile period.[1] Since the latter is often taken as an indication of the restriction

Table 5

1560–1629 [2]

No. of children	20–4	25–9	30–4	35–9	40–4	45–9	Total
0	1	2	6	16	34	61	120
1	1	16	19	24	32	6	98
2	6	31	49	35	9	0	130
3	2	9	14	9	4	0	38
4	0	2	0	3	1	0	6
5	1	0	1	0	0	0	2
Total	11	60	89	87	80	67	394
Average	2·18	1·88	1·84	1·53	0·83	0·09	

1647–1719

No. of children	25–9	30–4	35–9	40–4	45–9	Total
0	1	8	17	23	32	81
1	6	11	15	14	2	48
2	4	16	9	3	0	32
3	4	3	0	0	0	7
4	2	0	0	0	0	2
5	0	0	0	0	0	0
Total	17	38	41	40	34	170
Average	2·00	1·37	0·80	0·50	0·60	

[1] The changes which took place at Colyton are very similar to those which took place at the same
period in the Genevan *bourgeoisie*. See Henry, *Anciennes familles genevoises*, esp. pp. 75–81. The family
limitation which began amongst the Genevan *bourgeoise* in the second half of the seventeenth century,
however, became accentuated in the eighteenth, whereas in Colyton there was a reversion to the earlier
fertility patterns.

[2] In this table and subsequently in Tables 11 and 12 the period 1560–1629 is used rather than 1560–
1646 both because fertility was somewhat lower 1630–46 and because of the problem of the 'bridging'
families (see pp. 91–2 and Table 7 below).

of fertility within the family it is important to look further into the fertility characteristics of women in the period 1647–1719. The reason why a concavity to the upper side of a curve representing age-specific marital fertility often indicates family limitation is, of course, that most married couples want some children but not as large a number as might be born to them without any limitation of fertility. They will tend to concentrate their reproductive effort into the earlier part of the wife's fertile period. Age-specific fertility in the younger age-groups in these circumstances may remain high, but in the later age-groups there will be a progressively greater shortfall from the full fertility potential of the women in question, producing the characteristic concavity in the curve.

Table 5 shows the frequency with which women bore 0, 1, 2, 3, 4, or 5 children when living throughout a specified five-year age-group. At the foot of each column the average number of children born in the five-year period is shown. The figures when converted approximate closely to the rates shown in Table 4 as is to be expected (where they are a little lower it is because they largely eliminate the influence of the very short interval between marriage and first baptism – see p. 88, n. 2). It is possible to make an analysis of variance on the four age-groups over 30 in the two periods, with the following result.

	Sum of squares	Degrees of freedom	Estimate of variance	*F*
Total	490·00	475		
Age-groups	168·92	3	56·31	88·2
Periods	20·38	1	20·38	31·9
Error	300·70	471	0·6384	

A test for interaction produces an *F* which is not significant and the assumption of additivity can be retained. The difference between the two periods is very highly significant (beyond the 0·1 per cent level) and we may therefore say with confidence that there was a fall in fertility above the age of 30 between the two periods.[1]

The possibility of the existence of some form of family limitation immediately suggests a comparison of the fertility rates in the age-groups 30–44 of those women marrying below the age of 30 with the rates for those marrying in their thirties. Since the former will already in most cases have borne children before entering their thirties, it is to be expected that their fertility rates will be lower than those of women marrying after 30 who will have less reason to seek to restrict the number of their children. Table 6 shows that the expected pattern is present though it should not be forgotten that rather higher rates amongst those marrying at 30 or over are to be expected anyway because the interval between marriage and the birth of the first child is much less than the later birth intervals and this will cause the fertility rates of women bearing their first child after a marriage above 30 to appear higher than those who married younger even if the true fertility position were the same. The differences, however, are much too large to be accounted for on this ground. It is of

---

[1] I am greatly indebted to Dr T. H. Hollingsworth for his advice on statistical technique in this article and for his comments generally.

Table 6. *Age-specific Marital Fertility (children born per thousand woman-years lived)*
(In brackets the number of woman-years on which the rate is based)

1647–1719

	30–4	35–9	40–4	45–9
Women marrying				
–29	265 (215·5)	146 (191·5)	96 (146·0)	0 (108·5)
30+	316 (38·0)	284 (67·0)	116 (103·5)	43 (92·0)

interest incidentally to follow the short-term experience of the couples who had married before the plague visitation of 1645–6 and who survived the terrible year. It has sometimes been supposed that the 'instinctive' reaction of a population after a heavy loss of life is to increase fertility to fill the gaps created by death. Table 7 shows the age-specific fertility rates of women in families which bridged the plague year and where the age of the wife is known. Some were at

Table 7. *Age-specific marital fertility (children born per thousand woman-years lived)*
(In brackets the number of woman-years on which the rate is based)

	15–19	20–4	25–9	30–4	35–9	40–4	45–9
–1646	572 (3·5)	429 (28·0)	412 (51·0)	370 (40·5)	194 (15·5)	0 (4·0)	
1647+			174 (11·5)	247 (36·5)	154 (52·0)	127 (55·0)	0 (43·5)

the beginning of their child-bearing period when the plague struck, others were near the end, which explains how there are rates on both sides of the temporal division for most age-groups. The numbers involved were, of course, small, but the picture which emerges is nonetheless suggestive. Fertility rates dropped sharply and immediately to the levels which were to be characteristic of Colyton for the next two or three generations even though the women in question had displayed a fertility well above the average in the period before the swingeing losses of 1646.[1] The change from a high to a low level of fertility within these families was abrupt and complete, just as was the change to a later age at first marriage for women.

The examination of mean birth intervals can also throw much light on the question of family limitation. Table 8 shows the mean birth intervals 0–1, 1–2, 2–3, 3–4 and penultimate to last of completed families of four or more children in the three periods 1560–1646, 1647–1719 and 1720–69.[2] A completed family is one in which the woman reached the age of 45 in marriage and would therefore in almost all cases have completed her child-bearing. Only those women who married under 30 are included in the table, since if family limitation was to be found in the period 1647–1719 it is in such families that it would be most clearly apparent for reasons touched on above. To those in each group of whom the exact age at marriage is known have been added completed families [3] in which the age of the wife is not known when there were six or more

---

[1] It may be of interest to note that Creighton, in discussing the aftermath of the Black Death, quotes a passage from the *Eulogium Historiarum* that 'the women who survived remained for the most part barren during several years'. C. Creighton, *History of Epidemics in Britain*, 2 vols (Cambridge, 1891, 1894), I, p. 200. Creighton also quotes Piers the Plowman to much the same effect.
[2] The period 1770–1837 yields too few completed families to be worth including.
[3] Completed families here comprise any in which at least 27 years is known to have elapsed between the beginning and end of the marriage.

children born to the marriage in the periods 1560–1646 and 1720–69 an
where there were four or more children in the period 1647–1719, since in th
vast majority of these cases the wife was under 30 at marriage. Includin
such marriages increases substantially the number of cases which can b
studied (by almost three-quarters). The most striking feature of this table is th

Table 8. *Mean Birth Intervals (in months)*

	0–1	No.	1–2	No.	2–3	No.	3–4	No.	Last	N
1560–1646	11·3	87	25·2	87	27·4	84	30·1	77	37·5	7
1647–1719	10·3	23	29·1	23	32·6	26	32·1	18	50·7	34
1720–69	11·9	24	25·1	24	29·8	24	32·9	22	40·6	24

Birth Intervals 1–4 combined

	Mean	No.
1560–1646	27·5	248
1647–1719	31·4	67
1720–69	29·1	70

Notes. The smaller number of intervals 3–4 arises because when the interval 3–4 was also the las
interval it is not included in the 3–4 totals. The large number of last birth intervals 1647–1719 and th
reduced number 1560–1646 is a result of splitting families which bridged the year 1646 in the wa
described above.

A difference of means test may be applied to the means of the last birth intervals 1560–1646 an
1647–1719. The difference in the two means is 13·1 years. The standard error of the difference i
4·62 years. The difference of means is therefore 2·88 times the standard error of the difference, and th
difference is significant at the 1 per cent level. The same test applied to the means of all birth interval
1–4 shows the mean of 1560–1646 to be significantly different from the mean of 1647–1719 at th
5 per cent level (difference of means 2·15 times the standard error of the difference).

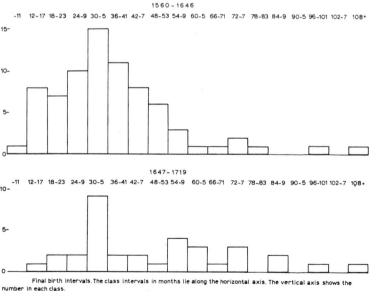

Figure 3

Final birth intervals. The class intervals in months lie along the horizontal axis. The vertical axis shows the
number in each class.

contrast between the middle period and the other two in the mean interval between the penultimate and last births. A marked rise in this interval is typical of a community beginning to practise family limitation.[1] It rises in these circumstances because even after reaching an intended final family size additions are nevertheless occasionally made either from accident (failure of whatever system of restriction is in use), from a reversal of an earlier decision not to increase family size, or from a desire to replace a child which has died.

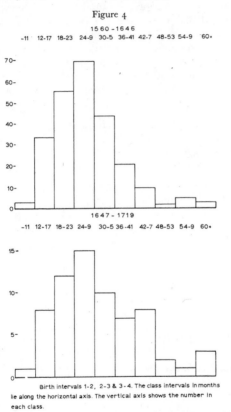

Figure 4

15 60 - 16 4 6

-11   12-17   18-23   24-9   30-5   36-41   42-7   48-53   54-9   60+

1647 - 1719

-11   12-17   18-23   24-9   30-5   36-41   42-7   48-53   54-9   60+

Birth intervals 1-2, 2-3 & 3-4. The class intervals In months lie along the horizontal axis. The vertical axis shows the number in each class.

Figure 3 shows the distribution of final birth intervals of the two periods 1560–1646 and 1647–1719 in the form of a histogram. In the earlier period the distribution is unimodal with a fairly clear peak about the 30–5 month interval. In the later period this peak is again apparent but there is also a suspicion of a second peak in the 54–65 month intervals, suggesting that while the 'natural' distribution continued to occur in some cases, there was superimposed upon it a different pattern which might be the result of family limitation.

Table 8 contains other points of interest. The mean interval between marriage

1 See Henry, *Anciennes familles genevoises*, esp. pp. 93–110

and first baptism did not change materially over the two centuries covered by the table. The later birth intervals, 1–2, 2–3, and 3–4, were always higher in 1647–1719 than in 1560–1646, though, rather surprisingly perhaps, the difference showed no tendency to grow greater as the rank of birth increased. It is also surprising to find the higher mean present as early as the 1–2 birth interval. One might have expected in the light of experience elsewhere that the early stages of family formation would have been as rapid in the middle period as either earlier or later, but this appears not to have been the case. The frequency distribution of all births 1–2, 2–3 and 3–4 (taken together since the numbers involved are small and the pattern much the same at each birth interval) shows that the reason for the higher mean in the period 1647–1719 does not lie in the shift of the peak frequency to the right but in the greater skewness of the distribution to the right. The median and modal figures underline this point. The frequency-distribution pattern is compatible with the view that family limitation was being practised. Some other changes in frequency

Table 9. *Means, Medians and Modes of all Birth Intervals 1–4*

	Mean	Median	Mode
1560–1646	27·5	26·6	24·8
1647–1719	31·4	29·0	24·1

distributions which might have occurred and which would have produced a higher mean would have shown a different pattern. For example, if there had been a general increase in the customary suckling period which would have increased the mean birth intervals by prolonging the period of lowered fecundity in the mother, there would probably have been a shift in the peak frequency to the right.[1]

Another tell-tale sign of family limitation is a fall in the age at which women bear their last child in families in which they are at risk to the end of the child-bearing period (45 years of age). This is likely to arise for the same reasons which tend to produce a very long final birth interval and will be most evident among women who marry young and have had several children well before the end of their fertile period. Table 10 shows the mean ages at the birth of the last child of women marrying above and below the age of 30. In the first of the three periods the mean age at birth of last child was much the same for

Table 10

	–29	No.	30+	No.
1560–1646	39·8	50	40·5	25
1647–1719	37·6	22	42·7	14
1720–69	40·4	14	41·4	5

women marrying –29 as for those marrying above 30, in each case about 40, and the same is true of the period 1720–69. But in the middle period the mean

---

[1] See the searching discussion of this question and the data presented in Henry, *Anciennes familles genevoises*, chaps. 4 and 5. It is of interest also to note that the mean birth interval after the death of the preceding child under one year of age (excluding last birth intervals) was 20·6 months in the period 1538–1646 (114 cases) and 22·7 months (15 cases) in 1647–1719 (data drawn from all families in which the date of the end of the union is known).

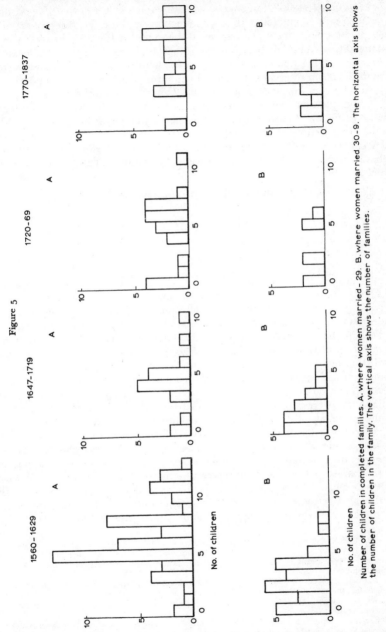

Figure 5

Women marrying −24 and 25–9 are brought together in the upper set of histograms. Since the number of women marrying −24 and 25–9 was much the same in each separate period (24 and 29 in 1560–1629, 9 and 8 in 1647–1719, 9 and 12 in 1720–69, and 10 and 10 in 1770–1837), this does not introduce much relative distortion and allows a clearer pattern to emerge.

age at birth of last child for women marrying under 30 was lower than for those marrying over 30 and lower than for women in the same age-group in the other two periods. Both these features are to be expected if family limitation were taking place.[1] The fall between 1560–1646 and 1647–1719 in the mean for women marrying under 30 was 2·25 years. This in combination with a steep rise in the mean interval between the penultimate and last births underlies, of course, the very low age-specific fertility figures found in the age-groups 30–4, 35–9 and 40–4 for women marrying under 30 (see Table 6). The eighteenth century shows a reversion to the earlier pattern in age at birth of last child as in the other fertility characteristics considered.

A convenient measure which reflects the combined effects of the changes already discussed is the mean size of completed families. Table 11 sets forth the chief statistics.

Table 11. *Mean Completed Family Size*

	−24	25–29	30–9
1560–1629	7·3 ± 1·3	5·7 ± 1·1	2·7 ± 0·8
1646–1719	5·0 ± 2·0	3·3 ± 1·7	1·7 ± 0·9
1720–69	5·8 ± 2·5	3·8 ± 1·7	2·4 ± 1·7
1770–1837	7·3 ± 1·6	4·5 ± 2·3	3·2 ± 0·9

Note. The figures after the means are the 95 per cent confidence intervals.

The extent of the decline between the first and second halves of the seventeenth century is underscored by the figures of completed family size.[2] Figure 5 gives more detail of the distribution of family sizes in the form of a series of histograms.

Perhaps the most striking single feature of the detailed distribution is that only 18 per cent of women marrying under 30 between 1647 and 1719 and living right through the fertile period had families of 6 children or more (3 in 17), compared with 55 per cent (29 in 53) in 1560–1629, 48 per cent (10 in 21) in 1720–69 and 60 per cent (12 in 20) in 1770–1837. Very large families, on the other hand, were rare at any time in Colyton, the largest during the full three centuries being only 13. Childless marriages were also rare in the period of high fertility before 1646. Of all marriages formed when the bride was under 35 and lasting till she was 45 or more, only 5 out of 70 were childless. Since a small number of marriages are infertile for physiological reasons the position in the earliest period may well represent a figure close to the minimum which can be expected.[3] It is notably similar to the Crulai figure, and is found also in the latest period 1770–1837 when marital fertility was again high at Colyton. In the other two periods, 1647–1719 and 1720–69, the proportion of childless

[1] The difference in mean age at birth of last child of women marrying under 30 between 1560–1646 and 1647–1719 is 2·25. The standard error of the difference of the two means is 1·24. The difference between the two means is therefore not significant at the 5 per cent level (the former is only 1·81 times the latter).

[2] The fall occurred at a time when age-specific death-rates, especially of young children, were rising so that the net reproduction rate fell even more sharply than the gross rate. It is doubtful whether the net reproduction rate of the population of Colyton reached unity during the period when fertility rates were at their lowest.

[3] See, for example, the tables of D. V. Glass and E. Grebenik reproduced in *The Cambridge Economic History of Europe*, vol. VI, pt. 1 (Cambridge, 1965), p. 114.

Table 12. *Childless Completed Marriages* (wife marrying −35)

	Childless	Total	%
1560–1629	5	70	7
1647–1719	4	22	18
1720–69	6	29	21
1770–1837	2	26	8
Crulai			
1674–1742	5	77	6

Note. The Crulai figure is calculated from Gautier and Henry, *La Population de Crulai*, Table VII, pp. 249–54.

families was much higher. It is interesting that the period 1720–69, an intermediate period in most other respects, had such a high proportion of childless marriages, though the absolute numbers involved are not large and are subject to wide margins of error. The difference between the first period, 1560–1629, and the two succeeding periods, 1647–1719 and 1720–69, is, however, not significant at the 5 per cent level even if the latter two periods are grouped together (χ^2 test).

Statistics of the mean size of completed families can, of course, be rather misleading, since many marriages were interrupted by the death of one of the partners before the wife had passed through her child-bearing period. Table 11 shows, for example, that in 1560–1629 the mean sizes of completed families born to women marrying −24, 25–9, and 30–9 were 7·3, 5·7 and 2·7 respectively. But if to these families are added all those cut short before the wife reached 45 the mean sizes fall to 5·2, 4·9 and 2·4 respectively. Marriages contracted in early life are, of course, more likely to be affected and the proportionate fall in family size is greater in their case. In all the tables expressing family size the importance of age at marriage is clear. At all periods the contrast between marriages contracted in the early twenties and those which took place when the bride was in her thirties is marked. The immense social and economic import of the fall of seven years in the average age at first marriage for women which took place between the beginning of the eighteenth and the early nineteenth century, therefore, is firmly driven home.

Before turning to the more general issues raised by the history of family formation in Colyton during the three centuries when the parish registers are the prime source of information about demographic changes, it is appropriate to touch upon the question of the completeness of registration. This is too large a topic to be treated here in its entirety, but one issue must be mentioned. Since the foregoing tables have been cast in a form which makes it easy to compare Colyton with industrializing countries today or with historical studies of the type done on French parish registers, it is important to know how accurate the Colyton statistics are. It is evident that when the figures err they will err by understating rather than overstating the levels of fertility reached. For example, although the families which are used for the calculation of age-specific fertility are subjected to a fairly rigorous test of presence in the parish,[1] there must be small a proportion of baptisms recorded in the registers

[1] For details see Wrigley (ed.), *Introduction to English Historical Demography*, chap. 4.

of other parishes which should ideally have been included in the fertility data for Colyton families. In addition to small 'leakages' of this sort there is a major source of 'leakage' which deserves attention. In some periods in English parishes many children who died soon after birth were never baptized [1] and some of these were buried without benefit of church service. No system of correction can overcome the difficulties arising from under-registration entirely, but some idea of the order of magnitude of correction which seems appropriate can be gained from a consideration of infant mortality and especially the frequency distribution of the apparent age at death of children dying under the age of one.

Table 13 shows the age at death of children dying under one for the parish of St Michael le Belfrey in York and for Colyton at two different periods. The

Table 13. *Age at Death*

	1st d.	1–6 d.	1–4 w.	1 m.	2 m.	3–5 m.	6–11 m.	Total
A	33	28	21	9	8	20	21	140
B	35	19	27	16	9	15	24	145
C	19	18	20	26	7	24	24	138

A. St Michael le Belfrey, York, 1571–86
B. Colyton, 1538–99
C. Colyton, 1600–49

register of St Michael le Belfrey during the years 1571–86 is very remarkable in that an exact age at burial is given (even down to an age in hours if the child died during its first day of life) and every care appears to have been taken to secure a complete coverage of vital events. The baptism register contains many entries of baptism by the midwife in the house and the burial of unbaptized children is also scrupulously set down. In Colyton in the same period only an apparent age at death can be calculated by comparing the dates of baptism and burial. Comparison of the A and B lines in Table 13 at least does nothing to undermine the view that in the sixteenth century children in Colyton were normally baptized very soon after birth and that consequently the 'leakage' was very slight. The comparatively high proportion of children buried on the day they were baptized is difficult to reconcile with any other view.[2] Line C in Table 13, however, presents a very different picture. In the period 1600–49 the proportion apparently dying in the first week of life was much lower. In all probability this period sees the beginning of the custom of delaying baptism in Colyton. Two calculations may now be made, one of which probably underestimates the amount of correction necessary, while the other perhaps overstates it. The first assumes that the number of deaths above one week is correct and a figure for deaths in the first week is calculated

[1] It would be more accurate to say that they never appeared in the baptism register. In some parishes it was the custom to baptize privately in the home if the child were in danger of death, but only to record it in the register after a subsequent public ceremony if the child survived its first dangers.

[2] It is interesting to note that at Crulai in the late seventeenth and early eighteenth centuries, where baptism is known to have taken place almost invariably on the first day of life, 30 per cent of all deaths under one were on the first day (99 in 331), compared with 24 per cent at Colyton, 1538–99. Gautier and Henry remark, however, that a proportion of these may well in fact have been born dead. Gautier and Henry, *La Population de Crulai*, p. 170.

on the assumption that they form the same percentage of total deaths as at Colyton, 1538–99, or at St Michael le Belfrey. This assumption might give an approximately correct answer if baptism usually took place within a few days of birth, but would tend to be on the low side since some of those apparently dying in the first week of life would in fact be more than a week old. Alternatively a figure may be calculated on the assumption that half the children buried at an apparent age of less than one month were in fact more than a month old and that the resulting figure of deaths above a month old formed the same percentage of total deaths as at Colyton earlier or at St Michael le Belfrey. Like the first method this gives, of course, only a very rough and ready correction, but this time probably on the high side. Use can also be made of the life-table mortality rates 1–4, 5–9 and 10–14 (a few of which are listed on p. 101, n. 1). Comparison of these with the United Nations specimen life-table rates also throws some light on the question of the likely order of magnitude of infant mortality rates.[1] These several exercises suggest that the fertility rates quoted in Table 4 understate the true position by between two and six per cent, with a low figure appropiate for the first period, 1560–1629, and figures in the upper part of the range more likely in the later periods. It appears most unlikely that differences in the degree of under-registration at different periods can serve to explain any of the major changes which appear in tables in the earlier sections of this article.

III

I have so far written of the striking changes in marital fertility which took place in Colyton between the first and second halves of the seventeenth century as if they were the result of a system of family limitation deliberate in the sense that social or individual action caused fewer children to be born, or at all events to survive long enough to be baptized, than would have been the case without such restraints. But is this a correct assumption? And if so, what were the means employed to reduce fertility so drastically?

Any explanation other than family limitation must take account of the fact that fertility fell much more steeply in the later years of the fertile period than the earlier, of the remarkable change in the mean age at first marriage for women, and, if possible, of the later reversion to a position not unlike that of the late sixteenth and early seventeenth centuries. Some of the explanations which might be entertained on one score are unacceptable on other grounds. For example, a fall in marital fertility might simply reflect a change in suckling habits, but this would not explain the much more drastic fall in fertility in the higher age-groups. Perhaps the only explanation other than family limitation which might cover the known facts is an economic reverse of such severity that the physiological condition of women of child-bearing age was affected by it (either from simple undernourishment, or from the absence in their diet of elements necessary for high fertility). This might plausibly be argued to be likely to affect the older age-groups more than the younger. Such an

---

[1] I hope to deal more adequately with the mortality experience of Colyton in a later article.

explanation has the additional attraction that it is fully consonant with the steep rise in child mortality which took place at that time.[1] This alternative explanation deserves further careful study, but suffers from several defects.

The first difficulty is that fertility in the higher age-groups was much higher among women who married late in life than among those who married early. This might be explained on the ground that those who had already borne several children were exhausted by this and that their physical condition deteriorated seriously as a result. But it is doubtful whether child-bearing would have had this effect on the mass of women. Gautier and Henry remark that this did not occur at Crulai, and that it is not apparent in modern Indian rural populations.[2] Again, the abrupt change to much lower fertility levels among the families which spanned the great mortality of 1645–6 creates a problem. It is difficult to imagine a change in economic conditions effecting such a swift and complete change in the absence of family limitation. It is possible, of course, that this fall in fertility was due to the after-effects of plague infection on the women who survived, but against this it must be noted that their fertility after 1647 was closely similar to the general pattern over the next two generations. But perhaps the most important difficulty is that although death-rates at all ages rose in the second half of the seventeenth century, and expectation of life fell by several years to the low 30's,[3] it was still as high in Colyton at this period as it was in Crulai at much the same time. Yet fertility rates at Crulai were almost as high as in Colyton in the sixteenth century, and moreover the pattern of age-specific rates in Crulai shows no sudden dip in the thirties. This undermines a main base of the argument from ag eneral worsening of economic conditions, unless indeed it is held that diet and other conditions of life in Colyton, though generally no worse than in Crulai, were nevertheless more deficient in certain vital constituents necessary for high fertility in women.

There are, however, difficulties also with the view that family limitation lay behind the change in fertility in Colyton. These difficulties fall under two main heads: the explanation of the rise in child mortality which accompanied the fall in fertility, and the question of the means which it is reasonable to envisage having been employed to secure a lower fertility. The first is a problem because it might seem natural to suppose that if a population began to limit its fertility drastically it would take the better care of those children who were born. If child mortality changed it would fall rather than rise. The second is a problem for the reason that Malthus expressed succinctly when he referred to the 'passion between the sexes' as a potent and unchanging feature of behaviour.

[1] The late seventeenth century was much more unhealthy for young children at Colyton than the preceding century, as is shown by these life-table mortality rates (the figures in brackets for 1600–49 are the rates which result from eliminating the deaths from plague in 1645–6. Rates per thousand).

	1538–99	1600–49	1650–99
1–4	88	97 (85)	162
5–9	30	54 (30)	45
10–14	16	41 (19)	37

[2] See Gautier and Henry, *La Population de Crulai*, pp. 98–100.
[3] I hope to publish the evidence for this statement on a later occasion.

et if the passion between the sexes is given free rein within marriage how an one explain a sudden fall in marital fertility in a period long before modern mechanical and chemical methods of birth control were practised? Both these re objections of weight and any answer to them is bound to be tentative. I am more concerned in this section of the article to set an argument in train than to suggest that a full answer can as yet be given.

It may be that the problem of the fall in fertility coinciding with a rise in child mortality is only a problem if viewed, anachronistically, in modern terms. f the reason for limiting family size had been prudential and consciously so rather in the way that a modern family may choose between an extra child or an expensive education for the existing children, then a concomitant rise in child mortality would be very surprising.[1] But the change may well have been of a very different type. It must be borne in mind that the view that pre-industrial societies normally did little or nothing to restrict the level of fertility within marriage is an extreme hypothesis. Societies at a low level of material culture frequently developed taboos upon intercourse during long periods of married life, and practised abortion or infanticide.[2] There is a very large literature about the connexion between the social activities of animals and the maintenance of population size at a level substantially below the maximum number which their habitat could support.[3] Both in primitive human groups and in an enormous range of insect, fish, bird and mammal species it is clear that methods developed within the group through social activity to prevent numbers from pressing too hard upon the food base confer a notable selective advantage. If numbers are allowed to grow too great the ecological balance of the area may be upset and the ability of the area to provide food for the population be impaired. Moreover, the group as a whole is more likely to be successful f its members are well fed and in good health than if the constant pressure of numbers makes it hard to keep adults vigorous. A tribe of Australian aborigines having only a limited food base on which to support itself behaves much as bird and animal communities do in similar circumstances. It throws up social controls which prevent so large a number of new mouths coming into existence as to prejudice the wellbeing of those already living. This may be done in animal populations either by preventing some adults from breeding in a given season, or by delaying the entry of adolescents into the breeding population, or by restricting the number of viable offspring, or by causing the early death

---

[1] Unless indeed the change in economic conditions had been so catastrophic that not even a fall in marital fertility as steep as that which took place in Colyton could ensure as good a life for the children of the small families of the late seventeenth century as their parents and grandparents had enjoyed in the much larger families of their childhood. There is, unfortunately, very little evidence as yet about the state of the Colyton economy in the late seventeenth century. Study of the Exeter wheat price series suggests that living was dear in this region at the beginning of the period of low fertility, though prices had fallen to low levels well before its end (in 1647 wheat was 62·72 shillings per quarter at Exeter, a level not surpassed until 1795, and prices stayed high for much of the 1650's and 1660's – but they had been very high before this, reaching 62·94 shillings in 1596). The state of affairs in Colyton may, of course, have been either better or worse than in the county or country as a whole.

[2] See e.g. N. E. Himes, *Medical History of Contraception* (Baltimore, 1936), and F. Lorimer, *Culture and Human Fertility* (Paris, 1954).

[3] This subject is brilliantly reviewed in V. C. Wynne-Edwards, *Animal Dispersion in relation to Social Behaviour* (1962). A. M. Carr-Saunders has also used this argument in *The Population Problem* (1922).

161

of many which are born, or indeed by many combinations and modification of these methods. But in all cases the effect is to keep population number fluctuating some way beneath the maximum – that is at a level which neithe prejudices the flow of food by creating too great a pressure on the availabl food base (over-fishing in Wynne-Edwards terminology; encroaching o capital rather than living off dividend in more familiar jargon) nor stunts th development of the adult members of the community but yet does not restric numbers much below the level imposed by these desiderata. It is importan to note that when a population has risen substantially above this level an a contraction of numbers is necessary it is normally secured, in part at leas by reducing the flow of new members into the community, and it is to b expected both that the number of births will fall and that the infant death rate will rise. Conversely, if numbers fall below the optimum range it i probable that there will be both a rise in fertility and a fall in the wastage c life among the very young members of the population. If therefore a mode drawn from the study of animal populations were made the basis of expectation it would occasion no surprise that fertility and child mortality should change i Colyton in the way that they did in the later seventeenth century.[1] Such model, incidentally, also makes the changes in mean age at first marriage o women (particularly the reversal of the usual age gap between the sexes a marriage) easier to understand, since this too is a reaction which might b expected in a population which was restricting its numbers to approach a optimum.

Populations whose economy is based upon hunting and the collection of foo appear to conform closely in their methods of population control to the genera model of animal communities. Pre-industrial populations whose economie are based upon the cultivation of the land are differently placed. In their cas the food base may be substantially broadened from time to time by technologica advance (for example by the development of a more effective plough or the introduction of a new type of food crop). Their population control problem are much less simple, since in periods following technological or organizational advance and an expansion of the food base they may be able to allow populations to rise for several centuries with only intermittent checks from epidemics and bad harvests, but they will be brought up against the same problem once more when the possibilities of any given advance in material culture have been exhausted. The Malthusian model under which populations tend to approach a maximum rather than fluctuate well below this is perhaps an aberration in the history of populations from the more general model to which most animal societies conform, rather as the classical model of full employment is a limiting case of Keynesian employment theory. At times when the potential of a technological or organizational advance has been fully used up populations may well have to relearn methods of social control of population size which could be forgotten as long as an expansion in the food base had made Malthusian

---

[1] The argument here is, of course, very general. Several other possible causes of higher child mortality can be envisaged. It may be, for example, that smallpox at this period was both more virulent and more widespread than earlier.

behaviour for a time possible and even appropriate.[1] In the absence of much more empirical work much of this discussion is inevitably speculative, but it may well explain why populations in the late fourteenth and fifteenth centuries remained at a lower level than before the Black Death in spite of the rise in real incomes which apparently took place among the peasants. Upon Malthusian assumptions this should have produced a fall in the age of marriage and a rapid rise in population.[2]

All the foregoing, of course, does not imply that the individual man or woman was conscious of this range of issues in the least, any more than the individual robin or rook is conscious of the problems of avoiding too large a population, but like robins and rooks people respond sensitively to social pressures. It would be surprising if there were not present in pre-industrial European populations a range of possible courses of social action which could secure a stabilization of numbers well short of the appalling conditions of control envisaged at times by Malthus. Populations before then and since have acted to secure this: it would be surprising if none in the intervening centuries had acted in the same way, and had done so not merely by altering socially acceptable patterns of age at marriage, but by changing normal levels of fertility within marriage (perhaps in ways which bore more heavily upon the lower sections of the social pyramid), and even by changes in social custom likely to produce higher child mortality.[3]

There remains the second general problem in accepting at its face value the evidence for control of fertility within marriage at Colyton, the problem of the methods used to produce this result. Once more one can plausibly argue that this is a problem only if approached with preconceived ideas, or more properly, since this is to some extent inevitable, with a particular set of preconceived ideas. It is quite clear that European pre-industrial populations could severely restrict their family sizes, not merely in the wealthy and leisured families, but throughout a whole community. When in the late eighteenth century rural populations in France still set in traditional economic ways began to limit the size of their families [4] they did not have at their disposal any of the modern chemical or mechanical means of contraception. They limited their families, so far as is yet known, by practising *coitus interruptus* or *reservatus*, and no doubt procuring many abortions, possibly also by infanticide. Any means which may have been available to French peasants of the Ile de

---

[1] The word Malthusian is not, of course, used here in the French sense. An interesting example of this cycle of events is afforded by the Irish population in the eighteenth and nineteenth centuries.

[2] In a recent article Bean argues that recurrences of plague in the fifteenth century were not sufficiently severe to keep population down to post-Black Death levels and that therefore it is reasonable to suppose that numbers were increasing. This view is advanced with proper caution, but is interesting as an illustration of the tendency to expect populations to rise unless some exogenous agency keeps them down. See J. M. W. Bean, 'Plague, Population and Economic Decline in England in the Later Middle Ages' *Economic History Review*, 2nd ser. XV (1963), 431–6.

[3] This possibility must have been in Krause's mind when he wrote: 'The usually cited infant death rates greatly exaggerate pre-industrial European infant mortality, especially among infants born to families which wanted to keep them alive.' J. T. Krause, 'Some Implications of Recent Work in Historical Demography', *Comparative Studies in Society and History*, II (1959), 177.

[4] See Gautier and Henry, *La Population de Crulai*, and J. Ganiage, *Trois villages de l'Ile de France au XVIIIᵉ siècle*, I.N.E.D. Cahier No. 40 (Paris, 1963).

France or Normandy at the end of the eighteenth century were also availabl
to English communities a century and a half earlier – and indeed to Europea
communities for many centuries before that.[1] Such means may perhaps b
regarded as being permanently at the disposal of European pre-industri
populations, requiring only the right sort of 'trigger' to bring them fortl
Circumstances in Colyton in the middle of the seventeenth century appea
to have been such as to produce this change. The parish register of Colyto
carries no clues to the methods of family limitation used. These may never b
known with certainty, but it is likely that there was scope for the quiet disposa
outside the ecclesiastical purview of abortions, and indeed of the victims c
infanticide if this was practised. The early hours of a child's life provide man
occasions when it is easy to follow the maxim that 'thou shalt not kill bu
needst not strive officiously to keep alive'. In the nature of things there canno
be much evidence about the frequency of *coitus interruptus* and similar metho
of avoiding conception in the absence of literary evidence on the subject
There is, however, a good deal of evidence from more recent times of the larg
scale upon which *coitus interruptus* may be practised and that it is an effectiv
means of controlling conception.[2] *Coitus interruptus* may well have been the mos
important method of family limitation in use in Colyton in the seventeenth an
early eighteenth centuries.[3] It was probably widely employed by Frencl
populations to secure a lower marital fertility a century later.

IV

Before it can be known whether the population history of Colyton in the seven
teenth century is typical of much of England or is an unusual variant from th
normal pattern, very much more work needs to be done. Family reconstitutior
is a laborious and expensive form of analysis and it may be some time befor
detailed studies of fertility using this method have been done sufficiently ofter
and widely to permit confident generalizations about regional or nationa
trends. It is much simpler, of course, to assemble evidence about the change

[1] Helleiner concluded recently that contraception and abortion may have been more widely practisec
in pre-industrial Europe than has usually been supposed. He takes issue with Mols on this questior
quoting literary evidence of *coitus interruptus* from Germany in the sixteenth and eighteenth centuries
In commenting on the big falls in births recorded during many French *crises* he writes, 'But when al
is said, the magnitude of the decline in births is such as to suggest to most students of the phenomenon
that people during crises had recourse on a considerable scale to birth control or abortion.' K. F. Helleiner, 'New Light on the History of Urban Populations', *Journal of Economic History*, XVIII (1958), 60–1.
[2] See, for example, Glass and Grebenik, *The Cambridge Economic History of Europe*, vol. VI, pt.I, pp.
113–18, esp. footnote 1 on p. 118.
[3] Sutter remarks that *coitus interruptus* is a technique which has sprung up independently in many
places and at many times. He writes '*Chaque couple pourrait l'inventer. Il ne nécessite, d'autre part, l'inter-
vention d'aucun corps étranger, ni d'aucune manœuvre féminine particulière*'. It is a technique '– *capable d'auto-
apparition et pouvant se diffuser sans propaganda. Ce n'est pas une manifestation culturelle comme les autres méthodes,
il est propre à l'espèce humaine et n'est pas une caractéristique ethnologique spécifique*'. H. Bergues, P. Ariès
E. Helin, L. Henry, R. P. Riquet, A. Sauvy and J. Sutter, *La prévention des naissances dans la famille.
Ses origines dans les temps modernes*, I.N.E.D. Cahier No. 35 (Paris, 1959), p. 345.
It may be of some importance that *coitus interruptus* is essentially a male act since in animal populations
in general the social activities which serve to maintain populations near an optimum are normally
a male preserve.

in the balance between baptisms and burials derived from parish registers and reliable transcripts. The *Cambridge Group for the History of Population and Social Structure* has instituted a survey of this sort depending largely upon the help of local historians, genealogists and others interested in work of this type. Each volunteer fills in standard printed forms on which are recorded the monthly totals of baptisms, burials and marriages in accordance with a cyclo-styled sheet of instructions. In this way it may be possible to compile, say, a 5 per cent sample of the totals of vital events for the three centuries between the institution of parish registers and the beginning of civil registration. Already returns for about 290 parishes are to hand. If it can safely be assumed that changes in the ratio of baptisms to burials similar to those which occurred in Colyton were produced by changes in fertility and mortality similar to those noted in Colyton, then it is already clear that the pattern of events in Colyton is repeated in other places. In a high percentage of the parishes for which returns are available the surplus of baptisms over burials was much less in the second half of the seventeenth century and the first few decades of the eighteenth than either earlier or later. In a substantial minority of parishes the change was sufficiently marked to produce surpluses of burials over baptisms for all or most of the decades during this period.[1] In general it seems that the Colyton pattern was most commonly found and was most marked in certain parts of the west, north, and, surprisingly, in Kent, but is less obvious in the home counties and the Midlands. Perhaps the constant baptism deficit in London which required a countervailing surplus of baptisms to occur somewhere else may have had something to do with this. The systematic analysis of the returns, however, has not yet begun and all conclusions must remain tentative.

V

Colyton's population history shows that in pre-industrial English society a very flexible response to economic and social conditions was possible. This may well have important implications for the general course of social and particularly economic change in England in the seventeenth and eighteenth centuries. It is now often asserted that during the early decades of the Industrial Revolution it was largely rising home demand which sustained the increasing output of industrial goods.[2] It is arguable that the growing home demand occurred because of rising real incomes spread broadly through large sections of the community.[3] The changes in real incomes and in the level of production were

[1] This pattern appears in the material which Drake analysed in the West Riding. He dealt with the parish of Leeds and a number of parishes in the wapentakes of Morley and Agbrigg. In them the change between the first and second halves of the seventeenth century is very striking. Population was rising rapidly in the first half of the century with surpluses of baptisms in most years. In the second half of the century the population appears to have been falling, and if the returns for all the parishes are added together it appears that in the period 1660–99 there were 72,310 burials compared with 70,723 baptisms. M. Drake 'An Elementary Exercise in Parish Register Demography', *Econ. Hist. Rev.* 2nd ser. XIV (1962), 427–45.

[2] Deane and Cole, for example, remark '. . . it seems that the explanation of the higher average rate of growth in the second half of the century should be sought at home rather than abroad'. P. Deane and W. A. Cole, *British Economic Growth, 1688–1959* (Cambridge, 1962), p. 85.

[3] This is the tenor of the argument used by Landes in a recent review of the Industrial Revolution

not very dramatic or abrupt, but spread out over several decades. If the Mal
thusian picture of demographic behaviour were correct this type of slow se
change coming over an economy and eventually helping to provide condition
in which decisive industrial advance can take place is very difficult to credi
since one would expect precarious gains in real incomes however achieved t
be wiped out quickly in a flood of additional babies produced by earlie
marriages (and possibly by increased fertility within marriage). If, on the othe
hand, populations behaved in a manner more likely to secure optimum tha
maximum numbers the establishment and holding of gains in real income ar
much easier to understand. The course of events in Colyton shows this to be
possibility. The balance between fertility and mortality was probably at a
times delicate and unstable under stress. Colyton itself shows that the ver
restrictive adaptation which appeared in the middle of the seventeenth centur
was beginning to give way after 1720 and that in the 1770s or 1780s de
mographic behaviour reverted to the sixteenth century type. Nevertheless fo
three quarters of a century in an extreme form and for well over a centur
altogether Colyton behaved demographically in such a way as to make possibl
an increase and even a steady growth in real incomes.[1] If changes in the eco
nomy and technology of the period made possible rising production and rea
incomes, demographic behaviour was not such as to prejudice them immediately

This forms an instructive contrast with the course of events in the sixteent
and early seventeenth centuries which do seem to fit what may be called
Malthusian model quite well. There is much evidence that over the countr
as a whole population in the sixteenth century was rising faster than productio
and that real incomes became depressed. One of the reasons why the 'industria
revolution of the sixteenth century' which Nef has documented had no chanc
of fructifying into a steady expansion in production and real incomes wa
that population behaved much in the way Malthus supposed to be almos
inevitable. The sixteenth century English economy and population was 'over
fishing'[2] and paid the penalty, just as the Irish population of the late eighteent
and early nineteenth century was 'over-fishing'. As with animal population
in similar circumstances a sharp adjustment was inevitable. It is possible that a
times in the late eighteenth and early nineteenth centuries the same cycle o
events came close to being repeated for the great surge of population increas
towards the end of the eighteenth century caused serious difficulties of whict

in Britain. See D. S. Landes, 'Technological Change and Industrial Development in Western Europe
1750–1914', in *The Cambridge Economic History of Europe*, vol. VI, pt. I (Cambridge, 1965), pp. 280–5
[1] In this connexion it is important to note that a decline of fertility as great as that which occurre
in Colyton in the seventeenth century must have had a marked effect on the age-structure of the popu
lation. The proportion of the population of working age must rise and the burden of unproductive mouth
be reduced. For example, the United Nations study, *The Aging of Populations and its Economic and Socia
Implications*, Department of Economic and Social Affairs, Population Studies no. 26 (New York, 1956)
Table 15, p. 26, gives 58·8 as the percentage of a stable population in the age-group 15–59 when th
gross reproduction rate is 2·0 and expectation of life at birth is 40 years, compared with 65·0% in th
same age-group when the gross reproduction rate is 1·0 and expectation of life at birth is 30. The rati
of productive to non-productive people in the first case is 1·43 : 1·00, in the second 1·86 : 1·00.
[2] I have discussed some aspects of this elsewhere. See E. A. Wrigley, 'The Supply of Raw Material
in the Industrial Revolution', *Econ. Hist. Rev.* 2nd ser. XV (1962), 1–16.

contemporaries were keenly aware. But if the new pattern of behaviour which can be seen in Colyton in the intervening period proved fragile and eventually gave way to a reversion to the older pattern, it may have helped to win a vital breathing space in the interim. Contemporary French population behaviour appears to have been very different and much more Malthusian (in the sense in which I have used the adjective in this article). Sauvy has estimated that towards the end of the eighteenth century French population was 100 per cent above the optimum level.[1] In consequence any adventitious increase in real incomes in the short term was not likely to be used to swell demand in the industrial sector but simply to secure a slightly better level of nutrition.

VI

In this article I have been unable to deal extensively with more than a small fraction of the interesting topics which spring to mind in studying the family reconstitution data of Colyton. Mortality remains largely untouched, and on the fertility side such things as pre-nuptial pregnancy rates, the interval between being widowed and remarrying, and bastardy rates. Moreover, though much has been written of the remarkable fall in fertility in the mid-seventeenth century, the equally remarkable recovery in the eighteenth century has not been fully analysed; nor have the implications of the high level of fertility during the reigns of Elizabeth and James I been sufficiently discussed. While the middle period is perhaps the most fascinating because it is the most unexpected, the significance of the earlier and later periods is also great. Each period is the more interesting and intelligible because a knowledge of the others provides a perspective in which to view it.[2]

The life of men in societies is a subtle and complex thing which can and does influence behaviour at marriage and within marriage. Since the disadvantages to society and to the individual of the unrestrained flow of births which it is within the physiological capacity of women to sustain are very great, societies take care at all times not to expose themselves to such strains. In comparing the sixteenth and the late seventeenth centuries in Colyton the contrast is not between a society producing children at a maximum rate and a society imposing maximum restrictions but rather between two points on a spectrum of possibilities, each some way from the furthest extremes. In the earlier period the control appears to have lain largely in conventional ages at first marriage which were even then so late for women as to cause them to spend on an average at least a third of their fertile life unmarried. But once marriage had taken place restraints upon fertility appear to have been slight. In the later period

---

[1] A. Sauvy, *Théorie générale de la population*, 2 vols (Paris 1956, 1959), I, 186–7. Sauvy sets the optimum between 10 and 12 millions at most in 1790 against an actual population of 24 millions.

[2] Colyton shows not only that it was within the power of pre-industrial communities to halt population growth, but also that their powers of growth were very remarkable. Over a period of about ninety years (1538–1629) when fertility was high and mortality comparatively low (expectation of life was about 40) baptisms stood to burials in the ratio of 1·61 : 1·00 – a ratio as high as this was common at this period. Rates of increase well above 1 per cent per annum were clearly possible – equivalent, say, to a doubling of population within about half a century.

after the great plague visitation of the mid 1640's the restraint through age at marriage became more pronounced and was compounded by new restraint within marriage. These in combination lowered fertility to the point where increase stopped.

It is likely that among the circumstances which produce large changes in fertility economic conditions often bulk large, but it also seems probable that the relationship is not direct and simple but indirect and flexible. Societies are unwilling to allow matters to reach a Malthusian extreme. But the buffer provided by a society's socio-demographic organization to cushion the shock of harvest fluctuation and economic *débâcle* may be either thin or thick, may be as inadequate as in parts of South-East Asia today or parts of the Beauvaisis in the seventeenth century, or so ample that the society has scope for further economic advance and is free from the periodic *crises démographiques* which are sometimes thought typical of all pre-industrial societies. The *mercuriale* may be a reliable guide to demographic fluctuations in parts of France in the seventeenth century, but some pre-industrial societies were much better buffered against the hazards of the weather than that. In the absence of a continuing advance in material culture a population will always find in time a rough equilibrium level of numbers, but the living standards which result from this will not be the same in all cases. Malthus proposed one limiting case, that in which living standards are minimized but numbers maximized. Other equilibria are also possible and will vary with the extent of the restrictions upon fertility developed within the society in question. If the restrictions are sufficiently severe the equilibrium may occur at a point substantially beneath the maximum level of population, with all that this implies for the likelihood of success in establishing a beneficent spiral of economic activity rather than becoming involved in that other chain of events which keeps the masses miserably short of food and prevents economic growth.

Peterhouse, Cambridge

Supplementary Note

This article deals solely with fertility and nuptiality in Colyton between the sixteenth and nineteenth centuries. I have described the mortality history of Colyton in a more recent article.[1] Expectation of life varied considerably during these three centuries and it seems clear that in some pre-industrial European populations both fertility and mortality varied considerably both in the long and the short term. The causes and consequences of these fluctuations, however, remain obscure in many respects. Nor is there much reason to hope that the understanding of population changes in the past will improve substantially until there is a far larger body of empirical evidence available.[2]

France is the only country which is approaching an adequate knowledge of its pre-nineteenth century population history, due above all to the work going forward at the Institut National d'Etudes Demographiques under the direction of Louis Henry. In other countries matters are less advanced, either for lack of suitable source materials or because research funds have not been available.

Family reconstitution is a complex, time-consuming operation, and even simpler forms of demographic analysis present considerable data handling and tabulation problems. Accordingly the facilities offered by electronic computers have an important bearing on the future of historical population studies. It is already possible to input data from Family Reconstitution Forms and obtain comprehensive computer tabulations of demographic characteristics. These are more exhaustive and more accurate than those obtainable by manual methods without a vast expenditure of labour. It should soon be possible to carry out reconstitution itself by computer, punching entries from suitable parish registers much as they occur in the original. The record linkage operations necessary to reconstitute families will then be carried out by a programme which parallels the logic of manual methods, but the capacities of a large computer permit a more sophisticated series of tests to be carried out before links are formed.

There is often a close connection between the devising of better methods of descriptive measurement and the formulating of more adequate explanatory hypotheses. The two have a symbiotic relationship to each other, so to speak. The general significance of the recent development of family reconstitution methods does not lie solely, or even primarily, in the addition to our knowledge of fertility or mortality in the past made possible by the new techniques. It lies rather in the creation of a means of articulating a large bulk of nominally ordered data within a single framework of reference. That framework is the life history of the family, and since the family was a key institution in all the societies of early modern Europe it is reasonable to hope that work on family reconstitution data which may at first sight appear to be dryly technical may prove highly useful in the wider study of the circumstances in which Europe changed into an industrial society.

1   See Wrigley, E.A. 'Mortality in pre-industrial England — the example of Colyton, Devon, over three centuries', *Daedalus,* 97 No 2 (1968) pp 246-80

2   I have tried to describe the extent of the present uncertainties in *Population and History* (London, 1969)

E.A. WRIGLEY   August 1969

The Foley Partnerships: The Iron Industry at the End of the Charcoal Era
B.L.C. Johnson
Reprinted from *Economic History Review,* IV (1951-2), 322-40

THE FOLEY PARTNERSHIPS: THE IRON INDUSTRY AT THE END OF THE CHARCOAL ERA

By B. L. C. JOHNSON

I

THROUGH the courtesy of a descendant of the Foley family, which for several generations in the seventeenth and early eighteenth centuries shared in the control of a not inconsiderable part of the charcoal-iron industry in Britain, a number of ironworks' account books have been made available for study by the present writer.[1]

Taken together with the Cartwright Hall MSS. (dealt with in an earlier paper in this journal)[2], which overlap to a small degree with the Foley MSS., they help to provide a wide coverage of the late seventeenth-century industry. The extent of this coverage can be measured from the earliest known list of furnaces and forges in Britain, compiled in 1717.[3]

All but three of the ironworks for which the Foley MSS. provide accounts, are shown in Fig. 1, which also includes works referred to in the accounts and in other contemporary MSS. prior to 1717. The table on pp. 324–5 lists the ironworks by regions, with the periods for which accounts have been examined.[4] The output of many of these works is summarized in an appendix.

It will be appreciated that these account books contain a formidable amount of information, only a fraction of which can be incorporated in a short paper. At least five different methods of book-keeping are represented, which vary widely in the detail recorded. Some accounts are mere summaries of the year's output and the balances of materials remaining in stock; others particularize every farthing of expenditure with an embarrassing wealth of detail, but with little attempt at classifying the information. A further difficulty encountered is due to the different periods covered by the accounts of the various works. As the list shows,

---

[1] The writer desires to acknowledge his indebtedness to Major H. T. H. Foley, M.B.E., J.P., who facilitated the examination of the MSS. material which forms the basis of this contribution.

[2] Raistrick, A. and Allen, E., 'The South Yorkshire Ironmasters, 1690–1750', *Econ. Hist. Rev.* (1939), IX, 168–85.

[3] Hulme, E. W., 'Statistical History of the Iron Trade', in *Newcomen Society Transactions*, vol. IX, p. 16. The general reliability of the 1717 list given in this work, is confirmed by the evidence in the Foley MSS.

[4] Dates written 1701/2 indicate one accounting year, usually Michaelmas to Michaelmas: 1688–9 indicates that the accounts cover more than a calendar year.

the accounts are concentrated for the most part within the years 1692–1717. Those relating to the period 1725–51 carry on, with only minor modifications, the story of the same works in the earlier phase. Certain of the

Fig. 1.

accounts for years prior to 1692, particularly of the Tintern and Whitbrook group of works, have no successors in the main period but have proved valuable for elucidating obscure clues in later MSS.

174

I. *Forest of Dean and South Wales*

FURNACES	Blakeney	1692–1706, 1707–15
	Bishopswood	1692–1706, 1707–17, 1725–7, 1728–33, 1748–51
	Elmbridge	1692–1706, 1707–17, 1725–7, 1728–33, 1746–50
	Gunns' mill	1705/6, 1710–12, 1730–33
	Redbrook	1697–1706, 1707–17, 1725–7, 1728–33
	St Weonards	1677/8, 1707–17, 1725–7, 1728–31,
	Tintern	1672/3, 1675/6
FORGES	Barnedge	1701–6, 1707–9
	Bishopswood new forge	1748–51
	Blackpool	1704–6, 1707–17
	Llancillo	1677/8, 1725–7, 1728–31
	Lydbrook (2)	1708–17, 1725–7, 1728–31, 1748–51
	Monmouth	1704–6, 1707–9 1725–7, 1728–33
	Peterchurch	1677/8
	Pontrilas	1677/8
	Rowley	1703/4
	Tintern (2)	1672/3, 1675/6
OTHER CONCERNS	Tintern wireworks	1674–7
	Whitbrook wireworks	1674–7
	Gatcombe anvilworks	1695–1705

II. *West Midlands*

FURNACES	Grange	1692–7
	Hales	1692/3, 1703–5
FORGES	Cookley	1692–7
	Cradley	1692–4
	Stourton	1692–7
	Whittington	1692–1705
	Wildon	1692–1705
	Wolverley	1692–7
OTHER CONCERNS	Bewdley storehouse	1692–1717
	Cookley slitting mill	1692–7
	Stourton slitting mill	1698–1705
	Wildon slitting mill	1692–1705
	Wolverley slitting mill	1692–7

III. *North Midlands*

FURNACES	Lawton	1696–1702, 1703/4, 1706/7, 1709–11
	Mearheath	1688–9, 1692–1710
	Staveley	1695–8
	Vale Royal	1696–9, 1700–2, 1703/4, 1706–8, 1709–12
FORGES	Bodfari (Flintshire)	1700–2, 1703/4, 1706–8, 1709–12
	Bromley	1692–1710
	Cannock	1692–1710
	Carburton	1695–8
	Chartley	1692–1710
	Consall	1688–9, 1692–1710
	Cranage	1696–1702, 1703/4, 1706/7, 1709–11
	Oakamoor	1688–9, 1692–1710
	Staveley	1695–8
	Tib Green	1702–9
	Warmingham	1696–1710
SLITTING MILLS	Consall	1688–9, 1692–1710
	Cranage	1696–1702, 1703/4, 1706/7, 1709–11
	Oakamoor	1688–9, 1692–4
	Renishaw	1695–8
	Rugeley	1692–1710

IV. *Sussex*

Ashburnham furnace and forge   1709–11

The account which follows relates what is known of the composition and financial basis of the several partnerships under which most of these ironworks were grouped, and attempts an interpretation of the pattern of production and trade in which these concerns were engaged.

II. THE PARTNERSHIPS

The concerns listed above were at no time combined under a single entrepreneur or pártnership. They did, however, enjoy one feature in common—Foley capital; perhaps, on occasion, acting alone but more usually through a number of partnerships to which it must have given a sense of unity. We have details of three major inter-related partnerships, which were constituted on a regional basis, covering works in:

(i) The Forest of Dean and the Stour Valley of North-east Worcestershire and South Staffordshire,

(ii) North Staffordshire,

(iii) Cheshire and Flintshire.

In addition, members of these partnerships continued to pursue interests in ironworks not covered by their partnership agreements. The full extent of the influence they exerted on the iron trade was thus much wider than even the collection of works accounts under consideration would indicate. A few examples of the interests which some of the ironmasters held outside these partnerships are given below.

(i) *The Iron Works in Partnership*

The largest concern, self-styled 'The Ironworks in Partnership' originated in 1692 in a partnership of five men, and at the outset controlled some fourteen active ironworks in the Forest of Dean and the Stour Valley of South Staffordshire and North-east Worcestershire. The antecedents of this group of works are not yet fully known. How the Forest of Dean works came into the partnership's orbit is not clear, but information is available concerning an earlier combine of works in the Birmingham region, centring on the Stour Valley. That the Foleys probably played a prominent part in this concern is indicated by a 1669 book of 'Stock and Debts' belonging to Philip Foley. Four furnaces, thirteen forges, four slitting mills and a warehouse are covered by this stock book.[1] Details of production and trade unfortunately are lacking, though an inventory of raw materials at the works suggests that production methods were the same as in the better documented period from 1692. The book does, however, provide a measure of the capital involved, a figure of £68,830. 8s. 3¾d. being given for the total of 'stock and debts'.

The deed of partnership which set in being the 1692 concern showed £39,000 as the total its members agreed to contribute, though only £36,277 was actually required to be paid up; £21,957 of this was described as 'total debts' and £14,320 as 'stock' at the works. This capital was distributed among the partners as under:

Paul Foley	1/6 share	Richard Avenant	1/4 share
Philip Foley	1/6 share	Richard Wheeler	1/6 share
John Wheeler	1/4 share		

John Wheeler was appointed 'cash-holder', in effect managing director, at a salary of £200. Paul Foley's interests lay in the Forest of Dean, near which he had his seat at Stoke Edith, and owned several ironworks. His brother Philip resided at Prestwood in Staffordshire, where the family had long associations with the iron trade. The Wheelers also, primarily, had Stour Valley interests, John Wheeler living at Wollaston Hall, near Stourbridge. Avenant, in addition to his financial commitment in the partnership, was in occupation of Shelsley forge on the Teme, which he held from yet a third Foley, Thomas (later Lord) Foley of Witley, nephew of the brothers Paul and Philip.

At the outset, this partnership held one defunct and two active furnaces in the Forest of Dean, two in the Stour Valley, six forges and three slitting

[1] For further details see Johnson, B. L. C., 'The Stour Valley Iron Industry, 1692–1705' in *Trans. Worcs. Arch. Soc.*, XXVII (1950).

mills, also on the Stour, and a storehouse (used as a transhipping agency, wholesale and retail store) at Bewdley. After 1705 the partnership gave up its Stour Valley works, though continuing to hold its Bewdley storehouse, and obtained control of more furnaces and several forges in the Forest of Dean and Pembrokeshire. Later, by leasing Ashburnham furnace and forge, a connexion was established with the Sussex iron industry, in which, however, the name of Foley was not altogether new.[1]

Changes in the personnel of the partnership paralleled the changes in works directly under its control, and had the effect of extending its indirect influence on the iron industry. Thus by 1707, shortly after the partnership had left the Stour Valley, Richard Knight had joined the concern, and a strong if indirect link was maintained with the Stour area through his forges there, some of which he had taken over from the partnership. Other of Knight's interests included, at various times, Willey furnace and Moreton forge in Shropshire, Flaxley furnace in the Forest of Dean, and a furnace and forge at Bringewood near Ludlow. By 1710/11 the partnership had capital amounting to £27,542. 12s. 1d., distributed thus:[2]

Thomas Foley (son of Paul)	6 shares
Philip Foley	3 shares
John Wheeler's executors	8 shares
Richard Avenant's executors	2½ shares
Richard Knight	3 shares
William Rea	2½ shares

William Rea, generally referred to as of Monmouth where he later owned a forge, began his connexion with the partnership in 1692 as manager of Wildon forge on the Stour. Rising to become a partner in 1704, Rea succeeded John Wheeler as managing director and enlarged his personal interests in the industry in the midlands, Forest of Dean and Lancashire.[3] Rea must have had intimate knowledge of the iron trade, and it is quite possible that he was responsible for the compilation of the 1717 list of furnaces and forges mentioned above, as it was he who forwarded it to John Fuller of Heathfield, and added a corrigendum to it.

No accounts have come to light for the years 1717–25, during which time the partnership's membership and its interests had shrunken

---

[1] Straker, E., *Wealden Iron* (1931), pp. 164, 267. Thomas Foley (father of Paul and Philip) was linked with Geo. Browne, executor of John Browne the gunfounder, in leasing Benhall Forge, near Tunbridge Wells, in 1652.
Among the Foley MSS. is a fragmentary account book relating to transactions of Thomas Foley and Henry Quintyne in the Wealden gun and cast-iron pot trade.

[2] The profit for 1710/11 was £2,542. 12s. 1d.

[3] From 1704 Rea managed Redbrook furnace, Monmouth forge and Blackpool forge. For some years he was closely associated with the Wheeler family as John Wheeler's trustee, obtaining the lease of Cradley furnace and forge, and Mill and Lye forge on behalf of John's widow, Mary Wheeler.

considerably; a trend which was to continue. The partners in 1725 were:

Thomas Foley, senior	£8,000. 0s. 0d.
Thomas Foley, junior	£2,666. 13s. 4d.
John Wheeler (son of John)	?
Mrs Cecilia Lane	£1,000. 0s. 0d.[1]

Their works were all in or near the Forest of Dean: they comprised six furnaces (two out of action) and three forges, with storehouses in Monmouth and Bewdley.

(ii) *The 'Staffordshire Works'*

Next in size to the 'Ironworks in Partnership' was a concern known as the 'Staffordshire Works', which between 1692 and 1710 controlled most of the ironworks within, and to the north of, the Trent Valley in Staffordshire. Two earlier groups of works were combined in this enterprise, namely the 'Moorland Works', and those of William Cotton and Partners. The Moorland works consisted of Mearheath furnace, Oakamoor and Consall forges and slitting mills, and Chartley forge. These, with the possible exception of Chartley, had been held by John Wheeler (the elder) prior to 1692. The other concern comprised three works lying farther to the South and East—Bromley and Cannock forges, and Rugeley slitting mill.

The financial structure of the Staffordshire works in its early years is not clear. While John Wheeler as managing director, and Obadiah Lane as local manager seem to have shared the balance of stock in the ratio of seven to one, capital seems to have been derived mainly from 'moneys took up on bond to stock the Staffordshire Works'. These bonds paid interest at 5%, and totalled £11,994. 10s. 6d. in 1693. The principal contributors among a total of twenty-nine were Philip Foley (£3,050), Lady Lyttleton and James Russell (each with £1,012), John Gray (£1,000), Jane and Samuel Fidoe (£1,000 between them) and Robert Foley (£250)—most of them South Staffordshire people. This method of raising capital appears to have been a temporary expedient. It is not met with elsewhere in the Foley MSS., and in 1707/8 the Staffordshire works were being financed by a relatively few partners. The new partnership, which was formed to operate the Staffordshire works in conjunction with works in Cheshire and Flintshire, was as follows:

Philip Foley	1/7 share
John Wheeler	1/7 share
Obadiah Lane's executors	2/7 share
Thomas Hall	1/7 share
Edward Hall	1/7 share
Daniel Cotton	1/7 share

The value of stock so divided amounted to £11,000 in respect of the Staffordshire works. By 1710 changes had resulted in the Staffordshire

[1] Possibly widow of Obadiah Lane, one time manager of Lydbrook forges in the Forest, and a partner and manager of the Staffordshire and Cheshire works. See below.

works' stock being shared equally among Philip Foley, Daniel Cotton, the two Hall brothers, and Wheeler's executors, the stock then standing at £11,927. The individual works operated by the partnership in Staffordshire hardly changed during the period covered by the accounts (1692–1710). One forge only, Tib Green on the Cheshire-Staffordshire border, was added in 1702/3 to those already listed above, though the function of certain works did alter in detail, notably Oakamoor which gave up slitting iron in 1693.

(iii) *The 'Cheshire Works'*

From 1707/8, as has just been mentioned, the Staffordshire works were closely linked with the 'Cheshire Works'. The latter comprised furnaces at Lawton and Vale Royal, forges at Cranage, Warmingham and Bodfari (Flintshire), a slitting mill at Cranage and a plating forge at Street. The linkage between the two concerns was provided by their being controlled by the same partners as ran the Staffordshire works, the partners' shares in the £13,500 'standing stock' being in the same ratio as in the Staffordshire works.

Prior to 1707 the Cheshire works had been mainly the concern of the Hall and Cotton families, the stock being apportioned in 1700 as under:

Daniel Cotton	£ 8,848
Edward Hall	£10,251
William Vernon	£ 2,327

Hall was responsible for Vale Royal furnace and Bodfari forge; Cotton for Lawton furnace and Cranage forge; and Vernon, from 1705, for Warmingham and Street forges. The name of Obadiah Lane also occurs in connexion with the latter two works, in which he held in 1701 an investment of £400, being a half share with Edward Hall. Daniel Cotton was probably the son of the William Cotton who preceeded him at Lawton furnace, and who (possibly on his death) had given up control of a section of the Staffordshire works in 1692. The Cotton family's interest in iron extended into North Wales where a William Cotton of Ruabon (? the same man) had held ironworks at Halton up to 1690, and to Yorkshire where another William Cotton was a partner in Kirkstall forge and other works.[1] Edward Hall was a brother of Thomas Hall of Cranage, also an ironmaster, related by marriage to the Cotton family.[2] With the Cottons the Halls had interests in Lancashire where Edward was in partnership with Daniel Cotton, William Rea and Edward Kendall from 1711, in the company which later became the Cunsey Company.[3] Kendall, a Stourbridge man, had been associated with John Wheeler as an agent in the Stour Valley-Forest of Dean partnership from at least 1702, though he was not a manager of any works under this concern. With William Rea, however, he became joint manager of the Staffordshire works in 1710.

[1] Raistrick, A. and Allen, E., op. cit., p. 169 ff. Also Raistrick, A., *Quakers in Science and Industry* (1950), p. 101.
[2] Earwater, *History of Sandback* (1890), p. 214.
[3] Fell, Alfred, *Early Iron Industry of Furness and District* (1908), p. 265.

(iv) *The 'Derbyshire and Nottinghamshire Works'*

One last group of works remains to be mentioned, the 'Derbyshire and Nottinghamshire Works' comprising Staveley furnace and forge, Carburton forge and Renishaw slitting mill. John Wheeler again figures as managing director but the precise financial structure of this concern, which appears to have lasted only for three years, 1695–8, is not known. Its close operational links with the Staffordshire works, and the inclusion in the accounts of the latter of certain of John Wheeler's running expenses, suggest it may have been an offshoot deriving capital from the Staffordshire partnership.

An important aspect of the financial make-up of these partnerships needs little further emphasis. Their intimate inter-relationship through sharing one or more partners, one with another, and in the case of three of the concerns, through having for a time a common managing director in John Wheeler, meant that in effect they operated as one company. Furthermore, through their extensive interests beyond the partnership, and the interests of their close relatives in the iron trade, the partners as a body must have been a powerful influence on the industry in the Forest of Dean and the North and West Midlands. In these areas, excluding central Shropshire where they seem to have been of only minor importance, the group controlled over half the pig-iron producing capacity (about 6,900 tons out of 10,350 tons) and a similar proportion of the bar-iron capacity of the area's forges (3,360 tons out of 6,660 tons).[1]

Before turning to a consideration of the iron trade itself, two further examples, drawn from outside the partnerships studied, will serve to confirm the inter-regional nature of the organization of the charcoal iron industry at this period.

Thomas (from 1711 Lord) Foley stood outside the partnership in which his uncles participated. In 1674 his name is associated with that of Thomas his father in the accounts of Tintern and Whitbrook wireworks in the Wye Valley. It seems he still held these works early in the eighteenth century when he also had Wildon forge on the Stour for a number of years from 1705. Whether on the Wye or the Stour, his works remained among the biggest and most faithful customers of the 'Ironworks in Partnership'.

Another important ironmaster, quite apart from the Foley family, was John Jennens of Birmingham. He must be regarded as distinct from the group we have been considering, although it is true he did business with the Foley partnerships; indeed, but for the references to him and his ironworks in the accounts our knowledge of him would be very scanty. Jennens' works included, in the immediate vicinity of Birmingham, furnaces and rod mills on the River Tame and its tributaries. Several of these works appear in Philip Foley's 1669 stock book. Farther to the north and east, Jennens had Kirkby furnace and Pleasley forge in Nottinghamshire, and Wingerworth furnace and New Mills forge in Derbyshire. It

---

[1] Based on the 1717 list of Hulme (op. cit.) modified from evidence in the Foley MSS.

may well be that his interests included other works as well, but as yet none of his accounts have been unearthed. Nevertheless, the wide range of his influence is clear. It is probable that the chief *raison d'être* for Jennens' widespread organization was (as will be demonstrated below for the several partnerships already described) to supply the workers in the iron trades of the Birmingham region with finished iron.

III. PRODUCTION AND TRADE

The close inter-relationships that have been shown between the personnel of the partnerships extended also to their manufacturing and commercial activities. Although there was vertical integration within each of the partnerships, considerable traffic took place between them, as well as with independent forge and slitting-mill masters. Iron at all stages of manufacture entered into this trade. Each group operated furnaces for the smelting of ore into pig or cast iron, 'finery' forges for refining the pig iron, 'chafery' forges for hammering the product into wrought iron bars, and slitting mills where certain types of bar iron were rolled and cut into rods. Most iron was retailed as bar or rod to the various finishing trades, though a small proportion of the product of the furnaces was in the form of castings such as fire-backs, smoothing irons, buckets and pots for direct sale to dealers and consumers. Charcoal was the exclusive fuel in the blast furnaces[1] and the finery forges, but in the chafery process in which refined blooms were 'drawn out' into bars under the tilt-hammer, and in the slitting mill, coal was used in a number of places, notably in the Stour Valley from 1669 at the latest, when iron of ordinary quality was being worked.

Of the concerns under review, the 'Ironworks in Partnership' was the most powerful. It may best be considered at two periods; the first 1692–1705 when it held extensive interests in the Stour Valley in addition to its Forest of Dean activities, and the second from 1706 till the middle of the century when it (or its direct successor) concentrated attention on the Forest of Dean. At all times however, from 1692 to 1751, the production in the Forest of Dean of a surplus of tough pig iron above the requirements of its own forges wherever situated was a characteristic of the partnership's activity. The following description of the contemporary iron industry will show how this situation arose.

As the Foley MSS. and other contemporary ironworks accounts abundantly show, two main types of pig iron were produced in Britain towards the close of the charcoal-iron era. These were *tough* pig iron, which worked up into the highest grade merchant bar comparable in quality to Swedish bar iron, and *coldshort* iron, much inferior in quality. Tough iron could only be made in Britain from the high grade non-phosphoric ores

---

[1] Only one exception can be cited from the Foley accounts. Redbrook furnace in 1716/17 cast four tons of pig iron 'that was made with stone coal', previously 'charket'. The coke-smelted pig was priced £6 a ton, compared with £7. 15*s.* 0*d.* for charcoal-smelted tough pig.

of the Forest of Dean and the Cumberland-North Lancashire area, and was in great demand for all purposes where a readily malleable material was needed, and for blending in the 'finery' forge with coldshort pig to make an intermediate quality of bar known as 'best mill'. By itself coldshort iron smelted from the phosphoric and lower grade ores of the coalfields and the Weald worked up into a more brittle metal, which was, however, well suited to the nail trade.

The Forest of Dean had for long been the principal source of tough pig iron and had concentrated on its manufacture. A high percentage of cinders, the iron-rich, slaggy residue of medieval and possibly earlier bloomery forges, was used, together with a variable, sometimes negligible quantity of iron ore.[1] Yarranton described the Forest pig as, 'of the most gentle, pliable, soft nature, easily and quickly to be wrought into manufacture', and went on to say 'the greatest part of this sow iron is sent up Severn to the Forges, into Worcestershire, Shropshire, Staffordshire, Warwickshire and Cheshire and there it's made into Bar iron...'.[2] The accounts confirm Yarranton's report. The bulk of the pig iron made at the partnership's furnaces travelled via the nearest Severn ports—Ashleworth, Newnham and Gatcombe—up river to the Stour Valley and Shelsley forges, some continuing up stream to Coalbrookdale and Pool Quay, and a little travelling overland to Jennens' forges in the heart of the South Staffordshire coalfield, and north to the Staffordshire works.[3] River transport also carried pig up the Avon for Clifford forge near Stratford, and for Redditch; while by sea, Blackpool forge on the East Cleddau in Pembrokeshire, had most of its pig iron from Forest furnaces.

Even after the major change in the partnership's composition in 1705/6, involving its withdrawal from the Stour Valley as a forge and furnace operating concern, the general pattern of distribution of its Forest pig iron did not alter, although by increasing its forge interests in the Forest of Dean, a larger proportion of the pig went to the forges mainly on the Wye and its tributaries. Some of the tough pig travelled west into the valleys of South Wales, no doubt to be blended in part with local coldshort iron.

The partnership's forges in and around the Forest of Dean, including also Blackpool forge, naturally used mainly tough pig iron, although the latter forge, and Llancillo forge, occasionally had small consignments of coldshort pig from South Wales furnaces, e.g. Kidwelly, Neath, and Llanelly (near Brecon). Charcoal was the only fuel, and tough merchant bar the principal product of all these forges. Their markets lay very largely outside the immediate vicinity of the Forest. Bristol, and the Severn towns of Gloucester, Tewkesbury and Bewdley took most of their bar iron output,

---

[1] The fact that from 1717 Lancashire ore was sometimes used in the Forest furnaces suggests that supplies of local ore and cinders were running low.

[2] Yarranton, *Englands Improvement* (1677–81), p. 57.

[3] For maps illustrating the economic geography of the iron trade see Johnson, B. L. C., 'The Charcoal Iron Industry in the Early Eighteenth Century', *Geographical Journal*, vol. cxvii (1951), pp. 167 ff.

Bristol forwarding bar to inland centres such as Frome and Warminster, the partnership's Bewdley storehouse (which they continued to maintain certainly as late as 1733, long after giving up their Stour works) acting as a wholesale agency for the Birmingham district. Even Blackpool forge, a hundred miles west of the Wye Valley, exported more than half its output to Bristol and Bewdley, and to small merchants in the Bristol Channel ports of Bridgwater, Barnstaple and Bideford.

Lydbrook upper forge, at least until the mid-1730's, had a specialized function which set it apart from the normal run of Forest forges. A large part of its production of refined metal was in the form of *Osmund*,[1] or wire iron, which required more working than merchant bar iron. Lord Foley's wireworks at Tintern and nearby Whitbrook took almost all this Osmund iron, though in 1672/3, when the Foleys held Tintern forges but apparently not Lydbrook, Tintern upper forge had supplied the wireworks.[2] Although concentrating their activities on wire-making, the wireworks also turned out small quantities of nail rods, a practice not usually associated so much with the *tough* iron district of the Forest of Dean, as with the *coldshort*-producing Midlands and the North.

Turning now to the Stour Valley side of their activities, we find the partnership in 1692 operating two medium-sized furnaces, utilizing the local coal measure ironstones to make a coldshort pig iron for blending with superior pig in their several forges. These drew mainly on the Forest of Dean for tough pig, additional supplies coming down the Severn from Shropshire, and even from Vale Royal in Cheshire (via Uffington on the Severn) and from Lancashire (via Chepstow and Bristol). The local furnaces could not supply all the coldshort iron needed,[3] and, despite the high costs of overland carriage of this low grade material, Mearheath and Lawton furnaces on the Staffordshire-Cheshire boundary sent appreciable amounts on occasion. With so wide a choice of pig iron, the Stour forges were able to make bar iron in its three main qualities, viz. merchant, or merchantable, bar, made from tough pig and retailed as such; best mill bar (made from a tough-coldshort blend) and ordinary mill bar (mostly coldshort). A good deal of the mill bar was subsequently slit and retailed as rod iron. In drawing out merchant and best mill bars charcoal was always used, but for the ordinary quality coal was deemed suitable, and its use meant an appreciable saving in fuel costs. This may well account

---

[1] The accounts occasionally use the term *Osborn* in place of Osmund.

[2] The detail of the wire-iron trade hardly belongs to the present account. The relevant MSS. are dated 1674–7 and the partnership association of the wireworks is not clear. No fewer than eighteen brands of iron, ranging from nail rods to 'superfine wire', were manufactured, and it is of interest that London came a good second to Bristol as a market for wire, whereas the metropolis is not mentioned anywhere in the accounts among destinations for merchant bar.

[3] The Stour Valley furnaces, Hales and Grange, although holding a humble position as coldshort pig producers, attained a considerable reputation as makers of forge hammers and anvils, commanding a wide market in South Wales, the Forest of Dean, North Staffordshire and Cheshire.

for the development of a small traffic in refined blooms from Shropshire to the Stour,[1] to be drawn out into bars in coal-burning chafery forges.

The slitting mills took over a major part of the mill bar from the forges and retailed the finished rod in small lots to nail factors and other iron-mongers, mostly in Birmingham and the growing industrial towns of what was later to become the Black Country, though a regular but small trade in rods was carried on with the Severn towns, Bristol, Gloucester and Shrewsbury in particular.

We are now in a position to review the activities of the biggest of the partnerships under consideration. By controlling ironworks in both the Forest of Dean and the Stour Valley a completely integrated combination was attained, which could supply both tough and coldshort pig iron to its forges, and through them and their associated slitting mills could manu-facture the whole range of bar and rod iron in demand. The navigable Severn was of inestimable value to the Stour Valley works, where both tough and coldshort pig could be obtained cheaply, and which were con-veniently situated to serve the growing market in Birmingham and on the South Staffordshire coalfield and its borders.[2] It was the necessity of blending the two main grades of pig iron to produce the mill bar iron so much in demand by the slitting mills that drew the forges to the Stour Valley end of the trade route, rather than to the Forest of Dean. For, on the basis of simple locational theory, the forges should have been attracted to sites close to their contributory furnaces to avoid wasteful transporta-tion.[3] The use of coal in chafery forge and slitting mill no doubt tended to reinforce the double magnets of the technical requirements of blending, and the nearby markets.

In its latter years, the partnership withdrew from direct control of the Stour forges, at the same time maintaining a hold on the midland market through Bewdley storehouse. The direction of the trade in pig iron did not change, however. The Stour forges, although under new control, con-tinued to consume the major part of the output of the Forest furnaces, and the trade pattern which had existed at least from the middle of the seventeenth century persisted despite changes in management.

[1] The use of coal in the chafery forge was by no means universal even in those areas where much coldshort iron was being used, and it is not unlikely that the Stour and North Staffordshire forges were pioneers of the process. Staveley and Carburton, Cranage and Bodfari for instance, do not appear to have used coal as a rule, and there is an interesting entry in the Bodfari Forge account of 1706/7 which records the payment made to John Critchley of Cannock forge 'for his trouble instructing the Hammerman to draw out iron with pitt coles'.

[2] It cost approximately one penny per ton mile to carry pigs up the Severn, in contrast with rates of between $5\frac{1}{2}d.$ and $8\frac{1}{2}d.$ per ton mile overland. Thus, in the case of Wildon forge near the confluence of Severn and Stour, it was slightly cheaper to bring Bishopswood pig iron up the Severn via Newnham than to bring it from Hales furnace a dozen miles away.

[3] Refining of pig iron into bar resulted in a weight loss of almost 30%. There was no discrepancy in transport costs of pig and bar iron by land or water which would counteract the effect of this wastage.

Before leaving the question of the Forest-Stour partnership it is convenient here to mention the Sussex subsidiary in which it was interested from *c.* 1709. As suggested above, it was probably through the Foleys that the partnership's capital became involved in the Ashburnham works. Although much of the pig iron made there was refined and drawn into bar locally, and found its way to local and London purchasers, a variety of products—pig iron, blooms, mill bars, and cast hammers and anvils—were shipped from Sussex through Bristol to the Bewdley storehouse for the midland market. It seems unlikely that such traffic could have prospered except under the aegis of an inter-regional partnership, for Sussex iron was not of exceptional quality, and would be in direct competition with the midland product.

Abandoning the chronological order of their appearance we may now review the activities of the Cheshire works, as it had certain important features in common with the 'Ironworks in Partnership'. The functions of the two furnaces held by the Cheshire partnership were very different, but complementary within the organization of the concern as a whole. Of all the furnaces listed in 1717, Vale Royal appears to have been the only one in the country dependent chiefly upon imported ores. High grade Cumberland ore was the principal raw material, brought in via Liverpool and the river-port of Frodsham. On occasion Forest of Dean cinders, and ironstone from Flintshire were imported via Frodsham and Chester respectively, and a local source of cinders on Rudheath to the east of Vale Royal was also used. But the material which was most consistently blended with Cumberland ore was Staffordshire ironstone which had to be carted overland a distance of about 15 miles. Even with the admixture of a proportion of the latter ore, the product of the furnace was normally tough iron, in great demand by forges in the North Midlands situated so far from alternative sources in the Forest of Dean and North Lancashire furnaces. Naturally, the Cheshire partnership's own forges at Cranage, Warmingham and Bodfari received the bulk of the output, but Vale Royal pig penetrated by land transport as far south as Heath forge near Wolverhampton, and east to Carburton in Nottinghamshire and Wortley near Sheffield. Nearer at hand, the Staffordshire and Tern Valley forges were regular customers.

Lawton furnace has the distinction of showing the lowest pig iron production costs of any of the furnaces in all the accounts. It lay on the fringe of the North Staffordshire coalfield which provided abundant ironstone for making coldshort pig. At times about one-fifth Cumberland ore, brought overland from Vale Royal, was blended to yield what was termed 'mixed pig', intermediate in quality and price between tough and coldshort.[1] Lawton pig was sent regularly to the Cheshire forges—Cranage and Warmingham—though not to Bodfari, but a more important market lay in the forges of the Staffordshire works, at Consall, Oakamoor,

---

[1] Mixed pig was also made at Vale Royal, but is not mentioned in any other contemporary accounts known to the writer. It seems to have been more customary to blend metal at the finery forge stage.

Bromley, Chartley and Tib Green. In addition, appreciable quantities went to George and Thomas Rock's Brewood forges on the River Penk, to the Tern Valley forges of Shropshire (e.g. Sambrook), and via Uffington on the Severn, down river to the Stour forges.

While the Cheshire furnaces served a fairly widespread market, particularly in the direction of Staffordshire, the market of the associated forges was more restricted in extent, being confined to an area roughly demarcated by Liverpool, Manchester, Newcastle-under-Lyme, and Wrexham, with Chester an important focus of trade in bar and rod iron. Cranage was the partnership's only slitting mill, but another subsidiary trade was engaged in, at Street forge—the plating of salt evaporating pans for the local salt industry.

The close financial relationship between the Cheshire and Staffordshire partnerships was reflected in a considerable trade in pig iron, and a less important traffic in blooms, which took place between them. It is significant that practically all of this trade was in one direction, towards the Staffordshire works, a facet of the centripetal nature of the whole midland iron trade.

It is no exaggeration to state that 90 % of the energy of the Staffordshire works was directed towards supplying the Birmingham and South Staffordshire finished iron trades with bar and rod. The local markets of Newcastle and Stafford absorbed but a small fragment of their output. The one large furnace, Mearheath, was very similar to Lawton in making coldshort pig iron from local coal measure ores but could not satisfy the demands of the Staffordshire forges, which were in some measure dependent upon pig iron from the Cheshire furnaces. Of the six forges for which accounts have been studied, three—Consall, Oakamoor and Chartley—were of the normal type, refining and drawing out iron into bar in the same works. Consall and Oakamoor (for a short while up to 1694) were slitting mills as well, and so could perform all three finishing processes. Bromley concentrated on finery work, and Tib Green exclusively so, both forwarding their blooms to Cannock forge. The latter was exceptional in doing chafery work only, for which coal from Wednesbury was utilized. All the forges, with the exception of Tib Green and Consall, forwarded most of the bar iron they made to Rugeley mill, a slitting mill of unusually large capacity, capable of dealing with over 600 tons of rod iron annually. Thus through Rugeley flowed the greater part of the output of the Staffordshire works, southward to the great midland markets.

During its brief career under John Wheeler's management, the Derby and Nottinghamshire works contributed in a small way to this stream, bar and rod iron produced at Carburton forge and Renishaw Mill respectively, travelling via Rugeley to Birmingham and the South Staffordshire towns. Although but a small trickle by comparison with the flood from the Staffordshire forges, this traffic does at least indicate that it was economically possible for Derbyshire and Nottinghamshire to supply the

Birmingham region, and by analogy it is very probable that John Jennens' works in these counties were engaged in the same trade. John Wheeler's accounts for the Staveley, Carburton and Renishaw works extend over only three years, but it is interesting to note that, when under the control of a Yorkshire partnership, these works no longer supplied the Midlands but confined their attention to the local, Hull, Newcastle and London markets.[1]

Seen then as an inter-related and, to a significant extent, inter-dependent collection of concerns, the Foley group of partnerships possessed an essential unity. Diverse in the detailed bases of its many operating units, one primary function of the group stands out above all others, its orientation towards the demands of the midland market, and in particular towards Birmingham and the industrial towns and villages of the adjacent coal-field. By sea and river, by road and bridlepath, raw materials and iron of various qualities and in its several stages of manufacture, moved towards this hub of the finished iron trades, where swarmed the blacksmiths and whitesmiths, the locksmiths, edgetool-makers, and gunsmiths, and, out-numbering them all, the nailers.

The University, Birmingham

[1] Cartwright Hall MSS. See also Raistrick, A. and Allen, T., op. cit.

APPENDIX

A. *Output of works, prior to 1688 (in tons)*

	Tintern furnace	Tintern lower forge	Tintern upper forge
1672/3	1,142 (62 weeks)	176	99
1675/6	1,034 (61 weeks)	—	—

	Llancillo forge	Pontrilas forge	Peterchurch forge
1677/8	150	89	54

B. *Output of furnaces, 1688–1751 (in tons)*

	Blakeney	Bishopswood	Elmbridge	Gunns Mill	Redbrook	St Weonards	Grange	Hales	Lawton	Mearheath	Staveley	Vale Royal	Ashburnham
1688/9	—	—	—	—	—	—	—	—	—	502	—	—	—
1692/3	273	739	597	—	—	—	130	210	—	769	—	—	—
1693/4	925	488	541	—	—	—	886	—	—	1,098	—	—	—
1694/5	810	753	689	—	—	—	NIL	—	—	315	—	—	—
1695/6	1,047	537	785	—	—	—	512	—	—	846	450	—	—
1696/7	794	777	694	—	—	—	152	—	627	444	250	155	—
1697/8	697	684	790	—	—	—	—	—	700	962	481	331	—
1698/9	995	656	346	—	—	—	—	—	709	853	—	377	—
1699/1700	725	825	736	—	616	—	—	—	650	828*	—	—	—
1700/1	1,251	695	529	—	—	—	—	—	850	—	—	805	—
1701/2	508	522	595	—	—	—	—	—	639	—	—	491	—
1702/3	922	674	293	—	158	—	—	—	—	670	—	—	—
1703/4	574	575	755	—	913	—	—	683	900	770	—	495	—
1704/5	917	810	552	—	531	—	—	466	—	855	—	—	—
1705/6	441	740	300	779	836	—	—	—	—	889	—	—	—
1706/7	—	—	—	—	—	—	—	—	794	578	—	640	—
1707/8	866	779	712	NIL	704	239	—	—	—	30	—	457	—
1708/9	553	NIL	495	NIL	678	175	—	—	—	559	—	—	—
1709/10	869	726	349	NIL	450	686	—	—	603	NIL	—	642	458
1710/11	628	532	336	562	862	168	—	—	571	—	—	647	—
1711/12	1,066	489	592	153	775	733	—	—	—	—	—	733	—
1712/13	435	526	275	—	899	NIL	—	—	—	—	—	—	—
1713/14	625	409	195	—	532	NIL	—	—	—	—	—	—	—
1714/15	614	150	683	—	633	293	—	—	—	—	—	—	—
1715/16	—	535	253	—	418	251	—	—	—	—	—	—	—
1716/17	—	201	568	—	513	519	—	—	—	—	—	—	—
1725-7	—	250	528	—	28	193	—	—	—	—	—	—	—
1728/9	—	—	468	—	657	230	—	—	—	—	—	—	—
1729/30	—	—	119	—	409	407	—	—	—	—	—	—	—
1730/1	—	—	NIL	467	317	201	—	—	—	—	—	—	—
1731/2	—	—	381	401	537	—	—	—	—	—	—	—	—
1732/3	—	—	399	—	478	—	—	—	—	—	—	—	—
1746-8	—	—	422	—	—	—	—	—	—	—	—	—	—
1748/9	—	482	NIL	—	—	—	—	—	—	—	—	—	—
1749/50	—	NIL	546	—	—	—	—	—	—	—	—	—	—
1750/1	—	474	—	—	—	—	—	—	—	—	—	—	—

NIL signifies no make. A dash indicates absence of information.

Figure covers 18-month period Michaelmas 1699 to Lady Day 1700.

C. Output of forges—bar iron (*in tons*)

(i)	Blackpool	Monmouth	Lydbrook (2)	Barnedge	Rowley	Llancillo	New Forge
1701/2	—	—	—	24	—	—	—
1702/3	—	—	—	25	—	—	—
1703/4	—	—	—	24	33	—	—
1704/5	164	188	—	19	—	—	—
1705/6	152	209	—	29	—	—	—
1706/7	—	—	—	—	—	—	—
1707/8	166	224	—	18	—	—	—
1708/9	158	136	184	NIL	—	—	—
1709/10	114	—	169	—	—	—	—
1710/11	204	—	203	—	—	—	—
1711/12	224	—	162	—	—	—	—
1712/13	230	—	188	—	—	—	—
1713/14	215	—	136	—	—	—	—
1714/15	211	—	161	—	—	—	—
1715/16	186	—	161	—	—	—	—
1716/17	54	—	198	—	—	—	—
1725–7	—	149	219	—	—	62	—
1728/9	—	266	170	—	—	120	—
1729/30	—	184	194	—	—	76	—
1730/1	—	175	152	—	—	33	—
1731/2	—	202	178	—	—	—	—
1732/3	—	218	230	—	—	—	—
1748/9	—	—	91	—	—	—	42

(ii)	Cookley	Stourton	Whittington	Wildon	Wolverley	Bromley*	Cannock	Charley	Consall	Oakamoor	Tib Green*	Carburton	Staveley
1692/3	113	70	145	274	160	159	161	114	170	182	—	—	—
1693/4	124	109	167	309	232	70	68	148	146	178	—	—	—
1694/5	155	97	154	308	163	131	157	130	42	264	—	—	—
1695/6	193	109	186	323	192	170	170	172	177	253	—	87	126
1696/7	160	163	194	288	183	137	150	136	155	238	—	95	100
1697/8	—	—	181	336	—	132	213	160	229	314	—	20	80
1698/9	—	—	183	337	—	153	62	134	154	243	—	—	—
1699/1700	—	—	235	345	—	237†	188†	235†	218†	352†	—	—	—
1700/1	—	—	246	282	—	—	—	—	—	—	—	—	—
1701/2	—	—	213	311	—	—	—	—	—	—	—	—	—
1702/3	—	—	215	307	—	156	181	146	167	213	99	—	—
1703/4	—	—	213	345	—	168	161	152	195	265	115	—	—
1704/5	—	—	204	311	—	160	194	148	—	271	134	—	—
1705/6	—	—	—	—	—	161	177	127	163	204	126	—	—
1706/7	—	—	—	—	—	120	215	66	163	159	92	—	—
1707/8	—	—	—	—	—	144	92	134	150	93	108	—	—
1708/9	—	—	—	—	—	188	219	142	156	181	41	—	—
1709/10	—	—	—	—	—	123	73	115	112	180	—	—	—

* Blooms only to 1699 after which bar iron in part.
† Figures cover 18-month period Michaelmas 1699 to Lady Day 1700.

C. *(cont.)*

(iii)	Bodfari	Cranage	Warmingham*
1696/7	—	149	54
1697/8	—	128	50
1698/9	—	149	83
1699/1700	—	148	—
1700/1	113	151	87
1701/2	119	160	88
1702/3	—	—	—
1703/4	156	146	103
1704/5	—	—	—
1705/6	—	—	104
1706/7	125	129	99
1707/8	118	—	95
1708/9	—	—	101
1709/10	114	177	96
1710/11	—	148	—

* Bars and blooms.

D. *Output of slitting mills—rod iron (in tons)*

	Cookley	Stourton	Wildon	Wolverley	Consall	Cranage	Oakamoor	Renishaw	Rugeley
1692/3	340	—	228	413	150	—	180	—	214
1693/4	258	—	255	298	172	—	70	—	724
1694/5	277	—	209	285	161	—	—	—	526
1695/6	279	—	214	532	132	—	—	138	468
1696/7	309	—	222	597	81	—	—	138	173
1697/8	—	—	294	—	129	—	—	79	374
1698/9	—	24	316	—	141	144*	—	—	496
1699/1700	—	165	257	—	198*	—	—	—	815*
1700/1	—	166	202	—	—	74	—	—	—
1701/2	—	211	231	—	—	51	—	—	—
1702/3	—	195	239	—	152	—	—	—	573
1703/4	—	187	271	—	186	—	—	—	597
1704/5	—	215	203	—	13	—	—	—	605
1705/6	—	—	—	—	138	—	—	—	490
1706/7	—	—	—	—	109	39	—	—	551
1707/8	—	—	—	—	117	—	—	—	368
1708/9	—	—	—	—	20	—	—	—	608
1709/10	—	—	—	—	12	47	—	—	603
1710/11	—	—	—	—	—	76	—	—	—

* Figures cover 18-month period Michaelmas to Lady Day in the following year.

Some Statistical Maps of Defoe's England
J.H. Andrews
Reprinted from *Geographical Studies,* 3 (1956), 33-45

SOME STATISTICAL MAPS OF DEFOE'S ENGLAND

By J. H. Andrews

The early years of the eighteenth century make a convenient point of departure for detailed studies in the evolution of modern English economic geography. To contemporaries, it is true, this seemed to be a period of rapid industrial and agrarian change, but in the light of later developments there is some justification for regarding it as a time of comparative calm, with a geographical pattern which appears in retrospect as a simple base-map on which to plot the more radical changes associated with the advent of canals, factory machinery, the coke-fed blast furnace and the steam engine. Hitherto geographical knowledge of this important period has been chiefly derived either from local records, often of the highest value but difficult to co-ordinate in a broad national survey, or from contemporary works of a narrative or descriptive character. Among the latter the writings of Daniel Defoe are of course outstanding: despite its avowed intention of avoiding 'meer geographical description' (II, 180),[1] his *Tour through the whole island of Great Britain* has probably contributed more to the geographical reconstruction of its period than any other narrative work. Its popularity is deservedly based on merits which were notably rare among Defoe's predecessors in this field: his travels were extensive, his interest in English topography was economic rather than literary or antiquarian, and although it is doubtful whether he actually visited all the places described in the *Tour*, he certainly made more use of direct observation, and less use of Camden's *Britannia* and other obsolete works of reference, than most of his contemporaries.[2] Nevertheless Defoe, in life and letters alike, was notoriously inclined to mix fiction with truth, and errors both of fact and emphasis are not difficult to discover in his work. Many of them can be detected and corrected by detailed investigation of local sources, but such studies do little to help those of Defoe's readers who seek a general but accurate impression of the economic geography of the whole country, and who wish to estimate the validity of those broad geographical comparisons which add so much to the interest of the *Tour*.

From this standpoint, a series of economic maps of contemporary England would make a useful supplement to Defoe's writings, especially as statistics were so obviously one of their author's weakest points.[3] Remarkably few such maps have so far been made available, however. In Darby's *Historical Geography*, the fourteenth century is better served in this respect than the eighteenth, Defoe's

[1] Volume and page references in brackets refer to Dent's 'Everyman's Library' edition of Defoe's *Tour*.
[2] The scope of Defoe's travels is indicated in J. Sutherland, *Defoe*, 1950. For estimates of the general validity and importance of his picture of eighteenth-century England see G. D. H. Cole, *Persons and periods*, 1938, pp. 20-41; G. M. Trevelyan, *England under Queen Anne*, vol. I (1930), p. 2; D. George, *England in transition*, Penguin Books, 1953, p. 29.
[3] Typical of Defoe's exaggerations are his estimate of London's population (I, 322; Cole, op. cit., p. 75) and of the volume of the coastwise cheese traffic (*The complete English tradesman*, 1745, vol. II, pp. 73 and 174; T. S. Willan, *The English coasting trade, 1600-1750*, 1938, pp. 85-6).

lifetime being represented only by two population maps for 1690 and 1700;[1] and except in the case of the iron industry[2] little has subsequently been added to them. In the illustrations to this article an attempt has been made to fill a few of the many gaps that still remain in the economic cartography of this period. Most of them, of course, will never be filled owing to the absence of appropriate statistical data, and a set of maps based on what little material has survived must inevitably have the appearance of a random harvest. All the maps in the present collection possess certain points in common, however. Thus each has some bearing on the economic geography of England during Defoe's working life; each refers to an aspect of the subject in which he showed particular interest; and each is based, with as little subsequent inference and adjustment as possible, on contemporary evidence which, whatever its limitations, was collected by one man or one official department using methods which purport to have been applied uniformly to the whole country. This evidence is sampled rather than exhausted in the present article, but the maps will suffice to indicate its somewhat limited range. A few more industries, such as glass[3] and salt,[4] could be added, but as in earlier periods the bulk of the evidence relates to shipping and maritime trade.[5]

Any survey of the economic geography of England in the first half of the eighteenth century must give first place to wool, 'the greatest and best of our trading produce, the soul and life of our whole commerce, and the fund of all our prosperity and success in that commerce'.[6] It is difficult to assess the value of the rough estimate of output by counties on which Fig. 1 is based: the figures combine to give a national total which falls short of the most reliable contemporary estimates,[7] but their picture of relative distribution may well be more accurate. Although it shows one or two surprising and inexplicable features, the map accords well with Defoe's statement that the lowland pastures of the East Midlands had begun to rival the chalk downs as the principal sources of English wool (II, 89),[8] and taken in conjunction with a map of the woollen industry[9] it reveals a pro-

---

[1] H. C. Darby (ed.), *An historical geography of England before 1800*, 1936, pp. 439, 524.

[2] R. A. Pelham, 'The west Midland iron industry and the American market', *University of Birmingham Historical Journal*, vol. II (1950), pp. 141-62; B. L. C. Johnson, 'The charcoal iron industry in the early eighteenth century', *Geographical Journal*, vol. CXVII (1951), pp. 167-77.

[3] Darby, op. cit., p. 420.

[4] A map of salt production could be constructed on the basis of the receipts from the salt duties. For an example of these figures see *Calendar of Treasury Books*, vol. XXVI (1712), p. ccclxxiv.

[5] Material not used in this article includes the lists of Customs receipts from individual ports in P.R.O. Audit Office, Declared Accounts, Customs (A.O.1), many of which are printed in the *Calendars of Treasury Books*. Lists of shipping belonging to individual ports are given by T. S. Willan, op. cit., App. 7, and J. H. Andrews, 'English merchant shipping in 1701', *The Mariner's Mirror*, vol. XLI (1955), pp. 232-5. Unpublished lists of fishing vessels are to be found in B.M. Add. MS. 11255. Accounts of goods imported and exported, which in a few cases specify individual ports, are listed in G. N. Clark, *Guide to English commercial statistics, 1696-1782*, 1939.

[6] D. Defoe, *A plan of the English commerce*, 1728, p. 115.

[7] G. E. Fussell and C. Goodman, 'Eighteenth century estimates of British sheep and wool production', *Agricultural History*, vol. IV (1930), pp. 131-51. These authors do not discuss the county figures used in Fig. 1.

[8] Defoe, op. cit., p. 198.

[9] Darby, op. cit., p. 506.

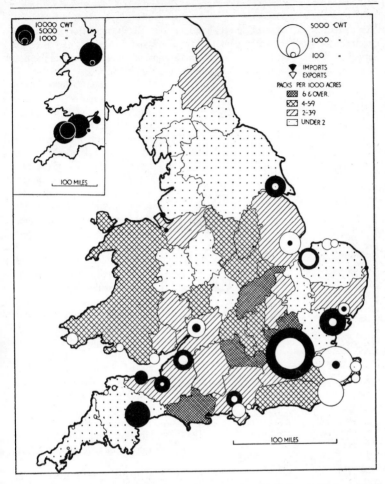

Fig. 1. Wool production and trade, early eighteenth century. Output by counties in packs of 240 lb. from B.M. Stowe MS. 354, f. 158. This estimate is catalogued as *c.* 1700, but was more probably somewhat later, since the list of which it forms part, omitting the separate figures for the counties, was published in a weekly periodical of 1712 (J. T. Rogers, *A history of agriculture and prices in England*, vol. VII (1902), p. 607).

Coastwise trade in wool, in 1719, from P.R.O. C.O. 390/8 C. For the definitions of the ports see Fig. 4. There is no record for Leigh in Essex, which probably had a small import.

Inset: average annual imports of Irish wool, 1703-06, from *House of Lords MSS.* (*New Series*), vol. VI, p. 108; vol. VII, p. 233. Imports of Irish wool were allowed only at Liverpool, Chester, Milford, Bristol, Bridgwater, Minehead, Barnstaple and Bideford.

nounced lack of coincidence between wool-growing and cloth manufacture. The pattern of the coastwise and Irish wool trades tells the same story: substantial quantities of wool were imported to Lancashire and Yorkshire, to the region served by Exeter and the ports of north Devon and Somerset, and to the East Anglian centres supplied through Colchester and King's Lynn.

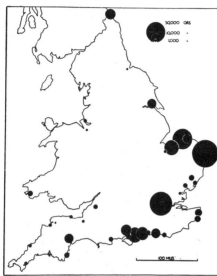

Fig. 2. Corn and malt exports in 1735. From P.R.O. Treasury Various (T.64), 277. To make the malt figures comparable with those for grain they have been reduced by 11 per cent as suggested by Gregory King in his estimates of corn, malt and ale production (B.M. Stowe MS. 292, f. 10). These figures were printed in *The Gentleman's Magazine*, vol. VI, p. 559, but with the Chichester figures mistakenly repeated under Chester and a number of other smaller errors.

There are no statistics of overseas wool exports (which were illegal except for an annual quantity of 1650 cwt. allowed to pass from Southampton to the Channel Islands),[1] but as much as one-tenth of the total clip was thought to be shipped abroad, and records of the work of the preventive officers suggest that the smugglers were most active in the coastal wool-producing regions nearest to France.[2] Apart from Ireland, Spain was the only foreign contributor to the English woollen industry, supplying, in 1715, 7524 cwt. of which 6880 cwt. passed through London.[3]

A complete evaluation of Fig. 1 is clearly impossible in a brief summary. It should be emphasized, however, that this was a period of rapid change in the pattern of the wool trade: imports from Ireland were rapidly decreasing, and there was soon to be a very considerable expansion of the import trade at Hull.[4]

With the assistance of a system of export bounties dating from the reign of Charles II, England maintained a large, though fluctuating, outward trade in corn throughout the first half of the eighteenth century.

This traffic provides the only available statistical measure of the pattern of corn

[1] 12 Charles II c. 32; 1 William & Mary c. 32.

[2] Of 58 seizures of smuggled wool made in the period 1676-82, 33 were in Kent, 11 in Hampshire, 5 in Dorset and 3 in Sussex (P.R.O. State Papers, Domestic, Charles II 422/176). The distribution of riding officers appointed after 1690 to prevent smuggling was similar (P.R.O Customs Registers, Series I (Customs 18)).

[3] P.R.O. Ledgers of Imports and Exports (Customs 3), 17.

[4] Detailed figures for the coastwise wool trade in 1735-43 are to be found in P.R.O. Treasury Various (T.64) 278-81.

	Exports	Imports
Wheat	125,911	116
Barley	21,661	94
Malt	219,060	—
Rye	39,481	—
Oats and oatmeal	596	3,261

production in the coastal regions, although of course the distribution of the export trade was also dependent on inland transport facilities, the relative accessibility of overseas markets, and the volume and composition of corn consumption in the hinterlands of the various ports and in the places they supplied by means of the coasting trade. Two exporting regions were especially prominent, namely Norfolk, served by the ports of Yarmouth, Blakeney, Wells and King's Lynn (I, 72), with the traditional barley and malt of this county providing 92 per cent of its total corn exports, and secondly the coastal plain of Sussex and Hampshire between Shoreham and Southampton, where wheat contributed just over half the total. Most of the remaining trade was shared among the ports of the south and east coasts, with some easily explained gaps in such regions as the Yorkshire Moors and the Weald. The coasts near the Thames Estuary present a misleadingly blank appearance, however, since much of the large corn surplus of Suffolk, Essex and north Kent found its way abroad only after having first been shipped to London. Corn exports from the west coast were inconsiderable, although most of England's very small oats trade came from this region; this was not wholly due to the absence of easily accessible overseas markets, for Ireland's corn imports were often drawn from the south coast of England rather than the west.[2]

On the whole, 1735 was a successful year for the corn trade.[3] Only rye fell short of its average, but although a normal rye surplus would have enlarged the symbols for Hull, King's Lynn and some of the other east-coast ports, the general appearance of the map would be little altered. The only important place to which Fig. 2 fails to do justice is Stockton.[4] In most years this port, like Hull, Berwick and sometimes Newcastle, exported considerable quantities of wheat, a trade which seems to have owed its existence to the fact that wheat bread had not yet become popular in north-east England.[5]

Although the quantitative contribution of hops to the total agricultural output was naturally very small, this map is interesting in that it is based on the earliest

[1] C. Smith, *A short essay on the corn trade and the corn laws*, 1758, pp. 114, 126.

[2] Between March 26th and July 8th, 1726, for example, Dublin imported 7700 quarters of English wheat, flour and meal, of which 5572 quarters came from ports east of Southampton (Marsh's Library, Dublin: MS. Z. 2. l. 7 (26)).

[3] The year 1735 seems to be the earliest with complete records of corn exports except for 1728 (P.R.O. Treasury Various (T.64) 274/58) which was quite unrepresentative owing to acute scarcity of corn. Figures of corn bounty debentures for 1674-81 given by N. S. B. Gras (*The evolution of the English corn market*, 1915, App. G) suggest that the distribution had remained fairly stable.

[4] Stockton is prominent in other years in the 1730s and in the similar lists for 1743-63 in the Liverpool Papers (B.M. Add. MS. 38387).

[5] G. E. Fussell, 'The traffic in farm products in eighteenth-century England, except livestock and livestock products', *Agricultural History*, vol. XII (1938), p. 359.

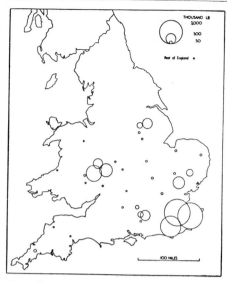

Fig. 3. Hop production in 1722. From P.R.O. Treasury Board Papers (T.1) 271/23. The figures refer to the collection districts for the hop duties, which were Barnstaple, Bedford, Cambridge, Canterbury, Cornwall, Derby, Essex, Exeter, Gloucester, Grantham, Hampshire, Hereford, Hertford, Lichfield, Lincoln, Lynn, Marlborough, Northampton, Norwich, Oxford, Reading, Rochester, Salisbury, Salop, Sheffield, Suffolk, Surrey, Sussex, east, middle, north and west Wales, Warwick and Worcester. The figure for the rest of England includes those for Bristol, Buckingham, Chester, Cumberland, Dorset, Durham, Isle of Wight, Lancashire, Leeds, Richmond, Taunton, Tiverton and York. There are no eighteenth-century records of the boundaries of these districts. The circles have been placed in positions which seem probable in the light of the parish acreage figures which begin in 1807 (*Parliamentary Papers*, 1821, XVII, pp. 345-70): hence the apparently incorrect positions of the circles for Salisbury and Sheffield.

official returns of English agricultural output by districts. These figures give precision to the oft-repeated statement that at this time hop cultivation was more widespread than in the nineteenth and twentieth centuries. In fact the total English acreage was only one-third of that reached in the peak period of the 1870s and the relative importance of the principal regions was much the same as at present, although several minor districts, such as Essex, Suffolk and the south-west, had more land under hops in the 1720s than at any time in the nineteenth century. Hops were a crop in which Defoe was especially interested, and both his strength and weakness as an economic geographer may be illustrated by comparing his brief summary (I, 82, 113, 118) with the official statistics: he gives due emphasis to Canterbury and Maidstone and mentions several other areas, such as Farnham, Essex and Herefordshire, but he seriously understates the importance of the west country and omits Lincolnshire and adjacent districts altogether.

In this period, as in modern times, coal was the chief constituent of England's coastwise trade, as well as the most widely distributed. Indeed the statistics used in Fig. 4 understate the latter aspect of the trade by grouping the imports of the smaller harbours together with those of the principal ports into a series of composite totals.[1] The geography of the coal trade has been summarized by T. S. Willan[2] so little further comment is necessary. The bulk of

[1] An appreciable proportion of the coal imports of Sandwich in Kent, for example, was actually landed at Margate, Ramsgate and Broadstairs.

[2] Willan, op. cit., chapter 5; see also J. U. Nef, *The rise of the British coal industry*, vol. I, 1932, chapters 1 and 2.

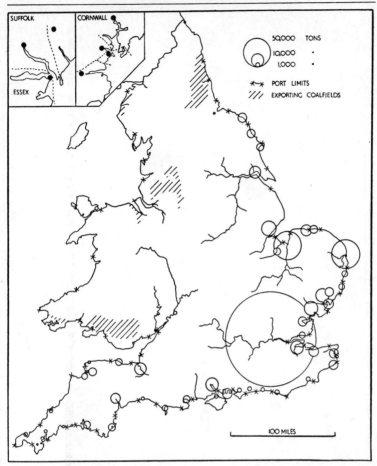

Fig. 4. Coastwise coal imports in 1723. Calculated from the receipts from the duty of 3s. per London chaldron of about 26 cwt. (P.R.O. Audit Office, Declared Accounts, Customs (A.O. 1) 797/1030). Each symbol relates to all ports within the limits shown, port limits being based on the lists of Customs officers in P.R.O. Customs Registers, Series I (Customs 18), 130; in several places without resident Customs officers the limits are uncertain. These statistical limits did not always correspond with the legal port limits determined by Act of Parliament or Exchequer Commission. The ports were Berwick, Newcastle, Sunderland, Stockton, Whitby, Scarborough, Bridlington, Hull, Boston, Wisbech, King's Lynn, Wells, Blakeney, Yarmouth, Southwold, Aldeburgh, Woodbridge, Ipswich, Harwich, Colchester, Maldon, Leigh, London, Rochester, Faversham, Sandwich, Deal, Dover, Rye, Newhaven, Shoreham, Arundel, Chichester, Portsmouth, Southampton, Cowes, Poole, Weymouth, Lyme, Exeter, Dartmouth, Plymouth, Looe, Fowey, Falmouth, Truro, Penryn, Gweek, Penzance, Scilly, St. Ives, Padstow, Bideford, Barnstaple, Ilfracombe, Minehead, Bridgwater, Bristol, Gloucester, Chepstow, Cardiff, Swansea, Llanelly, Milford, Cardigan, Aberdovey, Beaumaris, Chester, Liverpool, Poulton, Lancaster, Whitehaven, Carlisle.

Navigable rivers from T. S. Willan, *River navigation in England, 1600-1750*, 1936. Fig. 3.

Inset: Port limits not shown in the main map.

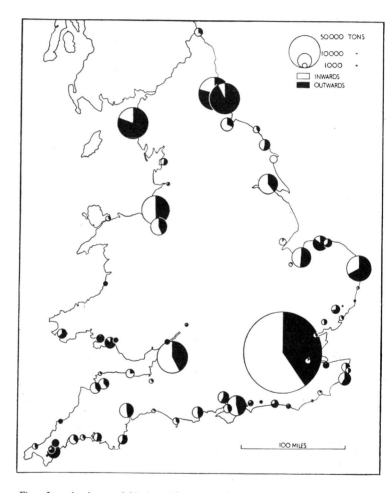

Fig. 5. Inward and outward shipping, with cargoes, in foreign (including Irish) trade, counting repeated voyages, in 1723. From B.M. Add. MS. 11256. The symbol for Maldon is based on the figure for 1737, the first recorded year at this port. The ports are the same as in Fig. 4 except that Leigh (Essex) is omitted, and Hastings, Neath and Preston are included. Ulverston is listed but no figure given. The symbol for London, which is also omitted, is an estimate based on other eighteenth-century figures given in *Second rept. from the committee on the improvement of the port of London*, 1799, App. D 2.

the traffic passed from the Northumberland and Durham coalfield to the rest of the east coast, with particularly large imports at London and at those of the outports with good facilities for the inland water carriage. The market area of Newcastle and Sunderland extended as far as south Devon, the trade beyond this point being dominated by the port of Swansea and its members. The Lancashire and Cumberland coalfields were of negligible importance, although the latter made up for this by the enormous volume of its Irish trade (Fig. 5).

This map shows much that Defoe has made familiar, notably the unrivalled pre-eminence of London and the way in which it had 'eaten up' most of the trade of the coast between Yarmouth and Portsmouth (I, 43), the position of approximate equality which had been attained by Bristol and Liverpool (II, 256), and the large number of smaller ports of roughly similar rank. But Fig. 5 also serves as a reminder that the total traffic of a port provides no direct measure of the value and variety of its trade, or of the geographical extent of its commercial connections by land and sea. The general commercial status of the ports of Defoe's England cannot be measured statistically; if it could, London's superiority would be even greater than Fig. 5 suggests, and the highest places among the outports would doubtless be filled by Bristol, Liverpool, Hull, Exeter and King's Lynn. Quantitatively, this pattern was distorted by the volume of the coal trade, and the statement that coal shipments to places outside the British Isles were insignificant in the eighteenth century[1] needs to be reconsidered in the light of the position of Newcastle as the second and Sunderland as the fourth port in the England of 1723. To a lesser extent the size of the corn trade explains the prominence of several minor ports, such as Wells and Blakeney, which ranked higher in volume of trade than Exeter and Plymouth respectively.

Data are available for an exhaustive analysis of the direction of outgoing traffic from every English port in 1714-17,[2] but limitations of space have made it necessary to divide foreign countries into four groups according to their positions in relation to the English coast. In detail, the 'foreland' of a port was affected by geographical variations in the demand for its products, the conspicuous position of Yarmouth in the map of traffic to southern Europe, for example, being due to its exports of herrings to Spain, Portugal and Italy (I, 67); but the outstanding feature of the map is a pronounced general tendency for each foreign country to trade chiefly with the nearest English coast, and Defoe was therefore justified in devoting particular attention to the comparatively few ports where 'they trade round the whole island' (II, 256). Among these London was of course outstanding, sharing in all the trades of the outports and enjoying a virtual monopoly in Asia and mainland Africa. Bristol and Liverpool were also distinguished by the range of their outward traffic, and to a lesser degree the same was true of Hull, King's Lynn, Newcastle and Exeter. Particular interest attaches to the stretch of coast between Hampshire and north Devon; this was a kind of 'no-man's-land' remote from the influence of

[1] T. S. Ashton and J. Sykes, *The coal industry of the eighteenth century*, 1929, p. 226.
[2] For other maps based on these figures see J. H. Andrews, 'Anglo-American trade in the early eighteenth century', *Geographical Review*, vol. XLV (1955), pp. 99-110; idem, 'Eighteenth-century "port forelands" in the Irish Sea', *Irish Geography*, vol. III (1955), pp. 114-17.

both London and Bristol, where no one port had achieved supremacy and where such minor centres as Southampton, Poole, Dartmouth, Plymouth and Falmouth succeeded in keeping a foothold in most of England's export markets.

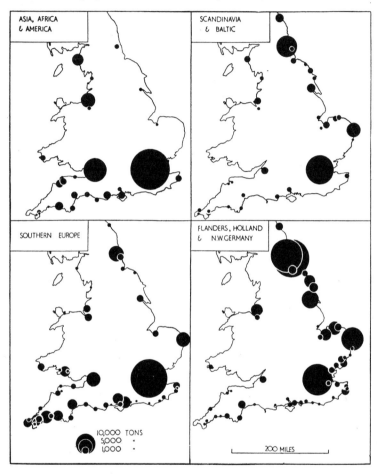

Fig. 6. Destinations of outgoing shipping with cargoes in 1715. From P.R.O. C.O. 390/8 B. Southern Europe includes the Channel Islands, the Canary Islands, Madeira and all continental ports south of Calais. Calais and the rest of the French coast are included with Flanders. Ireland is not included. Leigh is omitted and Grimsby, Milton, Hastings, Pevensey, Keyhaven, Christchurch and Neath included; otherwise the ports are as in Fig. 4.

If Defoe's *Tour* can be said to have a single theme, it is the unique place of London in England's commercial geography, and especially the wide extent of its trade connections (I, 12). This thesis, which Defoe has frequently been accused of overemphasizing, derives support from Fig. 7, as it does from several of the

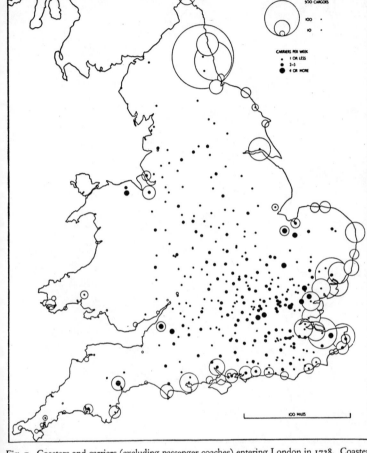

Fig. 7. Coasters and carriers (excluding passenger coaches) entering London in 1728. Coasters from W. Maitland, *The history of London from its foundation by the Romans to the present time*, 1739, p. 621. By an obvious error this alphabetical list transposes the figures for Swansea and Sunderland. Besides the ports shown in Fig. 4, Maitland gives figures for Blyth, Hartlepool, Milton, Folkestone, Hythe, Hastings, Lymington, Clovelly, Newnham, Neath, Tenby, Haverfordwest and Preston.
   Carriers from *A new review of London*, 1728, pp. 37-46 (B.M. Printed Books 1302. a. 5). Seventeen places in this list cannot be identified.

previous maps. Maitland's list of incoming coasters provides further evidence of the volume of the coal trade and suggests the importance of the short-range traffic in agricultural products mentioned in discussing Fig. 2. This account seems generally reliable and consistent with most other evidence,[1] but the list of land

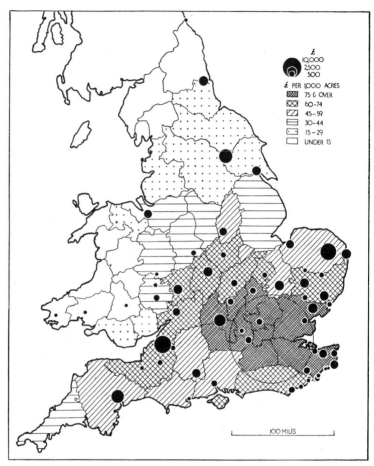

Fig. 8. Land tax assessments by counties, cities, boroughs, Cinque Ports and limbs of Cinque Ports in 1692. From A. Browning (ed.), *English historical documents*, vol. VIII (1660-1714), pp. 318-22.

carriers, one of a long series of such records which become numerous at the end

[1] T. S. Willan (op. cit., pp. 135-6, 139-40) states that the traffic to London from Essex and north Kent decreased in the early eighteenth century, but this statement is based on a misinterpretation of the Port Books (J. H. Andrews, 'The Thanet seaports, 1650-1750', *Archaeologia Cantiana*, vol. LXVI (1953), p. 41).

of the seventeenth century,[1] is more difficult to interpret. Each of these lists differs in detail from the others, and all of them sacrifice much of the reader's confidence by their omissions of what seem obvious places and their hopeless garbling of many names. The list used in Fig. 7, which its author claimed to be the most accurate to have appeared for twenty years, provides at least a minimum demarcation of London's urban field, and casts some interesting sidelights on the competition between land and water transport in coastal regions. In the south-east, to mention only one example, there was a sharp contrast between Kent, with its enormous volume of waterborne traffic and comparatively few carrier services, and Sussex, where, despite the difficulties of Wealden transport, communication with London was mainly by road.[2]

Several periods of English history have been illustrated by maps of the distribution of wealth as revealed by tax assessments,[3] and the pattern depicted in Fig. 8 is, in its broad outlines, characteristic of England before the Industrial Revolution. In particular, the map confirms Defoe's remark that England south of the Trent was 'the most populous part of the country, and infinitely fuller of great towns, of people, and of trade' (I, 253). An unusual feature of the assessment used in this map is its inclusion of figures for certain cities and boroughs, which provide, in default of population statistics,[4] some indication of the relative importance of the major towns. The figures lend support to Macaulay's well-known estimates: London was supreme, followed at a great distance by Norwich Bristol, York and Exeter.

[1] A. L. Humphreys, 'Stage coach and wagon lists, 1637-1840', *Notes & Queries*, vol. CLXXVIII (1940), pp. 39-40, 57-60. This bibliography is by no means exhaustive.

[2] G. J. Fuller, 'The development of roads in the Surrey-Sussex Weald and coastlands between 1700 and 1900', *Transactions and Papers, 1953*, Institute of British Geographers, no. 19, pp. 37-49.

[3] For another such map of this period see A. Browning (ed.), *English historical documents*, vol. VII (1660-1714), 1953, p. 459.

[4] The nearest urban population data to the period under review are the hearth tax returns of the 1660s and 1670s. Comparable figures for most English towns for this earlier period have been assembled by C. A. F. Meekings in *Dorset hearth tax assessments*, 1951, App. III.

Agricultural Changes in the Welsh Borderland. A Cultural Diffusion at the Turn of the Eighteenth Century
D. Thomas
Reprinted from *Transactions of the Honourable Society of Cymmrodorion,* Part I (1961), 101-14

AGRICULTURAL CHANGES
IN THE WELSH BORDERLAND

A CULTURAL DIFFUSION AT THE TURN
OF THE EIGHTEENTH CENTURY

By DAVID THOMAS, M.A.

INTRODUCTION

"ALL through historic time", wrote Professor E. Estyn Evans[1] when discussing the borderland between England and Wales (Fig. 1), "two forces have been at work, a tendency towards the fixation of the boundary, and a natural disregard of this by movements of men and their changing cultures". The concept applied to a political frontier and to physical movements of peoples in historic times earlier than those being considered here, but it has far wider application. In the latter part of the eighteenth and the early

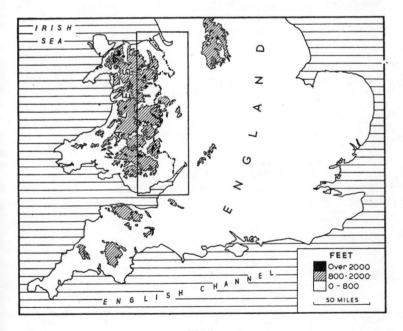

Fig. 1
The setting of the Welsh borderland, showing the frame of Figs. 2 and 3

[1] E. E. Evans, "An essay on the historical geography of the Shropshire-Montgomeryshire borderland", *Montgomeryshire Collections*, 40 (1922–8), 242.

years of the nineteenth centuries another type of diffusion was under way. The spread was one of new agricultural ideas and techniques ; methods which had their origins in the power of human inventiveness and the increasing willingness of farmers to benefit from the results of scientifically conducted experiments. The frontier formed was that between areas which had adopted the new ideas, and those in which farmers, for environmental or cultural reasons, still clung to traditional ways.

Naomi Riches[2] has described how improved agricultural systems had been adopted in some parts of East Anglia in the first half of the eighteenth century, but it was not until the very end of the century, when the work of Arthur Young, Sir John Sinclair, and William Marshall was combined with a set of exceptional economic conditions, that a rapid spread took place into the Welsh Borderland. The outbreak of war with France in 1793, a succession of bad harvests in 1794, 1795, 1799, and 1800, and the rapid growth of the population beyond the point where it could be supported by grain produced within the British Isles, led to an acute inflation in the price of agricultural produce. This gave great impetus to the diffusion of the new agricultural ideas, for not only did they increase output but they also lowered production costs. Every incentive thus existed for farmers to adopt the improved methods.

Three major sources of information document the spread of the "new husbandry" into the borderland at this period. The first results from the work of the itinerant surveyors of the newly founded Board of Agriculture and Internal Improvement, who were appointed to prepare reports on the state of agriculture in all the shires of England and Wales. The reports of the counties of north Wales were published together under the title, *General view of the agriculture of North Wales*, in 1794, and in the same year separate reports for the counties of Brecon, Chester, Gloucester, Hereford, Monmouth, Radnor, and Salop also appeared. The report for Glamorgan followed in 1796. The second source, the acreage returns of 1801,[3] refers to individual parishes. The acreages devoted to the cultivation of wheat, barley, oats, potatoes, peas, beans, turnips and rape, and frequently rye are shown, together with the general remarks of the parish incumbent.[4] Thirdly, the consolidated reports of the Board of Agriculture appeared between 1803 and 1814

---

[2] N. Riches, *The Agricultural Revolution in Norfolk* (Chapel Hill, 1937).

[3] Public Record Office, London ; H.O. 67 : for a general account of this material, see H. C. K. Henderson, "Agriculture in England and Wales in 1801", *Geographical Journal*, 118 (1952), 338–45.

[4] Certain problems arise in the use of the returns. Large numbers of the forms are missing and many of those extant are inaccurate. The way in which these and other problems are best resolved is discussed in D. Thomas, "The statistical and cartographic treatment of the acreage returns of 1801" *Geographical Studies*, 5 (1958), 15–25.

for north Wales,[5] south Wales, and individually for Cheshire, Gloucestershire, Herefordshire, Monmouthshire, and Shropshire.[6] Different surveyors were generally appointed for the later reports, most of which provide accounts quite separate from those of the earlier reports. Professor David Williams[7] has pointed out that none of the authors of the Board of Agriculture reports appeared to have made use of the acreage returns of 1801. Indeed, no attempt seems to have been made to use any statistical or cartographic material other than that acquired during the course of each investigation. This makes it possible to use the three surveys not only to throw light upon cropping, but also to gauge the accuracy of each by comparing one with another. Changing conditions at the turn of the eighteenth century are therefore documented by a series of agricultural surveys which are unique for the period before 1866, when the annual collection of agricultural statistics began.

The restricted field covered by the 1801 returns, which dealt with the acreages of crops only, has meant that comparisons between the three periods 1794–6, 1801, and 1803–14 are limited to the cropped land. Attention must therefore be concentrated upon changes in crop distributions and rotations between 1794 and 1814. The introduction of a new crop, such as turnips, which had not hitherto been grown extensively, or the adoption of more rational cropping methods are the indices of change. In this respect the diffusion of the popular Norfolk four-course system (wheat, turnips, barley, and clover) is particularly interesting. In spite of the intense economic pressure its spread was limited by the ecological requirements of the crops in the rotation. Wheat and barley were dominantly lowland crops while turnips required a fine tilth, especially at the germination stage. These characteristics, combined with the need for constant tillage inherent in the new system, ensured that turnip husbandry was best adapted to easily worked, lowland soils. In examining crop distributions and rotational practices the physical transition which exists in the Welsh borderland (Fig. 2) assumes great importance.

CROPPING CONTRASTS BETWEEN 1794 AND 1814

In the following discussion, regional divisions based upon the 1801 returns have been used as a framework for the analysis of the Board of Agriculture reports, partly because the acreage returns mark a

[5] Some parts of the north Wales report were written as much as thirteen years before it appeared in 1810. There is little reason to suppose that the section on cropping was not reasonably up-to-date at the time of publication.
[6] For convenience the Board of Agriculture reports of 1794–6 (quarto) are referred to hereafter as the earlier reports, and those of 1803–14 (octavo) as the later reports.
[7] D. Williams, "The acreage returns of 1801 for Wales", *Bulletin of the Board of Celtic Studies*, xiv (1950–51), 57.

mid-way stage in the period under review, but mainly because they lend themselves to more detailed and precise mapping. Fig. 3 is constructed by use of a technique modified from that outlined recently by Weaver for identifying crop combination indices.[8] These are calculated by objective means from the acreage returns for each parish and represent the groups of crops which were dominant or typical. To simplify the description of crop combinations a standard notation has been adopted.[9] For example, a wheat-barley combination is referred to as WB, and a wheat-oats-barley-peas combination has an index of WOBPe. The crop combination index for a parish also gives grounds for speculation about contemporary rotational practices. A parish in which the Norfolk system was well established would have a WBT index, or at least include turnips in its crop combination, but in a parish not influenced by the new ideas these characteristics would be absent from the index.

Within the area shown in Fig. 3 data are available for 507 parishes, of which 176 have a WOB index. The numerical strength of this combination and its association with the relief borderland (Fig. 2) suggests that it represents the true transitional border combination between those which are typical of highland areas (e.g. O, OR) and those which are specifically lowland (e.g. WB, WBT). From the point of view of cropping, therefore, three major areas can be distinguished : (i) the Upland area, (ii) the Borderland zone, (iii) the Lowland area.

(i) *The Upland Area*

The Upland area may be defined as consisting of those crop combination regions which were dominated by the hardier grains, such as oats and rye. Fig. 3 shows that in 1801 these regions were to be found in Merioneth, in the higher parts of Montgomeryshire, and also over a large extent of north-west Radnor. Had the evidence of the 1801 returns been available for the upland region of Glamorgan and Monmouthshire, it is most likely that poor-grain crop regions such as O and OR would also have been found here.

Kay, in his description of Montgomeryshire in 1794,[10] like so many authors of both the earlier and later reports, listed several rotations without stating exactly where they were pursued. The rotation containing a fallow year (first year—fallow ; second—wheat or rye ; third—barley ; fourth—oats ; fifth—oats with grass seed) was presumably that practised in the highland areas. Assuming that such a rotation were widely used on individual

---

[8] D. Thomas, op. cit., J. C. Weaver, "Crop combination regions in the Middle West", *Geographical Review*, 44 (1954), 175–200.

[9] W—wheat, O—oats, B—barley, R—rye, Pt—potatoes, Pe—peas, Be—beans, T—turnips and rape.

[10] G. Kay, *General View of . . . Montgomeryshire* (Edinburgh, 1794), 15–16.

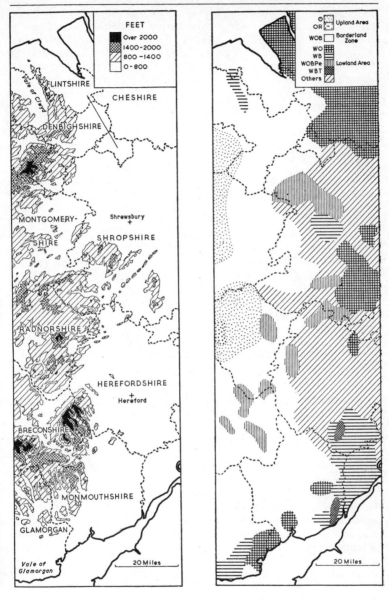

Fig. 2
Relief and county boundaries

Fig. 3
Major crop combination regions,
1801

holdings, an analysis of crop acreages by parishes would undoubtedly show a dominance of oats, with barley and either wheat or rye holding far less prominent places. In his report on Merioneth,[11] Kay, although not giving an example of a rotation in use, was far more specific about the standing of the various crops. The amount of cropland was small, but oats occupied the greatest proportion with barley and wheat sown only infrequently. Turnips and potatoes were seldom planted.

In his description of Radnor in 1794,[12] Clark made special reference to the mountainous hundred of "Rhydarogwy" (Rhayader) which was roughly co-extensive with the O–OR regions shown in Fig. 3.[13] Here, the practice was to plough up land which had been under pasture for some years, manure it as heavily as possible, reap a crop of barley in the first year, and thereafter grow successive crops of oats until the land did not return the seed. When this point was reached it was restored to grassland. Clark noted that this type of farming could only be practised in the drier areas. When later dealing generally with rotations in hilly areas[14] he mentioned that rye might replace barley after the initial ploughing of the grassland. In an appendix to the report,[15] two rotations were recommended to the tenants of the "upper district". On the "best tillage land" Clark suggested : first year—turnips, "strongly mucked" ; second—barley with clover ; third—clover ; fourth—wheat ; fifth—oats, or better fallow ; to be used for continuous cropping, while on the "poorest tillage land" : first year—oats ; second—fallow ; third—wheat ; fourth—peas ; fifth—oats ; sixth—fallow ; seventh—turnips ; eighth—barley ; to be followed by four or five years under clover or rye grass.

The dominance of unbalanced rotations containing the coarser grains which clearly existed in the Upland area in 1794 is broadly reflected by the acreage returns of 1801. In Merioneth and in the highlands of Montgomeryshire the O region signifies the dominance of oats (Fig. 3), while an examination of crop rank within each parish shows that wheat and barley usually held poor second and third places, followed by rye. In upland Radnor the acreage returns also suggest rotational systems which were generally consistent with conditions described seven years earlier. Oats were again important, for it was everywhere the most important crop, and in a number of parishes exceeded 60 per cent of the cropland acreage. But there are a number of anomalies. No evidence existed in 1801 of the use of barley in "Rhydarogwy" and, on the other hand, the obvious importance of rye in the two parishes

[11] G. Kay, *General View of . . . Merionethshire* (London, 1794), 12.
[12] J. Clark, *General View of . . . Radnorshire* (London, 1794), 11–13.
[13] W. Rees, *An Historical Atlas of Wales* (Cardiff, 1951), Plate 57.
[14] Clark, op. cit., 18.
[15] Ibid., 36.

forming the OR region (Fig. 3) was not mentioned by Clark in his account. Kay also made no reference to the standing of potatoes in upland Montgomeryshire, where in one parish they were the third most important crop in 1801. These inconsistencies are most likely due to omissions on the part of the authors of the written accounts, or the recording of evidence which related to part of the area only. It is unlikely that the small differences shown between 1794 and 1801 indicate any actual change in practice, for they would represent a regression in husbandry methods in a period of agricultural advance.

The ambitious rotation recommended by Clark in 1794, which included one more grain crop than the Norfolk four-course system, had evidently not been adopted in the better parts of upland Radnor by 1801 (Fig. 3). While the three WOBPe regions of the more lowland areas seem to represent his second suggested rotation, it will be shown later that this rotation was in use in these areas in 1794, and, in any case, was not found on the poor quality upland soils as Clark had intended.

The period 1794–1801 in the Upland area was one in which few, if any, improvements in agricultural methods were introduced. Between 1801 and 1814, on the other hand, Davies (Gwallter Mechain)[16] was able to report that the "county of Radnor is much improved in this respect, within a few years". In the "upper parts" of the shire he mentioned the following rotation as being in use : first year—turnips ; second—barley with clover ; third— clover ; fourth—wheat ; fifth—oats ; and then grass for two or three years. Thus the very rotation which Clark had suggested in 1794, and of which no trace could be detected in 1801, was now in use, though modified by the introduction of short leys in recognition of the more rigorous physical conditions. For the uplands of Montgomeryshire Davies's report[17] was much less enthusiastic. Oats were grown on newly ploughed land for as many as five years in succession. The only other crop mentioned is barley, which was grown exclusively on south-facing slopes. Montgomeryshire thus apparently lagged behind Radnor in the improvement of rotations, although it should be borne in mind that the report on Montgomeryshire was published four years earlier, and that the improvements in Radnor had been recently introduced.

Both the earlier and later reports of the Board of Agriculture devoted considerable proportions of their space to the discussion of rotational practices and the crops under cultivation in the Upland area. Comparisons between these written surveys and the less subjective, statistical returns of 1801 suggest that although the written reports were wide in scope, important details, such as the

[16] W. Davies, *General View of . . . South Wales*, I (London, 1814), 367–8.
[17] W. Davies, *General View of . . . North Wales* (London, 1810), 162–4.

OR region of Radnor (Fig. 3), were omitted or not recognized by their authors.

(ii) *The Borderland Zone*

The Borderland zone is not as easily delimited as the Upland area, for the distribution of the WOB crop combination region which defines the zone is frequently uncertain. This is especially true in areas such as north-west Shropshire or western Monmouthshire, where large numbers of the 1801 returns are missing. The zone coincides broadly with the relief border (Fig. 2) stretching southwards from eastern Flintshire, through Denbighshire, eastern Montgomeryshire, eastern Radnor and the Breconshire basin to Monmouthshire. On the Shropshire–Radnor border, where highland and lowland crop regions are closely juxtaposed, the zone is fragmentary (Fig. 3).

In his account of north Wales in 1794 Kay described the chief crops of Flintshire[18] as wheat and oats, with barley, beans, peas, potatoes, and clover grown in smaller quantities. A typical rotation where fallowing was practised was : first year—fallow ; second— wheat ; third—barley ; fourth—oats, continuously. In the "fertile vales" of Montgomeryshire[19] a hay crop was followed by wheat and then barley, oats, or perhaps peas. Kay's attenuated and unreliable description of Denbighshire[20] adds nothing to this information.

In Radnor[21] at the same period two systems were in use in the "lower districts" of the county. The first (first year—wheat ; second—peas ; third—barley and clover ; fourth—clover ; fifth— clover ; sixth—fallow) was the practice of the "good farmer" while the second (first year—wheat ; second—barley ; third—peas ; fourth—oats with clover ; fifth—clover ; sixth—fallow) was the practice on "middling farms". In Breconshire,[22] Clark described five rotations in use in the Talgarth hundred. Of these three had wheat, oats, barley, and peas in equal proportions, while the fourth, "the rotation of good farmers", included wheat, barley, peas, and clover leys. On coarse ground, wheat, oats, and barley were dominant. In the Vale of Usk a nine-course rotation was practised, including wheat, oats, barley, peas, and turnips. The report for Monmouthshire by Fox[23] is far less precise than those of Clark. Rotations of wheat, barley, and oats seem to have been dominant but two containing turnips were also mentioned, though none, unfortunately, were located.

The statistics of 1801 again reflect very broadly the conditions described in the earlier reports. In Flintshire, Denbighshire, and

[18] G. Kay, *General View of . . . Flintshire* (Edinburgh, 1794), 10–11.
[19] Kay (Montgomeryshire), op. cit., 16.
[20] G. Kay, *General View of . . . Denbighshire* (Edinburgh, 1794), 14.
[21] Clark, op. cit., 18.
[22] J. Clark, *General View of . . . Brecon* (London, 1794), 19–22.
[23] J. Fox, *General View of . . . Monmouth* (Brentford, 1794), 13–14.

Montgomeryshire the WOB region is consistent with Kay's accounts, while in Monmouthshire the areas where turnips were of importance emerge and can now be delimited (Fig. 3). Again in Radnor and Breconshire Clark's description is supported by the 1801 returns. Here, the absence of a WBPe region, the fact that in only four parishes did peas rank higher than oats, and the widespread occurrence of WOBPe regions suggests that the majority of farmers were still what Clark considered to be unenlightened.

The most striking feature to emerge from a closer comparison of the 1794 and 1801 surveys for the Borderland zone is the difference in quality between the work of different authors of the written reports. None of the written reports was as precise as the statistical data of 1801, but those of Clark, a land surveyor from Builth, were particularly discerning and detailed. For example, the 1801 figures clearly reflect even the nine-course rotation of wheat, oats, barley, peas, and turnips which he recorded for the Vale of Usk. One parish may be shown to have had a WOBPeT crop combination, while in a number of others the same crops held the first five places in 1801. The reports of Fox and Kay, on the other hand, are far less satisfactory. Kay particularly is guilty of many important omissions. He failed to distinguish the distinctive differences in crop rank order between coastal Flintshire, where wheat was the most important crop, and the inland limestone plateau where barley was most important and wheat consistently held third place. He also failed to recognize the obvious importance of barley (Fig. 3) in the Vale of Clwyd. These omissions probably arose because, unlike Clark, Kay's accounts for much of north Wales were based not upon accurate field observation but upon hearsay. This is especially so in the case of Kay's report on Denbighshire, one-third of which is concerned with the agricultural methods and views of one land owner, and in which such phrases as, "from the best authority" and "as I was informed", occur frequently.

The later reports of Davies (1810–14) covering the whole of Wales were far more uniform in their treatment than the earlier reports, roughly equal attention being paid to all counties. In Denbighshire and Flintshire he reported that the Norfolk rotation had been practised on one holding for eighteen years, and more generally throughout the two counties long enough to have given rise to the opinion that it was unsuited to the area.[24] As turnips were not mentioned in the earlier reports for the two counties and as they rarely exceeded 5 per cent of the cropland in 1801, it must be assumed that the spread of turnip husbandry into this area took place between 1801 and 1810. The crop must also have been introduced into the Vale of Clwyd during the same period, being

[24] Davies (1810), op. cit., 154–5.

associated, according to Davies,[25] with wheat, barley, and peas. Of these four crops, only turnips were of no importance in 1801. In Montgomeryshire, Davies[26] recorded variants of the Norfolk rotation on the lighter soils but on the "strong loamy soils" of the vales there had been little change since 1794. In Radnor and Breconshire[27] wheat, oats, and barley were still the major crops, with rotations containing the three grains, peas and sometimes turnips predominant in the river valleys. Here also there had obviously been little change.

In Monmouthshire, on the other hand, the later report[28] reveals a major transformation in agricultural practices between 1801 and 1812. In the extreme south-east of the county where wheat, barley, and turnips were the main crops in 1801 (Fig. 3), the Norfolk four-course rotation was in use eleven years later, but elsewhere there is little correlation between the results of the two surveys. Of the eighteen rotations which Hassall described in 1812, three were the Norfolk four-course system while eight others included turnips, often as frequently as any other crop. In 1801, turnips had barely gained a foothold in the county and were prominent only in the strictly limited south-eastern area already mentioned. There is thus clear evidence of the widespread introduction of turnip culture into Monmouthshire between 1801 and 1812.

Within the Borderland zone at this period, a comparison of the surveys of 1794, 1801, and 1810–14 has illustrated the progress made by crop-rotation reforms. Whereas in the Vale of Clwyd, a lowland enclave within the Borderland zone (WB, Fig. 3) turnips became established between 1801 and 1810, in the remaining parts of Denbighshire and in Flintshire the spread of the Norfolk rotation was quickly halted when it was found to be unsuited to the area. In Montgomeryshire, Radnor, and Breconshire, where a non-grain crop, peas, was already well established in rotations, turnips gained a footing only in a limited number of places, principally in the Vale of Usk. This evidence suggests that the Borderland zone, at this period, marked the physical limits of the area in which turnip husbandry was ecologically and technologically possible and beyond which it was excluded by rotations better adapted to prevailing environmental conditions. Monmouthshire was the only county in which turnips became firmly established in the early years of the nineteenth century ; a fact which suggests that the south-eastern part of Monmouthshire, like the Vale of Clwyd, should more properly be treated with the crop regions of the Lowland area.

[25] Davies (1810), op. cit., 156–7.
[26] Ibid., 160–1.
[27] Davies (1814), op. cit., 310–11, 332–6.
[28] C. Hassall, *General View of . . . Monmouth* (London, 1812), 38–43.

(iii) *The Lowland Area*

The Lowland area may be defined as including all areas shown on Fig. 3 which lie to the east of the Borderland zone. Here, crop regions containing mainly lowland crops occurred, although some crop regions, such as the WO area of the Cheshire Plain contained crops which were also characteristic of the Upland area. In these cases it is reasonable to assume that the existence of the crop was due to edaphic conditions rather than the effects of altitude. The greater parts of the counties of Chester, Salop, Hereford, Gloucester, the Vales of Glamorgan and Clwyd, and possibly also south-eastern Monmouthshire lay within the Lowland area.

In Cheshire in 1794, Wedge[29] described eight different rotations, in each of which oats was present and in only two of which was it not the most important crop. Precisely similar features emerge from his description of two typical dairy farms. The earlier report for Shropshire,[30] on the other hand, is far less helpful as it deals mainly with the eastern part of the county where the author lived. The only rotation quoted (first year—fallow ; second—wheat ; third—barley ; fourth—oats ; fifth—peas ; sixth—oats) occurred in the Clee Hills district. Clark's survey of Herefordshire,[31] like his work on Breconshire and Radnor, was extremely detailed. It is necessary and relevant here to mention only a number of the rotations which he quoted in order to establish the trends which were taking place. On the sandy land in the north of the county rotations including wheat, oats, barley, peas, and turnips were mentioned several times, while on the clay lands wheat, oats, and peas predominated. To the north of Hereford wheat, barley, and peas were the main crops but to the east of the town beans increased in importance. In the south of the county, around Ross-on-Wye, the old system (first year—fallow ; second—wheat ; third—barley ; fourth—peas ; fifth—barley ; sixth and seventh—rye grass and clover) was beginning to be replaced by the Norfolk four-course, while further west at the foot of the Black Mountains turnips were also being actively introduced.

The Gloucestershire report[32] gives no detailed information about land-use in the west of the county and the report for Glamorgan[33] is hardly more helpful. In the Vale of Glamorgan wheat, oats, and barley were the chief crops, but turnips seem to have been little known judging by the hints for sowing and using the crop which were included.

[29] T. Wedge, *General View of . . . Chester* (London, 1794), 14–17.
[30] J. Bishton, *General View of . . . Salop* (Brentford, 1794), 8–9.
[31] J. Clark, *General View of . . . Hereford* (London, 1794), 15–18.
[32] G. Turner, *General View of . . . Gloucester* (London, 1794).
[33] J. Fox, *General View of . . . Glamorgan* (London, 1796).

In 1801 the importance of oats in Cheshire is again evident. The crop featured in the crop index of nearly every parish (Fig. 3) and was frequently first rank crop. In Shropshire, the rotation reported by Bishton is reflected in the data of 1801, but because of the scanty evidence which he presented it is impossible to decide if the widespread use of turnips in rotations, suggested by the acreage returns, had been adopted before or after 1794. A comparison of the work of Clark and the returns of 1801, on the other hand, allows the date of the introduction of turnips to be established for Herefordshire. In the north and east of the county there was stability of practice between 1794 and 1801, for the crop regions of 1801 parallel Clark's description. Here obviously the introduction of turnips on the lighter soils had already taken place by 1794. In the Ross-on-Wye district the Norfolk rotation which was beginning to appear in 1794 had made considerable progress over the seven-year period. The 1801 statistics show two parishes with a crop combination index of WBT, while many more, although classified as WB, had turnips strongly represented in third place (Fig. 3). To the west, where rainfall was higher and the soil less sandy, the limited turnip husbandry mentioned in 1794 had not spread further by 1801. In Glamorgan, no evidence whatever existed in 1801 of the introduction of turnips.

Of the later reports for the Lowland area those for Shropshire[34] and Herefordshire[35] were generalized and contribute nothing to the argument. The report for Cheshire[36] merely reprinted the rotations given in the earlier report with the comment that they were still at the later date "an accurate account". But Davies's description of the Vale of Glamorgan[37] in 1814 was far more explicit. He reported thirteen rotations, all of which were consistent with the results of the 1801 survey. Wheat and barley were the most important crops and turnips were conspicuously absent. While there is no evidence of the Norfolk four-course system, it is noteworthy that of the thirteen rotations mentioned, eight included clover as a one-year crop between two of grain. The similarity between the standing of all crops in 1801 and 1814, and the contrast with the position in 1796, when oats were of importance, leads to the conclusion that clover was introduced together with a new crop system between 1796 and 1801.

It seems clear that the most active period in the diffusion of the "new husbandry" in the Lowland area was that before 1801. In Cheshire, where the use of the lighter Rotherham plough had already caused a major agricultural change, the heavy textured soils

[34] J. Plymley, *General View of . . . Shropshire* (London, 1803).
[35] J. Duncumb, *General View of . . . Hereford* (London, 1805).
[36] H. Holland, *General View of . . . Cheshire* (London, 1808), 129–33.
[37] Davies (1814), 323–6.

resisted any further change, but in Shropshire and Glamorgan the new methods had been employed before 1801 and in Herefordshire before 1794.

CONCLUSION

Comparisons between the three major sources documenting the agriculture of the Welsh borderland at the turn of the eighteenth century have yielded results which have application beyond the scope of this study.

It has proved possible, by using suitable statistical and cartographic methods, to contrast the merits of surveys of different kinds. While the statistical survey of 1801 was, to some extent, deficient in its coverage and accuracy, it gave detailed objective information. The written surveys, on the other hand, although giving a better overall picture, varied in accuracy and detail according to the competence of their authors. In spite of the fact that many written accounts were based upon questionnaire surveys and interview they were, on the whole, less specific and far more subjective. Great care is clearly needed when using such surveys, to detect views which either reflect the personal bias of authors and their informants, or are derived from faulty or incomplete evidence.

It has also been possible to establish the chronology of crop-rotation improvement in the Welsh borderland by identifying the introduction of new systems and new crops. The appearance of turnips in an area has proved a particularly useful index of change. In lowland Herefordshire and in a very small number of other lowland areas the improved methods had been introduced before 1794 ; similar changes had taken place in Shropshire and in a much more limited way in the Vale of Glamorgan by the year 1801. Between 1801 and the date of the later reports turnip husbandry actively penetrated into the Borderland zone. It became firmly established in south-east Monmouthshire and the Vale of Clwyd, but in the more upland parts of the zone physical conditions quickly halted the spread of the system. Other elements of the agricultural revolution were not as closely related to physical features and penetrated further into the Upland area. More rational systems replaced the continuous cropping of oats in Radnor and probably also in Montgomeryshire between 1801 and 1814, very much as the short clover ley, one element of the Norfolk four-course, had been introduced into Glamorgan at an earlier date. On the heavy drift lands of Cheshire only was there complete lack of change at the turn of the eighteenth century.

Lastly, it has been possible to demonstrate the applicability of Professor Evans's generalization about the Welsh border to this period, and to identify the two forces which he described. The diffusion of the "new husbandry" was quite clearly initiated and given impetus by human activities. But while some of the new methods were little affected in their spread, others underwent change or were prevented from diffusing further. The general improvement of rotations reached the whole of the area, but the spread of turnip husbandry was halted. In peripheral highland areas such as those in Flintshire and Denbighshire there was, at first, an advance of the Norfolk four-course rotation followed by a rapid retreat, which pointed to the fact that the system had been diffused beyond its physical limits. Hence, it is clear that the stabilizing force operating here was the physical nature of the borderland itself ; the same force which, in prehistoric and early historic times, had tended to fix political boundaries.

Supplementary Note

The ideas advanced in this paper, later to be expanded in book form and applied to the whole of Wales,[1] are of a kind familiar enough to geographers. At the time it was written the work of Hägerstrand upon the spread of innovations in Sweden was already well known, and since then economic and urban geographers have adopted contagion-diffusion techniques fairly widely. More recently an historical geographer, Grigg, has outlined in a valuable summary the sources available for studying the processes of regional change in English agriculture.[2]

Historians on the whole have been less happy with diffusion studies. In connection with this paper in particular they have pointed to the fact that the indices used to establish changes and attempted improvements in agricultural practices are lowland criteria, perfectly well applicable to East Anglia, but much less so in the Welsh border country. This, of course, is the point of the essay. The arguments of Arthur Young and his fellow propagandists were powerful. 'Improvement' was at first interpreted in their terms, but, very quickly, the problems encountered in adopting such methods in the agriculturally more difficult parts of the borderland encouraged a less dogmatic approach to change and in some areas appear to have halted the spread of lowland-based ideas altogether.

1   Thomas, D. *Agriculture in Wales during the Napoleonic Wars: a study in the geographical interpretation of historical sources* (Cardiff, 1963)

2   Grigg, D.B. 'The changing agricultural geography of England: a commentary on the sources available for the reconstruction of the agricultural geography of England, 1770-1850', *Transactions of the Institute of British Geographers*, 41 (1967) pp 73-96

DAVID THOMAS   August 1969

Changing Regional Values during the Agricultural Revolution in South Lincolnshire

D.B. Grigg

Reprinted from *Transactions and Papers of the Institute of British Geographers,* 30 (1962), 91-103

CHANGING REGIONAL VALUES DURING THE AGRICULTURAL REVOLUTION IN SOUTH LINCOLNSHIRE

D. B. GRIGG, M.A., PH.D.

THE agricultural revolution of the eighteenth and nineteenth centuries altered not only the structure and productivity of English agriculture, but also the agricultural geography of the country. The adoption of new farming methods together with changes in farm price structure led to a revaluation of the farming regions of England, especially in the arable east. The best example of this regional revaluation was the change in the relative status of 'light' lands and 'heavy' lands. The light lands (areas of soils developed on sands, gravels and limestones) were largely waste, sheep grazing or poor arable in the mid-eighteenth century; the 'heavy' lands (soils developed on clays) were either under grass or were wheat producers. But by the middle of the nineteenth century the light lands were among the best farmed regions in England, and produced an increasing proportion of the country's wheat output. The heavy lands by then had become marginal wheat producers, and the farming methods of these regions were generally backward.

This regional revaluation has been described in general terms, but the change has not been traced with any precision.[1] One means of measuring the change is to compare the average rent per acre of regions of light and heavy soils at different periods. The information on rents per acre in the agricultural writings of the time is not sufficiently comprehensive, and statistical records on a parish basis are needed. There are no such records for the eighteenth century,[2] but a series of parish assessments of land values for taxation purposes do survive for the nineteenth century, and can be used to calculate average rent per acre by parishes. In this paper these sources are examined, and then used to show the changing relationship between light land, heavy land and fenland in south Lincolnshire between 1815 and 1860.

The Sources

In the first half of the nineteenth century there were three taxes on land for which assessments on a parish basis are available; the Property Tax (1799-1816), the County Rate (1815, 1840 and 1847) and Schedule A of the Income Tax (1842-43 and 1859-60).

The Property Tax

The War Income Tax was first raised in 1799, but in 1803 the tax was revised and the name changed to the Property Tax.[3] Like the Income Tax, of which it was a forerunner, the Property Tax taxed property and profit under five schedules, A to E, both A and B taxing land. Schedule A taxed land, buildings, iron works and quarries together with some minor forms of property. The assessment to this schedule was based on the annual rent of these properties. Schedule B taxed only the profit made by farmers. The difficulty of calculating farm profit was recognized, and the assessment was based on an assumed profit equivalent to three-quarters of the annual rent. The tax was repealed in 1816 and many of the records destroyed. Receipts to both Schedules A and B do survive for most parishes in England from 1799 to 1816,[4] but because of the tax exemptions made on low incomes, these records are an incomplete guide to rent per acre. No assessments to Schedule B on a parish basis were produced, but the assessments to Schedule A were published for every parish in England for one year, 1815.[5]

The parish totals for these assessments are the sum of the annual rent for land, buildings and other minor forms of real property in the parish, and consequently they can be only used to calculate the rent per acre of land if certain precautions are taken. The assessments cannot be used for parishes which contained iron works or quarries, nor can they be used for urban parishes, where the total will consist largely of the rent of buildings. But for purely agricultural parishes the assessments can be used to calculate the average rent per acre. In such parishes about 70 per cent of the total assessment was made up, on the average, of the rent of land, and about 30 per cent of the rent of buildings.[6] The rent per acre for the parish can be obtained by dividing the assessment by the total acreage. This figure will be above the actual rent because of the inclusion of the rent of buildings. But when *comparing* one parish with another, the differences in the calculated rent per acre will be due primarily to differences in the value of land, for regional variations in the value of houses were small compared with regional variations in the value of land. Indeed, the rents of buildings can be assumed to cancel out. Thus the calculated rent per acre will give a fair representation of *relative* regional differences in rent per acre.

The County Rate

The Property Tax was suspended in 1816 and there was no comparable tax on land until 1842 when the Income Tax was instituted. The assessments to Schedule A for 1842-43 have been published on a parish basis, and it is possible to compare the Property Tax assessments for 1815 with the Income Tax assessments for 1842-43. However, the methods of tax collection had changed and it would be preferable to compare assessments with a greater administrative continuity, and this is possible by using the County Rate. This was a local tax raised to finance highway maintenance and other local works, on an assessment of the 'annual value of the messuages, lands, tenements and hereditaments' in each Poor Law parish. The assessment was made by local assessors and all parishes except liberties and franchises were liable to the tax.

Assessments to the County Rate for Kesteven and Holland survive for

1815.[7] For the next twenty-five years the Rate was raised on this assessment, but land values changed considerably in these years, prompting a revaluation of Holland in 1840 and of Kesteven in 1847. The assessments to the County Rate clearly have the same disadvantages as those to the Property Tax, for they include the rent of buildings. However, there seems little doubt that differences in assessments between 1815 and 1840-47 were due primarily to changes in the rent of land and not of buildings. As long as urban parishes are excluded, a comparison of rent per acre in 1815 with 1840-47 gives an accurate picture of regional trends in rent during this period.

Schedule A of the Income Tax, 1842-43 and 1859-60.

In 1842 the Income Tax was introduced, and this tax provides much more reliable information on the rent of land; the assessments have been used by a number of writers to show changes in agricultural rent.[8] The assessments for all five schedules for every parish in England were published for the tax years 1842-43 and 1859-60.[9] Schedule A taxed 'profits from lands, houses and every description of property in the nature of realty'.[10] Unlike the Property Tax, Schedule A was broken down into categories called 'cases', one of which was 'Lands'. This 'case' was an assessment of the value of cultivated and uncultivated land, woodland, lakes, gardens in excess of one acre, and some farm buildings. It did not include buildings, or land built upon, for purposes other than farming. The assessment was based upon annual value, which was taken to be rack rent.[11]

Thus the Schedule A 'Lands' provides a reliable guide to the rent of land alone. Three qualifications should be noted in using the assessments. First, where land was occupied by its owner an estimate of rent had to be made. Some critics thought this led to an underestimate, but according to Lord Stamp the difference from true rent was statistically negligible. Secondly, the 1842-43 assessment was thought to have generally underestimated land values.[12] This does not affect the regional pattern of rent, but it should be borne in mind when comparing 1842-43 and 1859-60. Lastly, the assessment, unlike those of the Property Tax and County Rate, did not include land which was built upon. As the total parish acreage has been used to calculate rent per acre, the figures for urban parishes will be an underestimate of actual rent.

From the sources discussed above it is possible to construct for any agricultural area in England the following maps: rent per acre in 1815 (Fig. 3), 1842-43 (Fig. 5), and 1859-60 (Fig. 7); and the percentage change in rent per acre between 1815 and 1840-47 (Fig. 4), and 1842-43 and 1859-60 (Fig. 6). The maps based on the Income Tax are reliable in both an absolute and relative sense. For the maps constructed from the County Rate and the Property Tax no more is claimed than that they show accurately relative regional differences in rent per acre and changes in rent per acre. Other contemporary evidence on rent per acre in the different regions of south Lincolnshire — in the Select Committee's on Agriculture for instance — suggest that the maps are probably accurate.[13] Before turning to the maps themselves, some consideration must be briefly given to the determinants of rent per acre.

The Nature of Agricultural Rent

Contract rent is an annual payment made by a tenant for the lease of farmland and farm buildings. Rent per acre is this sum divided by the acreage of the farm. The level of farm rent in the nineteenth century was determined by a number of factors of which only the most important can be discussed here.[14]

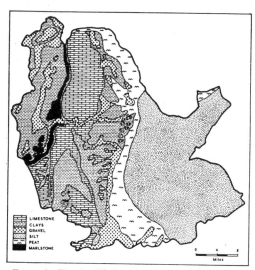

FIGURE 1—The simplified geology of south Lincolnshire.

The backwardness of farm methods in South Lincolnshire at the beginning of the nineteenth century made regional differences in the natural *fertility of the soil* important in determining rent; but because land use and crop selection were so much affected by differences in soil type, it was frequently difficult to differentiate the significance of this factor from that of the *type of farming.* Thus the average rent per acre of land under grass was generally higher than that under arable, whilst rough grazing bore the lowest average rent in the area.

Rent per acre was affected by the *size of farms*, for rent is paid for both land and buildings. Rent per acre tends to decrease as the size of farm increases, because the rent of buildings is proportionally more important in the rent of a small farm than a large farm. This factor was important in south Lincolnshire because of the pronounced regional variations in farm size. Farms were generally small in west Kesteven (see Fig. 2) and especially in the Fenland, whilst large farms predominated on the Heath and medium-sized farms in south-east Kesteven. The *position* of a farm often affected rent per acre, for farms remote from market towns were in less demand than those near to towns, where in addition farmers had to compete with urban users for the lease of land.

Rents were affected by other factors over a period of time. In the nineteenth century agricultural rents tended to follow, with a slight time lag, the course of *agricultural prices.* Rents in the country as a whole rose from 1800 to 1814 but were low and fluctuating in the 1820s and 1830s. They recovered in the late 1830s and rose steadily until 1878. This pattern closely followed the course of the general agricultural price level, but not all farm product prices followed precisely the same course.[15] In the 1820s and 1830s prices for animal products were generally more favourable than those for grain, whilst of the grain crops, malting barley fell least. One consequence of this was that not all parts of the country suffered equally in the post-Napoleonic War depression. Grazing regions maintained rents per acre better than arable areas. However the arable acreage greatly increased in the three grazing regions of south Lincolnshire in the years after 1815 (for reasons which have been discussed elsewhere[16]) and

thus became increasingly dependent on grain prices. One last factor affecting rent per acre must be noted. In the thirty years after 1815 there was very substantial *landlord investment* in south Lincolnshire farms — in underdrainage, fen drainage, fertilizers and farm buildings — and tenants paid for these improvements in increased rents, in spite of the generally unfavourable price conditions.

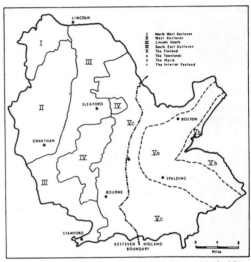

FIGURE 2—The agricultural regions of south Lincolnshire.

Agriculture in South Lincolnshire, 1815-60

In the first half of the nineteenth century farming regions in south Lincolnshire corresponded closely to regional differences in soil type (compare Figs. 1 and 2). Most of the area is low lying, the only significant relief feature being the Lincolnshire Limestone cuesta. This forms a scarp in the west striking south from Lincoln through Grantham to the Leicestershire border. The Lincolnshire Limestone dips gently east and the dip-slope (Lincoln Heath) formed a distinctive region (Fig. 2). The soils were shallow and nitrogen deficient and in the 1800s much of the Heath was still waste land. However, these soils had three important advantages: they were permeable and did not need underdrainage, were easily and thus cheaply cultivated, and were particularly suitable for turnips. South of Sleaford the dip-slope is covered by chalky boulder-clay, which gave a very different landscape and type of farming from those of the Heath proper. About three-quarters of the farmland in this region (south-east Kesteven) was under grass in 1815.

West of the Lincolnshire Limestone lies the low Lias clay plain of west Kesteven. This region, like south-east Kesteven, was mainly under grass. Both

231

the clay regions have impermeable soils and were badly drained. This meant that turnips were difficult to grow, for if sheep were folded on the wet soils their feet 'poached' the land and the sheep were liable to foot rot, whilst it was usually too costly to lift the turnips and feed them elsewhere. In wet years the clays held excessive sub-soil moisture which retarded plant development, whilst if there were heavy rains in autumn, sowing was delayed and yields were reduced as a consequence. But for all their drawbacks the clays had a considerable natural fertility, giving good yields of wheat and beans and carrying a fair grassland.

Northwards on the Lias clay plain fluvio-glacial sands and gravels cover much of the area. In this region (north-west Kesteven) there was still much waste land in 1815. Poor arable and rough grazing dominated the land use pattern, for the soils were nitrogen deficient, like those of the Heath. But also as on the Heath, these soils drained naturally, were easily cultivated, and included some of 'the finest turnip land in the county'.[17]

East of the limestone dip-slope there is only a narrow outcrop of the succeeding Oxford and Kimmeridge clays, as they are covered by the post-glacial deposits of the Fenland. The principal geological distinction to be made within the Fenland is between the peats, on the landward edge of the Fen, and the silts. The peats did not need underdrainage if they had adequate surface drainage, and were easily tilled. But the most important characteristic of the peats was their high nitrogen content, which gave large wheat yields, especially when the land was first broken up from grass. Unfortunately the nitrogen content was initially excessive and the straw grew at the expense of the grain. In the eighteenth century this was remedied by growing a series of oats crops to exhaust the soil before planting wheat. About 1810 'claying' was adopted instead. Clay was found everywhere beneath the peats and this was mixed with the surface soil, with beneficial effects on both the yield and quality of wheat crops. Turnips were not successful on the peats, the roots going 'fangy', and so coleseed was grown instead.

Silt soils occupy the greater part of the Fenland and vary from a light, sandy soil to a heavy clay. On the boundary of the peat and the silt are found 'skirty' soils, a mixture of peat and silt. Light silts are found near the sea, whilst inland the heavier silts are similar to the clays of Kesteven. Although the silts had a high natural fertility, they could not match the peats and needed more careful cultivation. Contemporary writers divided the fen not into two, but three farming regions, based partly on drainage efficiency: the Marsh, the Townland, and the Interior Fenland, all running parallel to the coast (Fig. 2). Although the Fenland as a whole was flat, a silt ridge near the coast lay slightly above the level of the Interior Fenland. On this ridge (the Townlands) the first settlement had taken place. The region was relatively free from drainage problems and had been enclosed at an early date: in 1815 it consisted mainly of excellent grazing lands. Seaward of the Townland lay the Marsh, which had been reclaimed from the sea over a long period, the last major enclosure being in the 1790s. Here the silts were lighter, and had long been used only as sheep grazing, but during the Napoleonic Wars much of the Marsh was ploughed up. Whilst both the Townland and the Marsh were relatively well drained, winter flooding was still a regular occurrence in much of the Interior Fenland, which lay inland from the Townland. In spite of the great drainage schemes of the late eighteenth century, only the northern Interior Fenland had been sufficiently well drained to allow regular cropping by 1815, and in the southern parishes summer grazing remained the major form of land use.

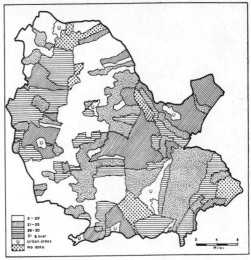

FIGURE 3—Rent in 1815 in shillings per acre.

Regional Changes in Rent, 1815-1860

Land use, soil type and the size of farm were the three most important factors affecting rent per acre in any one year. These factors were reasonably uniform within each of the major farming regions of south Lincolnshire, but differed sharply from region to region. It is not surprising then to find that rent per acre was more or less uniform within each region in 1815, 1842 and 1860 (Figs. 3, 5 and 7), but that there were marked inter-regional differences. There was also a regional trend in the pattern of rental change between 1815 and 1842, and 1842 and 1860 (Figs. 4 and 6). In the first period rental increases were greatest in the Fenland and the light lands, and least in the two clay regions. Between 1842 and 1860 increases were greatest in the northern Heath and north-west Kesteven, and least in the Fenland and the clay regions. Thus the overall pattern of increase 1815-60 was one of stagnation on the clays — which were highly rented in 1815 — and of rapid increases in the Fenland and particularly the light lands, which had been an area of low rent in 1815. This resulted in an overall decline in the regional differentiation of rent per acre. Two factors were primarily responsible for the changes of the period; the differential rate of farm improvement, and the shift in cost-price relationships in favour of the light lands.

(a) The Unequal Rate of Farm Improvement

The improvements in farming methods in this period came mainly in arable farming, and were associated with the spread of the Norfolk system. The principal characteristic of this system was the Norfolk four-course rotation of

233

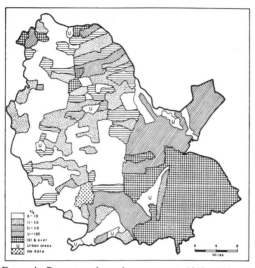

1. Turnips, 2. Barley, 3. Seed 4. Wheat, together with sheep flock. The key crop wa the turnip, which was adapte to light and medium soil and thus easily adopted o the Heath and in north-we Kesteven. But the syste could not be adopted on th clays or the peats, and on onˌthe sandier of the Fen silt However the great fertili of the Fenland soils was suc that the inability to adopt th Norfolk system was n deterrent to progress. Befor 1815 rents had been kept lo in the Interior Fenland b inefficient surface drainage particularly in the south. Bu

FIGURE 4—Percentage change in rent per acre, 1815 to 1840-47.

between 1815 and 1851, improvements to the outfalls of the main rivers an the replacement of windmills by steam pumps freed the Fenland from floods except in particularly wet years.

Between 1815 and 1851 the Norfolk system was generally adopted on th light lands and rents rose rapidly. Similarly drainage improvements in th Interior Fenland allowed a fuller utilization of the Fen after 1815. But i the clay regions the problem of underdrainage retarded technical progress an rents stagnated in comparison with both the Fenland and the light lands.

(b) Regional Changes in Cost-Price Relationships

Whilst grain prices remained high, the clay regions of England, with thei high natural fertility, could compete in grain production with the light lands even although farming methods were improving at a greater rate on the latte soils. But with the fall in grain prices after 1814 the wheat producers in the clay regions found it increasingly difficult to compete with light land producers for three reasons:

(i) The light lands rarely needed underdrainage, whereas it was essential on the clays.
(ii) Differences in soil texture between the light lands and the clays made the latter more expensive to cultivate even when they were well drained.

Production costs per bushel were thus lower on the light lands than on the clays. Light land farmers were able to concentrate expenditure on careful ultivation and the liberal use f artificial fertilizers, with consequent increase in ields. At the beginning of ie nineteenth century wheat ields were higher on the more aturally fertile clays than on ie light lands, but by 1815 iey were higher on the nproved light lands.

ii) Whilst all agricultural prices were low in the 1820s and 1830s, malting barley and wool prices were generally better than wheat or oats. Wool and barley were products of the Norfolk system and thus easily produced

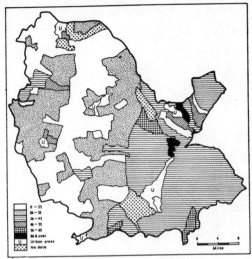

FIGURE 5—Rent in 1843 in shillings per acre.

on the light lands. The clay regions of south Lincolnshire were singularly unfortunate in this period. The clays grew only a poor malting barley and the considerable sheep flocks of south-east and west Kesteven were greatly reduced by attacks of foot rot in the 1820s. The farmers of these two regions consequently became increasingly dependent on wheat production.

Thus both production costs and farm price structure shifted in favour of he light lands after 1815. But at the same time the Fenland's competitive osition improved in relation to both the clay regions and the light lands. At the eginning of the century wheat yields in the Fen were twice the average yield lsewhere in South Lincolnshire, but rents were kept low by the frequent looding which often destroyed a farmer's whole crop. The improved drainage ifter 1815 removed this hazard. The fertile Fen soils needed far less fertilizer han the light lands, and the peats were friable and easily tilled once the surface Irainage was secure. Further, the exceptional fertility of the Fen soils allowed a greater flexibility in crop selection, and the 1830s saw the beginnings of special-zed arable farming in the Fenland. This land bore rents well above the average.

Rent per acre in 1815, 1842 and 1860

There are three distinct zones on all three maps of rent per acre (Figs. 3, 5 and 7). The regional differences in rent per acre were due mainly to three factors: soil type, the proportion of land under grass and the predominant farm size.

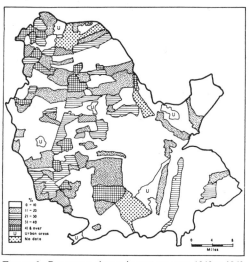

FIGURE 6—Percentage change in rent per acre, 1843 to 1860.

(a) *West Kesteven*

In all three years ren[t] per acre in west Kesteve[n] was above that of th[e] central zone, but belo[w] that of the east. Farm[s] on the Lias clay plain – to which this regio[n] corresponded — wer[e] predominantly smal[l] and the land was mainl[y] under grass.

(b) *The central zone*

The light lands remaine[d] a low rent regio[n] throughout the perio[d] in spite of the grea[t] improvements in farm[ing] methods. The roug[h] grazing land which ha[d] been important in 1815 was ploughed up, and by 1840 over four-fifths o[f] the farm land was arable. There were few small farms in this region, th[e] farm of over 300 acres being the dominant unit.

(c) *The eastern zone*

East of the Heath rent per acre rose sharply and the eastern zone bore a[] rent above that of the other two zones. The eastern zone consisted of th[e] boulder-clay region of south-east Kesteven and the whole of the Fenland. In south-east Kesteven over three-quarters of the land was under grass in 1815, and although this was reduced in later years, grass remained important in this region in comparison with the rest of south Lincolnshire. Average rent per acre was higher in the Fenland than in south-east Kesteven, but there were significant internal variations within the Fenland. In 1815 the northern parishes were better drained than the southern, and this was reflected in the rent per acre (Fig. 3). This difference diminished as drainage improved after 1815, but the northern parishes still had a[] higher rent per acre in 1860. This was due to the smaller average size of farm in the north, the proximity of Boston, the main Fenland market town, and the early development of specialized arable farming. Average rent per acre in the Fenland as a whole was influenced by farm size, for farms were smaller than in any other part of south Lincolnshire. In 1870 four-fifths of all farms in the Fenland were between 5 and 50 acres, compared with a figure of 60 per cent for the other area of small farms, west Kesteven.

Changes in Rent per acre, 1815-60

The factors influencing the rate of rental change in this period have already been discussed; their regional impact is clear in Figs. 4 and 6. Between 1815 and 1840-47 the greatest increases came in the Heath and in the Fenland, particularly in the south where drainage had been inefficient in 1815. The clay regions showed very little increase in this period, and in some parishes rent per acre actually fell. After 1840 the rate of farm improvement was slower and the regional pattern of rental increase was

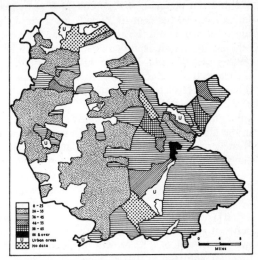

FIGURE 7—Rent in 1860 in shillings per acre.

less well defined (Fig. 6). The greatest increases in this period came in two light land regions which had lagged in the preceding period, north-west Kesteven and the southern Heath.

Over the period as a whole rental increase was least in the two clay regions, where rent had been relatively high in 1815; and highest in the Heath and north-west Kesteven, where it had been low in 1815; and intermediate in the Fenland. The net effect was to reduce the regional contrasts in rent per acre, but by no means to eliminate them. This is illustrated in Table I. In each of the years 1815, 1842 and 1860 the region with the lowest average rent per acre (in each year the Heath) is represented as 100, and the average rent of the other regions is represented proportionally.

TABLE I

Average Rent per acre by Regions
(The Heath = 100 in 1815, 1842-43 and 1859-60)

	1815	1842-43	1859-60
The Heath	100	100	100
North-west Kesteven	110	100	105
South-east Kesteven	150	110	102
West Kesteven	190	140	120
The Fenland	430	210	180

The table shows that whereas in 1815 there had been a difference of 340 per cent between the highest and lowest rented regions, in 1860 the difference was only 80 per cent. If the Fenland is not considered, regional contrasts ha fallen from 90 per cent to 20 per cent. Indeed by 1860 rent per acre was fairl uniform throughout the area outside the Fenland, only west Kesteven having regional rent significantly above the remainder of Kesteven. In spite of th greater rate of rental increase on the light lands, and the relative stagnation o the clays, rent per acre on the light lands was still below that on the clays. Th difference between south-east Kesteven and the Heath was small (only 5 pe cent), but west Kesteven was still rented at 20 per cent above the Heath, i spite of the greater demand for farms on the Heath. Part of the explanation lie in the fact that farms on the Heath were a great deal larger than those in wes Kesteven, but in terms of the contemporary technology and price structure, th clays were probably over-rented.

The decline in regional differentiation was due to a number of factors. First of all the spread of improved farming methods had reduced the farmer dependence on the natural fertility of his soils. Secondly, in 1815 there had beei a marked regional specialization in both land use and the type of product. Bu between 1815 and 1860 the spread of mixed farming had reduced this. This ha two consequences. The growth of the arable acreage in the old grazing region together with the virtual elimination of rough grazing meant there were les regional differences in land use and thus of rent per acre. In addition eacl region by 1860 was dependent for income on the same range of product whereas earlier in the century there had been more product specialization an dependence on one type of product. As rent was partially controlled by agricul tural prices, this factor led to a greater uniformity of rent per acre. Finally th improvement of transport facilities, especially towards the end of the period cheapened the import of lime, coal and other producer goods, and facilitate the movement of farm products out of the area. This reduced the differences i accessibility which had influenced rents locally at the beginning of the century

The above brief analysis of the maps of rent per acre illustrates the use o the assessments discussed earlier in this paper. As the assessments are available for all the parishes of England and Wales, it is hoped this technique will be o value to other students of nineteenth-century agriculture.

ACKNOWLEDGMENTS

The author wishes to acknowledge the helpful comments he has received from Dr. D. W. Harve on the use of the Income Tax, and is grateful to Dr. A. Garnett and Mr. I. S. Maxwell for criticall reading the paper. The University of Sheffield has made a grant towards the cost of the illustrations

NOTES

[1] G. E. FUSSELL, 'Light land farming a century ago', *Journal of the Land Agents Society*, 3 (1937), 577-80; G. R. PORTER, *The Progress of the Nation* (1847), 152; J. CAIRD, *English Agricultur in 1850-1851* (1852), 476.

[2] E. J. BUCKATZSCH, 'The geographical distribution of wealth in England, 1086-1843', *Economi History Review*, 2nd Series, 3 (1950), 180-202.

[3] A. HOPE-JONES, *Income Tax in the Napoleonic Wars* (1939), Chapter 2. See also P. K. O'BRIEN 'British incomes and property in the early nineteenth century', *Economic History Review*, 2nd Series 12 (1959), 255-67.

[4] The receipts are kept in the Public Record Office. Catalogue numbers are listed in A. HOPE-INES, op. cit, 126-8.

[5] The parish assessments can be found in *British Parliamentary Papers*, 19 (1818), 235.

[6] The author is grateful to Dr. D. W. Harvey for this estimate.

[7] The Kesteven assessments for 1815 and 1847 and the Holland assessment for 1815, together ith a description of the valuation procedure are kept at Lincoln Record Office, Kesteven County ouncil Deposit. The Holland assessments for 1840 are kept in the Muniment Room, Holland ounty Council, Boston.

[8] R. J. THOMPSON, 'An inquiry into the rent of agricultural land in England and Wales during the ieteenth century', *Journal of the Royal Statistical Society*, 70 (1907), 587-616; P. G. CRAIGIE, 'Ten ars statistics of British agriculture', *Journal of the Royal Statistical Society*, 43 (1880), 304-6.

[9] The parochial assessments for 1842-43 are in *British Parliamentary Papers*, 32 (1844), 451, and r 1859-60 in *British Parliamentary Papers*, 39 (1860), 157.

[10] J. C. STAMP, *British Incomes and Property* (1916), 15.

[11] J. C. STAMP, op. cit., 18, 41-3.

[12] J. C. STAMP, op. cit., 23, 38.

[13] For a survey on the other evidence on regional rents in South Lincolnshire see D. B. GRIGG, *ricultural Change in South Lincolnshire, 1790-1875*, unpublished Ph.D. dissertation (1961), ambridge University, 54-8, 116-27.

[14] D. R. DENMAN and V. F. STEWART, *Farm Rents* (1959). See also J. CAIRD, op. cit., 479-82.

[15] R. J. THOMPSON, op. cit., 596-602.

[16] See D. B. GRIGG, op. cit. (1961), 171-7. The remaining part of this paper is based on this ssertation and detailed references may be found there.

[17] Lincoln Archives Office, Jarvis 8.

[18] C. FORDHAM, 'Some notes on the value of agricultural land in the Midlands and Eastern unties between 1823 and 1947', *Journal of the Land Agents Society*, 48 (1949), 271.

Locational Change in the Kentish Hop Industry and the
Analysis of Land Use Patterns
D.W. Harvey
Reprinted from *Transactions and Papers of the Institute of British Geographers,* 33 (1963), 123-44

LOCATIONAL CHANGE IN THE KENTISH HOP INDUSTRY AND THE ANALYSIS OF LAND USE PATTERNS

D. W. Harvey, M.A., Ph.D.

Human geographers are invariably concerned with the analysis of patterns of economic activity. But these patterns are rarely a simple function of modern conditions, so that location studies should differentiate between the factors that govern the initial location of a particular form of production and the factors that govern the shift from a pre-existing to a new pattern. In a 'mature' economy such as that of Great Britain, the process of locational change may well be more important to the explanation of present distributions than the factors that governed initial location. Yet, in spite of this, geographers have tended to ignore the problem of exactly how a shift from one geographical pattern to another is accomplished. The lack of study focused directly on the processes of locational change stems, largely, from methodological problems of dealing with space and time in the same context. Thus, although the processes of locational change have not been entirely ignored, the complexities involved have often been wrapped up in general terms such as 'inertia' or 'historical momentum'. Unless these terms are broken down into more meaningful concepts, the analysis of location will inevitably lack penetration.

This paper is concerned with an examination of some of the processes that govern the evolution of land-use patterns. In particular it is concerned with the trend towards regional concentration of hop production in Kent during the nineteenth century, and with the three processes that appear to have accounted for this trend.

The Problem Isolated

Locational change in the Kentish hop industry was very complex and its explanation is even more so. It is not intended here to examine every aspect of change, but rather to isolate the tendency towards regional concentration and to discuss the factors that governed it.[1]

During the nineteenth century there were rapid changes in demand for hops which, together with technical adjustments in the hop industry, resulted in long-term fluctuations in the hop acreage (Fig. 1). The general trend was one of rising acreage from 1815 to 1861. After this date the repeal of the duty on hops, coupled with a rapid expansion of output in the brewing industry, led to a sharp rise in the hop acreage, which reached a maximum in the period 1878–85. After 1885 the acreage contracted rapidly so that by 1900 it had declined to approximately its 1860 level. This decline was mainly due to foreign competition, to technical change in the brewing industry, and to rising productivity in the hop industry.

These general trends were modified in the Kentish case by two further factors. First, there were sharp cyclical fluctuations in the hop acreage connected, before 1878, with the 'major cycles' of growth in the British economy as a whole.[2] This makes any analysis of changing location very difficult since at no period in the century was the distribution of the hop acreage anywhere near stable. Second, there was a persistent tendency throughout the century for hop production to become concentrated in Kent and Sussex at the expense of other producing areas. Between 1810 and 1878 the proportion of the national acreage located in Kent rose from 43 per cent to 65 per cent. It is not, however, the purpose of this article to explain either the cyclical fluctuations in acreage, or the shift of production towards Kent. These facts must, rather, be regarded as the given base against which locational change in the Kentish hop industry can be analysed.

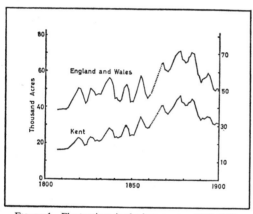

FIGURE 1—Fluctuations in the hop acreage 1807–1900.

The location of the hop acreage at any particular date between 1807 and 1861 can be ascertained from the returns to the Hop Excise. From 1867 until the end of the century the agricultural statistics provide the necessary data. The individual parish statistics are, in both cases, often suspect, and are difficult to use for comparative purposes. But the general pattern of distribution of hop cultivation can be fairly accurately illustrated from both sources.[3]

Figure 2 indicates the distribution of the hop acreage in Kent at selected dates throughout the nineteenth century. It illustrates, in a general way, the regional reaction within Kent to the basic changes in hop acreage shown in Figure 1. It suggests the existence of two core areas of hop production—one centred near Canterbury in east Kent, and one centred on Maidstone in central Kent. The east Kent district was less important, concentrated on a very high quality product and was, thus, susceptible to change in one sector of the market only. During the phase of depression after 1885, for example, the demand for high quality hops remained unimpaired, so that the hop acreage in east Kent remained fairly constant, while the acreage declined rapidly in the rest of Kent. Because it was affected by such special circumstances, the east Kent industry will not be considered here. Attention will be focused on that part of Kent roughly defined by the rim of the chalk scarp, the county boundary and Romney Marsh (Fig. 3).

Within this district the maps indicate that the hop acreage tended to be located in zones of declining density ranged around a central core area. Using a 'gravity model'[4] the centre of hop cultivation was determined for 1837 and 1855, and in both cases the centre determined was the parish of Wateringbury. To determine how density varied with distance, successive zones two miles in width were circumscribed around this centre (Fig. 4), and the average density

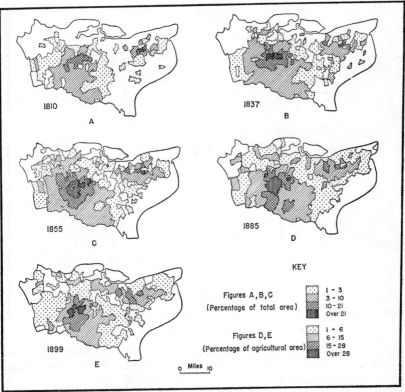

KEY

Figures A, B, C
(Percentage of total area)

	1 - 3
	3 - 10
	10 - 21
	Over 21

Figures D, E
(Percentage of agricultural area)

	1 - 6
	6 - 15
	15 - 28
	Over 28

0   Miles   10

FIGURE 2—Density of hop cultivation in Kent for selected dates in the nineteenth century.
(*Source:* Hop Excise and Ministry of Agriculture.)

of hop cultivation in each zone was calculated. Parishes which lay more or less equally divided between zones were counted in both zones in averaging out the parish statistics. The regular decline of density with distance is illustrated in Figure 5.

This regular distribution of the hop acreage according to distance from the main centre of cultivation appears to have little respect for differing soil conditions.

The hop plant is tolerant of a wide variety of soil conditions for it will 'grow and crop even in extreme adversity as far as its soil is concerned'.[5] Yet despite ·this the commercial production of hops is profoundly influenced by physical conditions and many studies have suggested that there is a close connection between hop yields and both soil drainage and soil texture.[6]

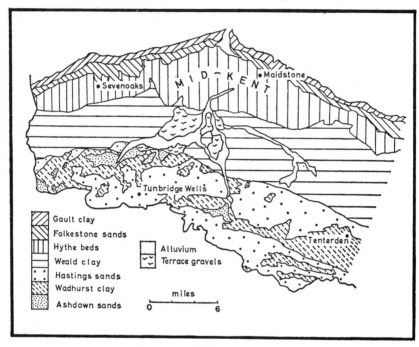

Gault clay
Folkestone sands
Hythe beds
Weald clay
Hastings sands
Wadhurst clay
Ashdown sands

Alluvium
Terrace gravels

miles
0   6

FIGURE 3—The Kentish Weald: generalized geology.

In the absence of detailed soil surveys, a definitive analysis of the relationship between hop cultivation and soil conditions is impossible. Generally speaking, however, soil conditions in the Wealden area are closely related to underlying geology. Using this as a basic guide (Fig. 3), certain interim conclusions may be reached.

There are certain soil groups which were completely negative for hop cultivation: namely, soils developed over open chalk, where drainage was far too rapid, and soils where drainage was impeded. The chalk soils are well distributed along the North Downs, so that although hop cultivation was carried on (nearly always on the clay-with-flint deposits) the North Downs tended to form a major negative area for hop growing. The high water-table soils are limited to the alluvium of the river flood-plains, but Romney Marsh formed a major negative area for hop cultivation because of its physical characteristics.

At the other extreme, there are certain soil groups of limited distribution that were ideally suited to hop cultivation. Most favourable of all were the well-drained loams developed over the Hythe Beds. An analysis of these soils distinguished thirteen soil series: five of these were very localized in distribution, two were derived from lime-free sand and were poorly drained and acidic, while the remaining six were derived from the 'ragstone' and were deep, loamy and well drained. These latter soils, together with those derived from Pleistocene valley gravels, predominated around Maidstone and this district—termed Mid-Kent—formed the highly favoured core area of hop cultivation.[7]

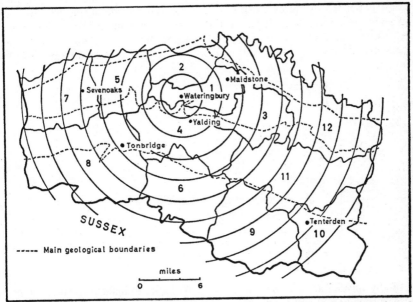

FIGURE 4—The Kentish Weald: showing the parish groupings used in Table I and the zones of equal distance constructed around Wateringbury.

There are soils elsewhere that were reasonably suited to hop cultivation. Some of the terrace gravels spread over the Wealden clays to the south of Mid-Kent were in this category. Some of the soils developed over the Hastings Beds in the High Weald were also favourable, although soil conditions are so varied here that N. B. Bagenall and B. S. Furneaux found hardly a single field with a uniform soil series throughout. They distinguished sixteen series; six were well drained and covered 41·5 per cent of the area they surveyed and undoubtedly some of these were suited to hop cultivation.[8]

But most of the soils throughout the district were neither absolutely negative to hop cultivation, nor particularly favourable. Most could be used, however, given the right economic conditions. The heavy, poorly drained soils associated with the Weald and Wadhurst Clays were probably the most marginal, although in many places they were ameliorated—the Weald Clay, for example, by beds of Paludina limestone or by river gravels. The soils developed over the Folkestone Sands were often not sufficiently retentive of moisture, while some of the sandy soils of the High Weald suffered from a similar disadvantage. The Gault Clay soils, on the other hand, tended to be too heavy for the cultivation of good quality hops. But none of these defects was sufficiently crippling to prevent hop cultivation completely.

The location of the core area of hop cultivation in Mid-Kent was, thus, closely defined by the excellence of the soils. But outside of this core area soil conditions appear to have played little part in determining the pattern of hop densities, for there was very little relationship between the zoning of the hop acreage around the centre and the distribution of suitable soil types. Only the

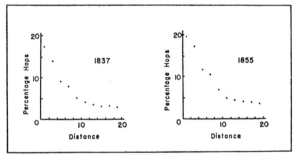

FIGURE 5—Decline of density of hop cultivation with miles distance from Wateringbury.
(*Source:* Hop Excise)

totally unsuitable soils were avoided. This indiscriminate cultivation of hops over such varied soil conditions in Kent puzzled many contemporary writers. W. Topley, for instance, could see no clear reason why hops were not cultivated in other parts of England if they could be so easily cultivated in Kent.[9] Clearly, therefore, causes other than physical ones must be sought if this pattern of hop location is to be explained.

The relationship between acreage distribution and distance from Mid-Kent was not simply a static one. The maps suggest that expanding demand resulted in either an increase in density in the central area or in a spread outward of acreage around the centre. The actual details of regional change are, however, rather complex. By dividing the district as a whole into twelve parish groups (Fig. 4) the regional reaction to the general trends of acreage change can be analysed in greater detail.

The density of the hop acreage for each region has been calculated for selected years throughout the century. The years chosen are those that correspond to the peak and trough dates in the cyclical fluctuations of the acreage. Table I thus indicates the main regional changes in Kent in relation to national trends.

Between 1810 and 1819 there was a phase of rapid adjustment in agriculture as a whole to meet rapidly changing price conditions. Hop cultivation remained one of the few profitable forms of agriculture after 1815 and the hop acreage tended to increase rapidly in many areas of Kent. After 1819, however, the importance of distance from Mid-Kent as a factor in hop acreage change can be more clearly demonstrated.

TABLE I

Percentage of Total Area under Hops by Parish Groups shown in Figure 4

Date	Parish groups											
	1	2	3	4	5	6	7	8	9	10	11	12
1810	13·2	4·2	5·8	8·0	2·0	4·7	2·0	1·4	4·8	0·9	2·8	1·3
1819	17·9	6·1	6·7	11·6	3·9	5·7	2·2	2·2	7·2	2·8	3·2	1·6
1823	16·2	5·7	6·0	11·0	4·0	5·2	2·0	1·9	5·3	2·1	2·3	1·4
1826	22·5	7·2	8·0	11·1	3·9	5·0	2·1	2·4	6·3	2·4	2·8	1·5
1831	17·3	5·5	8·6	10·9	4·0	5·0	2·2	2·0	6·4	1·6	2·2	1·7
1837	19·4	6·4	10·1	13·2	5·3	6·2	3·3	3·0	8·0	3·1	3·8	2·2
1840	11·3	5·0	9·9	9·4	4·8	4·8	3·1	2·5	6·6	2·8	3·2	2·0
1846	16·4	6·4	9·9	14·1	7·2	7·3	3·4	3·0	6·6	3·0	3·9	2·5
1849	14·9	5·6	8·5	12·0	6·9	5·9	2·6	2·8	4·9	2·5	2·5	2·0
1855	19·8	7·3	11·6	17·5	8·3	9·2	4·1	4·0	7·7	3·7	4·4	2·6
1859	19·6	6·7	10·2	14·9	7·2	7·2	3·3	2·8	5·4	2·5	3·2	2·0
1878	23·9	10·2	15·8	20·0	7·4	11·3	4·1	4·4	8·8	4·3	7·2	4·0
1885	22·0	9·2	13·6	19·5	6·1	12·1	4·0	4·3	9·2	5·0	8·0	4·6
1899	14·2	4·9	7·7	15·8	3·0	9·5	2·6	3·0	5·8	2·1	4·8	2·5

(*Source:* Hop Excise 1810–59, Ministry of Agriculture 1878–99.)

The general trend in the three parish groupings comprising Mid-Kent was one of expanding acreage in response to the overall rise in demand between 1819 and 1826. After this date two of the parish groups (1 and 2) tended to decline while the group to the south-east of Maidstone (group 3) continued to expand over the cyclical fluctuation culminating in 1837. All three groups remained static during the 1840s and expansion was only renewed after 1850 to culminate in the high densities of 1878—but even in 1878 the density was not very much higher than it had been in 1826, except to the south-east of Maidstone (group 3). The problem here is to explain why this favourably placed core area should have failed to expand its hop acreage between 1826 and 1846 when the general trend in demand for hops was upward.

After 1837 expansion was most rapid in those areas closest to the core area without actually being in it (groups 4, 5 and 6). These groups expanded very little before 1826, but after this date expansion was very rapid indeed until 1878. Farther away from the core area the expansion was not so marked, although the parish groups in the western Weald (groups 7 and 8) and in the eastern Weald (groups 11 and 12) expanded fairly steadily after 1826. But in the districts farthest from the centre (groups 9 and 10) the pattern of growth was rather different, for here the highest densities were almost reached in 1819; after this date the tendency was for the hop acreage to remain steady or to contract slightly.

There were thus three distinctive phases in the pattern of regional expansion in the hop acreage before 1878. The first phase from 1819 to 1826 saw the rapid growth of the central nucleus, while the other districts experienced little or no acreage change. The second phase, from 1826 to 1846, was characterized by stagnation in the core area, accompanied by a rapid expansion in the areas nearest to the core and a slight decline in the more remote districts. After 1846 there was a third phase of all-round expansion most marked at the centre and in the areas nearest to it.

Thus, even though the central area of Mid-Kent tended to stagnate at certain periods, there was a persistent tendency for the hop acreage to increase most in the parishes in, or near to, Mid-Kent. This tendency can be illustrated statistically by plotting the percentage change in the hop acreage for certain parishes against their distance from the centre of hop cultivation. This was done for one period of expansion and one period of contraction of acreage for each parish across the High and Low Weald (parish groups 4, 5 and 8 to 11 in Fig. 4). The statistical 'centre of gravity' varied throughout the century between Wateringbury and Yalding and since the latter parish lay within the area under consideration it was chosen as the central point.

During the phase of expansion from 1829–35 to 1856–61 a negative correlation coefficient (r) of −0.52 was obtained (Fig. 6, A), which indicates that there was a tendency for the percentage increase in the hop acreage to be more marked near the centre than farther away. The r^2 value of 0.27 indicates, however, that only 27 per cent of the variance in percentage change can be explained by the factor of distance from the centre. Thus, although the trend is significant it is not a full explanation.

The period of contraction of acreage from 1885 to 1899 (Fig. 6, B) shows a far closer relationship with a clear tendency for the percentage decline to become more marked with increasing distance from the centre. In this case the r^2 value of 0.50 indicates that 50 per cent of the variance is the result of distance. The figures in this case are in every way more reliable, especially as they may be expressed in relation to the agricultural land of each parish rather than in absolute terms. But both examples indicate that the factor of distance from the centre of cultivation was a significant one in accounting for the regional rate of expansion or contraction of the hop acreage during the nineteenth century.

The details of locational change were, of course, far more complex than the simplified account given here would suggest. But it has been shown that there was a persistent tendency throughout the century for the distribution of the hop acreage to be related to distance from the centre of production. A recognition of this tendency is essential to both the study of changing location and the understanding of the location of hop cultivation at any one particular time. This tendency, however, poses three specific problems. First, why did hop cultivation tend to concentrate in Mid-Kent? Second, what were the limits set to this concentration? Third, why, once these limits were reached, did the industry spread out and around Mid-Kent in a way more consistent with distance than with soil conditions?

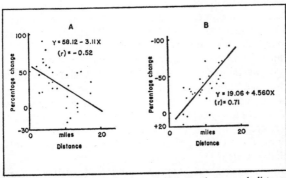

FIGURE 6—Relationship between hop acreage change and distance from Yalding for 28 parishes in the Kentish High and Low Weald.
A. Absolute change 1829/35 to 1856/61.
     (*Source:* Hop Excise)
B. Percentage change 1885 to 1899 in relation to agricultural area.
     (*Source:* Ministry of Agriculture)

The Problem Explained

The problems posed above can best be answered in terms of three specific processes—agglomeration, cumulative change, and diminishing returns. These three processes need detailed consideration.

Agglomeration

The process of agglomeration has been studied often in relation to industrial structures, but it has been largely ignored in an agricultural context.[10] There were, however, certain economies to be gained from establishing any new hop acreage in or near the existing locations. Economies of scale operated within the individual farm unit. Hop cultivation demanded the use of specialized equipment—oast houses, special implements, hop poles and so on—and it was in the grower's own interest to make an optimum use of all this equipment. The oast house was the most important item. It was scarcely economic to build on for less than ten acres of hops, while thirty acres was generally considered necessary to keep a well-designed oast house fully employed at mid-century Other buildings and items of technical equipment also encouraged the grower to keep up a certain minimum area under hops, since their inefficient use meant a higher cost per unit of output.

But the tendency towards concentration can only be fully explained in terms of the external economies of scale which accrued from establishing new acreage in the existing locations. Mid-Kent, for example, had long been the commercial centre of hop cultivation and possessed marked physical advantages. But by 1800 a whole range of capital assets had been built up which increased the attraction of the district from the point of view of hop cultivation.

Many of the Mid-Kent planters, for example, had accumulated quite impressive capital resources. Hop cultivation was, by nineteenth-century standards, an extremely expensive form of cultivation. The initial investment was heavy—anything between £60 and £100 per acre—and the annual costs of cultivation were also high—usually between £25 and £40 per acre. The accounts for one farm between 1838 and 1846 indicate an annual expenditure of £35 per acre on the hop land compared with £5 12s. on the arable.[11] The total capital requirements for successful hop cultivation were thus considerable; one agent stated that he would not accept a tenant unless he possessed at least £125 working capital per acre of hop land compared to £10 or £12 per acre of arable land.[12] At the same time there was a high element of risk involved in cultivating a crop with so unreliable a yield.[13]

High costs of cultivation were met, however, by a high turnover per acre. It was, thus, far easier for a farmer already cultivating hops successfully to finance further expansion than it was for the ordinary arable farmer, with a low turnover, to develop an initial acreage. Similarly, the successful hop farmer was able to build up capital reserves over a period of years and so he was better able to face the fluctuations in yield and market price so characteristic of hop cultivation. Thus the accumulation of capital resources from many years of successful hop cultivation created the capital by which further expansion could be financed. In this respect nothing, apparently, quite succeeded like success.

But the financial resources essential to hop cultivation were not entirely provided from within the industry. Much of the capital was provided by the country bankers and, more often, the hop factors and merchants of Southwark. For traditional reasons, specialized financial facilities—extended credit, advances, capital loans and so on—were far easier to obtain in the established locations than elsewhere.

Successful hop cultivation also required considerable skill, for it was 'too hazardous to be attempted where not well understood'. The skills were not only those of the planter who had to deal with complicated production and marketing arrangements, but also extended to the agricultural labourers of the district who were 'eminently skilled and with fair education'. The development of these skills further enhanced the position of Mid-Kent as the centre of hop cultivation, for 'the importance of having every man, woman and child already trained ... instead of having to train them is inappreciable'.[14] Hop cultivation also required a very large casual labour force at picking time; the development of a regular seasonal migration from London and elsewhere into this part of Kent gave another specific advantage to this district.[15]

One of the most important subsidiary facilities essential to hop cultivation was the supply of hop poles. Before the introduction of creosote in the 1860s and of wirework in the 1870s, the demand was very heavy; 3000 to 4000 poles were required to establish an acre of hops and 500 to 600 of these had to be replaced every year.[16] By 1800 much of the woodland along the North Downs and in the Weald, together with all available space in Mid-Kent, had been converted to the systematic production of hop poles. The development of a tradition of woodland management, designed for the production of hop poles, further encouraged expansion in and around the existing locations.

Hop cultivation also demanded enormous quantities of manure and fertilizer. The trade in manure and fodder was already developed by 1800 and it expanded rapidly during the century. By 1846 G. Buckland could write that the cost of 'oil cake and artificial manures considerably exceeds the rental'.[17] Accounts indicate that lime, dung, rags, sprats and ashes were also used.[18] In obtaining these Mid-Kent had the tremendous advantage of proximity to navigable water, but the building up of the trade in fodder and fertilizer was a further asset for the Mid-Kent hop grower.

Agglomerative advantages also existed in the process of hop marketing. The Southwark hop market, which dominated the hop trade, was one of the most unreliable of the London commodity markets. Prices shifted rapidly from day to day, and it was essential for the grower to sell his hops at exactly the right moment if he were to maximize his profit. Marketing thus required special facilities in warehousing and transport, adequate market information, and close contact between grower and factor. Once these facilities and contacts had been developed they could easily be expanded.

Prejudice in the hop trade also played its part. The parish 'mark' was very important, for every bag of hops was legally bound to have its parish of origin marked on it. Hops grown in a parish with a good reputation often sold more easily than hops from another parish irrespective of their intrinsic quality. Most Mid-Kent parishes carried a mark of high repute and this again meant a competitive advantage for the industry here. The hop market was far from operating under conditions of pure competition. The prejudices and imperfections contained within the marketing structure almost always operated in favour of the established locations.[19] Since external financial aid came mainly from the hop market, similar prejudices may also have guided decisions regarding loans and credit.

The structure of land-holding, farm occupance and landlord policy were also important. Hop cultivation generally required some outlay on the part of the landlord as well as the tenant, while some security was also essential for the tenant's capital outlay. This latter problem was largely overcome by the valuation system common to Kent, Surrey and Sussex whereby the incoming tenant paid for all manures and hop poles (the two most important items of outlay for the tenant).[20] But it was usual in the hop districts for long leases of up to 21 years to be granted. Undoubtedly the landlords in Kent pursued a policy of active encouragement to hop cultivation based on the higher rental that such cultivation yielded and the 'addition it made to the value of their woodland'.[21] Landlords who understood the special demands which hop cultivation made and who were favourably inclined towards it may well have been essential for the expansion of the hop acreage.

The advantages that have been listed here illustrate the marked economies to be had from locating new acreage in or near the traditional areas of hop cultivation. Some of these factors making for agglomeration were localized in distribution to the central area of Mid-Kent, but most were partially mobile in the sense that they could be utilized in districts close to Mid-Kent without too much extra cost. It is thus hardly surprising that the hop acreage tended to be zoned around a central core area since the costs of production were clearly affected by proximity to Mid-Kent. Economies of agglomeration would be more or less available according to distance from the centre and this factor may explain much of the peculiar locational pattern of hop cultivation within Kent. A. Lösch has summarized this tendency when commenting on the land-use structures that will emerge around centres of market activity:

> Other things being equal, profits decrease with distance from these centers, either because all shipments pass through them, or because with increasing distance their facilities can be enjoyed only with correspondingly greater difficulty.[22]

Although the factor of agglomeration was perhaps vital, it would be wrong to assume that it always operated with the same strength. Throughout most of the century it was a static factor that directed where an increase in demand could best be met, or where a decline in demand would result in contraction of acreage. But as the organization of the hop trade became more complex, as technical development brought increasing dependence upon subsidiary services, and as the transport system became focused on nodal points in the rail network, so the agglomerative pull around one specific nucleus became more important. This factor may well account for the persistent tendency for the areas in or close to Mid-Kent to grow at a more rapid rate than the more remote districts in the Weald.

Agglomeration was thus a vital factor affecting the distribution and development of the hop industry. Its main effect was one of concentrating the hop acreage in and around a central nucleus in Mid-Kent—but it was not the only process operating towards this end.

Cumulative Change

One of the most difficult problems associated with the study of locational change is that of determining how far the process of change is self-sustained. As G. Myrdal has pointed out:

> In the normal case a change does not call forth countervailing changes but, instead, supporting changes, which move the system in the same direction as the first change but much further. Because of such circular causation a social process tends to become cumulative and often to gather speed at an accelerating rate.[23]

This process of cumulative change appears to have been important to the development of the hop acreage. The development of hop cultivation in Kent had a profound effect upon social and economic structures; these changes in social and economic factors led, in turn, to the further expansion of hop cultivation. The tendency can be illustrated most readily by considering two basic elements in the farmer's costs—rent and wages.

The relationship between rent per acre and land use is a complex one. But all contemporary observers agreed that hop cultivation bore a higher rent per acre than any other form of land use apart from intensive market gardening and some forms of fruit cultivation.[24]

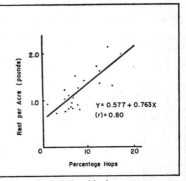

FIGURE 7—Relationship between rent per acre of agricultural land and percentage of agricultural area under hops for a block of 22 parishes in Mid-Kent *c.* 1840.
(*Source:* Land use and agricultural area from tithe awards; rent figures from British Parliamentary Papers, 1845, volume 38.)

There were, however, considerable variations in the value of hop land—a survey of rental values in Mid-Kent for 1867 indicated that the rent of hop land varied between 44s. and 105s. per acre.[25] Generally speaking, however, the greater the area under hops in any particular parish the higher was the average rent per acre likely to be. This can be illustrated by comparing the density of hops, as given by the tithe awards *c.* 1840, with the assessment of rent per acre on lands given in 1843.[26] The relationship is a fairly convincing one and yields a positive correlation coefficient of 0·80 (Fig. 7).

Once it was shown, however, that the hop land could bear a higher rent than other forms of land use, and that a particular district, such as Mid-Kent was particularly suited to that form of production, then there was a tendency for an all-round rise in rental values to take place. The value of the land was not simply assessed by what the land actually produced, but by what the valuer thought it could produce under the most advantageous system of management. No Mid-Kent landlord, for example, would tolerate a low rental because a farmer preferred to produce corn rather than hops. There were often instances of landlords deliberately raising the rent since, they argued, the tenant could easily produce more hops. The net result was that rents tended to increase on all classes of land independent of their form of cultivation.

A similar process is evident with regard to wages. These varied from district to district according to the form of land use, among other things.[27] In areas of high-quality hop production, such as Mid-Kent, day wages were higher than in the arable districts. The opportunities for remunerative piece-work were also far greater in the hop districts than they were elsewhere, so that the best labourers in the hop districts were invariably drawn into hop cultivation by the high wages offered. But the wages paid out and the competition for the best labourers varied from district to district rather than from farm to farm. Thus labour costs tended to be far higher in the hop districts than elsewhere independent of the sort of land use the individual farmer adopted. But there were other, more subtle pressures. Hop cultivation required more labourers per acre than other forms of cultivation. The net results of this was that the hop districts were faced with high social costs—cottage accommodation, provision of services, support of the poor, and so on. These social costs were often spread over a parish as a whole rather than over the hop growers only, so that parish rates and local taxes also tended to be higher in the hop districts than elsewhere.[28]

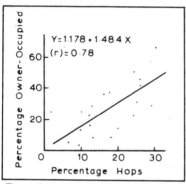

FIGURE 8—Relationship between percentage of agricultural land under hops and percentage of land farmed by owner-occupiers for 20 Mid-Kent parishes *c.* 1840.
(*Source:* Tithe Awards)

The effect of hop cultivation on the farming structure is more difficult to assess. There was undoubtedly a fairly close association between owner-occupancy and hop cultivation. Figure 8 indicates the relationship between density of hop cultivation and percentage of land under owner-occupancy for twenty Mid-Kent parishes *c.* 1840. The correlation is fairly close and gives a coefficient of 0·78. How far this relationship is evidence of a cumulative trend is difficult to assess, but undoubtedly the owner-occupiers were better able to adjust their acreage to changing demand conditions than were the tenant farmers who had to await a landlord's decision. At the same time, the existence of so many owner-occupiers could also be explained by hop cultivation since this was one of the few forms of cultivation which would allow the accumulation of sufficient capital reserves for the farmer to buy his own land. So that although there are sound historical reasons for the development of owner-occupancy in Kent (especially related to the prevailing law of gavelkind), it is very difficult to decide how far there is a one-way causal connection between this feature and the development of the hop acreage. It seems reasonable to attribute a certain cumulative element to both features.

The development of hop production undoubtedly influenced social and economic features. The net effect of these changes was the evolution of a distinctive pattern of overhead farming costs. The farmer in the hop districts was faced with a high rental, high wage costs, and high social costs irrespective of his farming system. These extra costs made his competitive position in ordinary forms of cultivation rather unsatisfactory. This provided an extra incentive to expand hop cultivation, provided economic conditions were favourable, in the already established locations which, once completed, further influenced the pattern of overhead costs. This process could continue until some sort of conformity of land use was established. Conformity, however, does not necessarily mean uniformity, for there may be more than one system of management that meets a particular pattern of overhead costs. In Mid-Kent, for example, the fruit industry formed an adequate alternative to hop cultivation.

Cumulative change was, thus, a further process that encouraged the concentration of hop cultivation into one district, by eliminating many of the alternative forms of land use. This pressure was a dynamic one, that inevitably led to conformity of land use within any particular district. Whether or not the farmer yielded to these pressures was a matter of individual choice; but the economics of the situation are clear. The net result was to reinforce the tendency towards concentration already determined by agglomerative processes.

Diminishing Returns

The concentration of hop cultivation was limited, however, by the rate of diminishing returns. Thus the process of spread outward from a central core area can be partially interpreted as 'the centrifugal effects of diminishing returns'.[29]

The tendency for overhead costs to rise with the development of hop cultivation has already been examined, but as the hop acreage expanded so the cost of many other factors of production varied. At first the cost per unit of output declined with scale of output, but after a certain limit these costs tended to increase. Some elements in the cost structure of hop farming in the central core area were thus more expensive than they were elsewhere—the rent of land and the cost of hop poles were two important examples at mid-century. The result was that the hop industry tended to be located elsewhere in order to avert these diseconomies; but the agglomerative pull meant that this relocation always took place with reference to distance from the centre. The interaction between the processes governing concentration and the centrifugal effects of diminishing returns can thus be regarded as the key explanation of the zoned distribution of the hop acreage. But this explanation depends very much upon ascertaining the point at which diminishing returns proved a serious barrier to an extension of the hop acreage.

The ultimate limit to hop cultivation was, clearly, a situation of monoculture where the entire agricultural area was given over to hop cultivation. But the statistics indicate that hops rarely accounted for more than 35 per cent of cultivated area, while 15 per cent was more normal. Simple percentage figures conceal much, however.

Sir Charles Middleton's account of his farm at Teston in the late eighteenth century indicates an interesting situation. Ony 40 out of the 260 acres were under hops, yet the whole farm was oriented to the needs of hop-growing. The hop ground made very heavy demands upon manure and fertilizer, and the account outlines how much of the farm was given over to the production of fodder crops:

> this year, I take it for granted, I shall be out of pocket by fatting stock more than two hundred pounds ... yet with all these losses attending feeding in this way, I find it answers on the whole; and without such expenses I could not possibly keep up the quantity of hop ground, in the state it now is. We look, in general, to hops for profit; and most farmers in this neighbourhood think themselves well off, if they do not lose by their arable.[30]

Because of the heavy manure requirements, 15 per cent of the farm was capable of dominating the rest. Under the Mid-Kent system, the bulk of the farm was a fertilizer factory which 'nothing but the all-receiving and frequently all-paying hop-garden would justify'.[31]

These heavy demands for manure could partially be met by bringing onto the farm either manure or cattle fodder, but both these alternatives tended to be rather expensive and to increase costs of unit output. Thus the farmer could cultivate 10 to 15 per cent of his land under hops without depending too heavily on external supplies of manure and fodder. But beyond this limit the farmer could only increase the hop acreage provided that dependence upon external supplies of manure and fodder did not result in increasing unit costs. When hop prices were high and fodder prices low, the farmer could obviously afford to cultivate a higher density of hops on his farm—in this respect the optimum density of hop cultivation fluctuated with prices and demand. But technical considerations were also important. The cost of obtaining fertilizer and fodder varied regionally, so that higher densities were achieved in Mid-Kent—with its access to cheap water transport—than in the remoter parts of the Weald. These costs also varied with time, so that with the cheapening of freight rates after 1850 and the development of a national trade in artificial fertilizer and cattle feeds, higher densities became possible.

There was thus some sort of optimum economic level for the density of hop cultivation. Empirical definition of this level is impossible because of the many variables involved. In the latter part of the century some farms had 80 per cent or more of their acreage under hops, but the large quantities of manure and fodder required clearly made this system expensive to operate. In general the farmer kept the proportion of hops down to the level where most of the fertilizer requirements could be provided from within the farm. This was true even on the smaller farms and there was surprisingly little variation in the proportion of the land under hops in different farm size groups (Table II). It can be assumed that 10 to 15 per cent of the agricultural area could be cultivated without difficulty, but at some point above this level, rising costs tended to check any increase in acreage. The evidence of actual densities suggests that this level lay somewhere between 15 and 35 per cent of the agricultural area throughout most of the century. It is impossible to pin it down more closely than that.

But in spite of its vagueness, this concept has considerable importance. In particular it serves to explain the changing fortunes of the Mid-Kent industry, for by 1826 the hop acreage appears to have reached an optimum level so that further expansion would have certainly meant rising costs per unit of output. This may account for the lack of expansion in Mid-Kent between 1830 and 1850. After 1850, however, declining costs of obtaining fertilizer and fodder in conjunction with a phase of very remunerative prices entailed a renewed expansion

TABLE II

Hop Cultivation and Land Occupance in Seven Mid-Kent Parishes, c. 1840

Farm size group	Percentage of agricultural land in group	Percentage of hop acreage in group	Mean percentage of hops on each farm in group
1–10	3·0	5·6	29·7
10–50	9·9	13·0	21·0
50–150	20·7	17·6	13·5
150–300	28·3	25·7	14·5
300–600	38·0	38·1	15·9
Owner-occupied	30·2	32·5	18·3

(*Source*: Tithe commutation awards for East and West Barming, Mereworth, Teston, Wateringbury and East and West Farleigh)

of hop cultivation in the core area. The development of the Mid-Kent acreage before 1878 may thus be interpreted as a function of fluctuations in the economic and technological conditions which determined the optimum density of hop cultivation.

Summary

There were three basic processes governing the tendency for the hop acreage to be ranged in zones of declining density around a specific centre of production. First, agglomeration of production allowed the grower to benefit from economies of scale in or near the established locations. The traditional centre of hop cultivation, Mid-Kent, accordingly exercised a powerful influence over the subsequent spread of the hop acreage. Second, the development of hop cultivation engendered strong cumulative pressures that tended to eliminate most rival forms of cultivation by imposing a specific pattern of overhead costs. Agglomeration meant economies of scale in the established locations, cumulative change meant cost diseconomies for rival forms of land use. The net result was a tendency towards concentration which was only effectively limited by diminishing returns after an optimum acreage density had been reached. The relative strengths of these three processes were by no means constant, however, and the fluctuating development of the hop acreage around the Mid-Kent core may be explained by the fluctuating importance of each process as economic and technological conditions changed.

Conclusions

This article has illustrated how two specific processes—agglomeration and cumulative change—can lead to concentration of production. It has also illustrated how diminishing returns, operating in the face of expanding demand, can lead to a spread of a particular form of production out into areas which possess no inherent advantages for that form, apart from proximity to an initial production centre.

It is unfortunately impossible in the remaining space to attempt any general survey of how these processes have, or might, influence forms of agriculture other than hop cultivation. In this there would be a major difficulty because of the lack of empirical knowledge on the subject; even such an important feature as the operation of internal and external economies of scale, with which the process of agglomeration is closely allied, has been given very scant attention in the literature.[32] But nevertheless some theoretical points can be made about these processes.

The importance of diminishing returns in agriculture has long been recognized. In the face of expanding demand the finite factor of land yields at a diminishing rate as its use is intensified, until it proves cheaper to move production to an alternative location, providing, of course, that land is available elsewhere. If all the factors of production (skill, technical knowledge, capital, labour, and so on) are completely mobile, then the alternative site chosen would obviously be determined by optimum physical considerations. But these factors are only partially mobile and the friction of distance acts in such a way as to make the spread out of cultivation partially a function of distance from the initial centre. This sort of process has been discussed in the greatest detail in terms of the diffusion of innovations and the evolution of settlement patterns, while gravity and potential models of economic activity may also have some relevance.[33] In fact it is not uncommon for agricultural distributions to be ranged around a series of nodal centres in declining zones of intensity; the location of fruit growing in either Kent or Worcestershire is one such example, while Lösch has noticed a similar feature in the pattern of cotton production in the U.S.A.[34] Further evidence is certainly worth looking for.

The case of cumulative change, however, is difficult. Any particular farmer should decide which crop or combination of crops to cultivate in terms of the demand (price) for each commodity and his relevant costs of factor inputs. But the cost of factor inputs will vary with the cumulative decisions of all the farmers in any particular district. This can have two diametrically opposed effects. The first would be declining costs in one form of production through economies of scale, and rising costs in all other forms of production because of the creation of a specific pattern of overhead costs. This will lead to concentration of production. The second effect could be a decline in factor costs for several lines of production through a fuller use of all factor inputs; one form of production may employ labour fully for certain limited periods only, and it will therefore benefit the farmer to adopt some complementary form of production to use up this unused factor at a time of the year when it is under-employed. This second tendency leads to diversification of production.[35] For most ordinary forms of production a modest degree of diversity is probably the most desirable situation, but for highly specialized forms of production—hops, fruit, market gardening, and so on—the cumulative tendency is probably dominant. The cumulative process which was demonstrated by reference to the hop industry, probably only applies, therefore, to highly specialized forms of agriculture which create very marked patterns of overhead cost.

The process of agglomeration also depends upon the variation in factor costs with the cumulative decisions of many farmers in any district. But in this context we are dealing with the problem of competition between different agricultural regions in producing the same crop, rather than with the factors that influence the choice from a variety of alternative crops within any one district. Agglomeration in agriculture is simply an example of those 'economies of specialization' which form a basic tenet of international trade theory. The pattern of international trade in agricultural produce is as much a result of these economies as is trade in industrial products; the Danish dairy industry and the Canadian wheat industry are typical examples where economies of scale and specialization result from the adoption by numerous producing units of similar forms of production. But, as B. Ohlin and subsequent writers have pointed out, trade theory does not cease to apply below national units; it can also be applied to inter-regional patterns of trade within any country.[36] The logic behind economies of scale through agglomeration of agricultural production into regional specialisms is just as strong as it is for inter-regional trade theory as a whole. In determining which region specializes on which crop or combination of crops, it is comparative advantage rather than absolute advantage which matters.[37] It may be, for example, that Mid-Kent has an absolute advantage over East Anglia in both hop and sugar-beet production, but it is nevertheless mutually advantageous for each district to specialize on one crop.

The difficulty that arises here, of course, is to differentiate between the economic and physical factors involved in regional specialization. The sort of situation that could arise may be demonstrated in the following way.

If we assume two crops making equal demands upon factors of soil and climate, and assume two separate districts of equal physical capacity and position relative to the market, then there is no physical reason why each district should not split its productive capacity equally between the two crops. If the two crops are not complementary, and there are no economies of integration, then economies of specialization will lead to agglomeration and each district will concentrate on one crop only. Which district concentrates on which crop may be determined by chance. If we now drop the assumption of equal physical conditions, and assume a situation where there are minor differences in productive capacity between the two districts, then regional specialization will still occur provided that the mutual economies of specialization are greater than the diseconomies of cultivating one crop under inferior conditions. Again, which district specializes on which crop may be determined by chance. Two districts of slightly different physical capacity are now cultivated under completely different cropping systems, but it is impossible to argue in this case that the cause of the difference is the difference in physical capacity even though there is a coincidence between the two distributions. It is, thus, dangerous to argue about agricultural distributions and physical capacity in a way that assumes that coincidence between the two is proof of causal connection.

The sort of confusion that may arise is illustrated by two recent articles on dairying in Great Britain. In an article on Cheshire, E. S. Simpson illustrates the stability of land use in the face of rapidly changing technology and economic conditions. Because stability exists, and because it is a district of certain physical characteristics, Simpson concludes that the stability 'gives some measure of the strength of the contribution of the physical environment to the agricultural economy'.[38] A similar feature of stability in the face of changing price support policy was noted by F. A. Barnes in an article on the Anglesey dairy industry. But the conclusion in this case is that 'events in Anglesey are demonstrating that once capital has been fixed in the necessary buildings, equipment and herds in an area of small farms such as this, dairying is strongly resistant to change'.[39]

Physical factors may well be a fundamental cause of stability in the Cheshire and Anglesey cases, but there are also good economic reasons for stability— as R. O. Buchanan has pointed out, 'the specialized area ... will fight to the last ditch rather than accept a change of specialization'.[40] The explanation of stability is undoubtedly very complex, but land-use systems grow and develop and the factors that govern evolution are so very complex that there is an inherent danger that physical coincidence will be read as physical causation.

The initial location of a particlar form of production in an empty area may be 'explained' (so far as it is rationally explicable) by a relatively simple interaction between demand factors and innate physical capacity assessed in terms of current technology. But once an initial location pattern has been developed, the factors that govern its subsequent evolution multiply in complexity. Fundamental changes in agricultural technology, transport technology, consumer taste, and so on, may alter the whole context of resources, distance and demand. But it is clear also that there are systematic economic factors that also govern the 'where' and 'how' of agricultural development. The factors of agglomeration, cumulative change and diminishing returns are only three elements in a complex matrix of causal interconnections. But their operation is surely worth consideration in any final analysis of the logic of locational patterns in agriculture.

ACKNOWLEDGMENT

The author is indebted to the Colston Fund in the University of Bristol for a grant towards the cost of the illustrations.

NOTES

[1] For a full account see D. W. HARVEY, *Aspects of agricultural and rural change in Kent, 1800–1900*, unpublished Ph.D. dissertation, University of Cambridge (1961).

[2] Ibid., appendix 2.

[3] Ibid., appendix 1. Generally speaking the acreages recorded by the Hop Excise are accurate, but the published parish statistics (contained in yearly volumes of the British Parliamentary Papers 1822–62) must be treated with care since acreages often appear to 'float' from one parish to the next. There are other minor errors in compilation and printing that make detailed use of the statistics difficult. But the general accuracy of the returns need not be doubted. For a critique of the agricultural statistics see J. T. COPPOCK, 'The statistical assessment of British agriculture', *Agricultural History Review*, 4 (1956), 4–21 and 66–79.

[4] For a full account of these models see W. ISARD, *Methods of regional analysis* (1960), chapter 11. In this case the gravity model adopted was given by the formula

$$g = \sum \frac{p}{d}$$

where

p is the density of hops in any parish
d is its distance away.

When the value for g had been ascertained for the parishes in and around the centre of hop cultivation, the parish with the highest g value was then designated the 'centre of gravity' of hop cultivation.

[5] B. S. FURNEAUX, 'Soils for hop growing', *Journal of the Southeastern Agricultural College, Wye*, 44 (1939), 30–6.

[6] A. D. HALL and E. J. RUSSELL, *A report on the agriculture and soils of Kent, Surrey and Sussex* (1911).

[7] W. A. BANE and G. H. G. JONES, 'Fruit growing areas on the Lower Greensand in Kent', *Ministry of Agriculture, Bulletin* No. 80 (1934).

[8] N. B. BAGENAL and B. S. FURNEAUX, 'Fruit growing areas on the Hastings Beds in Kent', *Ministry of Agriculture, Bulletin* No. 141 (1949).

[9] W. TOPLEY, 'On the comparative agriculture of England and Wales', *Journal of the Royal Agricultural Society*, Second series, 7 (1871), 269–84; and 'On the agricultural geology of the Weald', *Journal of the Royal Agricultural Society*, Second series, 8 (1872), 241–67.

[10] W. ISARD, *Location and space economy* (1954), chapter 8.

[11] LORD AMHERST, 'An account of Hall Farm, Sevenoaks', *Journal of the Royal Agricultural Society*, 8 (1848), 33–46. For a general summary of expenses see H. H. PARKER, *The hop industry* (1934), chapter 2 and appendix 2.

[12] 'Report of the Select Committee on the operation of excise and customs duties on hops', *British Parliamentary Papers* (1857, session 2, volume 14), qq. 3753–4.

[13] P. MATHIAS, *The brewing industry in England 1700–1830* (1959), 477; A. YOUNG, 'A fortnight's tour in Kent and Essex', *Annals of Agriculture*, 2 (1784), 70–7; and C. WHITEHEAD, 'On recent improvements in the cultivation and management of hops', *Journal of the Royal Agricultural Society*, Second series, 6 (1870), 336–66.

[14] *Maidstone Gazette*, editorial of 14 April 1846.

[15] J. Y. STRATTON, *Hops and hop pickers* (1884).

[16] H. H. PARKER, op. cit., 64.

[17] G. BUCKLAND, 'On the farming of Kent', *Journal of the Royal Agricultural Society*, 6 (1846), 273.

[18] Details of this trade are given in the Medway navigation accounts, Kent Archives Office, S/MN, A21.

[19] 'Report of the Select Committee on ... hops', op. cit. (1857), qq. 1162, 2168 et seq.

[20] 'Report of the Select Committee on agricultural customs', *British Parliamentary Papers*, (1847–48, volume 7), q. 6607; and T. B. GRAINGER and L. KENNEDY, *The present state of the tenancy of land in Great Britain* (1828), 249–51.

[21] 'Report of the Select Committee on ... hops', op. cit. (1857), q. 2621.

[22] A. LÖSCH, *The economics of location* (1954), 87.

[23] G. MYRDAL, *Economic theory and underdeveloped regions* (1957), 13.

[24] A. YOUNG, op. cit., 94; G. BUCKLAND, op. cit., 279.

[25] R. W. TOOTELL, 'Hop cultivation', *Transactions of the Royal Institute of Surveyors*, 11 (1879), 296.

[26] For the use of these returns see D. B. GRIGG, 'Changing regional values during the agricultural revolution in south Lincolnshire', *Transactions and Papers*, Institute of British Geographers, 30 (1962), 91–104.

[27] D. W. HARVEY, op. cit., chapter 5.

[28] Ibid., 257.

[29] W. ISARD, op. cit. (1954), 4.

[30] SIR CHARLES MIDDLETON, 'Queries relative to the farm at Teston, Kent', *Communications to the Board of Agriculture*, 2 (1800), 119–27.

[31] G. BUCKLAND, op. cit., 273.

[32] For this approach see E. O. HEADY, *Economics of agricultural production and resource use* (1952), 360–3.

[33] T. HÄGERSTRAND, 'The propogation of innovation waves', *Lund Studies in Geography*, Series B, 4.(1952); E. BYLUND, 'Theoretical considerations regarding the distribution of settlement in inner north Sweden', *Geografiska Annaler*, 42 (1960), 225–31.

[34] K. M. BUCHANAN, *Report of the Land Utilization Survey of Britain*, Part 68, *Worcestershire* (1944) (especially the maps on pp. 636, 648 and 649); and L. DUDLEY STAMP, ibid., Part 85, *Kent* (1943), 581. Also A. LÖSCH, op. cit., 87.

[35] For a full analysis of this process see T. BRINKMANN, *The economics of the farm business* (English edition 1935), 62–71.

[36] B. OHLIN, *Interregional and international trade* (1933); and W. ISARD (1960), op. cit., chapter 8.

[37] E. O. HEADY, op. cit.

[38] E. S. SIMPSON, 'The Cheshire grass-dairying region', *Transactions and Papers*, Institute of British Geographers, 23 (1957), 162.

[39] F. A. BARNES, 'Dairying in Anglesey', *Transactions and Papers*, Institute of British Geographers, 21 (1955), 137–56.

[40] R. O. BUCHAN, 'Some reflections on agricultural geography', *Geography*, 44 (1959), 12.

Supplementary Note

I suppose there is a natural tendency to look upon work past done with a certain amount of embarrassment and a certain amount of affection. My embarrassment in this case stems from the technical and theoretical naivete of the work. Correlation and regression techniques are misused for example. The data are not normalised, the observations are certainly not independent, and they are drawn in any case from areal units of varying size (and I therefore rode roughshod over all the technical complexities posed by spatial autocorrelation and the scale problem[1]). Under these conditions the inferences made must be regarded as tenuous. I prefer, therefore, to regard the graphs as portraying the *direction* of relationships and to ignore the correlation and regression measures. Fortunately, these technical results are embellishments rather than central pinions in the work. On the theoretical side I must also confess that I had very little understanding of the importance of location theory in analyses of this kind - a gap in my knowledge that I have since endeavoured to fill.[2,3] My feeling is that this study would have been far more percpetive of process and interaction if I had only possessed an adequate grounding in locational analysis.

The affection I have for the work is partly nostalgia for the three years I spent trying to understand the way in which the Kentish agricultural community worked and changed its whole style of living over an extended time-period. I found this kind of work intuitively satisfying and I believe that there is no substitute for really getting to know the place and time of action in order to achieve an adequate understanding of it. Here, the classical method of the historical geographer has much to recommend it. But my affection also stems from the way in which I found myself forced to reach out from this basic intuitive understanding for some kind of adequate framework which would somehow or other pin my thoughts together in a coherent fashion. This framework I eventually constructed out of rudimentary notions of spatial interaction, cumulative causation, and the like. In this, of course I was reaching out for some adequate theoretical framework. The lesson to be learned, therefore, is that historical geography can only progress through a careful integration of theory and empiricism.

1   Harvey, D.W. 'Pattern, process and the scale problem in geographical research', *Transactions of the Institute of British Geographers,* 45 (1968) pp 71-8

2   Harvey, D.W. 'Theoretical concepts and the analysis of agricultural land use patterns in geography', *Annals of the Association of American Geographers,* 56 (1966) pp 361-74

3   Harvey, D.W. 'Models of the evolution of spatial patterns in human geography' being pp 549-608 of Chorley, R.J. and Haggett, P. (eds), *Models in Geography* (London, 1967)

DAVID HARVEY   August 1969

The Urban Hierarchy and Historical Geography: A Consideration with Reference to North-East Wales
H. Carter
Reprinted from *Geographical Studies,* 3 (1956), 85-101

THE URBAN HIERARCHY
AND HISTORICAL GEOGRAPHY:
A CONSIDERATION WITH REFERENCE TO
NORTH-EAST WALES

By Harold Carter

The major part of geographical and sociological work which has been devoted to the concept of an urban hierarchy since it was first outlined has undoubtedly been aimed at refining the process by which towns are classified into grades. Alongside this have been parallel attempts to improve methods of defining urban fields. Christaller's earliest suggestions for grading towns[1] did not lend themselves to wide application, for the special criterion he used was not suitable for transference to very different conditions. Accordingly A. E. Smailes presented a much fuller scheme for England and Wales[2] which was mainly aimed at identifying the fully fledged town but also identified ranks above that level and varieties of sub-town below it. This scheme was based on the examination of the functional institutions[3] which each town possessed; more recently H. E. Bracey has elaborated this first assessment for particular areas.[4] Bracey's method is based on the examination of appropriate places, usually parish villages, in the countryside, and from data so collected he makes an attempt to estimate the degree to which various towns participate in the satisfaction of a standard array of wants arising in these villages. This has resulted in his identifying as many as six grades of towns. This method would be difficult to apply uniformly to the whole country and would run into great difficulties in areas of dispersed rural settlement. Above all, such analysis relies on an elaborate questionnaire with a comparatively large number of returns. The use of the questionnaire is equally essential in the survey being carried out by Smailes as chairman of the Geographical Association's Standing Committee on Urban Spheres of Influence. On the standard form nine items are listed with many subdivisions. Although intended primarily to identify spheres of influence, it is clear that the information can also be used to grade towns.

As geographers refine their means of analysis of the present landscape and of the functions of the visible objects which compose it, their methods will inevitably be utilized to examine past geographies. And these methods may be used not only to analyse a particular past period, but also to understand the moving picture of the past from which the present is derived, for it must now be axiomatic that study of past conditions and of historical process markedly aids interpretation of the present. It follows from this that a study of a past period, that is, historical geography as the purist would conceive it, should include a study of the contemporary hierarchy of towns and patterns of urban fields. If a series of such studies were put together (as suggested in Fig. 1) then a picture of town growth or decline would be vividly portrayed. Such a scheme would be of great value to the geographer for it would clarify the whole complex process of town growth or decay and depict it as simply as possible. From this simple depiction the geographical factors at work could be

269

isolated and emphasized. The relations between function and position and site, from which the particular role of the physical environment can be assessed, could also be effectively analysed and the present situation placed in its true perspective. Indeed such historical considerations are invoked in most modern *interpretations* of the urban hierarchy.

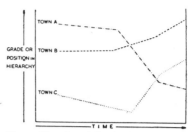

Fig. 1. Hypothetical Graph of Town Grade against Time.

It is unfortunate that there are many drawbacks to this ideal scheme. Attempts to construct hierarchies for past periods become not only impossible but even undesirable. The major immediate drawbacks can be listed and others subsequently noted during a consideration of north-east Wales.

(1) As already outlined at the beginning of this paper, as methods of identifying urban grades become more and more intricate, so does their application to the past become impossible. Questionnaires cannot be used and hence the earlier method used by Smailes, the selection of a complex of institutions, is the only one that can be successfully adopted.

(2) Not only do methods change but so do town functions. Though the basic function of towns, the service rendered for a tributary area, is constant, nevertheless a variety of other functions has been super-imposed upon it. The Industrial Revolution for example created towns that had no regional service function. It is therefore important that a 'trait complex'[5] of institutions that is in keeping with the whole range of town functions at any particular period under consideration should be used.

(3) There is the additional difficulty that even if the actual functions remain the same they are not represented by the same institutions. It is self-evident that Woolworths and head post offices, banks and secondary grammar schools are all of relatively recent origin. It is now clear that for any historical period a distinctive set of criteria must be chosen, possibly representing a changed array of functions, and an entirely new grading scheme constructed. This in turn means that there cannot be any direct link between grades in the hierarchy at one period and those at another since these grades may imply completely different concepts in their appropriate periods. This vitiates the whole idea of the dynamic picture which one might achieve as suggested in Fig. 1.

(4) Even if this were not sufficient to deter an historical analysis, there is the added factor that prior to the Directories which were published at the end of the eighteenth and the beginning of the nineteenth centuries, there is very little information which can be used in constructing a hierarchy and which is common to a large area. It is

true that for limited areas there is information sufficiently reliable and relevant to be employed[6] but, prior to the useful index provided by chain-stores, the simple classi-fication of a settlement as a market town is perhaps the only one that can be achieved. The only alternative is to use purely administrative criteria. This is satisfactory only to a limited extent since there is the obvious problem that administrative functions are slow to change and are often anachronistic when related to economic realities. The immediate danger is that the study becomes one of boroughs rather than of towns, and Smailes has succinctly pointed out[7] that the geographer is interested in *towns* not boroughs, that is, in the functioning settlement of urban status not in the settlement which possesses merely the external trappings of the borough. It is also true that the further one goes back the less significant becomes the distinction. If therefore, administrative criteria are to be used, then quite clearly a great deal of discretion is needed in their employment.

(5) Lastly a case must be made for the very attempt to construct hierarchies rather than the standard use of population figures. Apart from the obvious reason that borough boundaries are such that figures are often completely arbitrary, there is the basic drawback that uniform reliable data become available only at the beginning of the nineteenth century. Before the Industrial Revolution there was clearly a better balance between the population of a town and its significance as a regional service centre. It was this balance, among so many other things, that the Industrial Revolu-tion destroyed, but the absence of census data before this period precludes classifica-tion by population.

These considerations present a formidable, indeed an insurmountable array of difficulties. Nevertheless the problem is one which deserves further study even if no successful solution can be presented for the problems which arise.

The first example of a hierarchy constructed for a past period applies to the years 1830-35. A hierarchy in the past must utilize material covering several years. This seems permissible if the gap be short and if there were no vital changes during the interval covered by the material used. The author has elsewhere[8] constructed a hierarchy for the whole of Wales for that period, but the north-eastern part (Fig. 2) may be taken to illustrate the procedure. The type of information available may be summarized under appropriate headings with brief comment.

Fig. 2. North-East Wales

271

Market:
It is impossible to refine this simple criterion before the days of nation-wide department stores. It can be accepted as the basic qualification for urban status.

Numbers employed in Trade and Handicrafts, 1831 Census:
This is a fairly satisfactory measure of economic activity which has been used on other occasions for similar purposes.

Numbers of Shopkeepers; Commercial Directories, 1830:
This can be used to supplement the above since in many Directories the types of shops are enumerated and a more refined selection appropriate to the commercial functions can be made. The Directories are, however, open to errors and omissions.

Banks:
Banking was in an early phase of development in Wales and before the dominance of the 'Big Five' the exact definition of a bank is difficult. It is better to accept lists in contemporary Directories and assume that the significant have been included.

Insurance Agents:
Insurance agencies were also in a period of development but they can be included as an indication of the important centres where business would be sought.

SOCIAL FUNCTIONS

Theatres:
A relatively permanent theatre can be taken as an indication of the importance of a town. Theatres would, however, be more important in the Anglicized boroughs than in the 'Welsh towns'.

Newspapers:
At this period the development of weekly newspapers in Wales was in its infancy and consequently the publication of a weekly cannot be used as a criterion.

Grammar Schools:
The grammar schools in existence at this time were usually Tudor foundations and reflected former conditions rather than those of the period under consideration.

Numbers in Professions:
This can be used as indicative of the social life of a town though it is also a useful reflection of the all-round economic and administrative activity of a town.

ADMINISTRATIVE FUNCTIONS

Assize Towns and Quarter Sessions:
These are both useful but, although the location was often changed with changes in town status, there is the danger that past conditions were carried through and hence the contemporary position falsified.

Poor Law Union Heads:
This is one of the most useful criteria since the Poor Law Commissioners stated: 'The most convenient limit of Unions we have found has been that of a circle taking a market town as a centre and comprehending those surround-

ing parishes whose inhabitants are accustomed to resort to the same market.'[9] The chosen centre must therefore have played a prominent part in the servicing of the countryside.

The task is now to choose satisfactory criteria from this array. It must be emphasized that the writer does not maintain that he can identify any trait complex of institutions, that is any group of these indices tending to occur in standard association. In consequence it is a selection of significant and relevant data to give a satisfactory grading which has been made below:

Market Town and Poor Law Union Head	A
Market Town only (Minimum qualification)	A_1
Over 500 employed in Trade and Handicrafts, 1831 Census	B
Over 200 employed in Trade and Handicrafts, 1831 Census	B_1
Over 10 noted as in Professions, Pigot and Co's *National and Commercial Directory*, 1829-30	C
One or more Banks noted in above *Directory*	D
Theatre	E

This gives a suggested grouping in north-east Wales as follows:

ABCDE	Wrexham	Group 1
A_1B_1CD	Denbigh	Group 2
AB_1C	Ruthin	
ABD	Holywell	Group 3
A	St. Asaph	
A_1	Mold, Flint, Llangollen, Hawarden, Abergele	Group 4

The four groups in this grading can be justified as representing valid distinctions in rank and condition. Wrexham was clearly the head and, if Chester be excluded, the metropolis of the area. Denbigh and Ruthin both represent a stage below this. The fact that Denbigh was not a Union Head is to some extent an anomaly and perhaps AB_1CD for Denbigh and a simple A_1 for St. Asaph would have been a more suitable

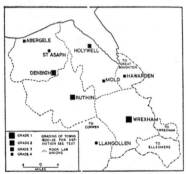

Fig. 3. Town Grades and Spheres of Influence in North-East Wales, 1830-35.

reflection of actual conditions. In comparison with Wrexham, Denbigh and Ruthin are deficient in commercial and economic, but tend to be equal in administrative and possibly in social functions. This is due to the industrialization of east Denbighshire which had progressed apace since the 1770's. This feature is reflected in the unique conditions at Holywell. This settlement, as its name implies, was in origin a small grouping of houses around a well, dedicated to a Celtic Saint.[10] It had been transformed into a town by the growth of industry, so that while it was fully represented in commercial and economic functions, it was partly deficient in social and administrative activities. The remaining towns are all small in size and status and either served to fill the gaps where the efficiency of the larger towns was at its minimum or were being revivified by the growth of industry.

This grading, for a period over a century ago, seems fairly satisfactory. The criteria are reasonably appropriate and fairly accessible. Moreover, if necessary, the Poor Law Unions could be used, along with supplementary material relating to coach journeys and carriers to market, to identify spheres of influence (Fig. 3).

Having now suggested and examined a grading of towns during the early nineteenth century, the next step is to attempt to carry this process still further back. Perhaps the most appropriate period to choose is one toward the end of the sixteenth century when sufficient time had elapsed for the decline of those medieval boroughs which did not achieve the transition from created strong point to functioning town, and also for the administrative system created by the act of Union with England and the Act of 1542 to have become operative. The criteria that can be used are now very limited. The following can be suggested.

Presence of Market: This must again be the basic qualification for town status and no town without a regular market can be considered.

Towns with a Chancery and Exchequer: These were created by the Act of Union, four towns to be the local capitals of Wales. They were Carmarthen, Brecon, Caernarvon and Denbigh. These can be accepted at their face value as regional capitals.

Assize Towns: Such towns can be accepted as those most convenient for general assembly and hence those most commonly used. The major difficulty is that Assize towns were created on a county basis. Thus in two neighbouring counties an important town in the one (in which there was a still more significant town) would be graded below an unimportant town which, because it was the largest in the other, was the one in which administrative functions were fixed. As long as this possibility is borne in mind, together with the fact that two towns were often nominated (since Assizes were held twice yearly), this criterion can be accepted.

Charter of Incorporation, 1485-1600: This is a much more debatable criterion. Generally incorporation is the process which 'unites and emphasizes all the tendencies contained in the heyday of charter giving and building of new towns. It is as if a common roof has been found for a massive and irregular building'.[11] But while this is so, and although Henry VIII in 1542 had 're-served to himself the right for seven years of annulling the little corporate towns of Wales that were reduced to mediocre rank' so that those that could present positive evidence of progress were confirmed in their status, the fact that incorporation applied only to the chartered Norman boroughs prevents its use as a common criterion.

Grammar Schools: At this period the founding of a Grammar School can surely be accepted as an indication of the importance of a town in the life of the area which it served and is therefore worthy of inclusion. It should be noted, however, that in this case the reverse proposition is not necessarily true, for the absence of a grammar school does not indicate a lack of status.

General Description: There is much comment available on these towns in the works of Camden,[12] Speed,[13] Leland,[14] and George Owen of Henllys.[15] This material can, in part, be utilized but only for limited areas. While kept in reserve to aid interpretation, therefore, this subjective and perhaps biased information cannot be utilized in grading schemes.

From the above the following criteria can be selected for the grading scheme:

Market Town	A
Chancery and Exchequer	B
Assize Town	C
Grammar School	D

In the north-east this gives:

ABC	Denbigh
ACD	Wrexham
AD	Ruthin
A	Caerwys

This scheme is thin and certainly not as complete as that envisaged in the ideal scheme as shown on Fig. 1. There seem to be no other measures that can be used and in many respects the comments of the writers noted above are more valuable than this attenuated list. But the minimum criterion, the presence of a market, cannot be waived. Denbigh stands out as the head of the hierarchy and was later to acquire a grammar school in the eighteenth century. It had already been chosen as the admin-istrative centre of the north-east and, if it is suggested that this was due to its borough tradition rather than its economic significance, then recourse can be had to contem-porary comment. Speed categorically states: 'Here stands the faire toune and goodly castle of Denbigh situated upon a rock, the greatest market towne in North-Wales.'[16] Wrexham appears to rank above Ruthin, while Caerwys, the only market town in Flintshire and a very minor one at that, is very much of an inferior: 'No goode town in the shire' says George Owen.[17]

If now any attempt is made to carry interest still further back it is clear that emphasis must change from the construction of grading schemes to the questions of origins. This is a special problem which cannot be dealt with here but nevertheless it has its interests in this context. In Wales prior to the Industrial Revolution there were two classes of towns. The first is the castle town consisting both of the true bastide and of the more haphazard collections of houses developed around a castle node and granted a charter. The second class contains towns that have 'native' origins, that is where urban functions have devolved on a pre-Norman settlement which thus served as a pre-urban nucleus. These nuclei were either *maerdref* (tribal caputs) or churches founded by Celtic missionaries in the Age of the Saints, or Roman forts and encampments. The first of the above classes, the castle town, was composed of settlements founded and favoured as towns and, as it were, given a strong push towards the higher grades of the hierarchy. The second class had no such advantages and it is therefore of great interest to examine why some of the former should have failed and many of the latter have become higher graded towns. Such an examination would have to be carried out in terms of the developing urban hierarchy and the nature of services rendered for tributary areas.

Having discussed why a grading scheme cannot be projected beyond the sixteenth century, we can, however, partly complete the sequence by relating the historical gradings to the modern hierarchy. An attempt can thus be made to construct a graph (Fig. 4) such as that envisaged in Fig. 1. For this modern period the type of grading suggested by Smailes is used but more detailed analysis is carried out, and this sug-

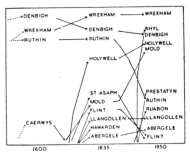

Fig. 4. Graph of Town Grade against Time in North-East Wales.

gests a breakdown of the fully fledged towns into two groups, Wrexham standing above them as a major town. Rhyl and Denbigh form the first group and Holywell and Mold the second; the remainder are classed as sub-towns in status. In detail the grading scheme is based on the simple possession of:

Three of the 'Big Five' banks	A
All or part of a range of chain stores	BB₁
Head post office	C

In addition, to complete the picture the presence of a grammar school (G), one or more cinemas (X) and the publication of a local newspaper (N) has been indicated, together with the population at the 1951 Census.

Wrexham	ABC	GNX	30,962	Major Town	1
Rhyl	ABC	GNX	18,745		
Denbigh	ABC	GNX	8,127	Fully Fledged	
Holywell	AB_1C	GNX	8,196	Towns	2
Mold	AB_1C	GNX	6,436		
Ruabon	AB_1	G-X	—		
Ruthin	AB_1	G-X	3,599		
Prestatyn	AB_1	-NX	8,809	Sub-Towns	3
Llangollen	A_1B_1	G-X	3,275		
Abergele	A	GNX	7,539		
Flint	A	--X	14,257		

The last two sub-towns could possibly be excluded, but at Abergele the surprising array of functions other than those primarily employed in the grading, and the population figures for both settlements, show that these must be retained for consideration.

From the diagram presented (Fig. 4), the following main points emerge for consideration.

(1) There has apparently been competition for the role of capital of north-east Wales which has resulted in a change of leadership in the hierarchy.

(2) There appears to have been an entry of small towns into the nineteenth-century grading which contrasts very markedly with the absence of such towns in the earlier grading. This is in spite of the many possibilities offered in the earlier period by the many medieval boroughs which had been founded.

(3) The growth of industry has added significant members to the hierarchy.

These three points can be discussed in turn and at the same time the efficacy of the diagram can be measured.

Denbigh was undoubtedly the acknowledged capital of the north-east in the sixteenth century and was clearly recognized as such by the Act of Union. This was no doubt partly due to its tradition as a walled castle town after which the shire itself was named. It had the advantage of being centrally situated within the county which includes part of the Hiraethog Moorlands, the Vale of Clwyd and the Clwydian range and extends eastward into the border lowlands (Fig. 2). It lacked, however, the major nodality which is nearly always found to be characteristic of the local capital before the days of industry. Although it was situated opposite and commanding the Bodfari Gap it was on no major through route. This is reflected by the fact that the Assizes were later moved from Denbigh to Ruthin which 'from its central situation . . . has been selected in preference to the town of Denbigh for holding the Assizes for the county'.[18] Ruthin could play the part of intermediary between western moorland, central vale and eastern lowlands much more successfully owing to its location in the peculiarly shaped county, while Denbigh had no major nodality to set against its eccentric position. Still, in the sixteenth and early seventeenth centuries Denbigh was undoubtedly the local capital by virtue of its being the service centre for the Vale of Clwyd. The comment of Speed that it was the greatest market town in North Wales has already been noted, while Leland recorded 'in the market place well builded, which is fair, and large, and paved of late years, the confluence to the Market on Tuesday is exceeding great'.[19] Ruthin at the period, 'not much inferior in goodness' to Denbigh as Owen noted,[20] was the local centre for the southern part of the vale.

The exact position of Wrexham in the hierarchy is not easy to assess. It appears on the earliest grading as intermediate between Denbigh and Ruthin and seems to have reached that status by carrying out service functions for the eastern lowlands. It did not have the advantage of a borough origin, but had developed as a small agricultural settlement. An early survey after the Norman conquest reveals it as 'an agricultural village of unfree status . . . and one of the manorial centres of the neighbourhood, but it already had a market of considerable importance'.[21] This seems to reflect on the validity of the grading scheme adopted for the early seventeenth century, for contemporary accounts suggest that these three towns were of roughly similar status. This problem will be taken up later.

Wrexham proceeded to climb in standing until, by the nineteenth century, it had displaced Denbigh as the capital of the north-east. The cause of this trend is easy to find. A town situated on the eastern lowlands and thus peripheral to the region united and linked together the diverse elements that composed the north-east much more successfully than an internal town, especially as ties between England and Wales became more vital. Denbigh, as already emphasized, was a town with only local connections, whereas Wrexham was a nodal point where routes from north and south met; not only was it the local capital of the eastern lowlands but a major route centre. This can be illustrated by examination of the Directories of the early nineteenth century. In Pigot and Company's *National and Commercial Directory* (1829-30) no coaches are recorded as passing through Denbigh and the only regular carriers to markets were to Chester (twice a week), to St. Asaph (twice a week) and to Ruthin (once a week). Compared with this Wrexham not only received a eulogy on its advantages — 'a large popular and respectable town . . . few towns have greater local advantages . . . its present trade arises chiefly from its central and great thoroughfare situation',[22] but the following coaches are recorded there:

To Chester:	Royal Mail	from	Hereford
	High Flyer	„	Shrewsbury
	Hark Forward	„	Oswestry
	Nettle	„	Welshpool
	Bang Up	„	Shrewsbury

The return journeys are also given. In addition to these coaches, carriers are recorded to Bala (weekly), Chester (daily), Dolgelley, Ellesmere, Liverpool, Llangollen and Llanrwst (all weekly) and Mold and Oswestry (three times a week). All this is indicative of the changes which had taken place, for in Ogilby's *Britannia*,[23] which indicates the position in the seventeenth century, it was Denbigh which was on the main route from Chester via the Bodfari Gap to the north-west, and on to Holyhead. Wrexham thus became the focus of all the routes which penetrated the north-east.

A similar hierarchy characterizes the Welsh borderland generally except where industrial growth has altered the entire scheme. Thus from the major English towns, such as Chester and Shrewsbury, there is a fall in grade to the controlling Welsh border towns, Wrexham and Welshpool, and from these a further fall in grade with distance into the Welsh mountain core. This is due not only to the fact that the quality of the land deteriorates and the population density decreases, but also because the border town has a much greater capacity for drawing to itself all the diverse streams of human movement which flow from the fractionated uplands. The urban fields in a valley system are usually thrown upstream and consequently it is the town at the lowland debouchment which ultimately brings together major services for the interior areas, such areas having only local services provided by small towns.

By 1830 the industrial development of the North Wales coalfield had confirmed Wrexham in its supremacy. This town, which for other reasons was becoming dominant in the area, was so situated on the coalfield that it became the centre of the growing industrial movement. Thus there was here no change in pattern as occurred so often elsewhere in Wales.

In this story of competition for supremacy Ruthin seems to have played a fleeting part. As Denbigh slowly lost control and as Wrexham grasped it, Ruthin seems to have risen almost to a state of equivalence with these towns before its growth, too, declined relative to that of Wrexham. The fluctuations of Ruthin's fortunes merit further consideration for, according to the evidence of Fig. 3, recent decline has been marked. This would not seem to be in accord with observed facts. Ruthin still serves a considerable area of the southern Vale of Clwyd (Fig. 5) and is still to a large extent the administrative centre for the whole of the county of Denbigh. These functions served to give an increase of 23.6 per cent in its population between 1931 and 1951, of which only 3.0 per cent was due to natural increase, the remainder consisting mainly of migration into the town. Thus although it has continued its main functions direct from the nineteenth century, it has simply not had the economic power to attract the modern trappings of urbanism in the form of chain stores which are so well represented at Denbigh, a mere eight miles away. The 1951 Census of Distribution[24] shows a hundred retail and service trades' establishments at Ruthin with sales which amounted in the census year to £638,000 as against 136 establishments at Denbigh with a turnover of £1,017,000. The ratio of shops in Ruthin and Denbigh is 1 : 1.36, the ratio of turnover 1 : 1.59, this difference probably resulting from the larger stores of the latter town. Ruthin has thus remained to a large extent unchanged while other towns have experienced that expansion which has been characteristic of the twentieth century. The marked downward pointing arrow on Fig. 4 which links Ruthin in 1830 with the town in 1950 is thus in a sense inaccurate and it would have been perhaps more apposite if the line joining Ruthin at the two periods were made horizontal, and all the other towns set in their appropriate relations according to that control. Some towns, e.g. Wrexham, would consequently appear considerably higher in 1950 than in 1830, and this is an appropriate comment on the difference in the ability of towns to dominate surrounding areas at these two dates. This effectively illustrates the danger of comparing gradings at different periods as is done on Fig. 4. It suggests that when such comparisons are being made a satisfactory link should be identified to function as a fixed control against which the remainder of the gradings could be

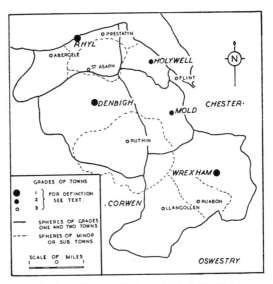

Fig. 5. Grades and Spheres of Influence in North-East Wales, 1950.

set. This, however, would introduce a major complexity to an already tenuous scheme. The crux of this matter is that two intertwined trends have to be separated:

(a) There is a general increase in the power of towns to dominate the countryside which is part of the general economic development of the country as a whole.

(b) There are the changing individual relations of a group of towns in a particular area.

It is a difficult and delicate task to disentangle these two trends. While the scheme suggested in Fig. 4 has proved useful, considerable doubt has been thrown on its validity.

The second feature of the graph noted above was that there appears to be a marked increase in the number of towns in the grading of 1830 when compared with the number in 1600, though this total was less than the number of boroughs. This feature is related to the consideration of Ruthin carried out above. It is a reflection of general social and economic conditions rather than of a decline and revival related to particular local factors. Although the Normans brought town life to Wales and attempted to create an economy based on them as an effective means of control, nevertheless the native way of life continued unaffected in the highland areas away from Anglo-Norman influence. In this part of the Welsh borderland there is very little interpenetration of highland and lowland, the curving line of the Clwydian Range and the Eglwyseg mountains presenting a sharp front to the east. There is thus no equivalent of the Vale of Gwent or the Severn Valley. Only in the richest lowlands was any effective break in the native way achieved and the hegemony of the market town introduced. Consequently the small boroughs or the more important native settlements had little opportunity to achieve a status which to the modern investigator can justifiably be considered urban. Flint provides a suitable example. It had been founded by Edward I and built on open land to be the capital of the county of the same name. By the beginning of the seventeenth century it had so decayed that only a few desultory houses are marked on Speed's plan. It had lost its market function, and even the Assizes had been moved to Caerwys, a very small settlement to the north of the Bodfari Gap but central within the county. George Owen's statement can again be recalled, 'No good town in the shire.'[25] Closely backed by the Clwydian Range and with no important through route, Flint had failed to capitalize on the opportunity which had been given it and had merely stagnated. This is equally true of Rhuddlan and partly of Mold. As already indicated the relative stagnation in the economic growth of the country together with restricted means of transport meant that there was no great need for towns. Perhaps it would be better to think of these as sub-towns in *contemporary terms* since Speed does write of the *town* of Mold. Here again detailed consideration seems to reflect the inadequacy of the grading scheme. Not only is the relation between gradings of different dates in question, but this applies to the whole concept of the grading for 1600.[26] It could well be argued that at that date, and especially in this area, urban functions, if not different in nature from those of the present, were at least developed to such a slight degree that the idea of a hierarchy is of little use. This in turn reintroduces a point which partially emerged in the consideration of the competition for the role of capital. In the early seventeenth century, when communications were poor and economic activity slight, there was little competion between towns. The prosperity of each town was based on the intensity of the agriculture of its immediate surrounds and the density of population so derived. Denbigh was the capital of the north-east by virtue of the rich agriculture of the Vale of Clwyd. Because of its prosperity and its tradition it acquired administrative functions which further enhanced its status. But as economic activity increased, and as regional service and wider nodality became more important than *local* service, Denbigh could not compete with Wrexham for reasons of situation outlined above. The hierarchy of 1600 is thus seen as virtually an expression of local conditions, and is not derived from the competition and consequent sorting of towns into fairly well defined grades which characterizes the modern hierarchy. The new entries into the hierarchy of 1835 show that, by that date, the modern pattern of competition and sorting was beginning to emerge. Only at this later period, therefore, can the idea of a hierarchy be confidently accepted and the principle of urban spheres of influence introduced. While this might be true it still does not preclude attempts to investigate the early stages in the emergence of the present hierarchy as an aid to an interpretation of urban spheres as the emerging human regions of the present time.

By the nineteenth century, therefore, with an ever quickening economic life and improvements in transport, many small settlements began to play a more dynamic part in the life of the countryside, functioning as small market centres and local intermediaries between the country and the larger towns. For example, the northern part of the Vale of Clwyd had no dominant town. It was an open, marshy area which had only been important in early times when it provided a defensive point on the route along the north Wales coast, a route long forsaken in favour of the direct route along the Dee valley. But in the nineteenth century St. Asaph and Abergele, together with the castle borough of Rhuddlan, developed slowly as the service centres of this piece of country and competed amongst themselves for the lead. This leadership was eventually snatched out of their hands by the rapid rise of Rhyl. South Flintshire, which was always closely linked to Chester, was served by Mold and Hawarden, the latter being the leader at that particular time of a group of settlements at the southern tip of the Dee estuary. Within the Dee valley Llangollen emerged as a minor centre. All these were small settlements with long histories which, under the stimulus of new economic conditions, took on the functions of towns.

The last feature that has to be invoked to explain the fluctuations in grade is the growth of industry. In the northern part of the coalfield Holywell became the focus of textile and metallurgical industries during the period 1775-85, and consequently that small settlement grew rapidly to become a fully fledged town dominating Deeside, and became the successor to the borough of Flint. The way in which the town fitted into the 1830 grading has already been noted,[27] and its growth effectively obliterated Caerwys. In the southern part of the coalfield Wrexham became the focus of industry as also previously noted.[28] Consequently its commercial advantages were backed by industrial expansion to confirm its place at the head of the hierarchy. In addition Ruabon became a secondary centre of industry to the south. There was also an extensive development of industry in lower Deeside, in an area including Flint, Hawarden, Shotton and Connah's Quay; the whole of this area is now virtually a small and slowly integrating conurbation. At the present time the actual criteria of urban status, such as grammar schools, banks and stores, are scattered throughout this complex, and hence it fails to emerge as significant in the urban hierarchy. By an analysis in time, however, the process at work can be identified and traced.

Also under this heading, and intimately associated with the growth of industry in this area and in Lancashire, must be included the rise of the seaside resorts. Abergele owed its appearance in the nineteenth century grading mainly to this function, but it was rapidly overtaken by Rhyl and Prestatyn. The former has risen high in the hierarchy to provide a dominant centre in the north of the Vale of Clwyd to match Ruthin in the south, but very different in nature as in origin.

The commentary on the graphs thus brings in the present situation (Fig. 5). In its broadest outline this is comparatively simple. Two lines of towns correspond to the north-south extent of the Vale of Clwyd to the west, and the border lowlands of east Denbighshire and Flintshire to the east. In the south these lines finish against a third line, that along the Dee, represented by Llangollen and Ruabon, and also by Corwen, which is outside the area being considered. This third line links with the south-east corner of the major system at Wrexham. Wrexham has retained its dominant role but the trend of dominance southward in the Vale of Clwyd has been reversed by the rapid growth of Rhyl. But while Rhyl presents a wide array of urban institutions, these are primarily for its visitors in the summer, and a field survey [29] has shown that its influence falls off fairly quickly southward, leaving Denbigh still as the focus and economic capital of the Vale of Clwyd. Since Rhyl is in Flintshire this also leaves administrative functions concentrated mainly in Ruthin.

Fig. 3 has already indicated the possible urban fields of 1835. Comparison with Fig. 5 will show that this was an emergent pattern. The concept of an urban field can be justified at that period, but it is only since then that the more intensive serving of the countryside merits the consideration of these fields as human regions, applicable to a study of regional geography. Indeed the system of urban fields on Fig. 5 provides the key to the identification of the human regions of the north-east, and a population map would clearly emphasize that the urban regions so distinguished form nodes of population. The lowland fringe of north-east Wales, which extends from Point of Air to Chirk, and is bounded on the west by the Clwydian Range and the Eglwyseg Mountains, can on this basis be divided into three.

(1) The Wrexham Region. This is composed of the concentration of settlement on the coalfield south of the Bala-Chester fault where by far the greater proportion of modern mining is concentrated. A whole series of somewhat formless mining settlements, including Brymbo and Gwersyllt to the north, and Rhos and Johnstown to the south, clearly constitute the heart of the Wrexham region.

(2) Middle Deeside. This area is much less of a simple concentration than the Wrexham region. This has already been indicated in the fractionation of its urban services. Mold, the town which might have served the area, is too far removed from the industrial core at Shotton and Connah's Quay, while the dominance of Chester in close proximity has tended to work against the emergence of one central focus. This is an area which has been characterized by very rapid growth in recent times, and still shows a degree of incoherence in its internal structure.

(3) Lower Deeside. Holywell is the local focus of this strip of country. It is a more lightly populated area, with a density which fades away towards its northern outpost in the Point of Air colliery.

Contrasted with these three major nodes of population and economic activity in the industrial parts of Flintshire and Denbighshire is the Vale of Clwyd. Here the pattern is rather different with a much more diffuse spread of agricultural population which is served by the two centres of Denbigh and Ruthin. This is an area which stands apart in all ways, a unit in itself with its twin capitals.

The north coast presents an entirely different aspect for here again there is a more intensive collection of population along the coast plain from Prestatyn to Rhyl and Abergele and this is continued along the coast beyond the area here considered. This fringe represents an entirely different grouping and is a human region in its own right. It is essentially an Anglicized resort and residential region penetrating toward the very heart of Wales. Nowhere does the influence of these towns as normal service centres penetrate very far inland. It is thus in many ways an alien fringe clearly marked off from the north-east as a whole.

It is clear that a marked link can be found between urban spheres of influence and the pattern of human regions in this area. The end product of the process which this paper has attempted to trace is this pattern of functional regions gradually emerging as the established influence of towns and the impinging forces of economic development mutually interact.

Although an appropriate conclusion may have been reached it will have become apparent by this stage that the simple idea of a graph of grade in the hierarchy against time cannot in practice be realized. Each hierarchy must be regarded as an end in itself. This is fully emphasized not only by the difficulties noted at the outset, but also by the problems which have arisen in the consideration of north-east Wales. But neither the construction of hierarchies for past periods, nor the general attempt to trace the growth or decline of towns by considering a series of such hierarchies and the spheres of influence of the towns in them, is undermined. Each hierarchy must, however, be examined intrinsically, and no inevitable link invoked between similar grades at different periods. The growth of towns has always been a problem of prime geographic interest because it is so explicitly a result of the interaction between a human demand and the physical environment, between function and situation. The type of study here presented is intended to break away from the general descriptive surveys by which this interaction is examined in many texts. This might justify a more widespread use of such past hierarchies which would be of value to the historical geographer as well as to the urban geographer, to whom towns must always be constructions in time as well as patterns in space.

[1] Christaller, W., *Die Zentralen Orte in Süddeutschland*, Jena, 1933, p. 46.

[2] Smailes, A. E., 'The Urban Hierarchy in England and Wales', *Geography*, vol. XXIX, 1944, p. 29 and p. 41, and 'The Urban Mesh of England and Wales', *Transactions and Papers of the Institute of British Geographers*, 1946, p. 87.

[3] The word 'institution' used in this context refers to the actual physical representative of a function in a town. Thus a bank is an institution representing the commercial function of a town.

[4] Bracey, H. E., *Social Provision in Rural Wiltshire*, London, 1952, p. 131, and 'Towns as Rural Service Centres', *Transactions and Papers of the Institute of British Geographers*, 1953, p. 98.

[5] Smailes selected for his hierarchy not merely an arbitrary collection of criteria but criteria which tend to recur in characteristic association thus forming a 'trait complex'.

[6] See Carter, H., 'Urban Grades and Spheres of Influence in South West Wales', *Scottish Geographical Magazine*, vol. LXXI, 1955, p. 43.

[7] Smailes, A. E., *The Geography of Towns*, London, 1953, p. 19.

[8] Carter, H., 'The Relations of Function, Position and Site in the Urban Geography of Wales, University of Wales', M. A. Thesis, 1951, unpublished.

[9] See Lipman, V. D., *Local Government Areas 1834-1945*, Oxford, 1949, p. 45.

[10] See Bowen, E. G., *The Settlements of the Celtic Saints in Wales*, Cardiff, 1954.

[11] Weinbaum, M., *The Incorporation of Boroughs*, Manchester, 1937, pp. 2-3.

[12] Camden, *Britannia*, translated as *Britain*, by Philemer Holland, London, 1610.

[13] Leland, J., *The Itinerary of John Leland in or about the Years 1536-39*. Edited Smith, L. T., London, 1906.

[14] Speed, J., *The Theatre of the Empire of Great Britain*, London, 1611.

[15] Owen, G., 'The Description of Wales', contained in the *Description of Pembrokeshire*, Edited Owen, H., Cymmrodorion Record Series, London, 1892-1936, vols. III and IV.

[16] Speed, J., op. cit.

[17] Owen, G., op. cit., vol. IV, p. 584.

[18] Nicholson, G., *The Cambrian Traveller's Guide*, London, 1813 (2nd Ed.), p. 1165.

[19] Leland, J., op. cit., p. 97.

[20] Owen, G., op. cit., vol. IV, p. 551.

[21] Ellis, T. P., *The First Extent of Bromfield and Yale, A.D. 1315*, London, 1924, Cymmrodorion Record Series, no. XI, p. 7.

[22] Pigot & Co., *National and Commercial Directory, North England and Wales*, London, 1828-29, pp. 1177-78.

[23] Ogilby, J., *Britannia*, London, 1675, vol. I, Map 26.

[24] H.M.S.O., *Census of Distribution and Other Services*, London, 1953, vol. I.

[25] See above, p. 91.

[26] See above, p. 94.

[27] See above, pp. 89-90.

[28] See above, p. 95.

[29] Survey carried out by students of Geography Department, University College of Wales, Aberystwyth, 1953.

Supplementary Note

Substantial advances have been made at various points since this paper was originally published, although together with a study of South West Wales[1] it can claim to be one of the first attempts to consider the development of an urban hierarchy through time. The ideas set out in these papers were eventually applied to the whole of Wales.[2]

The advances referred to can be most easily considered under four headings:

1 *The concept of a dynamic hierarchy* It is now accepted that a hierarchy of towns is not a static system but has evolved through time and is at present subject to change. This has brought into being attempts at considering the changing pattern as a stochastic process and of simulating change[3] and also of looking at the problem in terms of general systems theory.[4] There is undoubtedly some danger of introducing notions for their own sake and producing a jargon rather than an explanation.

2 *The use of new data sources* This is a minor operational point but certainly the use of material from contemporary directories, which was illustrated in this paper, has been widely extended.[5]

3 *The introduction of statistical objectivity into town ranking* There is a vast literature on this topic and this is not the place to review it but merely to record that the crude methods of the above study have given way to more sophisticated techniques. The most convincing analysis of this sort, using past British data, is that by Lucy Caroe[6] who employed principal component and factor analysis on nineteenth-century directory data for East Anglia. This was followed by a method of association analysis to produce rankings of settlements by trades and services.

4   *The development of comparability between rankings at different dates*   W.K.D. Davies has to a large extent offset the misgivings which were expressed in this paper as to the comparison of rankings at different periods.[7] By his method the total number of outlets of each function is used to derive a location coefficient for that function expressed as a percentage

$$C = \frac{t}{T}.100$$

where C is the location coefficient, t is one outlet of function t and T is the total number of outlets in the whole area. Each settlement can be assigned a *centrality value* for each function by multiplying the number of outlets by the location coefficient for the function and a *functional index* for each settlement can be obtained by summing centrality values. Since by this process each settlement is assessed against all other settlements in the area at any one time then changes over time can be effectively considered, for the functional index measures the proportion of the total activity in the area centred in each settlement. There are difficulties. The prime one is that the area is arbitrarily defined and regarded as a closed system which it cannot be. In addition the ranking by its nature assesses only relative and not absolute change and a strongly growing settlement can be recorded as showing *relative* decline. Lastly, one non-conforming and errant function can upset the whole process.

It is clearly now possible to approach the problem set out in the above paper with far more confidence and with more adequate techniques. But some difficulties remain and certainly the tendency for many workers on central place theory to consider exclusively commercial functions creates problems, for towns are more than retail centres and certainly in the past it is possible to argue that commercial functions followed others, such as administration, and in terms of explanation the leading functions must be sought. The problem of selecting functions still remains.

Perhaps it is appropriate to conclude by repeating that, owing to its fascinating intermingling of temporal and spatial relationships, the changing urban hierarchy will remain a topic of major interest.[8] One feels that at this stage fundamental empirical research might be more profitable than the exclusive concentration on method and technique and the elaboration of jargon, which has been so much a part of urban research.

1   Carter, H. 'Urban grades and spheres of influences in South West Wales', *The Scottish Geographical Magazine,* 71 (1955) p 54

2   Carter, H. *The Towns of Wales. A Study in Urban Geography* (Cardiff, 1965) Ch 1 to 4

3   Morrill, R.L. *Migration and the Spread and Growth of Urban Settlement* (Lund, 1965)

4   For a review of some notions see Haggett, P. 'The spatial structure of city regions'. SSRC/CES Joint Conference Papers, *The Future of the City Region* Vol 2 (1968). For an historian's view see Lampard, E.E. 'Historical aspects of urbanization' being pp 519-54 of Hauser, P. and Schnore, L.F. (eds), *The Study of Urbanization* (New York, 1965)

5   Davies, W.K.D., Giggs, J.A. and Herbert, D.T. 'Directories, Rate Books and the commercial structure of towns', *Geography,* 53 (1968) p 41

6   Caroe, L. 'A multivariate grouping scheme: association analysis of East Anglian towns', being pp 253-69 of Bowen, E.G., Carter, H. and Taylor, J.A. (eds), *Geography at Aberystwyth* (Cardiff, 1968) 1968)

7   Davies, W.K.D. 'Centrality and the central place hierarchy', *Urban Studies,* 4 (1967) p 61

8   Carter, H. *The Growth of the Welsh City System* (Inaugural Lecture, Univ of Wales Press, 1969)

H. CARTER   August 1969

Boroughs in England and Wales of the 1830s
T.W. Freeman
Reprinted from R.P. Beckinsale and J.A. Houston (eds),
*Urbanization and its Problems: Essays in Honour of E.W.
Gilbert* (1968), 70-91

Boroughs in England and Wales
of the 1830s

T. W. FREEMAN

Boundaries of local government units form an interesting study for a geographer, though strangely enough they have received little attention. They are not eternal and have been altered at various times. Here it is proposed to consider the efforts to make logical boundaries for boroughs in the 1830s: in many ways the attempt was remarkably successful and it is not without significance that the definition of the Poor Law Unions made in the same period was logical and perspicacious, as it embodied the idea that each should comprise a market town and the rural parishes from which it drew trade. In both the definition of the towns and of the unions one can recognize a concern with the distribution of population, with their movements, with the current and potential expansion of towns, with health, amenities and policing and much more that pertains to civilized living.[1]

The borough and town commission

William IV, according to the report of the Boroughs and Corporate Towns Commission,[2] authorized the commissioners 'to collect and arrange all information procured on the local circumstances of such of the Cities, Boroughs, Cinque Ports, and Municipal Corporations in England and Wales, as should be named and specified to us by one of Your Majesty's Principal Secretaries of State, touching the Metes and Bounds to be

---

[1] The substance of this article will appear in a forthcoming book to be published in Hutchinson's University Library, and thanks are due to Messrs. Hutchinson and the editor of the Geography section, Professor W. G. East, for permission to reproduce the material here. The author has pleasure in acknowledging his admiration for the work of E. W. Gilbert on administrative geography, notably in 'The boundaries of local government areas', *Geographical Journal*, 111, 1948, 172–98.

[2] The full title is *Report of the Commissioners appointed to report and advise upon the boundaries and wards of certain boroughs and corporate towns in England and Wales*, 1837, 3 vols. The towns are arranged alphabetically with no page numbers: the report covers pp. 1–11.

assigned to the same.' They were to advise on suitable ward boundaries within the towns as they were re-defined. In all, they dealt with 178 towns, for 91 of which they recommended that no division into wards should be made: many of the towns dealt with were—and in numerous cases still are—very small and yet neither Birmingham nor Manchester was mentioned as both were outside the categories considered.

The first job was to define the limits of the town. In many cases an old and extensive parish existed which was predominantly rural and the new boundaries were more restricted than those they replaced. In fact, rural and urban interests differed: as an example the Commissioners quote the defeat of the proposal to light Saffron Walden by the agricultural rate-payers within its wide bounds. The aim was to provide 'for the safety and convenience' of the townspeople by 'cleansing, paving and lighting the streets, and providing a daily and nightly watch.' Police services were regarded as 'necessarily confined to those whose houses are nearly contiguous' and therefore the costs might reasonably be resented by the rural inhabitants within the borough boundary. In some cases people excluded from the boroughs objected, generally because the rates charged by the boroughs were lower than those of the counties: similarly, many boroughs objected to the loss of land, such as Brecon, where it was said that the few rural inhabitants derived profit from the propinquity of the town and should therefore pay a tax for lighting and paving. No doubt they enjoyed these when they went to Brecon where, it is surprising to note, arrangements had been made to leave the gas lamps on all night and during the whole year. One wonders what went on at night in Brecon.

In some cases, in fact in virtually all, the new boundaries laid down by the Commissioners included some land used by the townspeople for agricultural or other purposes, or likely to be used for houses, industries or commercial premises. Some town boundaries were left unaltered though in several cases new ones were drawn, some of which seem arbitrary. Official direction was given that particular attention was to be given to suburbs: the nature of their population, whether commercial, manufacturing or agricultural, was to be noted and the 'extent and nature' of the ground separating the suburb from the main part of the town was to be considered as in no case was there to be a gap. Any natural features such as a river that could provide a suitable boundary, or historic lines such as parish limits, could be used. In spite of the respect for parishes, they were not used unless appropriate. As in many such enquiries, no rules could meet all circumstances: instances are given below (pp. 74, 81) of interlocking places that might have been united but in fact were not.

Ward boundaries within towns were to include approximately the same number of electors, but this plan could be modified to avoid making wards socially composed of the richer or poorer townspeople: ideally wards should be heterogeneous. As in the boundaries of the towns themselves, rivers, other natural features, or parish boundaries might provide suitable ward limits. In every street the fullest information on the inhabited houses, and the rates paid, was to be gathered, with detailed information on trade, manufactures, markets, roads and other concerns of the town. In short the need was for a comprehensive land use survey and all boundaries were to be shown on maps: the report itself was illustrated by excellent plans, most of which were based on Ordnance Survey materials provided by Lieut.-Colonel T. F. Colby and Lieut. R. K. Dawson of the Royal Engineers. The latter helped to establish the boundaries in detail, but who did the hand colouring in the report is not mentioned.

As a whole, the work of the commissioners shows great care and common sense. They noted the existence of 'liberties' which, by the parliamentary Act of authorization, were considered with certain towns, including Beverley, Coventry, Doncaster and York. In the last case the recognition of Liberties as part of the town would have spread York on one side to Tadcaster, which it has not reached over a century later: similarly Doncaster would spread over a vast area. This absurdity was apparently removed by Royal wisdom, for the division into wards of the 'Ainsty of York' and 'the Soke of Doncaster' was spoken of as 'disapproved by YOUR MAJESTY' (so written) so sense prevailed. Running through the reports is the view that for many purposes town and country had different problems: legal justice must exist everywhere, but street lighting belonged to towns. Poverty must be relieved everywhere but policing was an urban need. Gas lights could burn all night to brighten Brecon but the countryside rightly remained dark and asleep. Here and there in the reports it was recognized that a prosperous municipal authority could do more than the essential jobs conducive to health and protection from robbery and murder. In Preston—proud Preston—it was noted that the Corporation had recently enclosed a waste called the Moor, of some 240 acres, over which the burgesses had rights of pasture, as a place of recreation with public walks.

Of the 178 towns investigated, 71 were substantially reduced in area, 54 considerably enlarged, 33 left unchanged and 20 given only minor alterations. Many of those reduced were small towns with large parishes, including some historic places such as Tewkesbury, Thetford, Glastonbury and Godmanchester. Towns whose area were substantially enlarged included growing places such as Bristol, Liverpool, Newcastle-upon-Tyne, Portsmouth and Swansea. Those left unchanged were regarded as reasonably defined by existing boundaries which in some cases, such as Leeds, formed the parish, divided into eleven townships (whose names are now familiar as suburban areas) and one extra-parochial district. In Norwich the existing borough was made up of a large number of parishes in the old town and hamlets beyond it: in two other cases, Wigan and Winchester, the existing borough limits were regarded as reasonable. Some small towns appeared to be definable by their parishes, such as Huntingdon which had two parishes, St. Mary and St. John, extending beyond the town and two others within it. Minor alterations call for little general comment as most involved merely the drawing of a more logical boundary than the one in existence, for example at Plymouth (*v.i.*) where land had been reclaimed.

Some local reactions

Opposition to the union of towns has been rampant for over a century and the 1837 report gives one example in which all the modern arguments are put forward with emphasis. Plymouth possessed a boundary that had been defined in the reign of Henry VI and did not include 53 acres reclaimed on the east side by an embankment made in 1811 for the new high road to the town (and still the main road—A38). This was added, but the idea of uniting Devonport and Stonehouse to Plymouth, in fact not achieved until 1914, met a cool reception. The Commissioners thought that

'The advantages of uniting the three in one municipality are obvious. Uniformity of action would be combined with economy in the maintenance of a single official establishment, the same local Courts, the same Magistracy and the same Police.'

But the householders of Devonport passed a resolution saying that union with Plymouth would be disastrous for both towns, and the people of Stonehouse opposed union with either, as they feared that their affairs and 'interests, instead of being regulated and protected by their own council, would, by reason of such majority, be subject and liable to be controlled and directed by the council of the adjoining and more wealthy Town.' Later, it was stated that

the Manor or Township of East Stonehouse is a Town of rising and increasing importance, as well from the extent and respectability of its population, comprising nearly 10,000 inhabitants, as from the circumstances of its having three extensive and important Government Establishments within it; *viz*, the Royal Marine Barracks, the Royal Naval Hospital, and the Royal William Victualling Yard; and is situate between the large and populous Towns of Devonport and Plymouth, being distant from Devonport about half a mile, and separated therefrom by an arm or Creek of the Sea, passing under Stonehouse Bridge, as well as by certain Government Fortifications, and from Plymouth divided only by three Tollgates, set up on the three Turnpike Roads, bounding the manor of Stonehouse on the East.

Stonehouse was a separate parish, electing its own parish officers, levying its own rates and maintaining its own poor under a 'select vestry'; it was lighted 'adequately and efficiently,' but had no police because, it was claimed, the service establishments in various parts of the town were adequately guarded. There was a town hall, at which magistrates held petty sessions weekly and general parish business was transacted. The people of Stonehouse wished to be 'left in the undisturbed enjoyment of their present comfort, rights and privileges.' As none of the three towns showed any enthusiasm for union, the Commissioners reluctantly abandoned the idea with the comment that it was unnecessary to consider whether the people might 'be reconciled to such a connexion by a calm review of the mutual advantages which must result.'

Obviously the commissioners paid close attention to local views though they were of the opinion that places in effect one town on the ground should become one town. They noted in their consideration of Rochester that the town of Chatham, which was a separate Parliamentary borough, was so markedly continuous with it that both boroughs appeared to form a single town: but they were advised that this union would be unpopular. The two towns are still independent of one another. With differences of emphasis, much that was said in the Plymouth district is still said when any proposals for uniting towns or even counties are made. In various later enquiries investigators always considered the wishes of the inhabitants, but did not of necessity act upon them; nor did they necessarily accept all the local accounts of the excellence of the services provided, for they went to see for themselves.

Town extensions

These were made not only in some of the larger towns, but also in several of medium and small size. In every case the commissioners had enquired into the local circumstances, and carefully considered what growth was to be expected: naturally they could not forecast the expansion that followed the railway building of the 1840s. Almost all their reports on individual towns have some interesting data, but here it is proposed to deal with a few towns of varying size.

STOCKTON

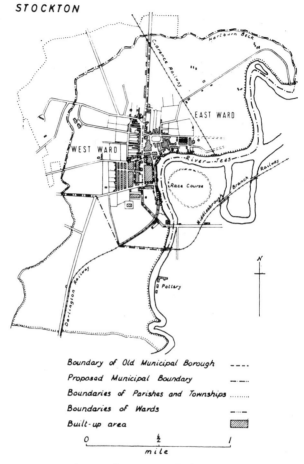

FIG. 17. Stockton: Built up area and administrative boundaries. Note the restricted early definition, long since archaic by the 1880's, the signs of growth, and the compromise boundary made by the Commissioners.

Stockton on Tees (Fig. 17) is a good example of a town in which industrial expansion seemed likely though by no means certain in the 1830s. Widely known for its pioneer railway to Darlington, it had two other railways[3] and was a port with wharves and coal staithes on the river. In

[3] One of these (unnamed) was paying a dividend of 23 per cent.

1835 the tonnage on vessels of its foreign trade was 10,347 inwards and 6220 outwards and of its coastwise trade 34,262 inwards and 272,366 outwards. Every week a steam packet sailed to and from London. The only manufacture in the town was of sailcloth at three factories, in one of which over 400 people were employed: the population of the township was 7,763 in 1,348 houses, of which only about one-quarter were in the old borough. This consisted of the old Lordship of Stockton, with the Bishop of Durham as Lord, and covered a small but obviously tightly settled area on either side of the southern part of the High Street. The commissioners proposed a boundary that included all the town and some of the surroundings, for here as elsewhere growth was seen on the main roads, and laid down the Hartburn beck as the west and north boundaries with the Middlesbrough railway and a road as the new boundaries on the south. This gave an area which covered most but not all of the Township. How far growth would continue was questionable, as

> lower down the Tees . . . has risen up within the last five years a great mass of houses, constituting Middlesbrough. The Stockton and Darlington Railroad runs down to the river in this point; wharfs and coal staithes have been built, and the place already presents the appearance of a busy port: larger vessels can come here than can get up to Stockton, and there is a great probability of the export of coal taking place almost entirely from hence. There is a steam packet exclusively between Middlesbrough and London once every week, so that in a few years it will probably deserve the name of a rival port to Stockton.

Banbury was a town of less than 4,000 people, reported to be clean and neat, and flourishing mainly through the prosperity of its markets and fairs as its manufacturers of horse girths and plush had declined. There were two existing definitions: the Parliamentary borough covered the entire parish, an area of nearly 6 square miles served by the fine Georgian church built to replace a large medieval church; the old municipal borough covered only one section of the town. Neither was reasonable. The parish was an area unlikely to be used for building in any conceivable time, and in the town as it existed the streets within the old municipal borough were watched, lighted and paved under the provisions of a local Act of Parliament but the others were not. The Commissioners said that all the existing town should be under one authority, and noted that there was considerable expansion along various roads leading from the town centre so they drew a boundary which included all these with some additional land where further growth might be expected (Fig. 18).

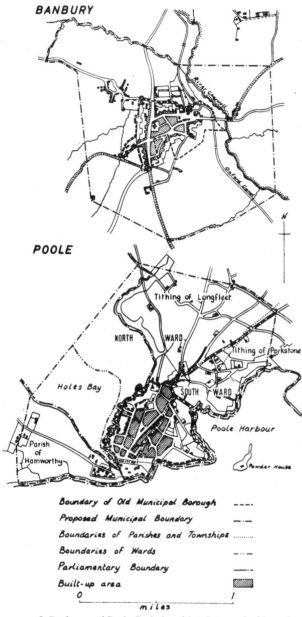

BANBURY

POOLE

N

Tithing of Longfleet

NORTH WARD

Tithing of Parkstone

Holes Bay

SOUTH WARD

Parish
of
Hamworthy

Poole Harbour

Powder House

Boundary of Old Municipal Borough   ----
Proposed Municipal Boundary   -----
Boundaries of Parishes and Townships ....
Boundaries of Wards   -----
Parliamentary Boundary   -----
Built-up area   ▨

0   1
miles

FIG. 18. Banbury and Poole. Both these historic towns had boundaries that were no longer realistic and the new ones were defined
in the expectation of considerable expansion of each town.

Poole in Dorset had two definitions, neither of which was realistic. The old borough covered only 170 acres, almost all of it built up, with 6500 people, between the Harbour and Hales bay. The parliamentary borough, which had become coincident with the municipal borough, covered approximately 9 square miles for it included not only the old borough but also the three tithings of Longfleet, Parkstone and Hamworthy. The newly-defined Poole covered slightly more than 2 square miles, and was fixed approximately one mile out on the main roads to Wimborne and Ringwood and rather farther out on the road to Christchurch as the village of Parkstone was developing: similarly at Hamworthy, connected to the old town by ferry, expansion was noted. At the time the new boundaries (Fig. 18) may well have seemed unrealistic, and wildly optimistic of future growth. In fact all of what was originally the parliamentary borough has been built up but the later growth of Poole was associated with that of Bournemouth, which had only 30 houses in 1841, and only 1700 inhabitants by 1861, though the first Improvement Commissioners were appointed as early as 1856 and the growth, rapid from 1870 when the railway came, was seen as possible by far-sighted people long before this date.

Bath is an interesting example of a medium-sized town where revision of boundaries was advised. There were some 51,000 people within the new municipal borough, for which the parliamentary borough provided a reasonable boundary. The old city, virtually the tightly built-up inner area, had well paved streets, a staff of watchmen, and gas lighting since 1819, but the outlying areas, where building had already begun and expansion was expected, had none of these advantages, which would themselves encourage development.

In York, as in Bath, the new municipal boundary was based on the parliamentary boundary, though with a few emendations: for example, the old village of Heworth was excluded as the people within it were almost entirely occupied in farming. But along various roads out of the town there were new houses, such as those along the Leeds road which were 'occupied chiefly by persons who have either retired from business or are engaged in business in the older part of the Town.' In fact there were ribbons of housing along all the main roads from central York, such as the 'continuous row of very good housing' along the Thirsk road to the village of Clifton. Here the claim was made that many of the people had rural rather than town occupations, but the Commissioners thought differently and recommended an extension of the boundary so that the growing suburban area of Clifton could enjoy such benefits as adequate policing and lighting: the policing was apparently provided already, but

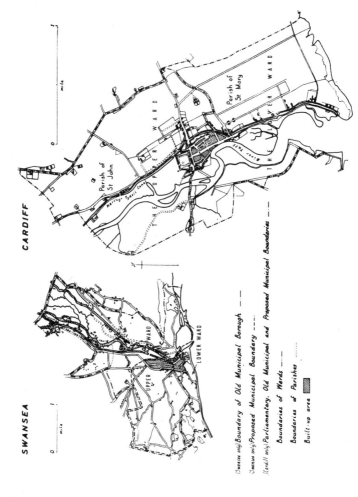

FIG. 19. Swansea and Cardiff. Swansea was generously defined as it was a major port and industrial centre in the 1830's. Cardiff was a smaller town in which growth came later, but the Commissioners were clearly aware of such possibilities.

the only lighting was one privately-owned gas lamp. And some of the people who claimed to be rural were cow-keepers selling milk to the city: it was not easy to define the boundaries and in fact they were drawn so that less than half the municipal area was built up.

Swansea, though larger than Cardiff in 1831, was a town of some 13,000 people within the old municipal bounds, but the Commissioners defined a parliamentary borough having a population of nearly 19,000. The town itself had the present High street and Wind street as its main artery, with parallel streets; it was reported to be 'in general clean and tolerably well built . . . of some reputation as a watering place.' Buildings included a handsome Court House, an Infirmary and Assembly Rooms, and there was an excellent market frequented by people from the surrounding district. The harbour was in active use and considerable improvements were planned; and much of the area surrounding the town was occupied by copper works and collieries and there were two large potteries. It was anticipated that numerous houses and possibly industrial premises would be added in the near future, so the parliamentary borough could become the new municipal borough. It extended for four miles up the river Tawe to Morriston, and from east to west for a distance of over three miles at the river mouth but only one mile near Morriston. Swansea had lighting for only eight months of the year, and protection was given by only three policemen. Such services did not exist beyond the old town, and it was hoped that the powers given to raise more money by local taxation would both improve the lighting and policing of the town in its new and expanded form (Fig. 19).

Of the larger towns expanded, Bristol is a notable example. The old municipal boundary included most, but by no means all, of the built-up area, but the new borough, made to coincide with the Parliamentary boundary, included an area extending about four miles from north to south and three miles from east to west. It included a considerable area to the east and northeast of the city, part of the parish of Westbury, all Clifton parish and the whole of Bedminster parish. The commissioners observed that though this new definition brought in many areas that were undeniably rural, the building in progress was so considerable that 'it is not improbable that the whole will at no very distant period become one mass of houses.' In all Bristol had 104,000 people in 1831, and for poor relief it had local powers under various Acts of Parliament, which could be transferred to the new town council elected on a ward basis. Clifton was lighted and protected by watchmen, but such benefits did not exist in Bedminster and Westbury, and other areas brought within the new boundaries.

Newcastle-upon-Tyne was a town and county, and consisted of part of the old large ecclesiastical parish of St. Nicholas, which had been divided into various parochial chapelries, of All Saints, St. John and St. Andrew. These with the area surviving as St. Nicholas parish, formed the old borough, but for the maintenance of the poor each of the parochial chapelries had outlying areas attached to it: for example, All Saints had Byker and Heaton, both then rural. The parliamentary borough became the new municipal borough, which survived unchanged until 1904, largely because the town was defined on spacious lines and covered nearly 8 square miles. The Commissioners noted that the northern suburbs, particularly Jesmond, 'are those to which the wealthy inhabitants resort, the situation being open, and removed from the trade of the town.' They also saw the improvements in the town centre in St. Andrew's parish,[4] associated with Robert Grainger, and their comment is worth reproducing.

> The Corporation are at present erecting a large and handsome Market-house, and individuals are at the same time building, on speculation, entire streets of shops and houses of a superior description in the immediate neighbourhood. There are various opinions as to the result of this speculation, but it is hoped that the situation, will attract inhabitants . . . the whole Northern part of the Town will present an appearance of comfort and beauty, exceeded by few commercial towns in the kingdom.

It was not proposed to unite Gateshead with Newcastle.

In Portsmouth, the ancient limits of the borough included the parish of Portsmouth, the part of Portsea parish which was called the Liberty and the whole of the harbour. This had ceased to be realistic as the population was increasing markedly: it was therefore proposed to define the new municipal borough on the same lines as the parliamentary borough, to include all of Portsea island (except for the parish of Wimmering in the north) and an area also in the north called the Salterns which had very few people. A proposal to include Gosport on the other side of the harbour was rejected on these grounds: it would be unpopular both with the people of Gosport and those of Portsmouth, and in any case Gosforth did not appear to be of sufficient size or importance to entitle it to separate municipal institutions. On the other hand Gosport and Portsmouth had obvious interests in common, but a crucial objection to their union was that they were on opposite sides of the harbour, over which travel at times of high winds was difficult. The arrangement of the wards of the

[4] Freeman, T. W., 1966, *The conurbations of Great Britain*, 196–7.

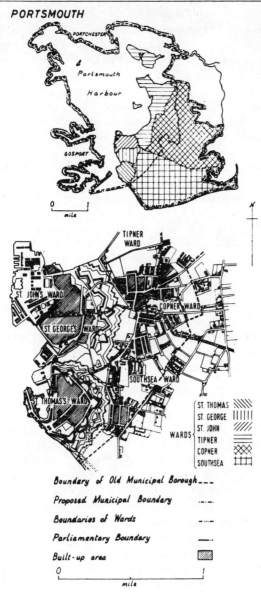

PORTSMOUTH

PORTCHESTER

Portsmouth

Harbour

GOSPORT

0   1
   mile

N

TIPNER
WARD

ST. JOHN'S WARD

COPNER WARD

ST GEORGES WARD

SOUTHSEA WARD

ST THOMAS'S WARD

	WARDS	
ST. THOMAS		╲╲╲
ST. GEORGE		‖‖‖‖
ST. JOHN		⫽⫽⫽
TIPNER		═══
COPNER		⊠⊠
SOUTHSEA		⊞⊞

Boundary of Old Municipal Borough _ _ _

Proposed Municipal Boundary _ . _ .

Boundaries of Wards _ .. _

Parliamentary Boundary _ . .

Built-up area ▨

0   1
   mile

FIG. 20. Portsmouth. The upper map shows the relation of
Portsmouth to other towns; the lower shows the fortifications which then dominated the naval base.

303

new Portsmouth was complicated by the fortifications of Portsmouth and Portsea, which had to be ward boundaries. Portsea was divided into two parishes, Portsmouth into one only. For the ward boundaries the Portsea and Arundel canal and the high road to London were chosen (Fig. 20).

From what has been written above, it is perhaps clear that the commissioners were far-sighted in their view that urban expansion was imminent, though they may have viewed the prospects of some places in an optimistic light. At least they did not have the modern fear of town expansion and they were not inhibited from speculating on the eventual size of a town by the existence of Green Belts designed to contain urban development within a defined perimeter. In short, they worked under quite different conditions from their modern successors. They gave great care to the delimitation of ward boundaries in order that each should contain equal resources in ratepayers: in Swansea, for example, there was a division into two wards of which the upper had 426 ratepayers providing £1,963 and the lower had 701 ratepayers providing £2,357. But in the whole town 2120 householders out of 3246 were excused for paying rates at all on the ground of poverty. There were 2208 houses in the lower and 1038 in the upper ward. Later, when rates were levied on all houses, this disparity of wealth ceased to matter and councillors were elected by all householders and their spouses, so that as the distribution of population changed new boundaries were drawn. It may be that the commissioners regarded wards as a modern equivalent of parishes, which in fact they failed to become.

Some unchanged boundaries

In the 1830s the commissioners did not change boundaries for the sake of making changes, and they found limits that needed no alteration in places as varied as Leeds, Norwich, Wigan, Cambridge and Cardiff. Leeds represented one of the vast parishes of the north of England; Wigan was a township: Cardiff was an historic town divided into two parishes; Norwich and Cambridge had useful boundaries which delimited both the old municipal and the parliamentary boroughs.

Leeds parish had become the old municipal and the recently established parliamentary borough by 1837: it covered an area of 32 square miles with a population of 123,000 in 1831. Virtually all of these, however, lived within an area little larger than modern central Leeds, though there were clear signs of expansion in areas such as Hunslet and Sheepscar, and also along main roads such as those to York and Huddersfield. The parish included eleven townships whose names are now familiar as quarters of the city: of these Hunslet, Holbeck, Beeston, Farnley, Wortley, Armley and Bramley lie to the south of the river Aire and Headingley, Chapel Allerton and Potter Newton, with the extraparochial district of Oswinthorpe (now Osmondthorpe), to the north of the river. These boundaries were retained by the city until 1912.[5] Economically Leeds was prosperous, with woollen manufacture as the staple industry though flax was spun and sent to Ireland for weaving. The Aire and Calder navigation was used for vessels of 80 to 100 tons, and a railway had recently been opened to Selby, with another planned to Derby. Manufacturers from the surrounding district sold their undressed cloth to merchants in the Cloth Halls, and there was a twice-weekly general market in Briggate, the main street. Industrial expansion was especially marked on the south side of the town, within the coalfield area, and the areas which became the northern suburbs, Headingley, Chapel Allerton and Potter Newton, were reported to be largely agricultural. The municipal services left much to be desired, as the paving materials and workmanship were so bad that repairs were frequent, lighting was inefficient and non-existent in the back streets, and the water supply was inadequate, though improvements were pending. Only the police services, under the care of the Mayor and alderman, was regarded as satisfactory.

Norwich differed from Leeds in history, appearance and the arrangement of parishes of which, with a small number of hamlets, there were over forty. Within the city there was a plenitude of parishes: the hamlets covered the outer area. In all the parliamentary and old municipal borough, to be unchanged, covered 11 square miles with a population of 61,000 people. The river Wensum was navigable for vessels of up to 100 tons, and the town was paved, watched and lighted under a local Act of Parliament: flagged footpaths existed in most of the principal streets. There were flourishing retail and cattle markets, and the textile industries were prosperous. Suburban expansion was notable on the west side of the town, which was graced by some fine private residences, mainly in the vicinity of the Cathedral.

Wigan was regarded as adequately defined by the Township around it, a diamond-shaped area rather more than two miles long from north to south and from east to west. The town had 22,000 people, and was increasing rapidly, as in addition to its canals (the Leeds and Liverpool, and the Leigh) it had a section of the railway later to become part of the main line to Preston. Most of the inhabitants were employed in coal mining or cotton manufacture, represented by some fifteen factories with two under construction. The main extension in progress was on the east,

[5] For the latter expansion see T. W. Freeman, *op. cit.*, 164–5, 168–73.

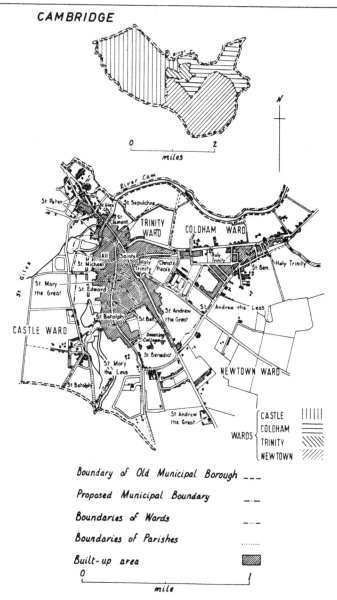

FIG. 21. Cambridge. Like many historic towns Cambridge was complexly divided into parishes and the extraparochial land of the colleges made the town fragmented in administrative responsibilities.

where building land was available on lease. Retail markets were held weekly, and fairs were held three times a year. The Highway rate was used for paving the streets and providing public lighting by gas: the police were paid out of the Poor Rates, and the night watchmen subsidized by a voluntary subscription collected from the townspeople. Water was supplied at a reasonable rate by a company.

Cambridge as an old municipal borough, and as a parliamentary borough, covered an area of 5 square miles south of the Cam and the Huntingdon road on either side of the Granta. It spread beyond the observatory on the St. Neots road, past Barnwell on the Newmarket road, and beyond New Town on the London road. Fourteen parishes existed, but the college grounds were extra-parochial except in the case of Downing which was in the parish of St. Benedict. Several of the parishes were spread all over the town: for example St. Benedict and Holy Trinity parishes were in numerous pieces, presumably representing various gifts of land at different periods. Twelve of the fourteen parishes were in the town and the two on its margins, St. Giles on the west side and St. Andrew the Less on the east, each covered more than 2 square miles. Most of the St. Giles parish was agricultural land but St. Andrew the Less included 'the populous suburb of Barnwell and New Town, consisting principally of recently erected houses, which are daily becoming more connected with the Town by the building of other streets.' The Commissioners distinguished the various parishes but failed to trace the four wards into which Cambridge had previously been divided, so a new ward division was made (Fig. 21). The town had in all 21,000 inhabitants, but there were no industries though there was a vigorous trade in coal, grain and timber along the Cam to Kings Lynn and beyond by coastal steamers. The main business was described as 'furnishing supplies to the Students and Members of the University' but the rural trade was also significant with several markets, for general merchandise in the Market Place, for pigs and cattle on St. Andrew's Hill, for hay in St. Giles parish and—less important—for corn and fish at the Peas Market in St. Edward's Parish.

Cardiff (*cf.* Fig. 19, p. 79) was regarded by the commissioners as a town having potential problems through its connexion with canal and coastal transport. In the 1830s the Merthyr Tydfil canal was in active use for carrying cargoes of coal and tin and for the export of oats, barley, butter and poultry to Bristol. The town had only some 6,000 inhabitants, but extensive improvements to its port were planned and an increase of population expected. There were two parishes, St. Mary and St. John, but the latter had 'the greater number of respectable Houses and Rate-payers,' many of them in what is now Queen Street. Public lighting with the care of roads and footpaths were provided under an act of 1774, and the Corporation also provided police and night watchmen, reported to be 'not very efficient.' Gas was available for private consumers from a company. There were already problems in the character of the population, as the Commissioners note:

> There are several Courts, Alleys and Lanes behind the principal Streets, occupied by families bordering on pauperism, and a similar class of people is found even in some of the new Streets, such as Charlotte-street, Caroline-street, and in Irish Town, and near the Canal; and although the Town is certainly thriving, and likely to continually generally to improve, it is to be apprehended that there will always be a shifting and pauper population in the suburbs, in consequence of the description of labourers required for loading and discharging the Vessels, for attending on the Wharfs, and for other casual occupations.

No change in the boundary, enclosing an area about three miles from north to south and one mile from east to west, was suggested.

These five towns all had boundaries that appeared satisfactory to the Commissioners. The extracts quoted will make it clear that they were conscious of the varied character of each town and in every case allowed for possible expansion. The division into wards followed the same principles as those noted on page 83, that is to give equal wealth and equal responsibility for representation on town councils. Awareness of poverty was keen and a desire to make good conditions of town living clear, but those who paid the Poor Law rates had the influence and power.

Towns reduced in area

Many of the numerous reductions in area were in comparatively small towns, where the old municipal boundaries coincided with the limits of the ecclesiastical parish. Of these, Godmanchester on the Ouse was an example, for the parish covered more than 7 square miles, with a population of *c.* 2,150, of whom a greater proportion were in the town, which could be better defined by drawing a line around the town to enclose about one square mile. Similarly, at Tewkesbury, the charter of 1698 gave the magistrates jurisdiction over the parish, which was four miles long from north to south and generally one to two miles from east to west: previously the municipal borough covered a smaller area. The population of the town in the 1830s was *c.* 5,500, with 94 in the rural area to the north and 183 in the rural area to the south. Tewkesbury had two main streets which were 'wide and respectable,' but the back streets were inhabited by the 'poor and labouring population'; it was added that the hosiery and lace trades were not prosperous. The proposal was to exclude the areas that were essentially rural: under a Local Act of Parliament, the town was lighted with gas and paved but watchmen were not employed.

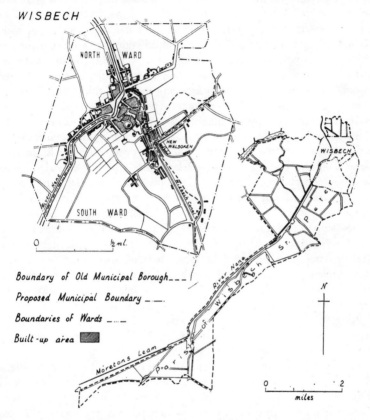

FIG. 22. Wisbech. Few towns were more curiously defined and the arrangements made by the Commissioners seem logical and far-sighted.

At Godmanchester, however, no lighting or paving was provided and in many small towns such amenities did not exist.

Some boroughs had curiously interesting problems of definition, such as Wisbech and Wenlock. Wisbech borough covered the parish of St. Peter which extended for three miles along both sides of the river Nene, so that an area of approximately seven square miles was included: the parish extended for a further six and a half miles on the south side of the Nene, giving a long narrow strip approximately half a mile wide. In all some 10 square miles were included. Within the parish there were 7250 people, living in some 1,500 houses: of these about 80 were outside the town, isolated one from another and widely separated by distance, and 30 to 40 of them were too poor to be a source of rates while the rest were 'not much superior in quality.' The town itself was located in the angle between the river Nene and the Wisbech canal, but it also extended for some distance along both banks of the river and beside the canal. On the east side of the canal there was a 'suburb,' New Walsoken, built during the previous twenty years, which had some 1,200 people, mainly labourers working in Wisbech. The commissioners included this area within the bounds of Wisbech, now to cover some 1,200 acres with some 1,700 houses and a population of approximately 9,000: all the rural area of the parish of St. Peter was left out. For its time, Wisbech was a large market town, and its trade had been stimulated by the improvements made in the river Nene. There was an iron foundry, a large brewery, and several yards for boat building and repairing boats. The trade included the import along the Nene of coal and general merchandise and the export of wool and agricultural products from the Fens, which included many types of seeds, hemp, peppermint and other unusual commodities. Though the improvements recently made in the town were clear, and both gas lighting and street paving were provided in Wisbech itself, such amenities did not exist in New Walsoken and it was hoped that these would be provided when the new boundaries were made: the people of New Walsoken were reported to be already negotiating with Wisbech Gas Company for public lighting. Wisbech, though now twice as populous as in the 1830s, is one of those gracious market towns retaining many of the houses and other premises that the commissioners saw on their tour (Fig. 22).

Wenlock offered quite a different, though not less interesting, problem: its ancient limits covered the seventeen parishes and the one extra-parochial district of the Franchise of Wenlock: several parishes were separated from each other by intervening parts of the country. It was agreed that these should no longer form part of the borough, and the boundary commissioners suggested that municipal government should be provided for only three parishes, Dawley, Madeley and Broseley, which together had some 17,000 people, many of whom were coal miners. There was no dominant centre that could be called a town and Dawley parish was outside the Wenlock Franchise area. The Revising Barristers however took a different view and made a borough consisting of the eleven parishes and the one extra-parochial district that lay within the common boundary line, so defining the widespreading Wenlock, an area of rural land with mining villages at intervals of a mile or two from one another, that still exists. Dawley remained outside the borough and in 1963 was designated as a New Town, though the site of 14 square miles also included the Madeley ward of Wenlock borough (with Ironbridge and Coalbrookdale, both famed for industrial history), parts of Oakengates U.D. and some rural areas.

Walsall borough coincided with the parish of Walsall but was divided into two Townships, known respectively as Borough and Foreign, of which the former covered the town. There were several large houses in course of construction, and the hardware trade was prosperous. Bloxwich, two miles away, was an industrial village separated from Walsall by rural land. The entire parish was used for the parliamentary as for the old municipal borough and of the population 6,400 were in the town area and 8665 in the 'Foreign' area. The town area had provisions for watching, cleaning, paving and lighting under an Act of 1765, which also provided powers to improve the town through street widening and other measures. The commissioners made a new municipal borough excluding all the 'Foreign' section except for a small area on which 'there is any probability of new houses being erected for many years to come.' Approximately one square mile was included, but the rapid growth of industry made this definition inadequate comparatively soon.

On page 71, reference was made to the struggles between the inhabitants of the town of Saffron Walden and the rural population of its parish, which was described as an agricultural district, measuring about 5 miles from north to south and $3\frac{1}{2}$ miles from east to west and containing an area of nearly 12 square miles. In all there were 990 houses of which 870 were within the 440 acres defined as the new borough: the total population was 4760. Though the town was neat, with many good houses and many signs of recent improvement, it had shown little sign of expansion during the previous seventy to eighty years and no great change was expected. Rather it seemed likely to remain a market town with a good general retail trade and malting as the only industrial activity. As noted on page 71, it was neither lighted nor watched, but it was said to be so peaceable that night watchmen were not required, especially if lighting could be provided.

Town and country

It has often been commented that the 'island' system of local government, which separated town and country, came with the legislation from 1872 onwards but study of the changes made in the 1830s show that the division between urban and rural was accepted much earlier as reasonable and even desirable. At the same time the Poor Law unions combined town and country in units based on the mutual interdependence of each, but the towns were recognized as units requiring special police protection, water supply, public lighting, street cleansing and repair, pavements for walkers, control of markets, and much more that came under the general heading of 'improvements.' Such views were firmly expressed by many people at the time, and received added support by various government commissions, notably in 1842, in the report on the 'Sanitary conditions of the labouring population of Great Britain.' Cholera epidemics due to defective water supplies stirred the fears of millions and the continuing growth of towns under the stimulus of mid-nineteenth century industrial expansion made provision for public health all the more urgent.

The first general outbreak of cholera came in 1831 and there were further serious epidemics in 1849 and 1854. The Poor Law Unions, established under an act of 1834, became the authorities for the compulsory registration of births, deaths and marriages from 1837, and such dark stains as the high infant mortality were revealed. In 1847, the Town Improvement Clauses Act consolidated a number of sanitary provisions previously found in various local Acts, and in 1848 the first Public Health Act established a General Board of Health, and local boards could be formed on the petition of the inhabitants, or on the initiative of the General Board if the death rate was over 23 per 1000. Town definition was for a purpose, and an urgently needed purpose, and it is perhaps a tribute to the social advance of the past century that one now takes the nineteenth century status symbols of a town, its drains, water supply, gas lighting and paved streets, for granted and looks to municipal achievement in the welfare services for the afflicted, recreational facilities, amenities such as public parks, attractive town centres and education for people of all ages.

Supplementary Note

The Reports of the Commissioners appointed to report and advise upon the boundaries and wards of certain boroughs and corporate towns in England and Wales, 1837, 3 vols, begins with a general discussion of the problem in eleven pages and then deals with the 178 towns regarded as boroughs. These do not include places such as Birmingham and Manchester which had lost all record of any charters though they may have possessed them at some time. But among the 178 towns there are a number that had failed to grow, such as Tewkesbury, Thetford and others mentioned in the text. For each town there is a map, on varying scales with hand colouring. At this time the Ordnance Survey (founded 1791) was preparing 1:63,360 maps but its other responsibilities included the preparation of town maps such as those reproduced in 1837. The Survey owes much to Lt Col Thomas Frederick Colby (1784-1852), of whom a biography was written by his one-time junior officer Joseph Ellison Portlock (1794-1864)[1]: Colby and his fellow-officers of the Royal Engineers held the view that the survey, though initially planned for military reasons, had a social and intellectual purpose and eagerly welcomed friendly relations with commissioners such as those of 1837. The maps are spendidly produced with hand colouring by unnamed illustrators. The commentaries on each town are full of interesting material and show local knowledge: many of the nineteenth-century commissioners went round the country collecting information. It was clear that some places would grow: for example the commissioners saw that Middlesbrough had such possibilities.

Material on the historical geography of the nineteenth-century is abundant and some of it made the more valuable by map evidence such as that available in this 1837 source. But there are other sources of this time such as Lewis, S., *A Topographical Dictionary of England*, London, 4 vols, 1831, with maps of England, London and a number of other towns in a fifth volume. The maps in volume 5 of Lewis's work, third edition 1837, are 'drawn by R. Creighton' and 'engraved by J. and C. Walker' and embellished by hand colouring.

1   Portlock, J.E. *Memoir of the Life of Major General Colby* (London, 1869)

T.W. FREEMAN   August 1969

The Pre-Urban Cadaster and the Urban Pattern of Leeds
D. Ward
Reprinted from *Annals of the Association of American Geographers,* 52 (1962), 150-66

THE PRE-URBAN CADASTER AND THE URBAN PATTERN OF LEEDS[1]

DAVID WARD

University of Wisconsin

THE purchase of land holdings for building purposes is an important step in the complex process of the physical growth of towns. The growth and characteristics of built-up areas may therefore be influenced by the pre-existing patterns of ownership. Fellmann[2] has demonstrated that lot subdivision and lot sales provided a framework which conditioned the expansion of the built-up area of Chicago. The West European city has, however, expanded over a long and closely settled rural landscape. The framework of land holdings to which the expanding built-up area of the West European city is adjusted is thus the complex and varied pattern of ownership of the rural landscape. In this paper it is proposed to examine the degree to which this pre-existing pattern of ownership has affected the urban plan of Leeds, a town of some half million people in northern England.

Earlier occupance of any area must necessarily limit and affect the freedom of choice for any subsequent development. The pattern of rural settlement in the form of village nuclei and of farm holdings antedates any settlement pattern created by urban development. In urban studies the influence of this pre-existing rural landscape is usually discussed by reference to the survival of old village nuclei within the suburban extensions of our towns. The past, however, leaves traces of itself in more complex ways than in mere residuary material

survivals conspicuous only by their relative rarity. It was, in fact, the land holdings attached to each building that were utilized for later urban developments. The urban plan was thus not simply superimposed on the pre-existing rural landscape by an arbitrary subdivision of this landscape into building units. Indeed since they were frequently the unit of purchase, these land holdings of the rural landscape acted as a framework within which much of the subsequent building activity had to be adjusted.

The antecedent pattern of ownership for Leeds has been obtained from the several tithe apportionments and maps relating to the parish of Leeds.[3] In 1836 by the Tithe Commutation Act landowners were able to call commissioners to commute tithes to a money payment in the form of a fixed rent on each holding. During the subsequent decade the parish of Leeds, like most other parishes in England and Wales, was surveyed and the ownership of each holding was thus recorded.[4] The tithe apportionment and map thus provides evidence concerning not so much the physical extent of settlements but rather the ownership of the fields attached to each building. The parish of Leeds was exceptionally large and was subdivided into no less than eleven townships (Fig. 1).[5] By the mid-nineteenth century the central parts of the township of Leeds were already well covered with buildings.[6] The several townships beyond this central area, however, were utilized for building purposes after the tithe survey was made. The relationship of the antecedent pattern of

---

[1] This paper presents some of the conclusions of an M.A. thesis on the more specific problem of the urban plan of Leeds and the factors that have conditioned its growth. The writer would like to express his gratitude to his tutor, Mr. Glanville R. J. Jones of the University of Leeds, for stimulating guidance and numerous helpful suggestions, and to Professor Andrew H. Clark of the University of Wisconsin for reading and criticizing the manuscript. The staff of the archives department of Leeds Central Reference Library and also of the Surveyor's Department of the Leeds City Council were extremely helpful in the two main repositories of the evidence used in this paper. The services of the University of Wisconsin Cartographic Laboratory are gratefully acknowledged.

[2] Jerome D. Fellmann, "Pre-building Growth Patterns in Chicago," *Annals,* Association of American Geographers, Vol. 47 (1957), pp. 59–82.

[3] Archives Department, Leeds Central Reference Library.

[4] For a discussion of this particular source of evidence see Hugh C. Prince, "The Tithe Surveys of the Mid Nineteenth Century," *Agricultural History Review,* Vol. 7 (1959), pp. 14–26.

[5] The parishes of northern England were in general very large and were frequently sub-divided like Leeds into units known as townships.

[6] For a discussion of the effect of land holdings on the urban plan within the township of Leeds see Maurice W. Beresford, *Time and Place* (Leeds: Leeds University Press, 1961), pp. 6–11.

317

Fig. 1.   Leeds: township and parish organization.

Leeds.[7] The domestic woolen industry demanded a distinctive holding, for a characteristic feature of the industry under domestic conditions was the duality of occupation of the clothier. The domestic clothier was at one and the same time manufacturer and farmer. The small holding represented the clothiers' agricultural interest although many were also used as cloth-drying grounds.[8] Moreover, large estates formerly leased as large tenant farms were more profitably exploited when subsequently divided into clothiers' holdings of one to ten acres. This development in the late eighteenth century resulted in the enlargement of areas of small holdings and fragmented ownership.[9]

In contrast to the southern townships, the northern townships of Leeds were characterized by large holdings (Table 1). Moreover, most of these large holdings were tenant farms, and each was a parcel of a compact landed estate. There were some small holdings in the old village nuclei and also some village farms with unconsolidated fields, but in general the large compact farm was the dominant unit of ownership in the northern area of Leeds. This was particularly true of the old common lands (common between the several villages), which were enclosed in the late eighteenth and early nineteenth centuries by Act of Parliament. The agricultural economy north and east of Leeds and the domestic woolen industry south and west of the town each had their distinctive land holdings. This distinction in the characteristics of land holdings is manifest in the contemporary urban plan of Leeds. The effect of land holdings on the urban plan of Leeds is most marked in the degree to which the formal layout of streets and buildings is adjusted to the framework presented by this earlier pattern of ownership. The precise arrangement of buildings within a holding is largely determined by the current concepts of practical planning. It is necessary, therefore to distinguish the effect of land holdings on

ownership and the present built-up area of Leeds can thus be established by the superimposition of the field and property boundaries derived from the tithe material on the latest editions of the six-inch and twenty-five inch (to one mile) Ordnance Survey maps. Over most of the contemporary built-up area a significant coincidence of the present pattern of building and the earlier pattern of ownership can be established.

DIFFERENCES IN THE ANTECEDENT PATTERN
OF OWNERSHIP

The degree and type of this coincidence of the present pattern of building and the earlier pattern of ownership is, however, quite varied. There are, in fact, significant differences in the characteristics of the antecedent pattern of ownership within the area covered by modern Leeds. Most of the southern townships of the parish of Leeds were characterized by small holdings and a fragmented pattern of ownership, whereas the northern townships had larger holdings with a more compact pattern of ownership. These differences were an expression of the former existence of the boundary of the domestic woolen producing area of West Yorkshire just to the north and east of

[7] There are many contemporary references to this boundary, but it is most clearly stated in an anonymous *Guide to the Town of Leeds* (Leeds, 1806).

[8] Although somewhat out of date, the most useful summary of the conditions in the domestic woolen industry is Herbert Heaton, *The Yorkshire Woolen and Worsted Industries* (London: Oxford University Press, 1920). Vol. 10 of *Oxford Historical and Literary Studies*.
[9] *Parliamentary Report on the State of the Woolen Industry* (London, 1806).

TABLE 1.—THE STRUCTURE OF OWNERSHIP IN THE LEEDS DISTRICT, *CA.* 1845

Township	Units of ownership in acres						
	1–5	5–10	Total as per cent	10–25	25–50	Over 50	Total as per cent
SOUTH LEEDS							
Armley	82	18	81	20	1	3	19
Beeston	33	22	57	21	9	8	43
Bramley	72	31	67	34	9	7	33
Farnley	25	17	52	18	12	9	48
Holbeck	57	11	88	7	2	0	12
Hunslet	109	27	86	20	1	0	14
Middleton	5	7	32	7	7	11	58
Wortley	88	41	86	17	3	1	14
NORTH LEEDS							
Adel cum Eccup	14	10	35	8	10	32	65
Chapel Allerton	67	38	61	33	19	13	39
Headingley	71	32	59	40	14	16	41
Potternewton	23	13	51	13	18	7	49
Seacroft	18	13	48	11	12	10	52
Temple Newsham	49	19	65	15	9	15	35

terraced[10] building of the period before 1919 from that on the more geometrical layout of buildings constructed since that date.

THE EFFECT OF SMALL HOLDINGS AND FRAGMENTED OWNERSHIP ON TERRACES

Of all building forms the terrace (Fig. 2) is perhaps the one which lends itself most readily to continuous and regular development. In Leeds, however, terraces are characterized by constant changes in alignment and frequent breaks within the built-up area. These characteristics are particularly well developed in the three southern townships of Hunslet, Holbeck, and Armley and can be related to the fragmented ownership and the small size of holdings in these townships. Before residential development took place in the late nineteenth century, over 80 per cent of the total land holdings in all three of these townships were less than ten acres in size (Table 1). There were very few areas of continuous compact ownership and the individual field was frequently the basic unit of ownership. Indeed, over 60 per cent of the total land hold-

ings in these townships was composed simply of a cottage and a plot of less than five acres (Fig. 3).

Thus, despite the facility with which a rectilinear arrangement of buildings and streets could have been extended over large areas as a unitary plan, in Hunslet, Holbeck, and Armley the urban plan is far from unitary, for the extent of each block of building was rigidly dictated by the older boundaries of ownership (Fig. 4). Each variation in the alignment or direction of terraces and streets coincides with the pre-existing property lines. Wherever the earlier property boundary was irregular and therefore cut across the rectilinear arrangement of terraces, it provides the most conspicuous confirmation of the thesis of continuity of ownership. The terraces are successively reduced or increased in length with each irregularity in the property line and are often reduced in length to only one or two houses (Fig. 4). The distorted corner houses which fit into the extremities of such irregularly shaped holdings reflect both the determination of the Victorian speculator to maximize his investment and also the degree to which building developments were conditioned by the shape of the earlier land holdings (Fig. 6).

In large holdings, the internal arrangement of individual terraces and streets usually reflects the desire of the land speculator to maximize the space available for building. Wherever holdings are small, however, the restric-

---

[10] Buildings which were constructed in units of four, six, eight, or even more dwelling units. In many English industrial towns the dwelling units were not only arranged in terrace rows, but were also placed back-to-back, so that each block of terrace housing contained two distinct rows of dwelling units, each fronting on the streets or, more frequently, the yards or courts on either side of the terrace (see Figs. 2 and 4).

Fig. 2. Terrace housing in units of four and eight back-to-back dwellings. Note the incomplete terrace or half back-to-back houses at the former field boundary.

tion imposed by the property boundaries determines the alignment of streets. Since there is sufficient room for only one street, any change in the shape of the holding will affect the alignment of streets and terraces. These conditions prevail north and south of Town Street, Armley where the alignment of several small holdings is perpetuated in the alignment of streets which have been determined by the direction of property lines (Fig. 4).

The effect of the antecedent pattern of ownership on the urban plan also is clearly revealed when only one holding has been developed or on the extremities of an expanse of built-up land. The present layout of the township of Wortley illustrates the effect of land holdings in an area of isolated rather than continuous building developments (Fig. 5). In Wortley there had been a less intense demand for land for building purposes because the township was cut off from the main built-up areas of Leeds by the Leeds-Bradford Railway. In the late nineteenth century only sporadic building took place here, but each unit of building was rigidly confined to the pre-existing holding which was often irregular in shape.

THE EFFECT OF LARGE HOLDINGS AND COMPACT OWNERSHIP ON TERRACES

In the northern and eastern parts of Leeds, the terrace has a more regular and well-ordered form. The larger and more compact holdings of the northern townships (Table 1) encouraged both a greater continuity of the terraces and also a wider spacing of the dwellings. At the end of the nineteenth century many of the landed estates on the periphery and beyond the limits of the existing built-up area of Leeds were developed for residential purposes. Although there were a few large units of ownership developed as large expanses of terrace housing in the southern townships, extensive blocks of terraces were largely built in the northern townships of Headingley and Potternewton. Almost all

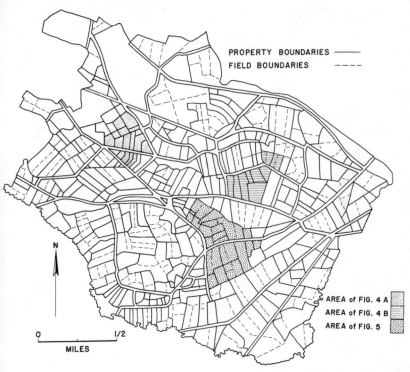

PROPERTY BOUNDARIES ——
FIELD BOUNDARIES   - - - -

N

0   1/2
MILES

AREA of FIG. 4 A
AREA of FIG. 4 B
AREA of FIG. 5

Fɪɢ. 3. Pre-existing pattern of ownership at Hunslet, Holbeck, and Armley.

the township of Potternewton, for example, consisted of three large landed estates (Fig. 7), although only one estate was utilized for residential building during the period before World War I. The size and quality of the dwelling units of these larger units of development were also markedly higher than in the smaller scale developments of the southern townships. Indeed the greater expense of the dwelling unit itself was matched by a more spacious layout of the individual terraces. Thus, in Potternewton the larger holdings permitted a greater control over the internal layout of streets, and the terraces were more regular over larger areas (Fig. 8).

The development of the small holdings of the southern townships for residential purposes was mainly in the period between 1870 and 1880, whereas the more ambitious residential developments of the larger holdings occurred chiefly in the period around the end of the nineteenth century. During the last decade of the nineteenth century the growth in the size of the building industry, the expanding sources of personal credit for house purchases,[11] the emergence of a cheap and swift system of public transport, and the establishment of minimum building standards by means of bylaws, all gradually affected and changed the precise demands and scale of operation of the house builder. There is thus

[11] The importance of Housing Associations in residential building in late nineteenth century Leeds can be gleaned from *The Royal Commission on the Housing of the Working Classes* (London, 1885), Vol. 1, p. 371.

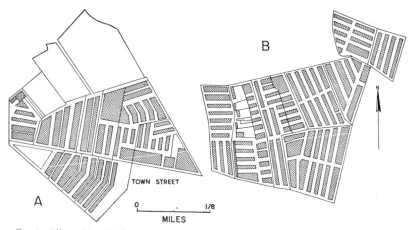

Fɪɢ. 4.   Effects of land holdings on the alignment of terraces at Armley. (For location of areas A and B see Fig. 3.)

in the plan of the physical additions to Leeds during the late nineteenth century a subtle distinction in scale between the small irregular terrace building of the earlier part of the period and the more substantial dwellings and more regular and well-ordered layout of terraces built at the turn of the century. The demands made on land by these two distinct scales of residential building resulted in the development of different parts of the town according to the characteristics of the pre-existing pattern of ownership.[12]

THE EFFECT OF THE PATTERN OF OWNERSHIP ON
SMALL-SCALE PRIVATE BUILDING DEVELOPMENTS
AFTER 1919

When a more open form of residential building was adopted in Leeds after 1919, the antecedent pattern of ownership again affected the urban plan. Between 1919 and 1933 the building industry continued to be founded on small-scale private enterprise; the general economic conditions of the 1920's did not favor large-scale speculation in residential building. In-

deed it was becoming increasingly obvious that the housing problem of Leeds was not that of a growing city but rather that of a city which had a great amount of derelict property. Slum clearance rather than the housing demands of an expanding population became the central theme of changes in the urban plan. The unit of development by private builders was thus small, for the housing demands of people dwelling in derelict property involved problems which required the attention of the municipal authorities.[13] Many of the surviving small holdings of the southern townships were thus developed by small-scale private builders.

---

[12] The role of local transport and the social desirability of the various districts is clearly important in the development of better quality dwellings, but the larger scale of building demanded large compact units of ownership which were located only in certain parts of the city.

[13] The reason why private industry was unable to provide an answer to the problem of rehousing slum dwellers is revealed by a statement by the Leeds Medical Officer of Health as early as 1922: ". . . the new housing schemes [i.e., a subsidy to private builders to aid construction] offered no material assistance to the overcrowding problem because the rents of the new houses were beyond the means of the majority of people living in the overcrowded districts." *Annual Report of the Leeds Medical Officer of Health* (Leeds, 1922). The demand of slum dwellers for new houses remained latent until there was some readjustment in the relationship of rent and income levels. Private house-builders in a city which has only a small annual increment of population and little if any increment to the income of the indigenous inhabitants have only a small and insecure demand.

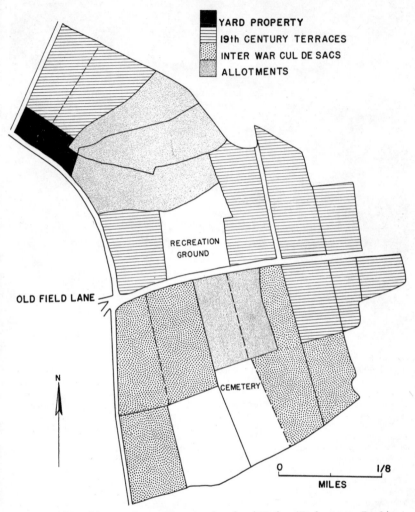

YARD PROPERTY
19th CENTURY TERRACES
INTER WAR CUL DE SACS
ALLOTMENTS

RECREATION GROUND

OLD FIELD LANE

CEMETERY

N

0   1/8

MILES

Fig. 5. Effects of fragmented ownership on the urban plan of Wortley. (For location see Fig. 3.)

This piecemeal, small-scale enterprise resulted in the use of several of the vacant holdings in Wortley for residential building. As a result, parts of Wortley now provide vivid evidence of the effect of fragmented ownership on the urban plan. To the south of Old Field Land in Wortley there were twelve fields with nine different owners. Each field today has its own distinct pattern of development. The few nineteenth century terraces are interspersed with cul-de-sacs built in the interwar period. Since the demand for land

Fig. 6.   Distorted corner houses on the extremities of an irregularly shaped holding.

for building purposes is not great in this area, some holdings are used as allotment gardens or are retained by the municipality for recreational use (Fig. 5). Fragmented ownership thus appears to exert a profound effect on the characteristics of the urban plan. The effect of fragmented ownership on the urban plan of Leeds is especially significant since large areas of the southern townships and also the cores of the old villages were characterized by this pattern of ownership. Discontinuous ownership is often preserved in the small holdings around old villages where today this pre-existing structure is reflected in the small scale and incompleteness of residential development.

THE EFFECT OF THE PATTERN OF OWNERSHIP ON
LARGE-SCALE PRIVATE BUILDING AFTER 1919

Private residential building, however, was not generally characterized during the inter-

war period by these small-scale developments. Whenever a particular district acquires a "desirable" residential status, the assured demand tempts the more speculative builder into more ambitious schemes. Especially during the 1930's the demand for semi-detached houses in the northern part of Leeds sustained many residential developments in such areas as Chapel Allerton and the northern parts of Headingley. Chapel Allerton was composed of several large estates divided into tenant farms, although in the old village nucleus there were several fragmented holdings. Over 40 per cent of the total holdings in Chapel Allerton were over ten acres in size. During the interwar period Chapel Allerton, like Potternewton at the turn of the century, assumed a "respectable" status in the hierarchy of residential areas north of Leeds. Like Armley, it is now one of the most completely built-up areas in the city. As in Armley, there is a uniform unit of develop-

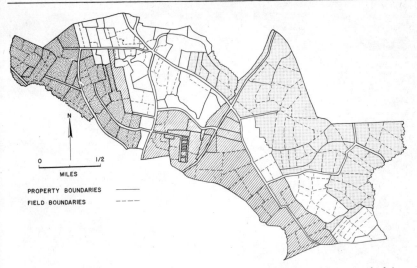

F<small>IG</small>. 7. Pre-existing pattern of ownership at Potternewton. (The shaded areas delimit estate lands.)

ment. In Armley the terrace was a ubiquitous constituent of the urban plan. In Chapel Allerton geometrical arrangements of semi-detached houses are characteristic. The significant aspects of terrace building were, however, the changes in alignment and breaks in their continuity. Similarly the changes in the layout of numerous geometrically arranged estates are as significant as the layout itself in understanding the urban plan of Chapel Allerton.

Over large areas of northern Leeds, despite the superficial similarities in the arrangement of buildings, the detailed changes within this uniform pattern are but a reflection of the pre-existing, and frequently surviving, pattern of ownership. Although breaks in the continuity of building patterns in parts of northern Leeds are fundamental, the larger unit of ownership and larger scale of enterprise resulted in less frequent changes in layout and greater independence of internal street plan than where terraces were confined to small holdings. The Meanwood district of Chapel Allerton township provides an example of the effect of larger units of ownership on the pattern of building and also illustrates the piecemeal process by which building development proceeds (Fig. 9). Each holding is purchased and developed independently. When several independent units of building eventually coalesce, the main determinant of variations in layout are the lines of ownership within which each estate has been built (Fig. 10). Farm holdings are not the only pre-existing units within which building developments have taken place. In Leeds the grounds of many detached mansions built in the northern townships in the mid-Victorian period have been utilized for building purposes. Frequently the old grounds are developed as a cul-de-sac of dwellings with distinctive contemporary architecture. Alder Hill Avenue is a particularly good example of this process, for the cul-de-sac fits precisely into the holding attached to a Victorian mansion which survives alongside the newer houses, although now divided into flats (Figs. 9, 11).

T<small>HE</small> E<small>FFECT</small> <small>OF</small> <small>THE</small> P<small>ATTERN</small> <small>OF</small> O<small>WNERSHIP</small> <small>ON</small>
M<small>UNICIPAL</small> R<small>ESIDENTIAL</small> D<small>EVELOPMENT</small>

The corporation also has actively participated in residential building. Unlike the private builder who often was catering for a limited though expanding demand, the corporation was concerned with the rehousing of

Fig. 8. Regular terraces in Potternewton. Scale: originally 6 inches to 1 mile. (Reproduced from the Ordnance Survey Map with sanction of the Controller of Her Britannic Majesty's Stationery Office. Crown copyright reserved).

slum tenants. The resettlement of these tenants was in houses built at a density of only 8 to 12 per acre, whereas most had previously been housed at densities of 60 to 80 per acre. The demand on land which was available for residential development in the Leeds area to absorb this planned redistribution of the population was clearly at a maximum. The corporation policy was to rehouse slum tenants in large housing estates on the periphery of the city. The dominance of small holdings and the relative absence of continuous blocks of land in single ownership has already been emphasized. The question of the availability of land

for corporation building thus became as critical as the litigation and compensation involved in slum clearance.

In the early phases of corporation enterprise the unit of development was small for the legislative machinery of compulsory purchase and rent subsidies had not been created. Most corporation estates built in the first decade of the interwar period were, like their private counterparts, small and related to single farm holdings. Stonegate Farm estate built in the mid-20's is a classic example of an estate within an old farm holding from which it takes its name (Fig. 9). After 1933, with the formation

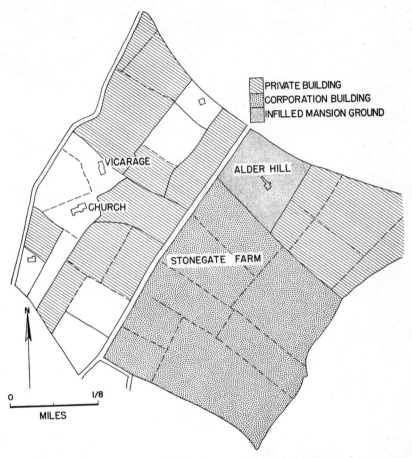

PRIVATE BUILDING
CORPORATION BUILDING
INFILLED MANSION GROUND

VICARAGE

ALDER HILL

CHURCH

STONEGATE FARM

N

0   1/8
MILES

Fig. 9.   Land holdings and variations in residential development at Meanwood.

of a special Housing Committee and increasing legislative framework for municipal land purchases, corporation enterprise took on its more characteristic large-scale form. The different demands of private and corporation enterprise attracted them to specific districts where the pattern of ownership was able to satisfy these particular demands. Thus, almost every corporation estate of any size has been built on a large landed estate. The corporation in fact purchased most of the pre-existing landed estates within the city limits irrespective of their location in relation to the city center. For this reason the corporation was obliged to ignore transport costs in order not to jeopardize the primary aim of rehousing slum tenants.

The largest corporation estate is located in the township of Seacroft, in the neighboring parish of Whitkirk. The village of Seacroft is conspicuous in the urban plan by the degree to which the compact village nucleus around

Fig. 10. A private estate of semi-detached houses located within a medium-size holding in northern Leeds. (By courtesy of "The Yorkshire Evening Post," Leeds.)

the green has survived. Over 80 per cent of the total area of the township was, however, concentrated in three large estates (Fig. 12). These estates were divided into large tenant farms, so that some 52 per cent of the holdings in the township were larger than 10 acres (Table 1). Corporation interest in the Seacroft estates was not new in the 1930's. During the late nineteenth century the corporation had purchased one of the large estates in Seacroft in order to establish municipal hospitals for the treatment of infectious diseases. Indeed by 1904 the corporation of Leeds owned some 250 acres in the township and was paying over half the rates despite the fact that the township of Seacroft was at that time beyond the municipal administrative boundary.

With the incorporation of Seacroft into Leeds in 1912 and the active participation of the corporation in house building after 1919 and more particularly after 1933, Seacroft was again highly suitable on account of the large areas under single ownership. As early as 1919, 81 acres of land were purchased on which 662 houses were erected. This estate represents one of the early smaller scale corporation housing ventures of the period before 1933. In 1933, however, a more ambitious scheme was approved whereby over 8,000 slum tenants were to be rehoused on landed

estates amounting in total area to over 1,000 acres. One estate of 800 acres, which bordered land purchased in 1900 in connection with the erection of hospitals but which had remained unused, was purchased as one unit in 1936. In 1947 an additional neighboring estate of 179 acres was purchased, so that with a minimum number of financial transactions the corporation acquired an estate of over 1,000 acres on which some 5,784 houses have been built.

In view of these particular demands of corporation enterprise after 1933 most of the large municipal housing estates are located on large landed estates in the northern and east-

Fig. 11. Alder Hill Avenue, a cul-de-sac of modern residences within the grounds of an older mansion.

PROPERTY BOUNDARIES ——————
FIELD BOUNDARIES — — — —

N

0   1/2
    MILES

Fɪɢ. 12.   Pre-existing pattern of ownership at Seacroft. (The shaded areas delimit estate lands.)

ern townships. One specific area of the south-ern part of the city has also been developed as a large-scale municipal housing estate. Ow-ing to the dominant pattern of fragmented ownership in the southern areas rather smaller housing estates have developed there. To the south of the highly fragmented pattern of ownership of Hunslet and Holbeck, the town-ship of Middleton had a compact pattern of ownership with no less than 58 per cent of its holdings over 10 acres in size. The township is dominated by the large holding of Middle-ton Park which along with the attached farm holdings was purchased by the corporation in

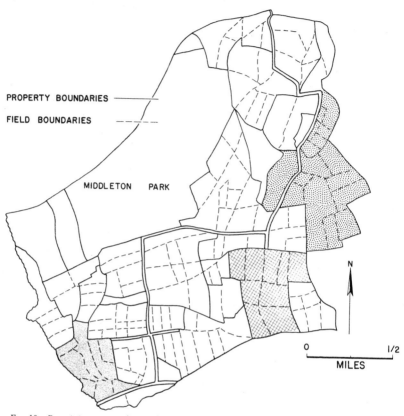

Fig. 13. Pre-existing pattern of ownership at Middleton. (The area of Middleton Estate is unshaded; the shaded areas delimit other estate lands.)

1920 as a unit of 326 acres (Fig. 13). Most of this area, which was a landscaped garden attached to the hall, was preserved as a park, and the residue was used for building purposes. In 1919, 57 acres had already been purchased here and in 1921 a further 44 acres were acquired to complete municipal ownership of a large block of land on which over 2,500 houses were built between the two world wars. Farther northward, the Belle Isle estate of 325 acres was purchased in 1937 as one unit to add to a smaller holding acquired in 1935. Building on this estate was interrupted by the war, but today the number of dwellings erected on it exceeds 2,500. Thus, on one of few areas of single compact ownership in the southern part of the city and in an area far removed from any existing lines of public transport, the corporation has actively developed two large housing estates of over 5,000 dwellings. Elsewhere in those townships south of the city center corporation enterprise is of more modest proportions than that in Middleton or to the north. Each estate tends to be completed as a single entity without regard to neighboring developments. The extensive blocks of corporation housing in the northern townships are here replaced by smaller self-contained units. In the absence of large units of single ownership the corporation could participate in residential building only on the same scale as private enterprise.

Certainly there are many areas where the contemporary pattern of building shows no relation to the pre-existing pattern of ownership. Frequently this negative conclusion is of great significance in emphasizing the role of compulsory purchase. Compulsory purchase of property by the municipal authorities is, however, an administrative mechanism which even today can be used only under exceptionally rigid conditions. Indeed, it is frequently only over property required for greenbelt purposes, or over those areas declared unhealthy and designated for slum clearance, that the local authorities can exercise the prerogative of compulsory purchase. As a result most areas between the central built-up district, scheduled for slum clearance, and the peripheral areas, zoned for green-belt purposes, have generally been free from large-scale compulsory purchase. Moreover, it is precisely within this intermediate zone that almost all the residential building in Leeds and many other cities has been concentrated since 1919.

Within this intermediate area, however, the construction of new arterial roads tends to destroy the possible effects of the pre-existing pattern of ownership. To alleviate the difficulties of road direction the local authorities have perforce to build roads independent of the structure of ownership. Complex purchasing problems are involved in the road building procedure, but, once constructed, a new road tends to determine the general orientation of the urban plan in its immediate vicinity. The cutting of both Scott Hall and Easterly Roads through the estate lands of Potternewton effectively destroyed the earlier pattern of ownership. Both the new roads and the powers of compulsory purchase granted to facilitate their construction prompted the owners of these estates to sell their whole holding and not merely the land for a road which they were obliged to provide. Ultimately both the corporation and the private builder built houses in units related to the road direction.

The pattern of ownership recorded on the tithe maps also was clearly subject to change over a period of some one hundred years. Although the tithe material would appear to be a very reliable representation of the pattern of ownership over which the nineteenth century additions to the town expanded, by the mid-twentieth century its significance is much reduced. Fortunately, another source of evidence is available for areas developed after 1942, for the Ministry of Agriculture survey of farm holdings of that date is extremely useful as a guide to the pattern of the building developments of the last two decades. Notwithstanding, however, the implications of major changes in the pattern of ownership after the tithe survey, the effect of property boundaries on the characteristics of the urban plan of Leeds occurs over sufficiently large areas to confirm its utility for this particular purpose.

OTHER MANIFESTATIONS OF THE EFFECT OF LAND OWNERSHIP ON THE URBAN PATTERN

In this paper only a few of the ways in which the pre-existing pattern of ownership affects the subsequent urban plan have been presented. The degree to which the particular shapes and sizes of land holdings satisfy or discourage particular contemporary building demands is but one important illustration of the diverse ways in which the factor of ownership affects the urban pattern. The question of the reluctance to sell land holdings on the part of certain landowners has been explored by Wise[14] in his analysis of Birmingham, where urban growth was not uniform on all sides of the old town but tended to move in a northerly and northwesterly direction. One of several factors involved in this differential growth was the fact that only two out of four lords of the manor cooperated in selling land for urban development.

Hoskins[15] has shown that the late survival of open fields with all their complicated property rights impeded the growth of such towns as Nottingham, Leicester, and Stamford. Most effective of all rights in preventing the sale of land for building developments were the Lammas pasture rights or the right of the burgesses to graze their animals after harvest on the

[14] Michael J. Wise, "The Growth of Birmingham," *Geography*, Vol. 33 (1948), pp. 176–190.
[15] William G. Hoskins, *The Making of the English Landscape* (London: Hodder and Stoughton, 1955).

open fields. Chambers[16] has examined the same problem in detail in Nottingham where, because of the late survival of open fields and common rights, all building was confined to the central core of the town. When the open fields were finally enclosed in 1845, many compact blocks were immediately developed by their owners without the slightest reference to neighboring allotments or owners. Although the pattern of streets was largely determined by the medieval footpaths and furlongs of the old open fields, the actual pattern of building was determined by the pattern of ownership established by the enclosure award.

In the process of land sales almost as important as the shape and size of parcels are the conditions of building leases, the covenants and stipulations they contain, and the particular policies laid down both by the landowners and developers who frequently operate in a very parochial way. Indeed, it is also important to take into account the almost whimsical decisions of estate developers which frequently are not only unrelated to the original cadastral pattern but also to the general current economic and social pressures. The most useful discussions of such factors are to be found in the Sir John Summerson's analysis of Georgian London[17] and a recent study of the London suburb of Camberwell during the nineteenth century by Dyos.[18] Such studies illustrate the fact that many estate developers have highly personal judgments as to what will maximize their return on their investment. The relevance of personal decisions and lease conditions to the growth and plan of Leeds would require a thorough analysis of such evidence as the numerous estate sale documents housed in the city archives and the West Yorkshire Registry of Deeds at Wakefield.

CONCLUSIONS

Without detailed analysis of other cities, any general conclusions on the effect of property boundaries and contrasting patterns of ownership on the growth and characteristics of towns must remain tentative. Indeed, it

must be emphasized that Leeds is one of the smaller "regional capitals" of Great Britain, where the "metabolism" of growth and change is perhaps at a minimum for a town of this size. Elsewhere urban growth over the last few decades has been on a different and more rapid scale, and the conditioning influence of the pre-existing pattern of ownership may well be less striking. Certainly a knowledge of the earlier pattern of ownership of the contemporary built-up area provides a refinement of the long-drawn distinction of "rectilinear" and "geometrical" patterns of building, for an interpretation of these patterns would appear to rest less on the formal layout of buildings than on the significant breaks in the continuity and alignment of buildings in residential areas.

The three conceptualizations[19] of urban structure do not embrace the conditioning influence of the pre-existing pattern of ownership. Fellmann[20] has demonstrated that even in Chicago, where the city was expanding over a newly settled landscape, the pre-building growth patterns, based on lot subdivision and lot sales, were only partly similar to those theorized as typical of the physical growth of cities. Rannells[21] has also criticized the applicability of these various theories to certain characteristics of the central areas of the city and stressed that even therein the boundary lines of ownership always remained as a mould constraining subsequent patterns of building. Although none of the theories of urban structure are completely satisfactory in themselves, they contribute collectively to an understanding of the product of individual aspects and factors of urban growth. It is, however, important to distinguish between theoretical patterns which are the concomitant of the individual factors of urban growth itself and the more amorphous and complex characteristics of the city as it really exists. It is clear that

[16] Jonathan D. Chambers, *A Century of Nottingham History* (Nottingham: University of Nottingham Press, 1952).

[17] Sir John N. Summerson, *Georgian London* (London: Pleides Books, 1945).

[18] Harold J. Dyos, *Victorian Suburb* (Leicester: Leicester University Press, 1961).

[19] Ernest W. Burgess, "The Growth of the City," in *The City*, R. E. Park, E. W. Burgess, and R. D. MacKenzie, eds. (Chicago: University of Chicago Press, 1925), pp. 47–62. Homer Hoyt, *The Structure and Growth of Residential Neighborhoods in American Cities* (Washington: Government Printing Office, 1939). Chauncy D. Harris and Edward L. Ullman, "The Nature of Cities," *Annals*, American Academy of Political and Social Science, Vol. 242 (1945), pp. 14–16.

[20] Fellmann, *op. cit.*

[21] John Rannells, *The Core of the City* (New York: Columbia University Press, 1956).

a necessary preoccupation with the structural corollaries of urban growth itself tends to underplay the role of the pre-existing pattern of occupance.

The growth and the characteristics of the urban plan of Leeds are fairly representative of the other industrial towns of northern England and to a lesser degree of Western Europe as a whole. In this paper the location, the size, and the shape of land holdings have been shown to have had a significant effect on the characteristics of the urban plan. It seems probable, therefore, that the conclusions yielded by this analysis of the urban plan of Leeds may well apply to many other towns in Western Europe. Certainly, urban growth, and particularly urban expansion over a long-settled rural area, creates an urban pattern which is the product of reciprocal factors to be found not only in the fact of urban growth itself, but also in the characteristics of the pre-existing and in part surviving rural areas.

The Lancashire Cotton Industry in 1840
H.B. Rodgers
Reprinted from *Transactions and Papers of the Institute of British Geographers,* 28 (1960), 135-53

THE LANCASHIRE COTTON INDUSTRY IN 1840

H. B. RODGERS, M.A.

NOT infrequently, over the last half-century, geographers, economists and historians have sought rational explanations for the tightly restricted distribution of the British cotton industry, and for the clear-cut pattern of regional specialization within its area of concentration in Lancastria. It would be difficult to justify adding to an already formidable literature were it not that some of the earliest series of official statistics which illuminate the origins of this locational pattern have been rather neglected, especially by geographers, and have never been mapped. It is the aim of this paper to analyse this material, to comment on maps constructed from it, and to assess its value in revealing the structure and distribution of the industry at the end of its first phase of rapid growth, technical revolution and locational experiment.

The Statistical Sources

Most of the evidence on which this study is based comes from a series of statistical surveys compiled for presentation to Parliament by the Inspectors of Factories. Their Returns of 1838 are the most valuable of these documents in a locational context, being virtually a census of the industries then covered by the Factory Act of 1833. For every parish in the kingdom a return was made of the number of factories in each of the chief textile manufactures, their power from both steam and water, and their employment.[1] Mapped in Figure 1, this material illustrates the distribution of the Lancashire cotton industry with great precision. Similar Returns had been made for 1835 and a comparison of the two tabulations (Fig. 3) reveals significant local differences in the rate of growth of Lancashire's cotton manufacture over a period which, though short, was one of especially quick expansion.[2] Two other maps are based on the survey of 1835. Since it shows more clearly than the later material those districts in which water-wheels were long preferred to the steam-engine, it has been used in drawing Figure 2, a map of the sources of power used in mills. The Returns of 1835 also contain an invaluable census of the power-looms then at work in the industry, and this, mapped in Figure 5, is the earliest sure guide to the regional separation of the spinning and weaving branches.

Though the Inspectors' Returns show the distribution of the industry with great clarity, they are much less informative on its structure, for they do not distinguish between its several branches. Fortunately, another contemporary document is complementary to them in this respect: a statistical appendix to a report for 1841 by Leonard Horner, the Inspector responsible for the greater part of northern England.[3] As an industrial survey this report is a model.

Every branch of the textile industries is treated individually: very full details are given of the fine-spinning, coarse-spinning and weaving mills, and of the 'combined' units which both spun and wove. Even the much smaller scale doubling, waste and smallware trades are surveyed most carefully.[4] Though all parishes of any industrial consequence are treated separately, some of the least important are grouped, often in so arbitrary a manner that the data for them are worthless.[5] A more serious inadequacy of Horner's inquiry is that, like his district, it did not include the extension of the Lancashire textile province into near-by Cheshire and Derbyshire. Fortunately, these areas had been covered by an earlier but less thorough survey made by S. Stanway, a Manchester accountant, for the Factory Commissioners of 1833.[6] This took the form of a sample survey of individual firms which, by happy accident, was fullest for precisely those areas omitted from Horner's analysis; and thus it permits the extension of Figure 4 to cover the textile districts of north-east Cheshire and north-west Derbyshire with tolerable accuracy and confidence. In a second respect Stanway's list supplements Horner's tables: the latter do not divide employment in the combined mills between the spinning and weaving departments, while the former supplies this information, though only for the towns close to Manchester. This material, being unsuitable for mapping, is presented in Table I (p. 148), and augments the fragmentary evidence of early specialization in weaving in parts of the region. Analyses of new investment in the various branches of the industry made by the indefatigable Horner during the years 1839-41 and 1844-45 are also used.[7] Short though the aggregate period is, this evidence of evolving regional specialization is too significant to be ignored, and it is mapped in Figure 6.

Apart from these official statistical surveys, evidence has been gathered from the many contemporary documents and accounts to which reference is made in the footnotes. But two of these other sources are important enough to merit inclusion in this bibliographical introduction, for they have supplied the water-hardness data plotted in Figure 1. It would be false and misleading to consider the locational influence of water-supply from the evidence of modern analyses of hardness, for these refer almost invariably to the pure brooks of the catchment areas and not to the lower, polluted courses of the rivers, which have long contained much harder water than their headstreams. A mass of mid-nineteenth-century data on water hardness is available in the local reports to the General Board of Health, made about 1850, and in the much fuller survey of the Report of the Rivers Pollution Commissioners of 1870.[8]

The Distribution of the Industry in 1840 and the Locational Factors

Figure 1 shows that cotton manufacture had already taken up a distribution which differed only in detail from that of the present day. The chief centres of the industry lay in the towns of the Manchester embayment, of the Calder–Darwen valley north of Rossendale, and of the coalfield of central Lancashire,

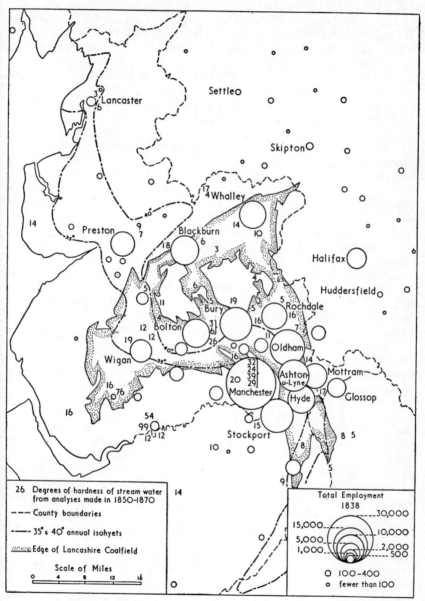

FIGURE 1—Distribution of employment in the cotton industry, 1838.

but it had spread also to the valleys of the gritstone moorlands east and north of Manchester and even into the West Riding. Even the relative importance of the main regions of manufacture has changed little since 1840 except that both north-east and central Lancashire now have larger shares of the employment in the industry. Apart from this the most notable locational tendency of the last century has been the peripheral contraction of the industry, for its distant outliers in extreme north Lancashire, in the valleys of north Derbyshire, and high up the Yorkshire dales were all to decay. Indeed, the manufacture has broken so little new ground since 1840, and lost so little old, that it is impossible to explain its modern location except by reference to its physical and economic environment a century ago. Since then new growth has simply been added to existing development in the districts already associated with the manufacture.

Of the factors which appear to have influenced the distribution of the industry in Lancastria during its first sixty years of growth availability of power seems to have been emphatically the most important. Two sources of energy were at work in mills, the steam-engine and the water-wheel. Though outmoded, water-power was by no means completely discarded; indeed, new sites were being developed and it still provided 13 per cent of the industry's energy.[9] In its resources of water-power Lancashire is extremely rich. A typical minor stream draining to the Manchester embayment, the Spodden, yielded 428 h.p. at eighteen sites spread over 5 miles of its course.[10] The larger wheels were more powerful, and much more reliable, than the steam-engines of the day, providing as much as 120 h.p. at a single site. But water-power was most restricted in its availability, for it is governed by the character of stream profiles. Far more was available in upland than in lowland Lancastria: little was developed below the 500-foot contour except where glacial diversion or the exhumation of a buried feature of the sub-drift landscape has caused local lack of grade along the lowland rivers. As late as 1840 streams still provided much of the power used in Bolton, Bury, Rochdale and throughout Rossendale, but they were never of much consequence in Manchester, Preston and Wigan.[11] Thus the growth of the industry during its water-powered phase involved its wide dispersion throughout, and indeed beyond, upland Lancastria. Its deep penetration of all the western Pennine and Rossendale valleys, its early growth in north-east Lancashire, its invasion of the West Riding and of upland Derbyshire must all be interpreted as a search for water-power. Figure 2 shows clearly that where the industry spread beyond what later became its dominant region it was to water-power sites.[12] Here is a reason for the later decay of these outliers of the industry. They had only this single specific advantage, and when river-power became outmoded, remoteness soon eliminated them.

Though many water-wheels rumbled on for decades, the progressive conversion of cotton manufacture to steam was well advanced by 1840. To the steam-powered industry location on the coalfield was not merely desirable but virtually obligatory; for the early engines were prodigal in their consumption of fuel, while the cost of transport of low-grade boiler coal was still high in

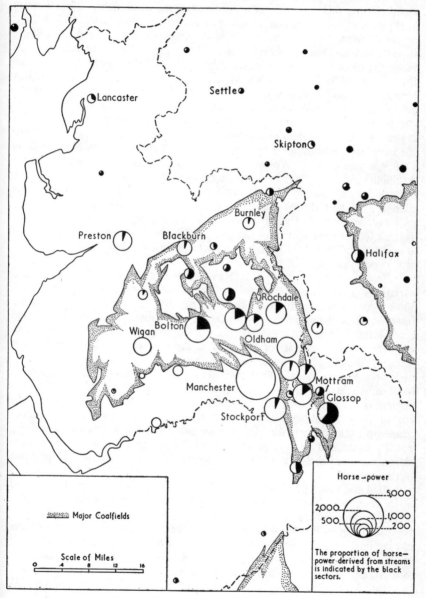

Lancaster

Settle○

Skipton○

Preston

Burnley

Blackburn

Halifax

Rochdale

Wigan   Bolton

Oldham

Manchester   Mottram

Glossop

Stockport

Major Coalfields

Scale of Miles

0   4   8   12   16

Horse-power

5000

2000
500   1,000
200

The proportion of horse-power derived from streams is indicated by the black sectors.

FIGURE 2—Sources of power in cotton mills, 1835.

relation to its very low pit-head value. When the first steam-mills were being built an overland journey of only 8 miles was enough to double the price of coal, and over difficult roads the cost of cartage was even higher. Thus Oldham coal priced at between 7 and 8 shillings a ton at its source brought 15 shillings at Saddleworth, only 5 miles away.[13] Water transport was less expensive where it was available, but for short hauls involving land carriage to and from the barge the canals were by no means cheap carriers. Household coal was one-third dearer in the late 'thirties at Manchester than at Hyde, only 8 miles away by water and on the worked coalfield.[14] Certainly the economies of canal transport were greater over longer distances, but the barge could not deliver truly cheap fuel to distant markets. Coal prices were consistently and appreciably higher in south-west than in south-east Lancashire during the early phases of the industrial revolution. Wigan coal sold for 7s. 6d. a ton on Merseyside in 1790:[15] a year later at Worsley near Manchester industrial grades averaged 4 shillings and ranged as low as 1s. 6d. a ton at the pit.[16] In 1823 the best coal, the type least affected by the cost of carriage, was 2 shillings dearer in Liverpool than in Manchester.[17] Nor did the lowering of freight rates brought about by railway competition destroy Liverpool's disadvantage, for canal and rail charges for coal brought from either St. Helens or Wigan were roughly equal at about 2 shillings a ton, a high figure set against the prevailing pit-head value of between 3 and 4 shillings.[18]

Fragmentary though these figures are, it is clear that pronounced regional variations in the price of coal survived the successive revolutions in transport. Thus a cotton firm incurred a substantial penalty in siting a mill more than a few miles from the nearest supply, especially since many of its competitors had coal almost literally on their doorsteps. Few mills in Oldham, for example, were more than a quarter of a mile from the nearest pit, and some, like the Ashtons' mill in Hyde, were 'supplied from rich coal measures immediately under the factory lands'. That the industry was extremely sensitive to these local differences in the cost of fuel is undeniable, for the coal bill was an important factor in the costs of production. An analysis for a typical mill put the cost of fuel at about one-fifth of the cost of labour;[19] thus a mill so far from the nearest pit that it paid twice the average price for coal was working under a penalty equivalent to a wage increase of 20 per cent. Much slighter wage claims were regarded by mill-owners as so ruinous that they provoked long and bitter disputes.

That the steam-powered cotton industry was virtually tied to the coalfield or its margins is demonstrated in Figures 1 and 3. By mid-century the manufacture had spread throughout the worked coalfield but extended hardly at all beyond its edges. Preston was and, remains the only important outlier, and this old regional centre with a long tradition of textile work could be supplied by canal and tramway from pits 8 miles away. The overwhelming importance of a local supply of fuel as a locational factor is illustrated with particular force in Figure 3, on which changes in the distribution of the industry between 1835

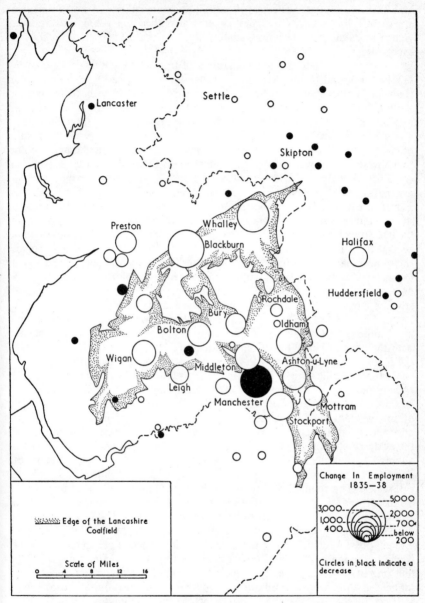

FIGURE 3—Growth and decline in employment in the cotton industry, 1835-38.
Both the decline at Manchester and the very rapid increase at Middleton reflect boundary changes.

and 1838 are plotted. The map needs little commentary. In north and west Lancashire, in the Yorkshire dales and even at Warrington, the manufacture was generally stagnant or declining, while within the coalfield it was growing with great energy.

Three other factors — the availability of transport facilities, of an existing labour force, and of supplies of soft water — may have had some influence on the evolving distribution of the cotton industry. It would seem to the present author that the importance of the last of these has been grossly overstressed and its influence misunderstood. It has been argued that Carboniferous east and central Lancashire are regions of soft water and Triassic west Lancashire of hard.[20] But this is simply an indirect way of putting the fundamental point, that surface water over most of the county tends to be soft and cheaply developed, where it has not been polluted by industry, while underground supplies are hard and expensive. Through its bolder relief and higher rainfall east Lancashire had, initially, far better resources of soft, surface water than the west of the county, where sub-surface supplies have been developed to supplement meagre stream resources. But for more than a century few streams in east and central Lancashire have contained soft water except in their moorland courses: their lower reaches have long been little better than industrial sewers, and a great increase in hardness is the inevitable consequence of pollution. A century ago Mersey water was analysed at 15° of hardness at Stockport though its head-streams showed only 5°: on the Irwell hardness increased from 4° at its source to 29° at Manchester, while the Douglas at Wigan was harder than Rostherne mere in Triassic Cheshire.[21] In effect, the cotton manufacture was associated with the zone of hardest water in Lancashire (Fig. 1); and the later growth of the industry was to be largely in the same districts.

Moreover, the various branches of the cotton manufacture have never been equally sensitive to the quality of their water supply. To the finishing trades, certainly, this was a factor of vital importance, but to the other branches a supply of soft water was of no greater value than to any other industry which had adopted the steam-engine. This distinction is demonstrated most forcibly in the evidence presented to the Rivers Pollution Commissioners in 1870. Firms in all branches of the industry were asked to put an actual cash value to the importance, in their operations, of a supply of clean, unpolluted and therefore soft water. The spinners and weavers who replied estimated the annual saving at an average of only £63, one-twentieth of their average annual fuel bill of almost £1300. The finishing trades reported that clean water was worth an average of £536 to each firm, while their fuel bill averaged £1100.[22] Here is the clearest possible evidence of the far greater importance of cheap coal than soft water to the manufacturing branches, and of the much greater concern of the finishing trades for the quality of their water supply. Though sources of water influenced the siting of mills of all types, for even the tiniest brooks were followed by chains of factories, this is a factor which has guided the local, rather than the regional, distribution of the industry.

A conclusion broadly similar to this may be drawn from a study of the influence of the canal network on the distribution of the cotton manufacture. In their courses through and even between the towns of east and central Lancashire the canals were picked out by lines of mills, but they quite failed to encourage the spread of the industry south and west away from the coalfield. Both the Bridgewater and the Leeds and Liverpool canals could bring coal and cotton, and even a water supply, to the districts they traversed, but no town on their courses away from the coalfield ever acquired a substantial cotton manufacture. The canals, too, influenced detailed siting rather than general location. Nor was the attraction of a pool of labour experienced in textile work sufficient to tempt the factory industry away from the cheapest sources of coal. The fate of the early mills in Lancaster, Altrincham, Nantwich and many other places shows that the existence of a textile tradition could not, alone, ensure success. Moreover, labour, in general, was mobile and moved to the industry: only in a few areas may the spread of mills have been, in part, a migration of the industry in search of workpeople to meet the shortage of hands which was a common complaint of the masters in times of prosperity. Thus the distress of large numbers of hand-loom weavers in north-east Lancashire may have accelerated the pace of factory growth here in the middle of the century. However, there was hardly a parish in Lancastria without a declining domestic manufacture at this time; but only those which were in other respects ripe for industrialization were colonized by the factory system.

This analysis of the factors which seem to have been responsible for moulding the distribution of the early cotton industry within Lancastria is, perhaps, involved; but the conclusions to which it leads are surprisingly simple. Cheap coal from local sources was clearly the vital factor. Contemporary observers were sure that this was so; for example, Baines wrote of Liverpool that 'the absence of coal in the immediate neighbourhood would form an impediment to the cotton industry' growing there. This assertion and its converse have proved true of almost every town in Lancastria. Only one beyond the coalfield, Preston, has acquired a substantial cotton industry: only one on the coalfield, St. Helens, has failed to do so.

The growth of the manufacture at Preston cannot be explained wholly in terms of the cheap water-transport of fuel, for the cost of coal here was much higher than on the coalfield.[23] But the strength of the textile and commercial tradition in this old regional centre, allied to the exceptional ability of some of its early mill-owners, appears to have offset this disadvantage; and the town stood on the threshold of the Fylde, for long among the county's richest rural regions and a source of both fresh labour and cheap food. There is evidence, too, that in Preston, a town of dear coal but cheap bread, wage-rates were low. Tentatively though these points are made, they seem to provide at least a framework for an explanation of the growth of this outlier of the cotton manufacture. But the reasons for the failure of the trade to take root in St. Helens, except weakly and impermanently, are more obscure. The prospect of intense com-

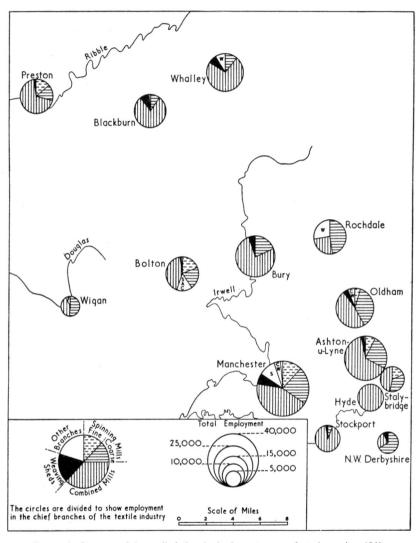

FIGURE 4—Structure of the textile industries in the cotton-manufacturing region, 1841.

The data for the four districts in Cheshire and Derbyshire are for 1833. In the sectors which show employment in 'other branches' the following symbols are used: W, woollens; CW, cotton waste; SAC, the spinning of all counts of cotton, both fine and coarse; F, flax. Table I gives the division of employment between spinning and weaving in the 'combined' mills of many of the towns shown.

petition with the established glass, copper and alkali industries not only for labour but also for the very limited water resources of the area must have discouraged textile entrepreneurs. Competition for labour seems also to have been the chief cause of the stagnation which followed the quick early growth of the industry at Warrington, already by 1840 a town of great industrial diversity with an increasing interest in the metal trades. It is most significant that by 1900 Warrington had a higher proportion of women among its cotton operatives (over 90 per cent) than any other English centre of the industry. Only where great variety of employment provoked intense rivalry for labour, as for example in Leeds, Derby and Bristol, were such high proportions of women workers characteristic.

The Origins of Regional Specialization

The Returns of 1838 show that the cotton manufacture in the North-west had taken up almost its modern distribution and that the surviving archaic features, especially its peripheral dispersion, were quickly decaying. From Horner's survey and from the other sources listed earlier it is equally clear that regional differences in the structure of the industry were already emerging. This regional specialization has always taken two forms. Firstly, there has evolved a partial separation of the spinning and weaving branches: the latter became the special interest of the towns north of Rossendale while the former remained the monopoly of the districts to the south. Secondly, within both the spinning and weaving areas, a complex system of local specialization in particular types and qualities of work has developed. It is true today, as it was a century ago, that no two cotton towns are alike in their industrial structure.

Three maps have been drawn to illustrate the origins of these two patterns. Figure 4 shows the detailed composition of employment in all the chief textile centres and thus summarizes both the major regional and minor local contrasts in the character of the industry. Figure 5 reveals the nascent specialization in weaving in some parts of Lancastria: on it are plotted the distribution of power-looms in 1835 and also an index of specialization in weaving, the ratio of looms to total employment in all branches of the industry. Figure 6 shows the character of new growth in the manufacture over the periods 1839-41 and 1844-45, and thus indicates, if only very generally, how the patterns evident in the two preceding maps were tending to change.

In examining Figure 4 it must be remembered that at this date most power-looms were operated not by separate and specialized weaving firms, but in the 'combined' mills which had developed through the addition of weaving sheds to spinning units. In such mills the importance of the weaving department varied enormously; in some it was dominant, in others negligible. None of the official statistics of employment distinguish between spinning and weaving in the integrated mills, and Stanway's list (the source of Table I) yields this information in sample form only for some of the towns close to Manchester. Clearly, therefore, Figure 4 indicates the relative importance of the two chief branches only very crudely, even when examined in association with Table I. But it is evident that in some towns, especially Bolton, Rochdale and Wigan, the spinning branch dominated the industry completely. Elsewhere the 'combined' mills were the largest employers, and in some parts of the region these were now dominated by their weaving departments. Surprisingly, the area of most active interest in power-looms lay not in the modern weaving belt of north-east Lancashire but in north-east Cheshire. In Stockport, Hyde and Stalybridge there were few specialized spinning mills, and in the integrated units which provided the great bulk of employment here weavers outnumbered spinners. But the map yields little evidence that weaving was yet the special concern of north-east Lancashire, though it reveals the early growth of specialized weaving sheds here. Unfortunately, the division of employment in 'combined' mills is not known for the towns north of Rossendale, though census data suggest that weaving was already their dominant occupation.[24] Figure 5 corroborates these conclusions but it also amplifies them. It confirms the importance of weaving in north-east Cheshire, where the ratio of looms to total employment was the highest in the region. Manchester had more looms than the north Cheshire towns but here the relative importance of weaving was slighter. Rather surprisingly, Bury and Oldham were also among the chief centres of cloth production.[25] North-east Lancashire had only a small proportion of the looms then at work, but it stood second to the Cheshire towns in the ratio of looms to workers, the earliest clear evidence of the attachment of this region to the weaving process.

The data contained in Figures 4 and 5 leave no room to doubt that the bulk of the weaving capacity of the period was located in the Manchester embayment and especially along its Cheshire flank, but Figure 6 suggests that this was not to endure for long. During the 'forties the growth of weaving, at least in separate units, was relatively most rapid in the later 'weaving belt' of the north, and there was remarkably little investment here in specialized spinning concerns. But the data on which Figure 6 is based are inadequate in two respects; they neither distinguish between the two types of employment in the 'combined' mills, nor do they extend into Cheshire. Thus this source yields no evidence as to whether the early prominence of weaving in the Hyde and Stockport districts persisted. Comparison of the Inspectors' Returns for 1835 and 1850[26] shows that by mid-century Cheshire was falling far behind Lancashire in the growth of powered weaving: in 1835 Lancashire had three times as many looms as Cheshire but by 1850 five times. However, in 1850, a much higher proportion of the Cheshire than of the Lancashire looms was in separate weaving units. Thus the Cheshire towns appear to have been among the pioneers not only of powered weaving, but also of the specialized weaving section.

Local specialization is at least as deeply rooted a feature of the cotton industry as the regional separation of spinning from weaving. By 1840 every cotton town had acquired a distinctive industrial personality which, in most cases, has changed remarkably little since. Then, as now, Manchester had a

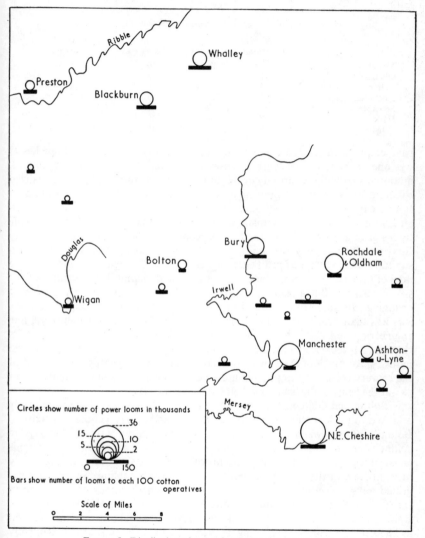

FIGURE 5—Distribution of power-looms weaving cotton, 1835.

more varied and better balanced range of textile industries than any other Lancashire town. What emphasis there was within its cotton industry lay on spinning which, if Table I correctly divides employment in the 'combined' mills,

TABLE I

The division of employment in 'combined' mills, from Stanway's lists

	Number of mills and total employed		Employment in spinning (%)	Employment in weaving (%)
Manchester	11	4921	50	45
Oldham	12	2896	48	44
Bolton	3	2741	86	13
North-west Derbyshire	3	586	58	41
Stockport	18	7335	42	56
Hyde	7	3869	38	60
Stalybridge	5	1809	43	56

gave employment to some 60 per cent of the textile workpeople. Manchester was one of the few towns with a considerable interest in fine-spinning; indeed, it housed over half the capacity of this branch, and many of the larger specialized spinning units produced only high counts of yarn. In contrast, the smaller spinning mills were generally, and the integrated units almost invariably, associated with medium and low qualities of work.[27] Other branches of the textile trades gave great breadth to the town's economy. The old smallware industry survived in many very tiny mills, and the new doubling branch, so far on a similarly small scale, was just beginning its growth. Though wool and flax were now of little consequence, Manchester was second among British centres of the silk industry.[28] But already the direction of the city's economic growth was changing. Its share of expansion in the basic branches of the cotton industry was less than proportional to its size, and in the future, newer industries, like engineering and chemical manufacture, were to contribute increasingly to its growth. Moreover, radical changes were taking place in Manchester's cotton industry, for much of the new investment was in weaving sheds. By the end of the century these were to provide more employment than spinning mills in this city at the heart of the 'spinning' belt.

Bolton and Oldham had none of Manchester's balance. They were firmly attached to the spinning branch and to the fine and coarse sections respectively. Bolton's industry was very highly specialized. Four-fifths of its mill-hands were spinners, and of these a higher proportion than in any other town was in mills engaged wholly or partly on high counts of yarn. It is significant, too, that only here, at least in the districts covered by Stanway's sampling, were there integrated mills concerned with fine-spinning. If Horner's survey of expansion in the 'forties is at all representative, interest in weaving was almost stagnant in Bolton, and it is clear that the town was already assuming its modern function as the centre of the fine-spinning branch. Oldham, in contrast, was quickly becoming the giant of the coarse-spinning towns. Though weaving was by no means as feebly developed here as it was in Bolton, the spinning of low-count

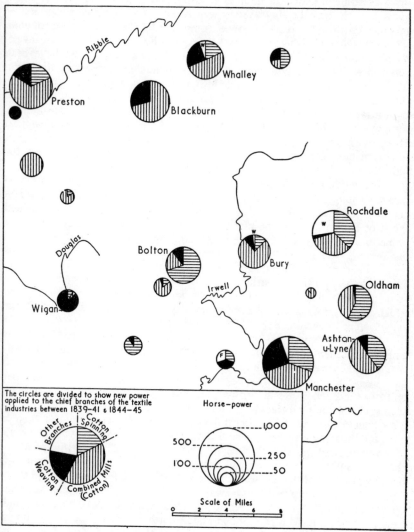

FIGURE 6—Expansion in the textile industries, 1839-41 and 1844-45.
The symbols used to indicate the minor branches are as in Figure 4.

yarns gave employment to two-thirds of the town's textile workers. The most curious feature of Oldham's spinning industry, and perhaps a cause of its mushroom growth, was the tiny average size of its units, many of which shared premises owned by 'room and power' companies.[29] These were more common in Oldham than elsewhere in south Lancashire. By reducing the initial investment required of an entrepreneur with little capital, they must have been responsible for a continual flow of new energy and enterprise into the town. Many small firms, reared in these industrial nurseries, graduated later to their own mill. Moreover, the availability of space and power for rent may have been a factor in the hardening of Oldham's specialization in coarse-spinning, for it was in this branch that the small firm, to which hired facilities would appeal most, stood the best chance of survival. Certainly, tiny coarse-spinning units in shared mills accounted for the bulk of investment in the 'forties, and the hitherto dominant 'combined' branch was beginning to fall behind.

Rochdale and Bury were following divergent paths of specialization — coarse-spinning in the former and weaving in the latter[30] — but they had in common some rather archaic characteristics. In both districts streams provided much of the power, and the old woollen industry, now transferred from the home to the factory, still flourished. Rochdale, a town always slow to change, had scarcely been reached by the weaving revolution, and though power-looms were widely used in Bury they wove fustians, an old fabric, rather than true cotton cloth. Nor did the structure of the textile trades of either town appear to be changing quickly. 'Combined' mills dominated the new growth in Bury, while cotton-spinning and the wool industry took the largest shares of the expansion in Rochdale.

The salient feature of the towns of the Cheshire flank of the Manchester embayment, their special concern with weaving, has already been discussed, though without reference to local contrasts within this district. Hyde seems to have been the most narrowly specialized of these towns: here every substantial mill of which details are known was integrated and had many more weavers than spinners among its hands. In total, the former outnumbered the latter by more than two to one. In Stockport the disbalance was not so complete, though here, too, weaving was the dominant trade. But the Ashton–Stalybridge group of towns showed more of the breadth and balance so characteristic of Manchester. Ashton, in particular, had not only adopted the power-loom quickly, but was also one of the few towns to have developed a fine-spinning industry. There is little evidence that the weaving revolution had spread from these towns on the threshold of the Pennines to the industrial villages of the moorland valleys. Neither in Mottram nor in Saddleworth parishes were power-looms widely used, although they had been adopted in Glossop and New Mills, and it is clear that in these remote districts the typical units were tiny, water-powered, coarse-spinning mills, relics of the first phase of technical advance in the industry.

Though the Manchester embayment and its moorland fringes still held almost three-quarters of the manufacturing capacity, the cotton industry was spreading in two directions, slowly westward into central Lancashire and more quickly northward into and beyond Rossendale. In central Lancashire Wigan and Leigh were the chief centres; St. Helens was its most westerly extension and Warrington a southerly outlier. Horner's report is less informative on this area than any other; but some, at least, of the characteristics of its cotton industry emerge. Spinning was the principal branch, and at Leigh part of the output was of high quality. The growth of powered weaving seems to have been slow, for few 'combined' mills or weaving sheds were recorded. Perhaps in reflection of the recent growth of the manufacture here, most of its units were of unusually large size: Wigan's three integrated mills, for example, each gave employment to over 600 hands. But there was little unity in the structure of the cotton industry in central Lancashire, and what there was did not endure. The new investment shown in Figure 6 was almost wholly in spinning mills at Leigh but in weaving sheds at Wigan. Thus the former was taking its place among the group of fine-spinning towns centred on Bolton, while the latter was showing closer affiliations with the Burnley–Preston line of weaving towns.

It has been stressed, in an earlier passage, that Horner's survey leaves completely obscure the origins of specialization in weaving in the line of towns on the northern flank of Rossendale. All that can be said with complete confidence is that 'combined' mills utterly dominated the industry here; but it seems very likely that these were concerned primarily with weaving. There is strong evidence, too, that separate weaving sheds were appearing more quickly here than in any other region. Even local contrasts are revealed only imperfectly by Horner's material, for the three constituent parishes for which details are given were of enormous size. But some divergent tendencies in their industrial growth are evident. Preston had a far greater interest in spinning than either the Blackburn or Whalley districts; and it housed a not inconsiderable section of the fine-spinning branch. Blackburn was the arch-type of the north Lancashire cotton town, with an almost total dependence on the 'combined' mill, a quickly growing interest in specialized weaving and a relatively stunted spinning industry. Whalley, a parish which then contained the Burnley group of towns, was the most archaic of the three, with its heavy reliance on waterpower and the remains of its old woollen manufacture. In Whalley, too, the contrast between the town and country branches of the industry was particularly well displayed. Coarse-spinning was mainly in the hands of tiny mills, mostly water-powered and rural in location. 'Combined' mills on the other hand were usually large and powered by steam, and these provided the bulk of the employment in the towns of the parish.

Conclusion

There are two very general conclusions to which this study leads. The first is that little has changed in the geography of the Lancastrian cotton industry over the last hundred years. By 1840 its general distribution had been shaped, at least in outline, and the pattern of local and regional specialization which had begun to crystallize has proved remarkably stable. The trebling of employment in the industry in the second half of the century led to no substantial territorial expansion, nor did the progressive separation of weaving from spinning over the same period initiate radically new tendencies in regional specialization. It is clear that by 1850 the industry had acquired an immobility born of maturity: the economies of concentration were obvious, and no changes in technique or in the economic environment of the industry profound enough to compel a shift in distribution transpired. Locationally, as well as technically, the industry has shown itself to be most conservative.

The second conclusion is that very different groups of factors have influenced the overall distribution of the industry on the one hand and the evolution of regional contrasts in its structure on the other. The sharp boundaries of the cotton-working province were set chiefly by physical factors — by the availability of water-power, of local fuel at low cost, and of ample surface water resources. But regional specialization appears to have been brought about by the accidents of tradition and invention, and by the play of historical and economic forces. The quick growth of weaving in the north Cheshire towns cannot have been unconnected with the early progress with the power-loom made in Stockport by Horrocks and other inventors. But Bolton's association with fine-spinning antedates, though it must have been strengthened by Crompton's invention here of the mule which made possible the growth of this branch. As early as 1795 fine work was regarded as traditional to the Bolton district, a skill 'rooted as it were to the soil' of the parish.[31] There is less obscurity in the growing attachment of north Lancashire to weaving, for the area was becoming industrialized at precisely the time when powered weaving was growing most quickly. But to attempt to rationalize the pattern of local specialization, if possible at all, is far beyond the competence of the present writer and the scope of this study.

NOTES

[1] Return of all the mills and factories ... June, 1838. *Commons Sessional Papers* (1839), 42, 1.

[2] Persons employed in the various mills and factories ... *Commons Sessional Papers* (1836), 45, 51.

[3] *Reports of the Inspectors of Factories, December, 1841* (1842), 33-76.

[4] Horner's Report also contains full data for the woollen and worsted trades: these were used in drawing Figure 4. But the Returns of 1838 are more informative on the flax and silk industries, and the employment in these manufactures as shown in Figure 4 was derived from these earlier Returns.

[5] Tabulation is complicated by the fact that the grouping of minor parishes varies with each branch of the industry surveyed. Still different groups are used in the tables of mills working short-time and idle. In general it is possible to abstract full details for every significant manufacturing parish. But it must be stressed that some minor centres of the industry cannot be identified. For example, a single total is given for the coarse-spinning mills in fifteen widely scattered parishes, which in total had about one-tenth of the employment in this branch. No distinction has been made, in tabulation, between mills working full-time, short-time and idle, for trade was soon to recover from the depression which prompted this survey.

[6] The full list of 151 mills is given in an appendix to A. URE, *The cotton manufacture of Great Britain* (1836). Of these mills sixty-five were in north Cheshire.

[7] *Reports of the Inspectors of Factories, 1841* (1842) and *1845* (1846).

[8] Rivers Pollution Commissioners, *First Report* (1870), 1, 111-26.

[9] In Bury, for example, 17 per cent of the power installed during the periods 1839-41 and 1844-45 was water-power.

[10] A. P. WADSWORTH, 'The early factory system in Rochdale', *Transactions of the Rochdale Scientific and Literary Society*, 19 (1937), 136.

[11] In many upland parishes steam-engines were installed only for use in drought. Thus the bulk of the power in normal use was from streams.

[12] Water supplied 45 per cent of the power used in cotton mills in the West Riding and 88 per cent in the valleys draining to the Trent.

[13] J. AIKIN, *Description of the country … round Manchester* (1795), 239, 558.

[14] Household grades cost 12 shillings a ton at Manchester (B. LOVE, *Handbook of Manchester* (1839), 44) and at Hyde 8 shillings (A. URE, *Philosophy of manufactures* (1835), 349).

[15] E. BAINES, *History; directory and gazetteer of Lancashire* (1824), 125.

[16] *Bridgewater account for 1791.* Manuscript in Chetham's Library.

[17] E. BAINES, op. cit., 201.

[18] W. LAIRD, *The export coal trade of Liverpool* (1846), 7-10 and 34.

[19] J. MONTGOMERY, *The cotton manufacture of Great Britain contrasted … with that of the United States* (1840), 122-4.

[20] H. W. OGDEN, 'The geographical basis of the Lancashire cotton industry', *Journal of the Manchester Geographical Society*, 45 (1928), 8-30.

[21] Rivers Pollution Commissioners, op. cit., 1, 111-26.

[22] Ibid., 2, 123-74.

[23] Wigan cannel, a special gas-making fuel, cost 15 shillings a ton in Preston compared with 10 shillings at its source. (Local Reports to the General Board of Health, 1851.)

[24] Unpublished data from the enumerators' books of the 1841 census have been furnished by Mr. K. L. Wallwork, to whom the writer is greatly indebted. These figures show that weavers outnumbered spinners by perhaps three to one in the Blackburn area. But many weavers here still worked at hand-looms, either in the home or in the factory, and it is impossible to distinguish between hand- and power-loom operatives.

[25] Only a joint total is given for Rochdale and Oldham, and even this includes some looms in Manchester.

[26] Return of the number of cotton, woollen, worsted, silk and flax factories … *Commons Sessional Papers* (1850), 42, 455. These Returns give only county totals.

[27] Throughout the region, except at Bolton, the 'combined' mills recorded in Stanway's survey were concerned only with the medium-coarse sections of the trade. This was quite rational, for power-looms were rarely used for the finest materials, and thus only coarse-spinners found it worth while to invest in them and to become integrated concerns. The same factor explains the large average size of fine-spinning firms, which could invest surplus profits only in additional mules. Coarse-spinners were generally small, for as they grew they bought looms and moved into the integrated section.

[28] The Returns of 1838 show that silk mills employed some 7700 persons in Macclesfield, 4200 in Manchester and 3000 in Derby.

[29] Of every ten spinning firms in Oldham, six shared mills. In the waste and doubling trades this was even more common, as many as six firms sharing a single engine.

[30] So many looms were recorded in Bury in 1835 that it is clear that weaving must have been the chief branch in the town's 'combined' mills.

[31] J. AIKIN, op. cit., 262. It may not be coincidence that the four towns which, by 1811, had taken up the mule most quickly and in the greatest numbers (Manchester, Bolton, Preston and Ashton) were in 1840 and still are today the great fine-spinning centres.

Supplementary Note

The distribution of the Lancashire cotton manufacture is one of the classic problems in the location of industry. Even during the nineteenth century there was speculation about the reasons for the remarkably compact and sharply defined pattern of location that it assumed so firmly and so early. A number of general explanations have been fashionable from time to time: the greater atmospheric humidity of east Lancashire, its soft water resources, the fixity of craft skills here and the early development of banking and credit facilities have all been suggested as the primary causes of the concentration of cotton manufacture into that distinctive region of eastern Lancastria in which the industry became so dominant.

One conclusion only was evident from the earlier literature; that the industry had colonised what was to become its region of concentration very early in its growth, and thereafter remained locationally stable. Thus if its distribution were to be analysed and explained rationally, this must be attempted in the context of the formative period of the late eighteenth and early nineteenth centuries. Not only was it necessary to secure an accurate and detailed statement of the industry's location at this time from contemporary sources, but it was also necessary to draw upon the evidence of the period in order to assess the relative influence of the various forces that may have helped shape the locational pattern. It is unprofitable and misleading, for example, to apply modern data on water hardness to the industrial environment of the mid-nineteenth century. A contemporary statement must be sought.

There was no difficulty in mapping the location of the industry in considerable detail from the Factory Inspectors' Returns of 1835 and 1838, a source surprisingly little used either before or since. One may observe, in passing, that it is odd that a parallel study of the wool-worsted trades of the West Riding has not so far appeared, though a study of the distribution of the early silk industry, using the Returns, is in progress. But the use of contemporary evidence in weighing the influence of the possible constraints on the location of the industry proved much more difficult. It was a pity that more exact information could not be gathered as to the relative importance of fuel and labour charges in the total costs of production, or that a more refined statement of sub-regional variation in coal prices was not possible. On the other hand very firm and direct evidence of the (rather slight) significance of the soft water factor came to hand from the Report of the Rivers Pollution Commissioners. One loose end, at least, is left interestingly dangling: the evolving pattern of sub-regional specialisation emerges clearly enough from the evidence, but the attempt to find reasons for such pronounced local contrasts in the developing character of the industry is a largely speculative one.

H.B. RODGERS   August 1969

**The British Hosiery Industry at the Middle of the
Nineteenth Century: An Historical Study in
Economic Geography**
D.M. Smith

Reprinted from *Transactions and Papers of the Institute
of British Geographers,* 32 (1963), 125-42

THE BRITISH HOSIERY INDUSTRY AT THE MIDDLE OF THE NINETEENTH CENTURY: AN HISTORICAL STUDY IN ECONOMIC GEOGRAPHY

D. M. SMITH, B.A., PH.D.

THE middle of the nineteenth century marked an important turning point in the development of the British hosiery industry. While the introduction of power-driven machinery during the latter part of the eighteenth century had brought about a revolution in the organization of other textile industries, a domestic system stubbornly persisted in the hosiery trade, which gradually stagnated. The domestic system suited the employers, and the operatives, known as 'framework knitters', were reluctant to leave their cottage workshops for the more regulated life of the factory, despite the unfavourable wages and conditions of employment in the domestic industry. By the middle of the nineteenth century the first steam-powered hosiery factories had appeared, however, and a fundamental change in the organization of the hosiery industry was about to take place.

During the first half of the nineteenth century the domestic industry suffered periods of severe depression, and the condition of the workers became so serious that in 1845 a parliamentary inquiry was held into the trade. The report which resulted[1] provides a mass of statistics and other information from which the distribution and organization of the hosiery industry at this critical stage in its development may be reconstructed in detail. In this paper it is intended to use this information to describe the main geographical features of the framework knitting industry in 1844, and to explain briefly how they had come about.

The Location of Hosiery Manufacturing in Great Britain

During the first half of the nineteenth century the distribution of hosiery manufacturing, like that of the other British textile industries, showed a high degree of concentration. In 1844 there were 48,482 stocking frames[2] in the British Isles, all but 108 of them operated by hand, and 90 per cent were situated in the East Midland counties of Derbyshire, Leicestershire and Nottinghamshire (Fig. 1). The most important concentration in England outside the East Midlands was in Gloucestershire, with 930 stocking frames in Tewkesbury and a further hundred or so in Northleach, Twining and a few other places in the county. The only other towns in England with more than a very small number of frames were Godalming in Surrey (102 frames), London (60), Wakefield (40), Chacombe (25) and Middleton Cheney (24) in Northamptonshire, and Thurley

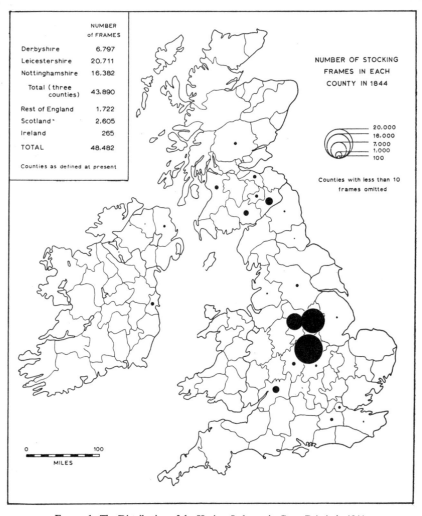

	NUMBER of FRAMES
Derbyshire	6,797
Leicestershire	20,711
Nottinghamshire	16,382
Total (three counties)	43,890
Rest of England	1,722
Scotland *	2,605
Ireland	265
TOTAL	48,482
Counties as defined at present	

NUMBER OF STOCKING
FRAMES IN EACH
COUNTY IN 1844

20,000
16,000
7,000
1,000
100

Counties with less than 10
frames omitted

MILES
0   100

FIGURE 1—The Distribution of the Hosiery Industry in Great Britain in 1844.

Note: In Scotland, Glasgow and the counties of Ayr and Renfrew are represented by one symbol.
Source: Report of the commissioner appointed to enquire into the condition of the framework knitters, British Parliamentary Papers (1845), XV, Appendix II, 12–13.

in Lincolnshire (20). In Scotland there were 2605 frames, the largest concentrations being in central Roxburghshire, with 1200 frames in the Hawick district and a further 150 round Denholm and Jedburgh, and the Dumfries area, with 500 machines. A total of 265 stocking frames existed in Ireland, the main centres being Balbriggan in the county of Dublin (100) and Dublin (44). There was no machine hosiery industry in Wales.

TABLE I

Employment Created by the British Hosiery Industry in 1833

Occupation	Number of persons employed
Production of yarn:	
Cotton spinning, doubling, etc.	3,000
Worsted carding, spinning	2,500
Silk throwing, winding	1,000
Total	6,500
Production of hosiery:	
Stocking making—men 13,000	
women 10,000	33,000
youths 10,000	
Seaming, winding, etc.—women and children	27,000
Total	60,000
Finishing:	
Embroidering, mending, bleaching, dyeing, etc.	6,500
Total	73,000

Source: First report from the select committee appointed to enquire into the operation of the existing laws affecting the exportation of machinery, British Parliamentary Papers (1841), VII, Appendix 3, 237.

It is difficult to estimate precisely how many people were employed in the hosiery industry at the middle of the nineteenth century, for a large number of women and children worked part time in such occupations as seaming and mending. The 1851 Census figures (58,900 in England of which 56,000 were in the East Midlands) did not include many of the part-time workers, and W. Felkin's estimate of 150,000 in 1866 appears to have been somewhat exaggerated.[3] The most accurate indication of the number of persons to whom the hosiery industry gave full-time employment is probably provided by figures for 1833 (Table I), which show that there were 33,000 persons actually working stocking frames and a further 40,000 concerned with ancillary processes and with the production of yarn for the industry. The total of 73,000 represents a little more than two persons to each frame in operation, and in addition there would have been many other women and children working only a few hours each day. If the same labour ratio is applied to the 42,652 stocking frames in operation in 1844 (the remaining 5830 were not at work at this time), and if allowance is made for part-time workers, the employment created by the whole of the British hosiery industry would have been over 100,000, of which about 90 per cent was in the East Midlands.

In order to explain the concentration which had developed in the East Midlands by the middle of the nineteenth century, it is necessary to examine briefly the early history of framework knitting. The manufacture of knitwear by machinery began in the village of Calverton, a few miles north-east of Nottingham, when the Rev. William Lee invented the stocking frame in 1589; before this stockings were either knitted by hand or made from woven fabrics. Important developments in industrial technology have generally been prompted by strong economic incentive, but this was not the case with the invention of the stocking frame. The usual explanation for Lee's remarkable achievement is that a young lady he admired was in the habit of paying more attention to her hand knitting than she did to Lee, and that he devised a knitting machine to remedy the situation.[4] Whether this is strictly correct or not, it appears to have been entirely a matter of chance that a machine for knitting stockings was invented in the East Midlands at this particular time.

Although William Lee worked stocking frames in Calverton for a number of years, it was in London and not in the East Midlands that the earliest important concentration of framework knitting developed. After failing to obtain a patent for his machine from Queen Elizabeth, and later from James I, Lee and his brother James took nine stocking frames to France. They were no more successful there, however, and when William died in Paris in 1610, James brought all but one of the machines back to England again. These were then set up in London, to form a nucleus round which the framework knitting industry gradually began to grow.[5]

Although James Lee soon returned home to revive framework knitting in Nottinghamshire,[6] the greatest expansion of the industry took place in London, and by 1664 there were 400–500 stocking frames in the city compared with about 150 in the Nottingham district and Leicestershire (Table II). At this time framework knitting provided employment for 1200 people in England.[7]

The relative importance of London during the seventeenth century is explained by the fact that the products of the framework knitters were still luxury goods, for which the city was the main market, and that knitted stockings were made almost exclusively from silk. London had for long been the main importing centre for silk yarn, and the establishment of silk manufacturing in Spitalfields, in the midst of the framework knitters, by Huguenot immigrants towards the end of the seventeenth century gave the city a further advantage.[8] By the end of the century there were 1500 stocking frames in the city, and by 1727 this had risen to 2500 (Table II).

At the beginning of the eighteenth century economic circumstances began to change, however, with the result that the advantages of proximity to the main luxury market and source of silk supply in London tended to be diminished. The production of cheaper goods made from wool and worsted quickly extended the market for machine-knitted hosiery, but to take full advantage of conditions of high elasticity of demand, cheap labour was essential. In London wages were generally higher than in other parts of the country[9] and the practice of reducing labour costs by employing large numbers of apprentices was restricted by the Company of Framework Knitters, which regulated the trade.[10] However, the practical control of the Company did not extend outside the London area, and manufacturers seeking cheaper labour began to move out of the city.

TABLE II

The Framework Knitting Industry: Number of Machines, 1641–1844

	Great Britain	Derbyshire, Leicestershire and Nottinghamshire		London	Leicester	Nottingham
		Number	Proportion of Total in Great Britain (%)			
1641	100(−)	×	×	×	×	×
1664	650	150(+)	25	400–500	×	×
1695	×	×	×	1,500	×	×
1727	8,000(+)	3,500(+)	45	2,500	500–700	400
1753	14,000	10,000(+)	71	1,000(−)	1,000	1,500
1782	20,000(+)	16,750[1]	84	500(−)	×	×
1812	29,582	25,168	85	100	1,650	2,600
1833[2]	33,000	28,000	87	×	×	×
1844	48,482	43,890	91	60	4,140	3,490

Source: G. HENSON, *The civil, political, and mechanical history of the framework knitters of Europe and North America*, (1831), *passim*; augmented from other sources.

Note: [1] The figure for the three counties in 1782 is an estimate; neither Henson's figure (13,000), nor Felkin's (17,350) are in accordance with statistics for the rest of the country.
[2] The figures for 1833 do not include machines out of work, and the total in existence was probably not much less than in 1844.
(+) indicates 'more than'; (−) indicates 'less than'; × indicates no data available.

Most of this movement was to the East Midlands, where labour and capital were available in three fairly large county towns (Derby, Leicester and Nottingham) which were as yet uncommitted to any other form of industrial specialization.[11] The area also had the advantage of local supplies of wool suitable for the requirements of the framework knitters, and the building of the first successful silk-throwing mill in Britain at Derby between 1718 and 1721 broke the London monopoly of silk supply. The East Midlands already contained an active

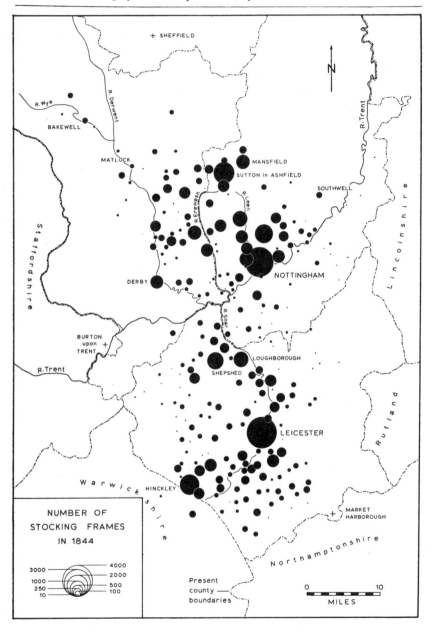

NUMBER OF
STOCKING FRAMES
IN 1844

3000 ——— 4000
1000 ——— 2000
250 ——— 500
10 ——— 100

Present
county ———
boundaries

0 ——— 10
MILES

nucleus of framework knitters, and the trade had probably been established in the Nottingham district long enough to have developed external economies associated with skilled labour, the manufacture and repair of machines, and finishing and marketing facilities. The presence of this early nucleus of framework knitters, which was probably the crucial factor in attracting the trade from London to the East Midlands, was the direct result of the invention of the stocking frame at Calverton, and the subsequent return of James Lee to Nottinghamshire. However, the eventual concentration of the domestic hosiery industry almost exclusively in the counties of Derbyshire, Leicestershire and Nottinghamshire would not have occurred if the area had not possessed certain advantages over other parts of the country in terms of the supply of labour, capital and materials, at the time when economic circumstances necessitated the migration of the trade from London.

By 1727 the three counties, with 3500 stocking frames, already had more than London (Table II); between 1732 and 1750 another 800 machines were brought to Nottingham from London, and a similar movement to Leicester took place.[12] The capacity of the industry was increasing rapidly with the expanding market, and by 1753 there were about 14,000 stocking frames in Britain, over 10,000 of them in the East Midlands. The number of frames in London had fallen to less than 1000 by this time, while the number in Nottingham had risen to 1500, and in Leicester to 1000 (Table II). The development of factory cotton spinning in Derbyshire and Nottinghamshire gave the framework knitting industry further impetus during the last three decades of the century, and by 1812 there were 25,168 stocking frames in the East Midlands—85 per cent of the total in Britain, compared with 71 per cent in the area in 1753 and only 25 per cent in 1664 (Table II). By the beginning of the nineteenth century the concentration of the British hosiery industry in the East Midlands had thus been completed.

The Location of Hosiery Manufacturing in the East Midlands in 1844

Within the East Midlands the distribution of hosiery manufacturing at the middle of the nineteenth century was largely confined to a well-defined area extending from the Matlock district, Mansfield and Southwell in the north to Hinckley, Lutterworth and almost as far as Market Harborough in the south (Fig. 2). Within this area a number of more important concentrations existed.

FIGURE 2—The Distribution of the Hosiery Industry in the East Midlands in 1844.

Note: The figures include all frames, whether they were at work at the time or not. The total figures for the counties of Derbyshire and Leicestershire include an addition made by the compiler of the statistics to compensate for frames not at work, and not included in the returns made; in the map these additional frames have been distributed over those places for which there is no return of the number of machines not at work. Figures for Thurmaston, and Broughton Astley with Primethorpe and Sutton, in Leicestershire, are not shown in the main list, but are included later in the Report. *Source: Report of the commissioner appointed to enquire into the condition of the framework knitters, British Parliamentary Papers* (1845), XV, Appendix II, 4–11.

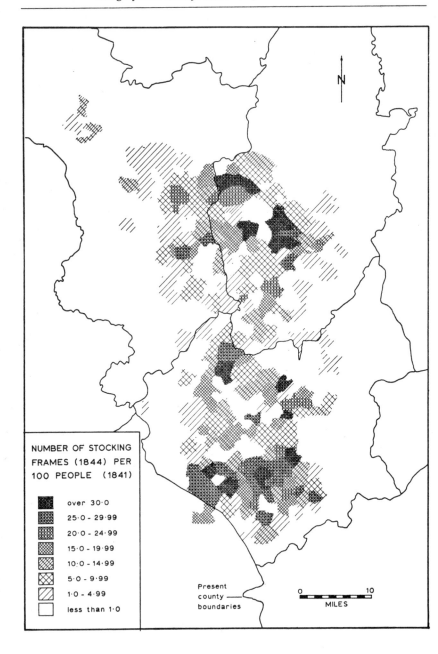

NUMBER OF STOCKING
FRAMES (1844) PER
100 PEOPLE (1841)

- over 30·0
- 25·0 - 29·99
- 20·0 - 24·99
- 15·0 - 19·99
- 10·0 - 14·99
- 5·0 - 9·99
- 1·0 - 4·99
- less than 1·0

Present
county
boundaries

0   10
MILES

In the north there were over 4000 frames in the Mansfield and Sutton-in-Ashfield district, to the south-west of which a number of prominent centres are also shown in the area between the rivers Derwent and Erewash. A large concentration existed in the Nottingham district, with 3490 frames in the town itself, almost 1400 in Arnold, about 3000 in the Leen Valley villages to the west, and a further 1500 or so in the villages to the east of the town. In Leicestershire there was a large concentration round Shepshed, with about 1200 frames, and Loughborough (900), extending up the Soar valley to Leicester, which was the most important hosiery manufacturing town in Britain and contained 4140 frames. A further concentration existed in the villages to the south of Leicester, and to the west there were about 3500 frames in Hinckley and its neighbouring villages.

Figure 3 illustrates the relationship between population and framework knitting, and shows the extent to which different areas were dependent on the industry as a source of livelihood. The highest ratios of frames to population were not in Nottingham and Leicester, where other industries also existed, but in the secondary centres of the framework knitting industry and in some of the villages. In Sutton-in-Ashfield, with a population of 5670, there were 34·7 frames per hundred people, in Shepshed (population 3872) there were 31·7 and in Hinckley (population 6365) the ratio was 27·7. In some of the villages to the north-east of Nottingham even higher ratios were recorded, and in the area to the south of Leicester a number of villages had over thirty frames per hundred people. As each frame generally provided support for three people, these figures represent a remarkably high degree of economic dependence on the framework knitting industry. In places where other industrial activities were beginning to develop, however, the ratio of frames to population tended to be much lower.

This brief examination of the distribution of the domestic hosiery industry in the East Midlands reveals two important features which require some explanation: first, the high degree of dispersal, with framework knitting in over 250 towns and villages in the three counties, and secondly, the compact nature of the hosiery manufacturing district as a whole. The dispersal of framework knitting in the East Midlands began during the seventeenth century, and it appears that in Nottinghamshire the industry spread first among villages in the west of the county, where an abundance of waste land had already attracted unusually large village populations.[13] Those villages which provided industrial employment, and others in open parishes where settlement and building was

FIGURE 3—The Relationship Between Population and the Hosiery Industry in the East Midlands.

Note: The number of stocking frames includes those which were not at work. Figures for the number of frames per hundred people have been mapped by parishes, or subdivisions of parishes (that is townships, hamlets and chapelries) as defined for the purpose of compiling population statistics in the 1841 Census.

Source: Report of the commissioner appointed to enquire into the condition of the framework knitters, British Parliamentary Papers (1845), XV, Appendix II, 4–11; and *Census of Great Britain, 1841,* Population Tables.

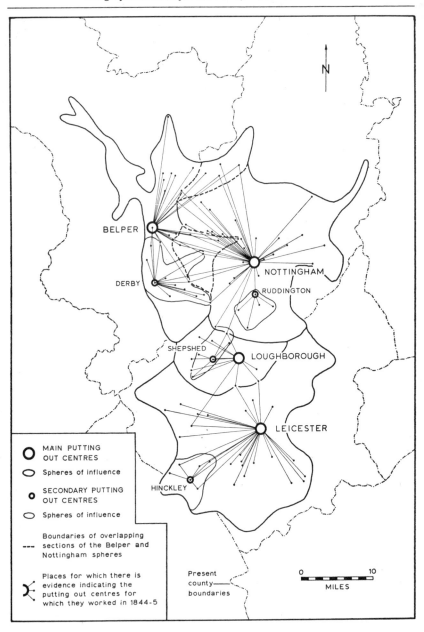

not prevented, attracted further labour when the eighteenth-century enclosures created agricultural unemployment and rural depopulation.[14] Surplus labour in the country villages was quickly absorbed by the rapidly expanding framework knitting industry, and the domestic system spread the manufacture of hosiery into almost every open parish in the three counties.[15]

TABLE III

The Framework Knitting Industry: Cost Structure, 1833

| | Variable costs | | | | | | Total |
| | Materials | | Wages | | Finishing | | |
	Cost (£1000)	% of Total	Cost (£1000)	% of Total	Cost (£1000)	% of Total	Cost (£1000)
Cotton goods	245	28	505	57	130	15	880
Worsted goods	449	52	335	38	86	10	870
Silk goods	120	50	108	45	13	5	241
Total	814	41	948	48	229	11	1991

Source: First report from the select committee appointed to enquire into the operation of the existing laws affecting the exportation of machinery, British Parliamentary Papers, (1841), VII, Appendix 3, 237.

The importance of labour as a factor of production in the framework knitting industry is indicated in Table III. In the industry as a whole in 1833, 48 per cent of the total variable costs were made up of wages, compared with 41 per cent for materials and 11 per cent for finishing, and in the cotton branch, the largest section of the trade, labour costs made up as much as 57 per cent of the total. The importance of labour is further emphasized by similar figures for 1844, which show that in the whole industry labour costs made up 40 per cent of the market value of finished goods, and that in the manufacture of cotton hosiery the proportion was as high as 60 per cent.[16] It is clear that in these circumstances the distribution of the framework knitting industry would have been closely related to labour supply, and that the high degree of dispersal reflected the need to seek surplus labour wherever it was available during the rapid expansion of the industry in the eighteenth century.

FIGURE 4—The Organization of the Domestic System in the East Midlands Hosiery Industry in 1844.

Note: Information on the putting out centres for which they worked exists for about two-fifths of the places engaged in the domestic hosiery industry in 1844, and this, together with other less precise information, enables the spheres of influence of the main putting out centres to be determined fairly accurately. For the sake of clarity, a number of less important places putting out work locally have been omitted.

Source: Report of the commissioner appointed to enquire into the condition of the framework knitters, British Parliamentary Papers (1845), XV, Appendices I and II, Evidence of witnesses.

Strong though the tendency for disperal was, other factors operated as restrictions on the spatial expansion of the domestic hosiery industry, confining it to the well-defined area indicated in Figures 2 and 3. The most important restriction appears to have been imposed by the organization of the industry, for the main towns acted as organizing centres from which work was put out to the surrounding country areas, and to which the finished goods were brought by the village workers.[17] The spatial organization of the industry is illustrated in Figure 4, which shows that the main putting out centres were Belper and Nottingham in the north (with spheres of influence covering the framework knitting districts of Derbyshire and Nottinghamshire), Leicester in the south (controlling much of Leicestershire) and Loughborough in the centre (with a rather smaller sphere of influence). Within the areas served by these towns it is also possible to distinguish smaller districts centred on other places (Derby, Ruddington, Shepshed and Hinckley) which operated on a more local scale as secondary putting out centres. It is evident from this map that the development of framework knitting in some areas, such as the northern parts of Derbyshire and Nottinghamshire, and south-eastern Leicestershire, was restricted by distance from the main organizing centres of the industry and by difficulty in communicating with them.

Inaccessibility cannot explain the absence of framework knitting in some places quite close to the main putting out centres, however. In some areas the presence of other activities restricted the development of the industry: thus in the coal-mining district of eastern Derbyshire the ratio of stocking frames to population was generally low (Fig. 3), and in the more prosperous agricultural areas of eastern Nottinghamshire and Leicestershire and south-western Derbyshire, framework knitting was virtually non-existent. In Derby the manufacture of hosiery was of secondary importance to the silk industry, and in some of the villages to the west of Nottingham the machine lace industry was beginning to compete with the hosiery trade for labour and capital. To the south of Hinckley the extension of framework knitting across the county boundary into Warwickshire was restricted by the domestic silk-weaving industry centred on Coventry; the only place to the south of the county boundary in which hosiery manufacturing was of any importance at the middle of the nineteenth century was Wolvey, with 150 frames in 1844.

The attitude of local landowners to the framework knitters, whose presence during periods of depression invariably led to high poor rates, also restricted the growth of the industry in some areas. On the Duke of Rutland's extensive estates on the borders of Leicestershire and Nottinghamshire poor rates were kept low by the deliberate exclusion of stockingers,[18] and similar restrictions were imposed on a more local scale by other landowners. In Papplewick, a few miles to the north of Nottingham, for example, it was reported in 1844 that the landlord had prohibited all manufacturing, and that framework knitters had also been expelled from the adjoining village of Linby.[19]

Compared with the various factors associated with labour supply the

TABLE IV

The Framework Knitting Industry: Type of Yarn Used, 1844

	Derbyshire		Leicestershire		Nottinghamshire		Total	
	Number of machines	Percentage of total	Number of machines	Percentage of total	Number of machines	Percentage of total	Number of machines	Percentage of total
Cotton	4,380	74·6	6,933	37·5	12,440	85·3	23,753	61·1
Wool and Worsted	2	—	11,457	62·0	61	0·4	11,520	29·6
Silk	1,454	25·4	105	0·5	2,094	14·3	3,653	9·3
Total	5,836	100·0	18,495	100·0	14,595	100·0	38,926	100·0

Source: *Report of the commissioner appointed to enquire into the condition of the framework knitters, British Parliamentary Papers* (1845), XV, Appendix II, 12.

Note: Frames not at work are not included.

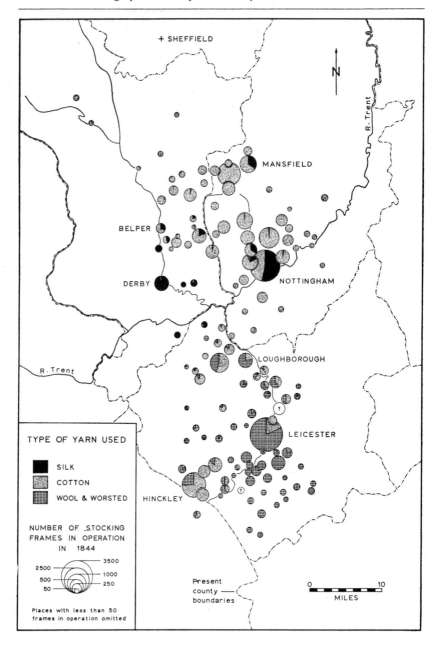

organization of the putting out system, and land ownership, the availability of raw materials had relatively little effect on the distribution of framework knitting in the East Midlands, but supply of yarn did influence the type of goods produced. During the eighteenth century Derbyshire tended to concentrate on silk goods, Nottinghamshire on cotton goods and Leicestershire on woollen goods, and the extent to which this still persisted in the middle of the nineteenth century is indicated in Table IV. In 1844 Derbyshire still had 25·4 per cent of its machines working with silk, but by this time there were almost three times as many using cotton yarn. In Nottinghamshire 85·3 per cent of the machines were concerned with cotton and almost all the rest with silk, but in Leicestershire virtually no silk was used, and wool and worsted replaced cotton as the most important raw materials.

Variations from place to place in the type of yarn used are shown in detail in Figure 5. In Derby, with its important silk-spinning industry, almost all the 620 machines in operation in 1844 were producing silk goods, and the use of silk also extended to a number of places near by. The most important town for the manufacture of silk hosiery was Nottingham, however, with almost 1800 machines in the district using silk produced locally or in Derby, and a further 255 machines were working with silk in Mansfield. The machines in Nottinghamshire and Derbyshire not using silk were exclusively concerned with cotton goods, made from yarn spun or doubled in the mills of the Derbyshire valleys and the Mansfield and Nottingham districts, but to the south the importance of wool and worsted spinning in Leicester was reflected in the gradual replacement of cotton as the main material used. In Leicester over 80 per cent of the 3620 machines in operation were using wool, worsted or merino, and in the villages to the south the only places using cotton were in the Hinckley area.

The Domestic Hosiery Industry and the Landscape

One final aspect of the framework knitting industry which deserves some consideration is its effect on the landscape of the East Midlands through its influence on domestic architecture. In the middle of the nineteenth century the factory was a rare innovation in the hosiery industry, which was still carried on almost entirely in the workers' own homes, or in small workshops attached to them. The intricate task of working a stocking frame required as much light as possible, and when a room in an existing cottage was converted into a domestic workshop it was often necessary to enlarge the

---

FIGURE 5—Type of Yarn used in the East Midlands Hosiery Industry in 1844.

Note: The number of stocking frames includes only those which were at work at the time of the survey. No information exists for Thurmaston, to the north of Leicester, and Broughton Astley with Primethorpe and Sutton, to the south. The figures for wool and worsted in Leicester and Loughborough include large quantities of merino.

Source: Report of the commissioner appointed to enquire into the condition of the framework knitters, British Parliamentary Papers (1845), XV, Appendix II, 4–11.

windows. Examples of cottages adapted for domestic industry in this way are comparatively rare today, but a few still survive in the East Midlands.

As the industry grew it was not long before houses with built-in work-rooms were being erected specially for framework knitting. These were some-times built singly, but more often in rows, and their characteristic feature is a line of elongated workshop windows often running the whole length of the building. These houses bear a strong resemblance to the weavers' cottages in Yorkshire, and the silk weavers' houses which still exist in large numbers in Coventry, Macclesfield and Leek. Framework knitters' houses may still be seen in many parts of the East Midlands, but the best surviving examples are in the Nottingham district, where there is a marked distinction between the two-storey houses with ground-floor workrooms found in villages such as Calverton and Woodborough to the north-east of the city and the three-storey houses with top-floor workrooms in Nottingham itself and in places to the west, such as Bramcote and Stapleford. The rapid expansion of framework knitting and of the new machine lace industry during the first half of the nineteenth century led to the erection in Nottingham of large numbers of courts and tenements, many with domestic workrooms, when the failure to enclose the open fields which surrounded the town created an acute shortage of building land.[20] Nottingham soon became notorious for its slums, and although these have now disappeared isolated buildings still survive to give some indication of the appearance of the more congested parts of the town when the domestic hosiery industry was at its height.

Framework knitting was not carried on exclusively in domestic workrooms, and its effect on the landscape was not confined to the distinctive appearance of the workers' dwellings. In some places the need for space to accommodate extra machines led to the building of additional workrooms, or 'frameshops', on to existing houses, and from this it was only a short step to the erection of work-shops completely detached from the operatives' houses. Buildings of this kind had a long row of windows placed just under the eaves to provide maximum light in the workroom. These workshops were generally of two storeys, and in many cases they were built on to or behind the house of a master hosier to provide room for machines worked by his apprentices and journeymen; the upper floor housed the stocking frames and the ground floor was used for storage. A number of interesting examples of framework knitters' workshops still survive, most of them in Leicestershire villages such as Shepshed and Wigston Magna.

It is difficult to determine precisely where domestic production ended in the hosiery industry and where factory production began. The back-garden workshop, though an essential part of the organization of the domestic industry, represented the factory in an embryonic form, and some of the larger workshops of hand-operated machines may be more appropriately regarded as rudimen-tary factories than as appendages of a cottage industry. It was the application of steam power to hosiery manufacturing, however, and not the erection of large numbers of workshops for hand-operated machines, which brought about the eventual decline of the domestic hosiery industry. The first steam-powered hosiery factories in Britain began working in the eighteen-forties, and during the second half of the nineteenth century factory production gradually replaced the domestic system.

The decline of framework knitting in favour of the factory hosiery industry had an important effect on the economic geography and landscape of the East Midlands. Changes in the distribution of hosiery manufacturing took place, and lead to the development of a greater degree of concentration in the main centres of the industry; red brick factories and terraces of workers' houses typical of the Victorian industrial scene replaced the knitters' cottages and workshops as characteristic features of the industrial towns and villages of the East Midlands. Despite these changes, the framework knitting district of the middle of the nineteenth century has remained the most important hosiery manufacturing area in Britain, and its landscape still recalls the days of the domestic system.

Conclusion

In conclusion it is appropriate to summarize briefly the main factors affecting the location of the domestic hosiery industry in Britain, as revealed by this study. The distribution of framework knitting in the East Midlands at the middle of the nineteenth century has been reconstructed in detail, and has been shown to represent a compromise between factors favouring dispersal of production on the one hand and concentration on the other. Spatial variation in the cost of labour, which occupied a dominant position in the cost structure of the domestic industry, were of the greatest significance in influencing the distribution of framework knitting, and the need to seek labour wherever it could be obtained at a suitable price led to a high degree of dispersal. The extent of this dispersal was restricted, however, by other factors, in particular by the organization of the domestic system which imposed spatial limits beyond which distance from the putting out centres made the search for cheaper labour uneconomic. Within the framework knitting district itself details of the distribution pattern were determined by land ownership, population distribution, communications and the extent to which other industries could compete for labour.

The factors responsible for the location of the hosiery industry at a national level are a little more difficult to evaluate. The initial location of the industry in the Nottingham district, dependent as it was on Lee's invention at Calverton, was entirely a matter of chance, and framework knitting might eventually have died out completely in the East Midlands if the main concentration had remained in London. However, at a critical point in the history of the industry the East Midlands appears to have had a distinct advantage over other parts of the country in terms of production costs, and as this prompted London manufacturers to move their machines to the Nottingham and Leicester districts the major part of the framework knitting industry returned to its original birthplace. This serves to emphasize the fact that, fortuitous though the circumstances surrounding the initial location of an industry may be, its successful development in that location is possible only if economic conditions permit. From the geographical point of view the most important feature of the early history of the framework knitting industry is that the invention of the stocking frame took place, quite by chance, in an area which was to prove eminently suitable as a location for the manufacture of hosiery.

NOTES

[1] *Report of the commissioner appointed to enquire into the condition of the framework knitters*, *British Parliamentary Papers* (1845), XV. The main statistical returns are to be found in, 'Statistics of the hosiery manufactured by machinery in the United Kingdom, compiled from an actual census taken in 1844', by WILLIAM FELKIN, in Part II of the Appendix to the Report, 4–13.

[2] The term 'stocking frame' includes all machines on which knitwear was manufactured. Although most of the frames were concerned with stockings and socks, gloves, shirts, cravats and other types of fancy goods were also produced on some machines.

[3] See W. FELKIN, *A history of the machine-wrought hosiery and lace manufactures* (1867), 517, and F. A. WELLS, *The British hosiery trade* (1935), 188.

[4] See G. HENSON, *The civil, political and mechanical history of the framework knitters of Europe and North America* (1831), 38.

[5] W. FELKIN, op. cit., 59.

[6] He joined Aston, a former apprentice of William Lee, who had been making improvements to the original machines, and they began making further stocking frames about 1620; ibid., 59–60.

[7] G. HENSON, op. cit., 60.

[8] F. A. WELLS, op. cit., 27.

[9] In the early part of the eighteenth century, artisans' wages averaged about 15s. a week in London compared with 10s. in the provinces. W. FELKIN, op. cit., 72.

[10] The maximum number of apprentices any master was allowed at one time was three. For details of the activities of the Framework Knitters Company, see J. D. CHAMBERS, 'The Worshipful Company of Framework Knitters', *Economica*, 296 (1929), 329; and F. A. WELLS, op. cit., 32–53.

[11] See E. M. RAWSTRON, 'Some aspects of the location of hosiery and lace manufacture in Great Britain', *East Midland Geographer*, No. 9 (1958), 19–22. Rawstron points out that deterrents to the growth of new industry, in the form of a preoccupation with other pre-existing economic activities, seem to have existed in much of lowland Britain at this time.

[12] G. HENSON, op. cit., 69.

[13] J. D. CHAMBERS, 'The vale of Trent 1670–1800, a regional study of economic change', *Economic History Review*, Supplement 3 (1957), 4 and 13 (footnote 8). The large populations of these villages are evident from the Hearth Tax of 1674.

[14] W. G. Hoskins points out that in Leicestershire the enclosures resulted in a movement of population to the larger framework knitting centres, such as Leicester and Hinckley, and to large open-field villages such as Wigston Magna, which became one of the largest framework knitting villages in the county. See W. G. HOSKINS, *The Midland peasant: the economic and social history of a Leicestershire village* (1957), 212.

[15] W. FELKIN, op. cit., 475.

[16] *Report of the commission on framework knitters* (1845), Appendix, Part II, 19.

[17] For further details of the organization of the domestic industry, see Ibid., Appendices Parts I and II, *passim.*, and F. A. WELLS, op. cit., 69–84.

[18] W. PITT, *A general view of the agriculture of the county of Leicester* (1809), 324.

[19] R. MELLORS, *In and about Nottinghamshire* (1908), 326. The expulsion of framework knitters was partly responsible for a fall from 515 to 271 in the population of Linby parish between 1801 and 1841.

[20] See J. D. CHAMBERS, *Modern Nottingham in the making* (1945), *passim*, and W. G. HOSKINS, *The making of the English landscape* (1955), 217–18.

Supplementary Note

The location of most manufacturing industries in Britain is the result of a long process of evolution. Attempting to reconstruct this process or to identify the distribution pattern of an industry at some critical point in the past, is a field in which much basic research remains to be done. In the case of some industries, such as engineering, there is very little reliable quantitative data relating to plant location in the early stages of development, while in others, such as textiles and iron smelting, the situation is much better. The textile industries are particularly well documented, for during the first half of the nineteenth century the unfortunate social consequences of the Industrial Revolution and the gradual replacement of domestic production by the factory system attracted the scrutiny of a number of important government inquiries. The main focus of their attention was working conditions but a large amount of information on industrial location was also collected and published in various parliamentary papers.

The study of the hosiery industry at the middle of the nineteenth century provides some indication of the wealth of material available for certain industries at certain points in time. Similar data can be found on the cotton industry, the wool and worsted industry, the manufacture of silk under both the domestic and the factory system, and the machine lace industry. This material enables the location of these activities to be identified at a number of dates before the first useful census returns, and also provides remarkably detailed information on such subjects as the use of steam compared with water as a source of power and the age structure of the factory population.

To date, very little research has been done on these sources. Studies of the cotton industry in Lancashire[1] and the East Midlands[2] show something of what can be achieved by using the returns of the factory inspectors, and a report of one of the parliamentary inquiries has provided material for an interesting socio-economic study of the Coventry silk industry.[3] The growing popularity of the field of industrial archaeology is also increasing the use of some documentary sources on plant location in the early nineteenth century. But many of these sources are still largely neglected by the geographer. Since the quantitative revolution and the emergence of the new model-building geography, historical inquiry has almost become unfashionable in certain branches of locational analysis, a tendency which has been reinforced by the quite proper preoccupation with contemporary problems of industrial location and development planning. However, the modern economic geographer would be well advised not to overlook industrial Britain in the nineteenth century as a laboratory in which to test his theories and run his models.

1   Rodgers, H.B. 'The Lancashire cotton industry in 1840' *Transactions and Papers of Institute of British Geographers*, 28 (1960) pp 135-53, reprinted *infra* pp 337-55

2   Smith, D.M. 'The cotton industry in the East Midlands', *Geography,* 47 (1962) pp 256-69

3   Prest, J. *Industrial Revolution in Coventry* (1960)

D.M. SMITH   August 1969

The Population of Liverpool in the Mid-Nineteenth Century
R. Lawton
Reprinted from *Transactions of the Historic Society of Lancashire and Cheshire,* 107 (1955), 89-120

THE POPULATION OF LIVERPOOL IN THE MID-NINETEENTH CENTURY

BY R. LAWTON, M.A.

"LIVERPOOLE", said Daniel Defoe, "is one of the wonders of Britain".[1] And so it must have seemed to himself and his contemporaries. For, although possessing an ancient charter, its real growth dated only from the development of its overseas trade and commerce in the late seventeenth century. This development initiated a rapid expansion which has continued to the present day. People flocked to the flourishing town from all parts of the British Isles. Building sprawled out along and behind the river as the docks were extended to north and south during the nineteenth century.[2] One by one old agricultural villages on the periphery of the town were engulfed. A great new city, the hub of a great new urban region of Merseyside, was created.

This development of modern Liverpool is of great interest from many viewpoints; of historian, economist, sociologist and geographer. Numerous aspects of it have been dealt with. But others remain little known, among them the precise nature of population development. It is with one facet of this problem that this paper deals. The decennial returns of the census of population enable us to trace changes in numbers and distribution of the people from 1801 onwards. Not until 1841, however, did detail concerning birthplaces, population structure (by age and sex) and occupations become reliable. Only in 1851 was the format used in subsequent censuses established. Thus, for a period of immense importance in the growth of Liverpool, there is much valuable information concerning its population.

During the century or so after the first census of 1801 the major lineaments of present-day Liverpool were created.[3] In 1801 Liverpool alone existed of the present-day Merseyside urban region. The main built-up area was entirely within the bounds of the borough and mostly concentrated within the old township of Liverpool. Here a population of 77,653 was crowded into a restricted area and overcrowded courts and alleys presented many social and health problems, particularly in the town centre. By 1851 the population

[1] Defoe, *A Tour through England and Wales*, Everyman Edition, Volume II, Letter X, p. 255.
[2] Of the *present* dock system Salthouse dock (opened in 1753) is the oldest, but the rest were developed during the period between 1821 and 1913.
[3] It is true that in the post-war period there has been a considerable economic revolution on Merseyside, but the genesis of modern Liverpool and the region around it lies essentially in the nineteenth century.

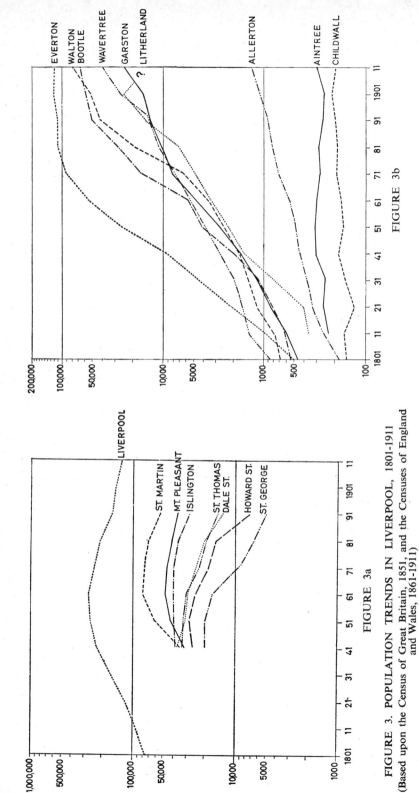

FIGURE 3. POPULATION TRENDS IN LIVERPOOL, 1801-1911
(Based upon the Census of Great Britain, 1851, and the Censuses of England
and Wales, 1861-1911)

Total populations are shown on a logarithmic scale in which changes in trends
as well as numbers are accurately portrayed.

Graph (a) deals with Liverpool Registration District and the Sub-Districts

Graph (b) shows populations of townships around Liverpool.
The totals for Litherland are affected by boundary changes between 1901 and 1911.

had grown five-fold to 375,955 (see Figure 3). As the line of the docks extended, so the built-up area grew and reached out further into its hinterland. As Liverpool township became fully built over the town extended into the adjacent districts of Kirkdale, Everton, West Derby and Toxteth Park. Into this area people flocked from all over Britain. Liverpool became a cosmopolitan city.

The general outlines and nature of this development have been traced elsewhere.[4] Here we are concerned with the nature of the population of Liverpool in a single year; 1851. It is possible to analyse this in very great detail. For the census of that year the enumerators' books, which record house by house and person by person the full details required by the Registrar General, can be inspected at the Public Record Office.[5] They contain for each person residing in Liverpool on the census night of 31 March 1851 details of name, place of residence, age and sex, relation to the head of the household, occupation and birthplace (by parish and county). It is from these books, entry by entry, that I have drawn my material. For a city of over 375,000 people I have had to be content with samples. Seventeen areas were selected, eight from within the borough boundary, nine from outside, ranging in size of sample from 153 to 1,138 and totalling, in all, 13,932 people (*see* Figure 4).

Area I is representative of the crowded wards of the commercial centre. Around this core was a ring of very high density areas ranging from crowded dockside districts (areas V and VI) to busy trading and servicing areas (areas II and IV). These were all at about their peak population in 1851 and were destined to lose population, on aggregate, from this time onward (Figure 3a).

Already, indeed, many of those who could afford to do so had moved away from their place of work or business into areas on the outskirts of the town or even beyond it into adjacent town-ships.[6] Furthermore, as the line of the docks was extended, industry and commerce went with them and housing spread along the river and behind it to a depth of a mile or more. To the mid- and latter-nineteenth century belongs much of the blanket of terrace housing wrapped around the Georgian and early Victorian town which is the core of the present city. Thus, while the Scotland Road area (area VII) was associated primarily with a working-class population in fairly crowded conditions, the Abercromby Square sample (area III) consisted of spacious residences of merchants and traders interspersed with better-class artisan property.

By 1851 new things were to be seen on the map. The built-up area, hitherto confined to a single block growing outwards from the old town, began to reach (and was ultimately to engulf) old villages away from the river. The first to experience this was Everton

[4] See, for example, W. Smith (*Ed.*), *A Scientific Survey of Merseyside* (Liverpool, 1953).
[5] Public Record Office, H.O. 107 (various).
[6] Movement was also going on "across the water" into Wirral, though this does not concern us here.

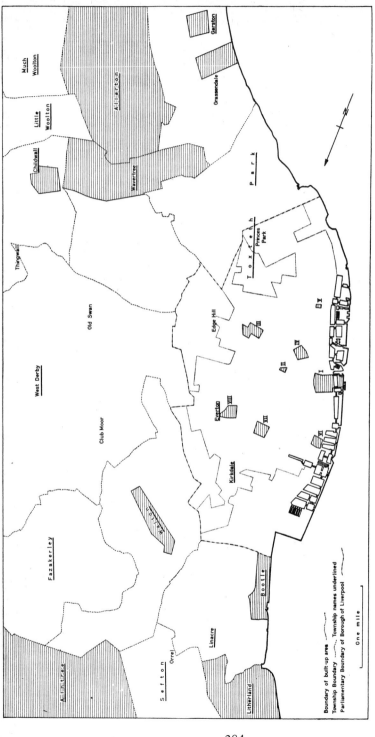

FIGURE 4. LIVERPOOL IN 1851

Based upon the Borough Engineer's Survey map of the Borough of Liverpool and of the Townships immediately adjacent (1851)

The sample areas are shaded.

Area I lies between Dale Street, North John Street, Lord Street-James Street.

Area II—between Lime Street and Skelhorne Street.

Area III—Abercromby Square and parts of Crown, Oxford, Chatham, Chestnut, Mulberry, Cambridge, Bedford and Grove Street.

Area IV—between Bold Street (part) and Gradwell Street-Parr Street.

Area V—Bell Street and Courts.

Area VII.—Dryden Street, Oswald Street and parts of Scotland Road and Little Homer Street.

Area VIII.—Everton Village.

Walton—Walton Village.

Bootle—Derby Road and streets off (e.g. Pleasant, Everton, Sheridan, Princes and Bedford Place).

Litherland—All the township west of the Leeds-Liverpool Canal including, chiefly, Seaforth and part of Waterloo.

Aintree, Allerton and Childwall—the entire townships.

Wavertree—All that part south of Dunbabin Lane-Penny Lane, including Mossley Hill.

384

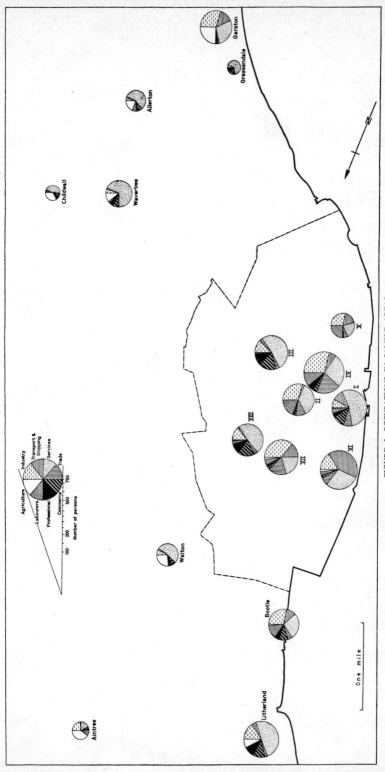

FIGURE 5. OCCUPATIONS IN SAMPLE AREAS.

The symbol is proportionate to the total of *gainfully employed* population and shows the proportion of people occupied in each of eight main groupings.

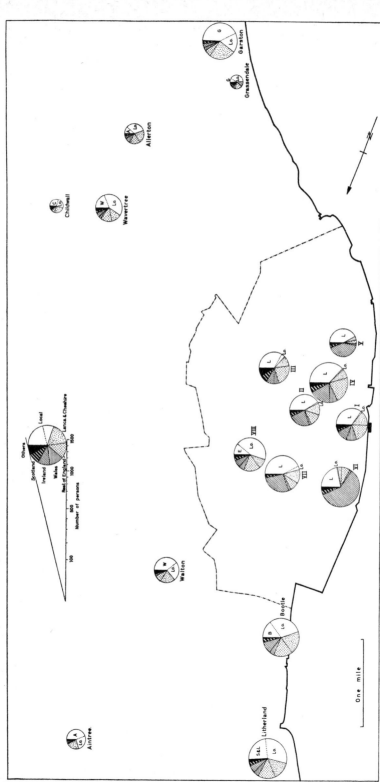

FIGURE 6. BIRTHPLACES OF THE POPULATION OF SAMPLE AREAS.
The size of the symbol is proportionate to the total population of the sample area.

The locally-born group is divided as follows:
(a) Those living in the township of their birth distinguished by the initial letter of the township, e.g. L—Liverpool, W—Wavertree, etc.
(b) Those born in local townships (Lo) including all those townships within the present-day boundaries of Liverpool, Bootle, Huyton with Roby, Litherland and Crosby.

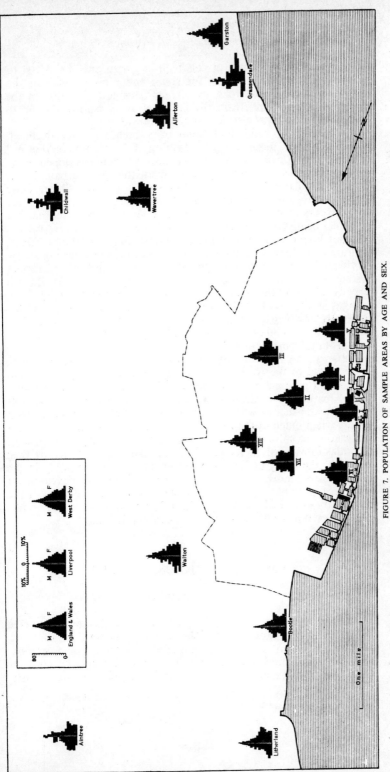

FIGURE 7. POPULATION OF SAMPLE AREAS BY AGE AND SEX.

Each diagram shows the percentage in the *total* population of 5-year age-groups (0—4, 5—9, 10—14, and so on to 80+). Males are shown to the left of the central line and females to the right.

village (area VIII). Thus a place which had been one of the first to receive the merchant looking for space and prospect near to the town was being linked to it by terrace housing advancing up the slopes of Everton hill from the crowded areas behind the north docks. Its society was also in a state of transition.

As such inner residential areas of a higher quality declined, and as it became increasingly the fashion of those who could afford to do so to live away from their business, so there developed outer residential areas, spatially divorced from the main urban fabric. Such old villages as Walton, Wavertree, Allerton, Bootle and Litherland received migrants from town. Secondly, residential parks and districts of new origin developed, one of the best and earliest examples being Grassendale Park. Another example of a new district, Mossley Hill, is contained in the Wavertree sample. Garston village, with its own docks and industry, is a special and interesting study. At this time, before the development of an adequate public transport system, the range of influence of the city was limited. It did not penetrate beyond the sandstone ridge of the Liverpool upland. Such villages as Childwall and Aintree felt the influence of the town only indirectly. They lost rather than gained people in the late nineteenth century (Figure 3b). Their absorption by Liverpool dates only from the post-1918 era.

Thus each of these seventeen areas illustrates, in its several way, some aspect of the cosmos that was Liverpool. Together they help us to paint in some detail a portrait of the character of its population. Separately they draw attention to distinctive zones of different economy and society within the city. As this study is concerned with a time when much of the modern city had begun to take shape, this material is of substantial value in an appreciation of the Liverpool of today, not least in its problems of planning. Further to this, however, the study of Liverpool's population is a type-study in the genesis of a conurbation. The first stage of suburban development was already under way and with it the corresponding decline of the city centre as a residential area. This is typical of other major conurbations of nineteenth and twentieth-century Britain.

ANALYSIS OF THE 1851 SAMPLES

A. OCCUPATIONS

The Liverpool of 1851 was a centre of trade and commerce, rather than of manufacture.[7] The economy focussed on the port, and the evolution of the urban fabric and development of population was intimately related to this feature. Liverpool's contacts were world-wide and its imports went to all parts of the country.

[7] See F. E. Hyde, "The Growth of Liverpool's Trade, 1700–1950" in *A Scientific Survey of Merseyside*.

These contacts can be seen in the enumerators' books in many ways. The merchants were East India merchants, in the American (especially West Indies) trade and the like [8] The town attracted people concerned in such trade either as permanent settlers or on business visits. In addition, vast armies of labourers were needed to unload and transport cargo from ship to warehouse. Thus *service* industry (trade, commerce, transport, *etc.*) was the dominant element in the occupational structure. Liverpool had its industry, of course, but much of this was directly connected with its trade (*e.g.* in sugar refining, soap and salt manufacture) or its ships. Ship-building was on the decline as the demands of docks and ware-houses restricted available riverside sites, and the industry trans-ferred to the Cheshire shore, But ship-repairing was still important.

Difficulties inherent in my method of sampling preclude a complete picture of the economy from occupations. In the first place, the strong coincidence between place of work and place of residence in the working-class districts means that specific industries may be omitted. Thus for a full account of soap works, sugar refineries and the like one must go to other sources such as the directories of the period. Secondly, the classification of a host of occupations into a few significant categories is not easy. Bearing in mind the nature of Liverpool in 1851, I have deliberately not followed the census classi-fication of the tabulated and published summaries. I have plotted the employed population only—the size of symbol is related to numbers. I have separated the very large group of service industries into domestic and other personal services, shipping and transport, commerce, trade, and professions. Manufacture and craft industry were of much lesser significance and have been confined to a single grouping. The resulting classification and diagrams are occupational rather than industrial. Thus a "clerk" may be classified under "commerce" while he was in point of fact employed in an industrial establishment. However, in the majority of cases some further des-cription was attached to such occupations and this facilitates the process of classification. Thus, only those returned as dock labourers are included in the transport and shipping section. Labourers alone are given a separate classification. It is usual also to distinguish between warehouse porters and railway porters, and so on. The classifications draw attention to the general nature of the economy of Liverpool and to certain distinct zones within it (Figure 5).

The inner city areas (I and II) present certain common character-istics, though contrasting facets. Each was primarily a servicing area. In the first (I) we are in the very heart of the commercial centre. Residential buildings were few and confined to courts and alleys off the main streets. These unattractive, crowded and insani-

[8] The numerous merchant households of Abercromby Square (area III) in-cluded a Jamaican-born timber merchant, two East India merchants, a general merchant whose wife and two elder children were born in Barbados, one whose wife and elder children were born in the U.S.A., two Brazil merchants, and two German-born merchants.

tary dwellings were inhabited primarily by unskilled workers employed in or around the docks; dock labourers, porters in the corn and cotton warehouses, and the like. Much of the population was transitory. In the hotels and lodging-houses were many concerned in commerce visiting the city on business, and those who catered for them swelled the domestic service element in this area.

From many of the main streets private residences had largely gone; whole blocks in Castle Street were returned as uninhabited and elsewhere it was the "office keeper" rather than the banker or merchant who remained. They, together with the clerks rather than the merchant, formed much of the commercial group. Occasionally, as at the Bank of England in Castle Street, the bank manager's place of work was still his residence. But this was rare. Thus in 1851 the business core of an actively growing Liverpool was already dying from a residential point of view. This character is further displayed in other ways (*e.g.* by its predominantly adult population) as we shall see in due course.

The second central area (II) shows a very varied occupational structure. Many of the people were engaged in trade and craft industries, typical of the large city with its considerable consumer hinterland. There were many domestic servants employed in hotels and lodging-houses. Most of the traders were small rather than big business men and were often craftsmen, such as tailors and cabinet-makers, making, as well as selling, their own goods.

The third inner area (IV) was part of the "new town" as described by Defoe, which developed largely in the eighteenth century. In 1851 Bold Street formed one of the principal shopping streets. Gazetteers and directories of the time indicate this, and the traders' advertisements often stress that their goods were made in their own workshops. This is reflected in the very large trading element in the population, with large numbers of shop assistants, still at that time chiefly male, housed on the premises. Most "industrial" workers were engaged in a substantial craft industry which supplied consumer goods like clothing and furniture. There were cabinet makers, gilders, upholsterers, tailors, watch-makers, jewellers, *etc.* The direct links with port industries and trade in this area were few, though there were a number of Irish labouring families in some of the cellars of residential streets behind Bold Street (*e.g.* Fleet Street).

One of the reasons for the limited number of well-to-do merchants and traders in the town centre is to be seen when we consider the Abercromby Square area (III). Here, in part of what Wilfred Smith described as "Liverpool's Bloomsbury", is a fine example of the merchant-class residential area of the town proper. These classes inhabited the larger houses but some of the adjoining streets (*e.g.* Mulberry Street) were occupied by skilled artisans and traders. To supply these households an army of servants gathered (up to a dozen in some households) and formed *in toto* the major element in the working population.

In contrast to the "town" areas already discussed, the dockside areas were almost exclusively bound up with the port. The dominant occupations were dock labourers, porters and artisans associated with ships and shipping, such as riggers, shipwrights, carpenters, and boiler makers. The high proportion of the population not gainfully employed (especially in area V) reflects a high birth-rate and relatively few openings for female labour, though many worked as charwomen, washerwomen and in other forms of domestic service. These influences had penetrated inland, especially in the north dock areas, and affected the Scotland Road sample (VII). The working element in the population was again a relatively low one associated primarily with large families in a crowded residential area. Much of this population was concerned with varied craft industries and small trade, but unskilled labour (mostly of Irish origin) had settled in the courts of the area and was often concerned in dockside industry. Their womenfolk swelled the "trade" section in such occupations as "orange dealer".[9]

So far we have been primarily concerned with sample areas lying within the continuously built-up area of the town proper. Everton village (VIII) is clearly in a zone, and a state, of transition. The large merchant households with their considerable domestic staffs are there, but so too are artisan and even occasional labouring households. Moreover, with no agricultural group left, it was, by 1851, closely and completely bound to Liverpool.

Migration of population, especially of the well-to-do merchant, trading and professional elements was actively taking place to formerly agricultural villages on the periphery of the town. Such people were, in the main, carriage folk, who could manage the journey to work thus entailed, but involved with them were numerous servants in their households. Moreover, there remained in such villages a considerable agricultural population, while the spread of new building involved many builders' craftsmen and labourers.

Though still spatially divorced from Liverpool, Walton village was becoming linked firmly in occupations and society to the city. For, superimposed upon a considerable agricultural foundation, were a number of commercial and professional households which, with their associated domestic staffs, were prominent in the occupational structure of this small village.

Some of this outward growth was bound up with the river itself. Thus Bootle had a two-fold development at this time: first, swelling the old village which was set back some distance from the river; second, the growth of a new, riverside Bootle. Our sample is this new Bootle. It was linked with commerce and shipping and already involved in new dock construction. Thus it had not only the large households of merchants moving from town, but artisans, sailors and labourers directly linked with the docks. The docks did not actually

---

[9] Even the Liverpool of today abounds in its market women and flower sellers.

front on to Bootle until the 1880's,[10] but the Sandon and Huskisson system nearby was opened in 1851 and 1852. Moreover, it was rapidly being built-up and a large proportion of the craftsmen were employed in the building industry.

Litherland (including in my sample Seaforth and Waterloo chiefly) lay further afield and was much more the fashionable better-class residential area. The "industrial" element in the population was chiefly involved in the building trade. The rural society on which this pattern had been recently superimposed was much obscured by the growth of Liverpool. Thus only a relatively small section was still agricultural. There were many merchants and traders and a large domestic service group.

In contrast to this the agricultural population of the southern portion of Wavertree township (*i.e.* the Mossley Hill area in the main) and of Allerton township was still prominent. Indeed in these cases the "big houses" were as yet relatively few and included some of Liverpool's most prominent citizens, for example, in Allerton, Joseph N. Walker of Calderstones, Thomas Brocklebank of Springwood, Hardman Earle of Allerton Tower, John Bibby of Harthill, and Theodore G. Rathbone of Allerton Priory, and, in Mossley Hill, Muspratt, the chemical manufacturer, Lawrence, merchant, magistrate and county lieutenant, and Kinderman, a Prussian-born merchant.

Beyond these the outer villages remained largely agricultural. Childwall, basically a small farm hamlet in character, had, however, the Hall with its large domestic staff and the Abbey Hotel, even then, it would seem, a house of some repute attracting business men visiting Liverpool. Aintree, a larger village, shows a structure typical of the mid-nineteenth century rural township community, with varied crafts serving local needs adding diversity—and a considerable measure of self-sufficiency—to a largely agricultural population.

Garston village and Grassendale Park are particular cases with distinctive features. Grassendale, one of the earlier residential parks of Merseyside and still in the course of construction, was exclusively the residence of carriage folk and their establishments. Garston, however, was a fairly large agricultural village to which had been added docks and industry. It was these new features which accounted for much of its working population. The commercial element was limited, for business in Merseyside was centred in the city of Liverpool and Garston *village* was not an important city man's residential area. Its industry was, however, intimately related to an important element in Liverpool's trade—that in salt. Garston Saltworks was the main employer of industrial labour and was as important as the numerous craft trades, which were especially connected with building and which made up about half of the "industrial" group.

[10] The Bootle docks of Langton, Alexandra, Hornby and Gladstone systems were not completed until 1881, 1881, 1884 and 1910–14 respectively.

B. POPULATION AND MIGRATION

Contemporary reports, the evidence of the census and vital statistics, and the polyglot origins of the population of present-day Liverpool leave us in no doubt that the natural growth of population, resulting from excess of births over deaths, could not alone account for the rapid rate of growth of Liverpool's population in the mid-nineteenth century. Figure 8 shows the relationship between the rate of total population growth and the change due to the balance between births and deaths. By 1851 the peak of inner Liverpool's growth had passed and there was a progressive decline associated with outward movement, and little or no natural increase of population. Even so, in 1851 out of a total population for the Registration District of 258,236, 53·2% were born outside Lancashire. In the West Derby District the high natural increase did not alone account for the total increment. A large immigration into the District continued until the end of the century. Even in 1851, 39·2% of a total population of 153,279 were born outside Lancashire.

A very high proportion of the population was Irish by birth. One-sixth of the considerable total of Irish immigrants in England and Wales up to this date was to be found on Merseyside (chiefly in Liverpool).

Although there were many people drawn to Liverpool from adjacent areas, Liverpool's power to attract population was country-wide. The general pattern of such immigration can be plotted from published census returns of birthplaces for 1851. But the manuscript returns give us very much more significant detail. For each person the township and county of birth is given. Not only does the proportion of immigrants differ from sample area to sample area, but so do the patterns of their birthplaces. These differences were in part the outcome of contrasts in the economic structure of different areas of Liverpool, in part of contrasts in social structure. In their turn they helped to strengthen these contrasts, especially social contrasts, in different parts of Liverpool. Moreover, as we shall see, they strongly affected the demographic structure.

A general map has been produced showing the birthplaces of the inhabitants of the seventeen sample areas under eight main headings: first, locally-born, using that term to cover all townships now within the built-up area on the Liverpool side of the river. This section is subdivided where relevant to show the proportion living in their native township and those from adjacent townships; second, short-distance immigrants from Lancashire and Cheshire the majority of whom are from quite close at hand. Other sections (giving medium and long-distance migrations) are from the rest of England, Wales (chiefly in these cases from North Wales), Ireland, Scotland, and a last group from overseas.

These birthplace tables present some problems of interpretation so far as the study of population movement is concerned. For

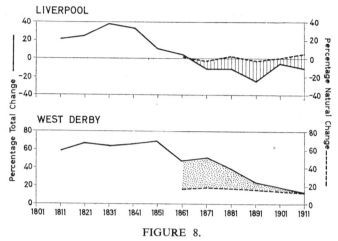

FIGURE 8.

POPULATION CHANGE IN LIVERPOOL AND WEST DERBY
REGISTRATION DISTRICTS, 1801-1911

(Based on the census of Great Britain, 1851, and the Censuses of England
and Wales, 1861-1911)

The graphs show the percentage intercensal changes in

(a) total population

and (b) due to natural change, i.e. the balance between births and deaths.

The difference between the two lines represents the change due to the balance
of migration.   Outward migration (as from Liverpool between 1871 and 1911)
is shaded, inward migration (as in West Derby 1861-1911) is stippled.

Vital statistics on which these changes are based are first available for the
decennium 1851-61.

example, the head of the house at 58 Crown Street was born in York, but the record of family birthplaces suggests that he reached Liverpool by a very indirect route. His wife and eldest son (aged 23) were both born in Bristol, his second son (21) in York, his daughter (19) in Hull, and three other sons (17, 15, 13) in Leeds. One cannot assume that "birthplace" is synonymous with "migrant from". But the family record helps to trace details of movement in many cases. The vast majority of households show no such complexity and it is fair to say that the diagram is a valid indication of the amount and pattern of population movement into Liverpool up to 1851 (Figure 6).

In the samples covered as a whole the proportion of those born outside the immediate locality was everywhere high, though less notable in outer areas. Short-distance migration (from Lancashire and Cheshire, but much of it from close at hand) varied in amount but was most notable in outer areas, especially in former agricultural villages recently affected by the growth of Liverpool. Medium and long-distance immigration was important in all but the villages unaffected or recently affected by the growth of the town. It was least in Aintree and Childwall. Thus a distinction can be clearly made between those areas in town and outer areas of new development. In town the proportion of longer-distance immigrants was generally high and was most marked in the inner districts. Moreover, many of these migrants came from far afield, notably in certain districts from Ireland, for which Liverpool was the principal point of entry into England. In the outer districts, however, much of the recent population increase had clearly been supplied from the local area, notably from Liverpool itself, while longer-distance immigration was less prominent. This contrast is, in part, bound up with the general nature of urban development in Liverpool and is probably typical of the majority of the great cities of Victorian England. It represents the suburban movement of the well-to-do from already decaying residential areas in the town centre. Moreover, a great many of the merchants and professional people involved were local men or to judge from their families' birthplaces had long been established on Merseyside (Figure 9). Often it is the servants in such households who were recruited from far afield. This is particularly noticeable in the sample from Wavertree township, but is typical also of Litherland, Walton, Allerton and Grassendale and in the town proper in Area III.

The long-distance immigrant was initially attracted, often as not, to the varied opportunities of the town centre. The attraction of Liverpool, lacking as it did large manufacturing industries requiring specific skill, was general rather than particular. Much of the *labour* (as opposed to commercial and professional classes) needed in a great port was unskilled. The craft industries were such as were attracted to large and growing towns all over England at this date. Thus few specific regional connections developed on economic grounds, such as, for example, one finds in the migration

FIGURE 9a

FIGURE 9.

BIRTHPLACES OF

(a) MERCHANTS, BANKERS, ACCOUNTANTS, BROKERS, ETC. IN ALL SAMPLE AREAS.

(b) DOMESTIC SERVANTS IN AREA III.

The symbols are on identical scales and are proportionate to the numbers born in the township in which they are placed. Where only the county of birth is given in the returns, an open symbol has been used and placed in the centre of the county of birth.

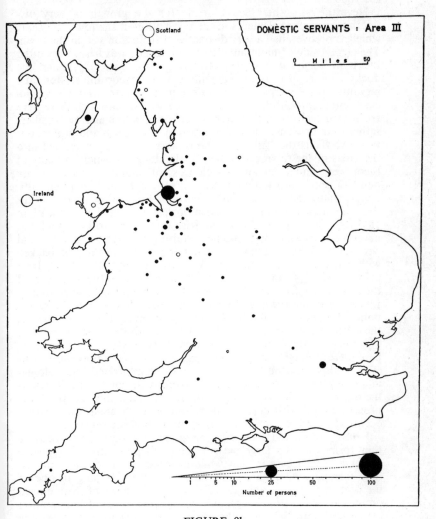

FIGURE 9b

of Staffordshire miners and iron workers to north-east England in the 1860's.

Nevertheless, other factors made for the growth of very distinctive immigrant elements in the population of the town, elements which, moreover, had a very distinctive distribution within the town. The largest single immigrant element in the city was Irish. Very often the Irish occupied unskilled labouring jobs, especially round the docks (Figure 10). Their womenfolk were important as domestic servants. The Liverpool Irish were not, of course, *wholly* a single-class community. But they tended to be so. For although there were Irish-born craftsmen, they were often poor tailors and dressmakers rather than artisans, and the proportion in business and professions was low. Thus the Irish immigrants were chiefly concentrated into the areas of the town centre behind the docks in which so many of them were employed and which was, of course, at their precise point of entry into the country. Not all stayed in Liverpool. Ultimately many moved on to other parts of England or abroad. Thus the very high proportion of Irish-born enumerated in area VI in 1851 (59·7%) comprised not only Irish immigrants to Liverpool, but many persons and some families awaiting passage to America and elsewhere. There were numerous lodging-houses in the area packed with such emigrants. In area V, however, the very large Irish colony (41·4%) was composed of permanent settlers. Many of them, to judge from the birthplaces of their families, had moved to Liverpool in the previous four or five years, that is after the severe potato famines of 1845–47. As one moves away from the river, so the Irish element in the population tended to decrease. They were prominent in the Scotland Road area (VII) (27·8%); many of them here were immigrants of some eight or ten years previously. But even in this area the Irish tended to be concentrated into colonies inhabiting the poorer courts in very crowded conditions. Towards the outskirts of the city and into the residential districts beyond, the proportion of Irish-born declines and in such areas they mostly occupied unskilled jobs as labourers or as domestic servants.

I have considered the Irish immigrants at some length because they formed such a large part of the city's population. They were rather a special case in that while in terms of the distance moved they formed long-distance migrants, they were settling in one of the nearest points to Ireland in Britain. Often many of them moved on in due course from Liverpool. As the great swell of immigration of the Irish into Britain in the mid-nineteenth century declined, the Irish element in the population of Liverpool decreased. By 1911 only 4·6% of the population of Liverpool borough and 6·7% of Bootle were Irish *born*, though, of course, a very high proportion of the population was of Irish descent. However, socially and economically, these distinctive nineteenth-century "colonies" left their mark on present-day Liverpool. The strong social stratification of nineteenth-century Liverpool and the gulf between unskilled worker and merchant at opposite ends of the whole gamut of

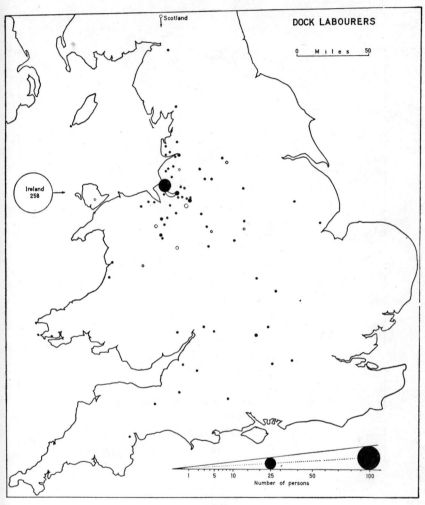

FIGURE 10.
BIRTHPLACES OF DOCK LABOURERS AND STEVEDORES IN ALL
AREAS.
Note the overwhelming emphasis on immigrant Irish labour.

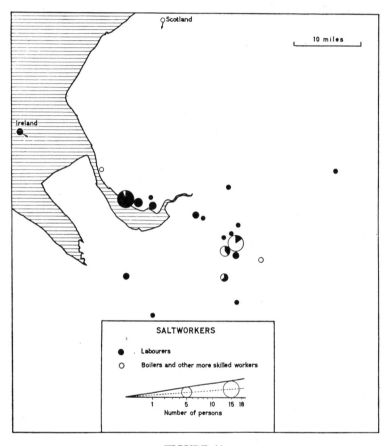

FIGURE 11a

FIGURE 11.

BIRTHPLACES OF (A) SALT WORKERS, AND (B) AGRICULTURAL LABOURERS IN GARSTON.

The symbols are not on the same scale.

Attention is drawn to the migration of more skilled salt workers from the Cheshire salt area, contrasting with the mainly local birthplaces of salt works labourers and farm workers.

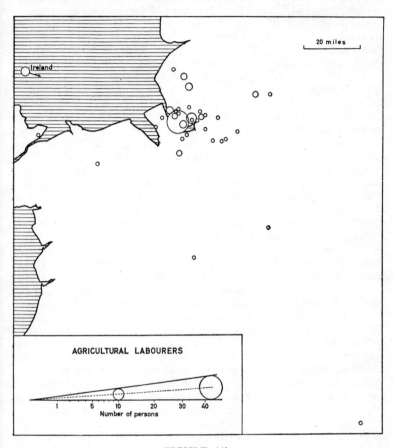

FIGURE 11b

occupations linked with the port has tended to perpetuate these features. Liverpool had too its Welsh and Scottish colonies. But they tended to be smaller in numbers, to be less concentrated in distribution, and found in a wider range of occupations and society. Nevertheless, the Welsh were prominent in domestic service, and as small traders and craftsmen, especially in the building trade. The Scots had similar jobs, but were also quite important in the merchant class, as for example, in the Abercromby Square area, and as doctors.

The single exception to the general rule that in Liverpool there appears to have been little direct recruitment of labour from areas of similar economy in other parts of Britain, was in Garston. Of the substantial immigration from Lancashire and Cheshire one part came from adjoining rural townships of south-west Lancashire. The other, major part (85 people) came from the Cheshire salt area and worked almost wholly in the Garston salt works. Of the 70 persons in my sample employed at the works, 33 came from this area. They were mostly employed in the more skilled work as salt boilers (see Figure 11a). The labourers were more widely recruited from adjacent agricultural townships and from Ireland in the main. This distribution is in marked contrast to that of the birthplaces of agricultural labourers in Garston (Figure 11b).

There is much evidence therefore from these detailed samples to support the contention that long-distance migration into Liverpool— as to other large towns—up to 1851 was of considerable importance, more important indeed than many previous writers on the general theme of population migration in nineteenth-century Britain have suggested.[11] It is true that many people followed a short distance drift from adjoining rural areas to town, or from town to outer residential districts, but in the city centre in particular, the least proportion of longer-distance immigrants was 42·0% (in area VII) and even in outer areas a general figure was about 25% to 30% of the total population. The main exceptions to this are Garston village and Aintree, both with a distinctive or separate existence, and the latter losing, rather than attracting, population by migration.

Thus the nature of immigration was affected by the economic structure of Liverpool and the character of its urban growth. In its turn it added distinctiveness to the population and strengthened social and economic contrasts between different parts of Liverpool. Moreover, the nature of the immigration made its mark on demographic characteristics, notably on age and sex structure.

C. AGE-SEX STRUCTURE

As compared with England and Wales in 1851 (*see* Figure 7), Liverpool Registration District had a considerably lesser proportion

[11] See A. Redford, *Labour Migration in England, 1800–1850* (1926). Professor Redford was, however, writing of an earlier period when much migration *was* short range.

of people in the groups 5 to 14. In West Derby District there were more in the 0 to 9 groups but less in the 10 to 19 groups than in England and Wales. The reasons are to be sought in a high birth rate, the effects of which were, however, soon negatived by a high infant and child mortality rate most pronounced in the crowded and insanitary residential areas of the inner parts of the city.[12] Another notable feature was the bulge in the middle age-groups, especially those between 20 and 44. This represents the effects of a large number of immigrants which accounted for so much of the rapid increase in population. The greater bulge in the female side of the pyramid in West Derby district was because of the large numbers of women (often unmarried women) employed "in service" in the better-class households of many parts of that district. Finally the "hollowing" of the upper age-groups, especially in Liverpool, represents, in part a higher death-rate than was general in England and Wales as a whole.

One or two examples will suffice to show the relationships between this and other population features already described. These features were not constant throughout the Liverpool of 1851. The numerous immigrant population of the inner districts, especially areas I and VI had a relatively low birth-rate. Much of their population was composed of immigrants of mature years and individual households were generally small, partly because of the high death rates accompanying crowded conditions, partly because of the relatively high proportions of transitory population (*see* page 111). The middle age-groups are considerably swollen by this immigrant element. In the town centre (I) the 10–29 *female* age-groups were particularly large and must be related to the large numbers of women drawn into employment in the numerous hotels and lodging-houses of the area. The inflated male groups from 15-44 represent the large number of "commercials", merchants and travellers in particular. Indeed, in the town centre as a whole this increased middle group is characteristic, though there were significant variations in it. Thus around Abercromby Square (area III), there was a large excess of female population, especially between 15 and 34 related to the very large domestic establishments of many of the houses there. Areas II and IV were less irregular because in the many artisan and labouring-class households typical of much of these areas there were large families. Even there, however, much of the population was composed of adults who had come into Liverpool from other parts of the country. In area IV many of these were to be found in the large shops of Bold Street where there were large numbers of shop assistants (largely male) "living-in" on the premises. Areas V and VII, each with a large immigrant Irish community, had high birth-rates and a broad base to the population structure, but much of this was quickly negatived by a high infant death-rate,

---

[12] A graphic picture of these is given in the early reports of the Liverpool Medical Officer of Health from 1847 onwards. See also Sheila Marriner, "History of Liverpool 1700-1900," in W. Smith, Ed., *op. cit.*, especially pp. 114-116.

and the bulge in the middle age-groups was due wholly to immigration of people of mature years. This insistence upon the significance of immigration into Liverpool as an important factor in its demographic structure is stressed by an examination of birthplaces in relation to age. The vast majority of those under fifteen years old were born in Liverpool. It was their parents who were the migrants.

In the outer areas the old villages affected by outward movement of people from town had common characteristics of a large excess over the general figures for England and Wales in the middle age-groups due to immigration. Much of this was due to large domestic staffs, generally giving a bigger bulge to the female side (notably in Grassendale, also in Litherland, Wavertree and Allerton). This factor more than counteracted the large size of many families, and indeed in many cases these families were of mature years. Bootle, with its varied male occupations (labouring and craft industry as well as commercial) had rather less stress on the female side. Garston is unique among the outer areas affected by the growth of Liverpool in that it had an excess of male population. It was still, in part, an agricultural community and farm labourers remained, while dock workers and those employed in the building and salt trades were important. Moreover, it was not an area where there was the same outlet for female labour in domestic service (the chief employer of women throughout Victorian England as a whole) as, say, in Mossley Hill or Allerton.

Aintree is the best example of the rural township of declining population. The narrow base in the lowest age-groups indicates a relatively low birth-rate. The hollowing of the pyramid in the middle groups between 20 and 49, especially on the female side, indicates emigration of population, in its turn a factor contributing to a further lowering of birth-rate. Generally speaking men tended to remain (mainly as agricultural labourers) rather more than the women. It is a characteristic not unfamiliar in similar rural townships elsewhere in Britain.

Thus, social conditions (especially in relation to birth and mortality rates and their variations) and economic factors (in relation to the attraction of immigrants) played an important and varying role in the creation of distinctive demographic zones.

D. CONCLUSION.

Therefore, in the Liverpool of 1851 there was a well-marked zoning. Even using a relatively limited number of samples, certain distinctive districts can be distinguished not only in terms of the period and type of development of their buildings, or of economy and society, but also in respect of population structure. This has been viewed from a number of points which are, however, intimately related to one another. A few samples in which the population for particular areas is plotted from a number of viewpoints side-by-side stresses these inter-relationships. For selected areas the proportion of *all* the population in particular occupation groupings has been separately plotted for male and female. This can be compared with a chart of birthplaces and an age-sex diagram in which the difference between percentages of different age-groups is compared with the figure for England and Wales. These have been plotted for male and female ¦separately and have the merit of drawing attention to the precise nature and degree of contrasts with the figures for the rest of the country (Figure 12).

Area I shows a relatively high proportion of both male and female gainfully occupied. This is to be related to a large immigration from outside the local area and is reflected in the difference in age and sex structure between the area and the country as a whole. Because of the low birth-rate there is a considerably lower proportion in ages 0–14 and, in the 15–44 age-groups, high immigration gives a large excess over the average figures for England and Wales. To a certain degree this can be correlated with particular occupational groups. For example, the very large excess of female population between 15 and 29 is closely linked to the demand for female labour in the service occupations associated with hotels and lodging-houses and domestic staffs. Other central areas (II and IV) show similar characteristics though with varying emphasis. Thus, because of the large number of men employed as shop assistants in the Bold Street shopping area, the male immigration bulge in the ages 20–55 is bigger than that in the equivalent female grouping.

Area III, an example of the better class "town" residential district, shows the immense influence that a single occupational group could exert on population structure. The excess of female population over the average for England and Wales is here very marked and is linked, in the main, to the great demand for domestic servants in the large houses in the Abercromby Square area. It is therefore associated with considerable immigration and a large percentage in the female age-groups, especially between 15 and 49. This has much in common with a similar district in Everton Village (VIII).

Area V, a dockside residential district of poor class housing, had a large immigrant population particularly from Ireland. But families were large (accounting for the large proportion of the female population not gainfully employed) and the birth-rate high. Thus, the lower age-groups (0–14) were large relative to England and Wales. But the high level of infant and child mortality led to a rapid lowering of this difference so that in the group 15–19 the Liverpool figures are below those for the country as a whole. Thereafter adult immigration swelled the groups between 25 and 44. Similar characteristics are shown by area VII, another example of a relatively crowded working-class district.

These contrast markedly with the dockside area VI where much of the very large immigrant population (chiefly from Ireland) was in transit to America and often consisted of single men rather than

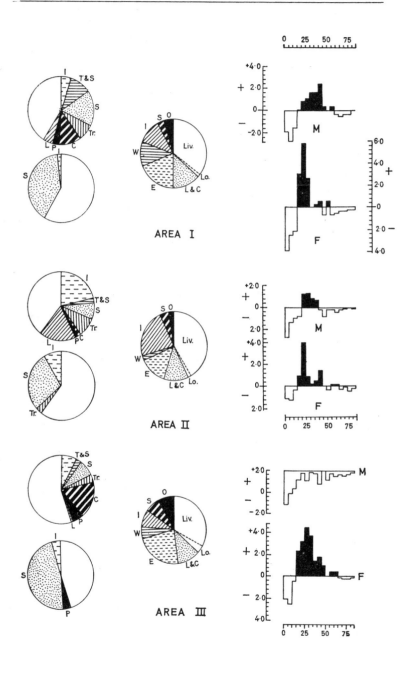

AREA I

AREA II

AREA III

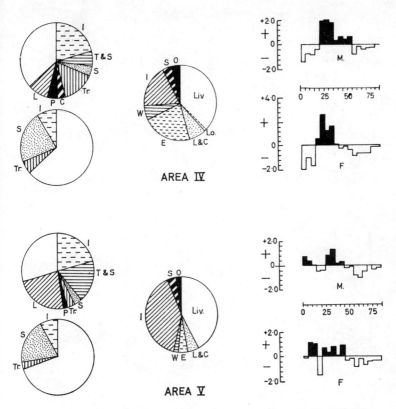

FIGURE 12. COMPARATIVE DIAGRAMS OF POPULATION
STRUCTURE IN SAMPLE AREAS.

These show in each case

(a) in the left hand circles—the proportion of *all* males and females (i) not gainfully employed (white); (ii) in the occupational categories shown in figure 8 (shaded, and with the initial letter as in figure 5); males above, females below.

(b) in the middle circle—birthplaces grouped as in figure 6, the groups indicated by the initial letter.

(c) age and sex showing the difference between the percentage in each male and female group (0—4, 5—9, and to 80+) and the corresponding figure for England and Wales as a whole. Age-groups are on the horizontal scale, percentage differences on the vertical. N.B. For Area III vertical scale for male population should read 0, −2·0, − 4·0.

The symbols in (a) and (b) are *not* proportional to the number of people in each sample.

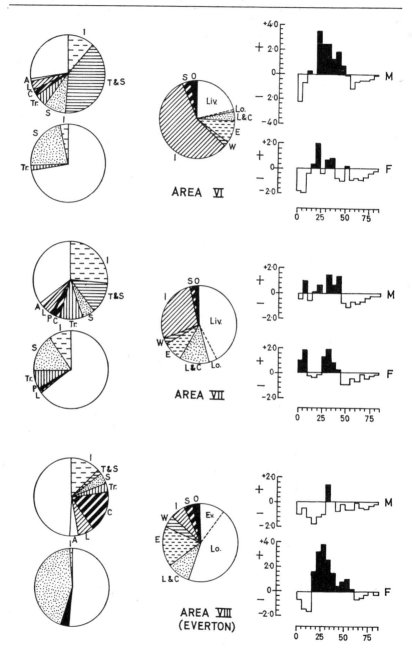

AREA VI

AREA VII

AREA VIII
(EVERTON)

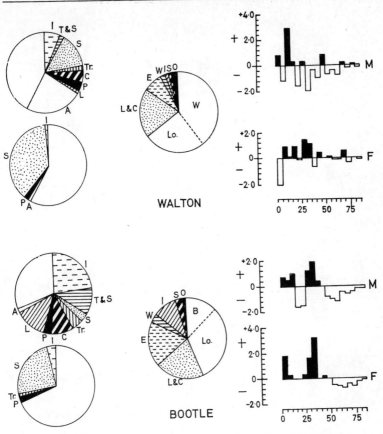

FIGURE 12. COMPARATIVE DIAGRAMS OF POPULATION
STRUCTURE IN SAMPLE AREAS.

These show in each case

(a) in the left hand circles—the proportion of *all* males and females (i) not
gainfully employed (white); (ii) in the occupational categories shown in figure 8
(shaded, and with the initial letter as in figure 5); males above, females below.

(b) in the middle circle—birthplaces grouped as in figure 6, the groups indicated
by the initial letter.

(c) age and sex showing the difference between the percentage in each male and
female group (0—4, 5—9, and to 80+) and the corresponding figure for England
and Wales as a whole. Age-groups are on the horizontal scale, percentage
differences on the vertical.

The symbols in (a) and (b) are *not* proportional to the number people in each
sample.

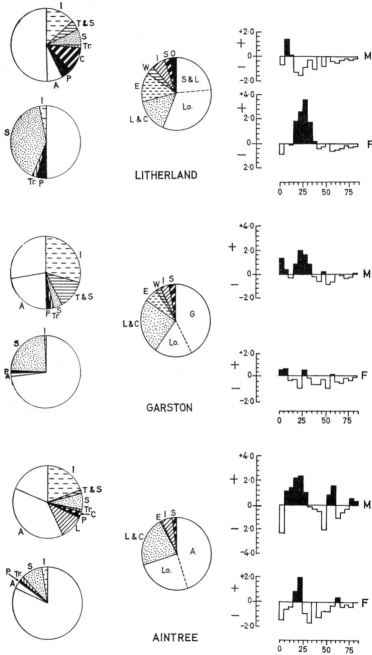

FIGURE 12. COMPARATIVE DIAGRAMS OF POPULATION
STRUCTURE IN SAMPLE AREAS.
(For interpretation see previous page.)

families. There were relatively few children and a pronounced excess of men between the ages of 25 and 49.

The outer residential areas were gaining much of their growing populations by an outward movement from Liverpool itself. Thus, in cases where an old agricultural village had superimposed upon it a suburban character, the population characteristics were composite. In Walton agriculture was still an important male occupation and those men and their families were usually born in Walton itself. The merchant households were not very numerous but employed quite large numbers of domestic staff. The striking numbers of boys in the 10–14 male group is due to boarders at Walton Academy.

Where the development of population associated with the spread of Liverpool was leading to the creation of *new* settlement as in the riverside area of Bootle township, the picture is clearer. Here a balanced occupational structure associated with a range of classes of people was linked to considerable immigration, much of it from the local area. The comparison of percentages in different age-groups with England and Wales shows two distinctive features. First, an excess in the younger age-groups of both sexes linked to high birth-rates and large families; second, a swelling due to adult immigration between 25–39.

Where the residential development had been chiefly associated with the moving of upper classes from the town, as in Litherland, there is a considerable similarity to the age-sex pattern in such districts as the Abercromby Square area and Everton. The large domestic service group is linked to an excess of population in the female groups between 15 and 39. The considerable numbers of people born locally but outside the Seaforth and Litherland township point to the large element of outward movement from town already commented upon.

Aintree is in complete contrast to any of the samples previously considered. It was still very much the agricultural township. There was little employment of women and as a result there had been much movement of women in the age-groups 25–54 to employment elsewhere. Agriculture and varied craft trades were more able to give the men employment and this, rather than any positive attraction, accounts for the greater proportion of men than women and the excess of males between 5 and 29. But the people as a whole were local people and the township was losing population by migration and even at this time beginning to decline in total numbers (*see* Figure 3). As the middle age-groups moved out (note the relatively smaller groups 25–49) so the population became an ageing one and the birth rate declined, giving a much lower figure than was typical for England and Wales in the 0–4 group.

Although these zones were by no means absolutely clear-cut, one can draw certain positive conclusions from them. Central Liverpool was, by 1851, a zone of banking and commerce, though it also had its labourers and small-scale traders and craftsmen. It was, however, very much in decline as a residential area. Indeed

TABLE I

SAMPLE AREAS: CUMULATIVE TOTALS OF OCCUPATIONS

The upper figure refers to total numbers, the lower to
(in Column 1) the percentage of the *total* population not gainfully employed.
(in other columns) the percentage of the *gainfully employed* population engaged in main groups of occupation.
A cumulative total for all samples is shown in the bottom line.

	Not Occu-pied	In-dus-try	T'ns-port	Ser-vice	Trade	Com-merce	Pro-fes-sional	La-bour	Agri-cul-ture	Total Occu-pied	Total
I	336	41	57	302	49	61	17	24	3	554	890
	37·8	7·4	10·3	54·6	8·8	11·0	3·1	4·3	0·5	100·0	100·0
II	392	132	11	157	53	8	5	81	2	449	841
	46·7	29·4	2·4	35·0	11·8	1.8	1·1	18·0	0·4	100·0	100·0
III	425	50	11	225	17	71	44	5	1	424	849
	50·1	11·8	2·6	53·1	4·0	16·7	10.4	1·2	0·2	100·0	100·0
IV	584	213	44	197	144	27	36	78	1	740	1324
	44·1	28·7	5·9	26·6	19·4	3·6	4·9	10·5	0·1	100·0	100·0
V	413	72	46	56	16	1	3	63	1	258	671
	61·7	27·9	17·8	21·7	6·2	0·4	1·2	24·4	0·4	100·0	100·0
VI	680	101	264	199	40	18		11	20	653	1333
	50·6	15·4	40·4	30·5	6·1	2·8		1·7	3·1	100·0	100·0
VII	643	192	69	108	94	13	11	29	10	526	1169
	54·9	36·6	13·1	20·6	17·9	2·5	2·1	5·5	1·9	100·0	100·0
VIII	567	59	7	218	18	78	42	16	3	441	1008
	56·1	13·4	1·6	49·4	4·1	17·7	9·5	3·6	0·7	100·0	100·0
Walton	336	17	4	113	4	9	12	2	53	214	550
	61·1	7·9	1·9	52·8	1·9	4·2	5·6	0·9	24·7	100·0	100·0
Bootle	814	122	45	120	21	43	24	61	5	441	1255
	64·8	27·7	10·2	27·2	4·8	9·8	5·4	13·8	1·1	100·0	100·0
Litherland	763	89	24	279	17	63	58	3	42	575	1338
	56·9	15·5	4·2	48·6	3·0	11·0	10·1	0·5	7·3	100·0	100·0
Aintree	165	32	2	25	4	2	2	18	61	146	311
	53·0	21·9	1·4	17·1	2·7	1·4	1·4	12·3	41·7	100·0	100·0
Allerton	151	8	3	110	1	12	6	12	36	188	339
	44·5	4·2	1·6	58·4	0·5	6·4	3·2	6·4	19·1	100·0	100·0
Childwall	67	3	1	46	1	7	4	3	34	99	166
	40·3	3·0	1·0	46·5	1·0	7·1	4·0	3·0	34·4	100·0	100·0
Wavertree	359	15	4	218	2	23	17	7	33	319	678
	52·9	4·7	1·3	68·3	0·6	7·2	5·3	2·2	10·3	100·0	100·0
Grassendale	77	4	—	51	1	11	9	—	—	76	153
	50·2	5·3	—	67·1	1·3	14·5	11·8	—	—	100·0	100·0
Garston	561	148	65	139	9	2	10	2	121	496	1057
	52·9	29·9	13·1	28·0	1·8	0·4	2·1	0·4	24·5	100·0	100·0
Total	7333	1298	657	2563	491	449	300	415	426	6599	13932
	52·6	19·7	9·9	38·9	7·4	6·8	4·6	6·3	6·5	100·0	100·0

412

TABLE 2

CUMULATIVE TOTALS AND PERCENTAGES OF BIRTH PLACES

The upper figures in each group refer to total numbers, the lower to the percentage these form of the total for each area. A cumulative total for all the samples is shown in the bottom line.

The totals shown in these two tables are not everywhere identical. This is because of a small number of cases of inadequate classification (or omission of information) which has not allowed proper analysis.

Initial letters in column I refer to township of birth, *e.g.* E = Everton.

	LOCAL L'pool	Other	Lancs. & Chesh.	Rest Eng.	Wales	Irel.	Scot.	Rest	Total
I	307	9	126	165	105	104	27	41	884
	34·8	1·0	14·3	18·6	11·9	11·8	3·1	4·6	100·0
II	342	12	101	110	19	198	36	18	836
	41·0	1·4	12·1	13·2	2·3	23·7	4·3	2·2	100·0
III	286	31	91	187	45	69	68	70	847
	33·8	3·7	10·7	22·1	5·3	8·2	8·0	8·3	100·0
IV	492	11	105	283	86	241	57	49	1324
	37·2	0·8	7·9	21·4	6·5	18·2	4·3	3·7	100·0
V	285	—	29	27	14	277	27	13	672
	42·5	—	4·3	4·0	2·1	41·4	4·0	1·9	100·0
VI	282	7	47	94	25	798	47	36	1336
	21·1	0·5	3·5	7·0	1·9	59·7	3·5	2·7	100·0
VII	495	37	146	97	26	325	27	16	1169
	42·3	2·3	12·5	8·3	2·2	27·8	2·3	1·4	100·0
VIII	E.103	L'p area 442	101	171	52	66	34	26	995
	10·4	44·5	10·2	17·2	5·2	6·6	3·4	2·6	100·0
Walton	W.221	L.A.135	115	45	11	8	7	12	554
	39·9	24·4	20·7	8·1	2·0	1·4	1·3	2·2	100;0
Bootle	B.175	L.A.378	256	225	45	122	38	14	1253
	14·0	30·2	20·5	17·8	3·6	9·8	3·0	1·1	100·0
Litherland	S&L 317	L.A. 415	201	197	48	82	37	36	1333
	23·8	31·1	15·0	14·8	3·6	6·1	2·8	2·7	100·0
Aintree	A.139	L.A.81	69	3	1	15	3	1	312
	44·5	25·9	22·1	1·0	0·3	4·8	1·0	0·3	100·0
Allerton	A.37	L.A.115	70	60	30	11	13	3	339
	10·9	33·9	20·6	17·7	8·9	3·2	3·8	0·9	100·0
Childwall	C.50	L.A.42	42	16	2	6	3	6	167
	29·9	25·1	25·1	9·6	1·2	3·6	1·8	3·6	100·0
Wavertree	W.130	L.A.270	89	92	19	33	21	23	677
	19·2	39·8	13·1	13·6	2·8	4·9	3·1	3·4	100·0
Grassendale	G.13	L.A.61	19	27	11	7	6	6	150
	8·7	40·7	12·7	18·0	7·3	4·7	4·0	4·0	100·00
Garston	G.447	L.A.179	258	78	25	41	26	3	1057
	42·3	16·9	24·4	7·4	2·4	3·9	2·5	0·3	100·0
Total	4121	2225	1685	1877	564	2403	477	373	13905
	29·6	16·0	13·4	13·5	4·1	17·2	3·4	2·7	100·0

this was true, although to a lesser degree, of other central areas (*e.g.* II and IV). Moreover, as the town centre declined from this point of view it was increasingly given over to the poorer classes. Some merchants and traders still lived at their business, but increasingly they were to be found in better-class residential districts on the outskirts of the town (*e.g.* Abercromby Square and Everton). However, even these were in a state of transition. The merchants were beginning to go further afield to suburbs like Allerton, Wavertree, Litherland or new residential parks like Grassendale, where they formed a new element in a hitherto largely agricultural community.

The considerable single-class districts which did exist were to be found chiefly *around* the centre of the town with its varied commercial functions, rather than *within* it. They were found in the crowded labouring-class districts behind the docks. Here the alleys and cellars teemed with a numerous and largely immigrant population, chiefly employed as unskilled labour in and around the docks. Where skilled workers were found their crafts were often associated with shipping.

Indeed, the Liverpool of the mid-nineteenth century looked almost wholly to the sea. It was its life and very substance; its influence coloured the development of the town at every turn—its changing morphology, its industry and trade, and, not least, its people.

Supplementary Note

The Census enumerators' books are now regarded as an essential basis for the study of mid-nineteenth-century Britain. Yet only in 1951, with the release to the Public Record Office (Home Office Papers) of the 1851 books, did they begin to attract attention. In 1961, under a hundred years' confidentiality rule, the 1861 enumerators' books were added to those of 1841 and 1851: these have been described by Beresford.[1] Although collectively of great value in comparative studies, those for 1851 are to be preferred where a single year's records suffice. The 1841 Census, the first to be conducted by the Registrar General's Office, established in 1837, is poorer in occupational and birth place data, the books for 1861 are often in poor condition and some are missing.

While primarily of interest in local and regional studies, the enumerators' books are of unique value for the study of nineteenth-century society as a whole. However, their bulk, range and complexity in cross-tabulation creates problems in analysis which call for selective handling, Since this paper on Liverpool was written in 1955 much methodological work by urban historians and historical demographers has led to better techniques of analysis, including sampling and the use of computers.[2] It is thus apparent that descriptive analysis is but the beginning of their usefulness which now extends to theoretical studies.[3]

While the enumerators' books have been used mainly in the study of urban areas,[4] they also illuminate rural England at a crucial stage of its development[5] and, in combination with the numerous contemporary Town Plans and Small-Scale maps,[6] may be used to portray the changing face of both our towns and villages in remarkable detail.

1   Beresford, M.W. 'The unprinted census returns of 1841, 1851 1861 for England and Wales', *The Amateur Historian,* 5, no 8 (1963) pp 360-9

2   Armstrong, W.A. 'Social structure from the early census returns', being pp 209-37 of Wrigley, E.A. (ed), *An Introduction to English Historical Demography* (London, 1966)

3   Taylor, P.J. 'The locational variable in taxonomy', *Geographical Analysis,* 1 (1969) pp 181-95

4   Dyos, H.J. *Victorian Suburb. A Study of the Growth of Camberwell* (Leicester, 1961); Dyos, H.J. (ed), *The Study of Urban History* (London, 1968)

5   Lawton, R. 'The economic geography of Craven in the early nineteenth century', *Transactions and Papers of the Institute of British Geographers,* 20 (1954) pp 93-111; Sheppard, J.A. 'East Yorkshire's agricultural labour force in the mid-nineteenth century' *Agricultural History Review,* 9 (1961) pp 43-54

6   Harley, J.B. 'The town plans and small-scale maps of England and Wales', *The Amateur Historian,* 5, no 8, (1963) pp 251-9

R. LAWTON   August 1969

Agricultural Changes in the Chilterns 1875-1900
J.T. Coppock
Reprinted from *Agricultural History Review,* 9 (1961),
1-16

Agricultural Changes in the Chilterns 1875–1900[1]

By J. T. COPPOCK

WHILE the broad outlines of the agricultural depression which affected British agriculture from the late 1870's until the end of the century are well known, few local studies have been made. The Chilterns and the adjoining clay lowlands (Fig. I) provide a suitable area for investigating the changes which occurred, for they contain a wide variety of country within a small compass. The Chilterns themselves, rising to over 800 feet, have stony soils of low fertility, the clay lowlands to north and south are poorly drained and difficult to cultivate, while the gravel terraces of the Thames and the Icknield belt below the escarpment have free-working loams which make good arable soils.

In the 1870's the Chilterns were primarily rural. It is true that many of the towns were growing rapidly, but they were still small, and most of the land, though much interrupted by blocks of woodland, was used for agriculture. In those parts nearest London there were also numerous parks and mansions. The clay vales to the north, where there were few parks and little wood, were almost entirely farmed, but south of the Chilterns parks were again numerous. There were marked regional differences in the kind of farming practised, differences of fairly long standing, determined mainly by soil and by nearness to London markets. The easily worked loams of the Icknield belt and the Thames terraces were almost entirely arable, as were the Chilterns, where the only extensive stretches of grass lay in the landscaped parks or along the few streams. The amount of grass decreased with elevation; a typical farm at Swyncombe, for example, had only 7 out of 372 acres under grass. On the clays to the north, more land was under permanent grass, though the proportion varied from all-grass farms in the low-lying Vale of Aylesbury to mixed farms with a preponderance of arable around Bletchley. Generally between one and two-fifths of the land was under the plough, and a farm at Waterstock, with 208 acres of grass and 118 of arable,

[1] The cost of extracting the statistical data on which this paper is based was met by a grant from the Central Research Fund, University of London. The author is grateful to Mr J. Bryant who drew the maps. Statements which are not supported by references are either derived from the parish summaries of the agricultural returns (which have been extensively used in the preparation of this paper) or generalizations made from sources too numerous to list.

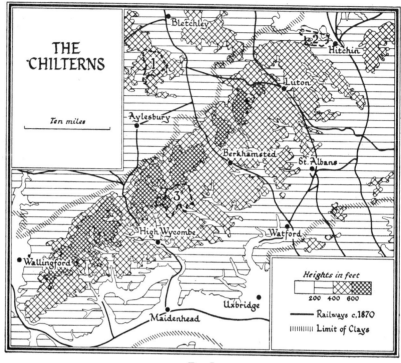

FIG. I

was fairly representative.[1] The clays of south Hertfordshire and Middlesex were nearly all under permanent grass, but the reason for this was only partly the heavy soil. London, with its large population of horses and dairy cattle, made heavy demands on the adjacent counties for hay, straw, and other fodder crops, and four-fifths of the grass was cut for hay each year (Figure IIa).

The stock kept and the crops grown also varied considerably. On the Chilterns and in all the main arable areas, the Norfolk four-course rotation, or some variant of it, prevailed (Figure IIb). Cereals, turnips, and clover accounted for four-fifths of the arable, the remainder being occupied by other fodder crops such as peas and vetches. On Hoo Farm, Kimpton, for example, there were in 1870 113 acres of wheat, 88½ of barley, 73 of clover, 20 of beans, and 99½ of turnips.[2] The better land supported an additional

[1] *Second Report, Commissioners on the Employment of Children, Young Persons, and Women in Agriculture*, Appendix, Part II, Parliamentary Papers, XIII, 1868–9, p. 326.
[2] Accounts, Hoo Farm, Kimpton, Hertfordshire Record Office.

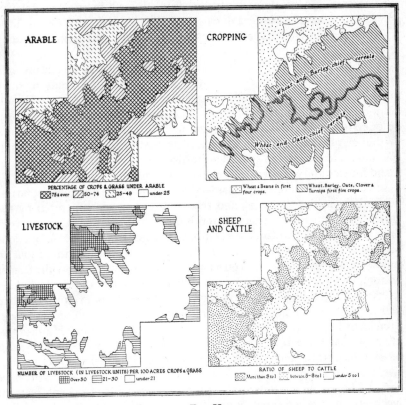

Fig. II

corn crop and usually carried more wheat and barley than oats. Thus, in the Hertfordshire Chilterns, where soils were generally better than further west, a five-course rotation was common and wheat and barley were the leading cereals;[1] in the poorer Oxfordshire Chilterns, a four-course rotation, with oats the second cereal, was general. On the clays, cropping was more varied, and rotations often longer.[2] Wheat was everywhere the chief crop, occupying a third or more of the arable. Beans were also a characteristic crop, and a larger proportion of land was bare-fallowed; but some oats, barley,

[1] H. Evershed, 'Agriculture of Hertfordshire', *Journal of the Royal Agricultural Society*, xxv, 1864, p. 272.
[2] *Second Report on the Employment of Children*, etc., *loc. cit.*, p. 75; *ibid., First Report*, Appendix, Part I, Parliamentary Papers, XVII, 1867–8, p. 124.

clover, and turnips were also grown. On Manor Farm, Upper Stondon, wheat, occupying 99 acres, and beans, 52 acres, were the leading crops in 1868, the remainder of the arable being occupied chiefly by 50 acres of clover, 37 of turnips, 24 of barley, 22 of oats, and 18 acres of fallow.[1] On the little arable on the clays to the south of the Chilterns, wheat was again the leading crop.

Specialized cropping was rare. Market gardening was important only on the Middlesex gravel terraces and potatoes were grown only in small quantities, except in the market-gardening areas and on the sandy soils around Leighton Buzzard. Wheat and barley were the principal cash crops; on one Hertfordshire farm they accounted for 84 per cent of crop sales.[2] Within easy reach of London, however, oats, hay, roots, and straw were sold; the importance of oats in south Hertfordshire was probably due to the demand for oats and oat straw rather than to the quality of the soil.

Most observers noted the considerable uniformity of cropping on farms, particularly in the Chilterns, and their impressions are supported by the agricultural returns. To what extent this uniformity was due to lease restrictions it is impossible to say; clauses in leases ranged from general injunctions to cultivate the land in a husband-like manner to specific instructions to follow a particular rotation, as on a farm at Mapledurham, where the farmer was enjoined to cultivate the land on a four-course system and was forbidden to take two crops of the same kind of grain in succession or to crop more than half the land with grain.[3] There were limitations on growing other crops; a tenant of a 640-acre farm on the Ashridge estate was prohibited from growing more than two acres of potatoes.[4] There were also restrictions on the disposal of hay, straw, and roots grown on the farm. It is true that such restrictive covenants were not necessarily enforced and practice seems to have varied from estate to estate; only one specific example of the enforcement has been noted, where a tenant on a farm at Chenies was ordered to plough up and fallow a field sown to oats because of "too great a liberty in the extent of his White-Strawed Cropping."[5] The object of the covenants was, of course, to protect the land, and farmers were usually allowed to sell crops, hay, and straw when sufficient dung could be brought back to replace their manurial value.[6]

The importance of livestock varied inversely with the proportion of

---

[1] Bedfordshire County Record Office, DDX 159/3.

[2] 'Remarks concerning a Herts Farm', *Herts Illustrated Review*, I, 1893, pp. 647-8.

[3] Agreement, April 1883, Blount MSS., Bodleian.

[4] Hertfordshire County Record Office, Leases, Ashridge Estate.

[5] Bedford Office, Bedford Estate Reports, 1887.   [6] Evershed, *loc. cit.*, p. 284.

arable,[1] except on the clays to the south of the Chilterns where the hay crop severely limited grazing (Figure IIc). On the Icknield belt and on the Chilterns sheep were the principal livestock, especially on the higher parts where water was scarce. They were arable sheep, folded on roots, and were kept primarily to manure the soil. Horses accounted for one third of the total livestock, and a few dairy cattle, beef cattle, and stores were also kept. Stocking on these farms is exemplified by Hoo Farm, Kimpton, which carried 702 sheep, of which 408 were breeding ewes, 32 cattle, 23 horses, and 75 pigs. Lower down the Chilterns, where water was more abundant, fewer sheep and more cattle were kept (Figure IId). South of the Chilterns farms kept mainly cattle, and nearer London some dairying was practised. The chief areas of livestock farming were, however, the clay lowlands to the north, especially the area around Aylesbury, which Read had called "the pastoral garden of the county."[2] Cattle were the chief livestock, but both arable and grass sheep were kept. The mainly grass farms near Aylesbury fattened beef cattle, particularly Herefords, but the mixed farms, which covered most of the clays, practised dairying and rearing as well as fattening. Dairying was typical of the poorer grassland and was still largely concerned with butter production; only in well-placed areas was much milk sold.[3]

Stocking, too, was affected by lease restrictions, though less frequently than the use of the arable land. Some leases merely enjoined the farmer to stock the farm adequately; but occasionally restrictions were more specific, as on Park and Rose Farms, Mapledurham, where the tenant was required to keep a sufficient flock of sheep and to pen and fold them on the farm.[4]

This brief statistical account inevitably minimizes the rich variety of farming; nevertheless, the prevailing impression is one of considerable uniformity within regions which differed markedly from each other.

In the late 1870's a series of bad harvests coincided with a period of falling prices. Although the weather improved, grain prices, particularly of wheat and barley, continued to fall; they were joined in the 1880's by a similar, though smaller, fall in the prices of livestock and livestock products. These falling prices were met in two main ways; part of the burden was shouldered by landlords, who remitted and later reduced rents, and part by farmers, who

---

[1] No winter returns of livestock were made, but there is evidence of fattening of cattle in winter in the arable areas.

[2] C. S. Read, 'Report on the Farming of Buckinghamshire', *Journal of the Royal Agricultural Society*, XVI, 1855, p. 281.

[3] J. C. Morton, 'Dairy Farming', *Journal of the Royal Agricultural Society*, 2nd Series, XIV, 1878, p. 689, and report of Daily News Special Commissioner, reproduced in *Bedford Times*, 13 September 1879.

[4] Agreement, April 1883, Blount MSS.

attempted to reduce their losses by farming less intensively, by avoiding expensive cultivations, and by concentrating on those products which were least affected by the fall in prices. But none of these remedies was adopted uniformly over the whole area.

The reductions in rents are the best documented of the changes and were almost universal. At first landowners granted temporary remissions; in 1880 for example, the duke of Bedford allowed 25 per cent off the year's rent to all tenants on the estate.[1] But gradually, as it became clear that this was not a temporary recession, there were permanent reductions. These were made necessary both to retain existing tenants and to attract new, and it was said that in parts of Hertfordshire no rent at all was paid, the landowners being glad merely to keep a tenant on the farm.[2] There was often a succession of reductions; the rent of Flint Hall Farm on the West Wycombe estate, for example, was reduced by £30 in 1882 and by a further £40 in 1886. Revenues from rents fell steadily; on the West Wycombe estate the rental fell by 19 per cent between 1876 and 1888,[3] and on the Bedford estates in Bedford-shire and Buckinghamshire average farm rent fell by 48 per cent between 1876 and 1895.[4] Reductions were most marked on heavy arable clays, which were expensive and difficult to work, and on poor soils which gave a low return; on the thin soils of the Oxfordshire Chilterns, for example, rents fell by 50 per cent between 1880 and 1893.[5] On good grassland, or where there was easy access to a market, reductions were much less; in the Vale of Aylesbury reductions were generally 20–25 per cent, and near the railways south of the Chilterns from 10–25 per cent.[6]

The most general of the agricultural adjustments was an extension of the grass acreage (Figures IIIa and b). Since wages changed little, labour costs, the largest single item in the outgoings of the arable farmer, could be reduced only by curtailing expensive cultivations. It is difficult to be sure how much land was laid to grass. The agricultural returns show a progressive increase in the amount of permanent pasture; and while this may be due in part to a more complete enumeration of the smaller holdings, which would tend to be largely grass, there is no reason to suppose that it does not reflect an actual

[1] Bedford Estate Reports, 1880.

[2] *Royal Commission on Agriculture, Reports of Assistant Commissioners,* Parliamentary Papers, XVI, 1881, p. 368.

[3] Rentals, West Wycombe Estate papers.

[4] Duke of Bedford, *The Story of a Great Agricultural Estate,* London, 1897, p. 224.

[5] *Royal Commission on Agriculture, Minutes of Evidence,* Parliamentary Papers, XVI, Pt. I, 1894, p. 57.

[6] *Royal Commission on Agriculture, Report of A. Spencer on the Vale of Aylesbury and the County of Hertford,* Parliamentary Papers, XVI, 1895, p. 17.

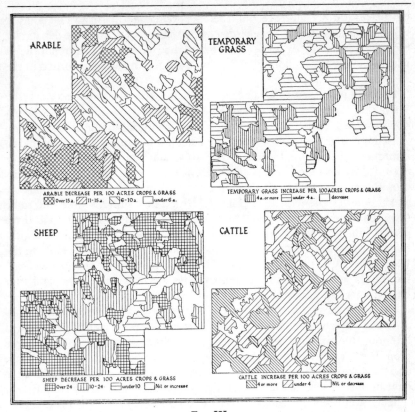

ARABLE

TEMPORARY GRASS

ARABLE DECREASE PER 100 ACRES CROPS & GRASS
◩ Over 15 a. ▨ 11-15 a. ◹ 6-10 a. ☐ under 6 a.

TEMPORARY GRASS INCREASE PER 100 ACRES CROPS & GRASS
▥ 4 a. or more ☐ under 4 a. ☐ decrease

SHEEP

CATTLE

SHEEP DECREASE PER 100 ACRES CROPS & GRASS
▦ Over 24 ▥ 10-24 ☐ under 10 ☐ Nil or increase

CATTLE INCREASE PER 100 ACRES CROPS & GRASS
◹ 4 or more ▨ under 4 ☐ Nil or decrease

Fig. III

trend. Naturally the permanence of price reductions was not appreciated at first and many farmers simply left leys down for more than one year; these would be returned as temporary grass, and only later would they be regarded as permanent. It is true that the assistant commissioner who reported on Bedfordshire in 1895 thought that the amount of permanent grass was being overestimated and that of temporary grass underestimated;[1] but the returns themselves suggest that an expanded temporary grass acreage often concealed the extent of the conversion of arable to permanent pasture. His observation that fields were allowed to lie in grass for a number of years with the intention of ploughing them when prices improved is probably correct;

[1] *Report of H. Pringle on the Counties of Bedford, Huntingdon, and Northampton*, Parliamentary Papers, XVII, 1895, p. 41.

but prices did not improve, and the fields remained in grass. The point at which such leys should be regarded as permanent is in any case debatable; cropping records on a number of farms on the Panshanger estate show fields which, having been under a ley for two or three years, are recorded in the succeeding year as pasture.[1]

Farmers increased their acreage under grass in a number of ways; by sowing more temporary grass and allowing it to stay down longer, by laying down arable to permanent pasture, and by abandoning arable to colonization by self-sown grasses and weeds. The contribution made by each varied in importance in different parts of the area. The proportion of the arable occupied by leys increased nearly everywhere, and in the Chilterns the increases were on such a scale that, despite the diminishing arable, the acreage of temporary grass expanded (Figure IIIb). The Chilterns were said to be unsuited to permanent grass, though they could support leys of up to three years.[2] But these leys were left down and subsequently recognized as permanent pasture; in 1901 Rider Haggard noted that most of the grass in the Oxfordshire Chilterns was originally seeded as two- or three-year leys.[3] On the clays the increase in temporary grass was often ephemeral, and after bad seasons had passed the acreage was reduced (Figure V, Stewkley).

On better land, particularly the claylands where mixed farming was practised and the establishment of good grass was known to be possible, land was intentionally laid down as permanent grass, either directly or under a nurse crop. But "it is a very expensive luxury;" the seeds alone cost 30s. an acre, and the duke of Bedford estimated the total cost at £15 an acre.[4] It is likely to have been widespread, therefore, only on the estates of wealthy landowners. The duke himself laid down 1,308 acres on the 28,274 acres of his Bedfordshire and Buckinghamshire estates between 1880 and 1897. The landowner usually provided the seeds and the tenant the labour; in 1880, for example, two arable fields on stiff clay at Hill Farm, Potsgrove, were laid down to permanent pasture, the duke of Bedford providing the seeds on condition that the fields were not again ploughed up.[5] The farmer himself sometimes provided both seeds and labour, though he had frequently to obtain the landowner's consent first. In general, once the fields were laid down to permanent grass they were subject to the same prohibitions on ploughing up as the existing grass; a lease on a Datchworth farm stated that the tenant was not

[1] Panshanger Estate Papers, Hertfordshire County Record Office.
[2] *Royal Commission on Agriculture, Minutes of Evidence*, 1894, *loc. cit.*, p. 57.
[3] Rider Haggard, *Rural England*, London, 1902, II, p. 118.
[4] *Royal Commission on Agriculture, Minutes of Evidence*, Parliamentary Papers, XVII, 1881, 618, and Duke of Bedford, *op. cit.*, p. 197.
[5] Bedford Estate Report, 1880.

to break up fields which at the determination of the tenancy should have been under seeds for six years.[1] Increases in permanent grass were widespread, particularly on the clays, and in the Oxfordshire Chilterns and in north-east Berkshire (though here accessibility to markets rather than the nature of the soil was the important consideration).

Much was made by contemporaries of the abandonment of cultivated land and of fields that "tumbled down to grass." Agricultural historians have perhaps been too influenced by the "terrible map, dotted thick with black patches" (Clapham's phrase) which accompanied Pringle's report on Essex in 1893. But there is no evidence that abandonment was widespread here; a return in 1881 of abandoned farms and fields in Buckinghamshire, for example, gave a total of 1,102 acres, out of 403,673 acres of agricultural land.[2] It is possible that abandoned land might escape enumeration (though there was no fall in the total acreage returned); but Pringle himself could find none in Bedfordshire. Some of the farms on owners' hands through lack of tenants may well have been neglected; land on such farms at Wallington and Bygrave was said to be almost out of cultivation.[3] But even the extent of land on landowners' hands seems to have been exaggerated. Although one witness reported, at second hand, that on Lord Camoys's estate in the Oxfordshire Chilterns only two out of thirty tenants remained in 1882, this area seems to have been exceptional.[4] Spencer suggested in 1895 that rather more than 20 per cent of the cultivated area was in hand in Hertfordshire, and agricultural returns for 1887 of the acreage of land farmed by owners suggest that over most of the area the proportion was even smaller.[5] Moreover, farms were sometimes taken in hand to prevent the land being neglected by tenants who had lost heart or resources. This seems to have been the practice on the Bedford estate. What is clear is that standards of farming fell. Lord Macclesfield's agent said in 1892 that he did not know a parish where the land was being well farmed, and that he had just taken over one farm without a clean acre.[6] A bad season might lead to temporary abandonment; this is suggested by the laconic entry "thistles" in the cropping record of one farm in 1880.[7] The increase in the acreage of bare fallow, particularly in the Chilterns (Figure IVc), may also conceal such temporary neglect. Fields did tumble

[1] Hertfordshire County Record Office, Abel Smith Papers.
[2] Manuscript figures, parish summaries 1881, Ministry of Agriculture.
[3] Spencer, *loc. cit.*, p. 22.
[4] *Royal Commission on Agriculture, Minutes of Evidence*, 1881, *loc. cit.*, p. 847.
[5] Spencer, *loc. cit.*, p. 22.
[6] *Royal Commission on Labour, Report upon the Poor Law Union of Thame*, Parliamentary Papers, xxxv, 1893–4, p. 52.
[7] Panshanger Papers, Digswell Lodge Farm.

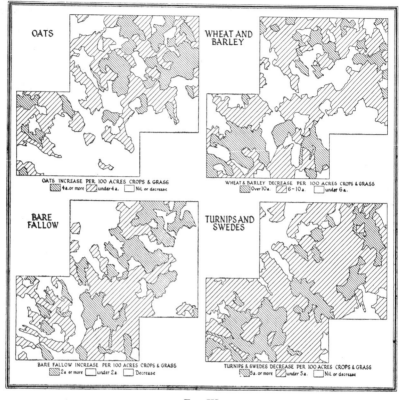

FIG. IV

down to grass; one such field is recorded on Great Green Street Farm at Chenies in 1887, where the land became covered with couch and weeds which provided only poor herbage. Self-sown grass was auctioned annually in Bedfordshire and was let at very low rents;[1] but even here the extent was exaggerated and an observer who had been told that a good deal of land around Toddington was "laying itself down with twitch" found the fields fairly clean.[2] It seems likely that in so far as self-sown grass was widespread, it was to be found chiefly on poor arable clays and on very light land.

In whatever way land was converted to grass there was everywhere a reduction in the tillage acreage. The fall was least on the free-working loams

[1] Pringle, *loc. cit.*, p. 22.

[2] *Royal Commission on Labour, Report upon the Poor Law Union of Woburn*, Parliamentary Papers, xxxv, 1, 1893–4, p. 18.

at the foot of the escarpment, and on the predominantly pastoral clays around
Aylesbury and in south Hertfordshire, where the need and scope for additional grass were limited. It was greatest on mixed farms on the clays and on
the steep slopes and stony soils of the western Chilterns, especially in Oxfordshire. Three sample parishes show the range of variation, Stewkley (Bucks.)
representing the heavy clays, Pirton (Herts.) the Icknield belt, and Great
Missenden (Bucks.) the Chilterns (Figure V). That they are fairly typical of

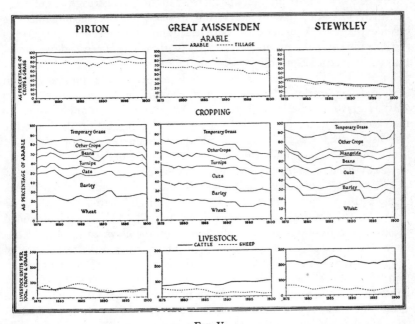

FIG. V

the areas in which they lie is confirmed by the maps in Figures III and IV.
  Of course, these averages conceal considerable variation between different
farms. It is possible to find farms which delayed conversion of arable until
the 1900's. Furthermore, the process on any one farm was not as continuous
as the graphs suggest; fields would be laid down at intervals between which
the arable acreage was constant. A change in tenancy was frequently the
occasion for an increase in the grass acreage since it was hard to find good
tenants for arable farms on indifferent or heavy soils. Thus, on the 260 acres
of Lodge Farm, Chenies, 81 acres were laid down to grass for a new tenant in
1884. The change in emphasis is well seen in a sale catalogue for the War-

grave Manor Estate, which, though largely arable in 1876, was advertised in 1896 as being mainly grass and having only 100 acres of arable, and that of high quality.[1] The great majority of farms increased their grass acreage between 1878 and 1900, and although the sequence of events and the proportion of arable converted to grass varied from farm to farm, there seems to be no doubt that the picture of steady conversion was true of the farms of any area as a whole.

In so far as it was deliberate, this increase in the grass acreage was effected primarily to reduce labour costs; but it was generally accompanied by changes in the stocking of farms. With less arable fewer sheep were needed to fertilize the land, and numbers fell, particularly where sheep had been most numerous, on the High Chilterns, below the escarpment, and in the clay vales (Figure IIIc). There was a corresponding increase in the number of both store and dairy cattle, save in the areas which remained largely arable (Figure IIId). In favoured parts, such as south Oxfordshire, the numbers of cattle increased at a faster rate than the grass acreage, suggesting that here the increase in stock was the cause and not the consequence of more abundant grass; but more commonly the increase in numbers of cattle seems to have been a by-product of the expanding grass acreage.

The extension of dairy farming was the most significant of the livestock changes; progressive farmers like Lawes established dairies because, as he put it, "foreign nations cannot so easily sell us milk."[2] Dairying had tended to increase in the traditional livestock areas on the clays north of the Chilterns ever since 1865, when the cattle plague decimated the population of the London cowhouses. Transport was the chief limitation on the production of milk for sale, and within two or three miles of a railway station farmers began to substitute milk-production for butter-making. With the decline in arable farming, other favourably placed farms along the railway lines adopted dairying as their grass acreage expanded, though they had frequently to await the construction of suitable buildings; a prospective tenant at Digswell insisted on a cowhouse for forty cows as a condition for taking over the farm. In addition to the London market, local markets for milk were provided by the condensed milk factory at Aylesbury and by the biscuit factory at Reading; the considerable increase in dairying in the Oxfordshire Chilterns is undoubtedly due in part to this local demand. The growing towns in the area, such as Watford, also provided local markets. The absence of water precluded dairying in the higher parts of the Chilterns, and the chief areas in which dairying increased lay in the lower south and in the major

[1] British Museum, Wargrave Manor Estate, Maps 137 c. 13.
[2] *Royal Commission on Agriculture, Minutes of Evidence*, 1881, *loc. cit.*, p. 949.

valleys. Figure VIa shows the general correspondence between areas of greatest increase and the major valleys, most of which carried railway lines from London. In the clay vales to the north there were both an increase in the number of dairy cattle and a further switch from butter-making to milk-

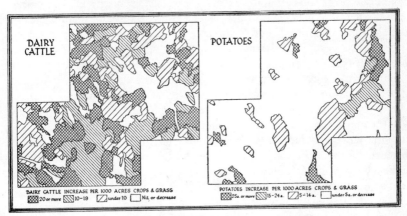

DAIRY CATTLE

POTATOES

DAIRY CATTLE INCREASE PER 1000 ACRES CROPS & GRASS
20 or more   10-19   under 10   Nil, or decrease

POTATOES INCREASE PER 1000 ACRES CROPS & GRASS
25a. or more   15-24a.   5-14 a.   under 5a. or decrease

Fig. VI

selling, especially for the London market.[1] Unfortunately there are no records by which this change in the use of milk can be measured; but one contemporary writer reported that in 1888 some 60,000 gallons of milk were sold each week out of the Vale of Aylesbury, more than half of it to London, and that "Aylesbury butter has lost its prestige."[2]

The increased interest in cattle-keeping was partly due to the immigration of livestock farmers from the west country and from Scotland, who were attracted by the low rents and the ease with which farms could be got. On the Knebworth estate, for example, in 1895 Scottish farmers outnumbered English by nine to six,[3] and so numerous were the newcomers when Rider Haggard made his survey of Hertfordshire in 1901 that he was led to ask "But where are the home people?"[4] The Scots were particularly associated with dairying while the Devon and Cornish farmers were said to be more concerned with stock-rearing.

On the reduced acreage of arable there were also adjustments in cropping (Figure IV). Restrictive covenants could no longer be enforced, both because of the difficulty of finding tenants and because farmers' working capital had

[1] Evidence of Mr Perkins, *Journal of the British Dairy Farmers Association*, VI, 1890, p. 126.
[2] R. Gibbs, *A History of Aylesbury*, Aylesbury, 1888, pp. 666-7.
[3] Spencer, *loc. cit.*, p. 14.   [4] R. Haggard, *op. cit.*, I, p. 510.

been reduced; on the Bedford estate, where the strict enforcement of cropping restrictions has previously been noted, there was relaxation,[1] and on the claylands convenience had become "the controller of rotations."[2] Apart from the increase in temporary grass, the most general changes were the greater emphasis on oats at the expense of wheat and barley, and the marked reduction in the acreage of other fodder crops, especially turnips on light land and beans on heavy land. Oats replaced wheat as the leading cereal over most of the western Chilterns, and replaced barley as the second cereal in the Hertfordshire Chilterns, where the oat acreage increased despite the falling arable. Fewer sheep were one cause of the reduced turnip acreage, but high labour requirements were also a factor, and the place of turnips in the root break was partly filled by an increase in the acreage of bare fallow. On the clays beans occupied a smaller proportion of the diminished arable and the acreage under mangolds rose; but while there was a marked increase in bare fallow in the early years of the depression, this expansion was not maintained (Figure V, Stewkley, other crops). The least change in cropping occurred on the loams of the Icknield belt.

As with the laying down of land to grass, these generalizations conceal differences between farms. These can be illustrated by the Panshanger estate, where cropping records for a number of farms in close proximity permit comparison of the average acreage under different crops for the periods 1874–6 and 1889–91. On Lower Handside Farm, for example, the acreage under wheat fell 8 per cent, while the acreages under barley and oats rose 5 per cent and 8 per cent respectively. On Digswell Lodge Farm the wheat acreage declined less than 1 per cent, the barley acreage 11 per cent, while the oat acreage increased 10 per cent. At Attimore Hall the oat acreage rose 2 per cent, and acres under wheat and barley declined slightly, while on Birchall Farm the wheat acreage rose 5 per cent, the barley 1 per cent, and the oat acreage fell 4 per cent. Nevertheless, although there was much variation from farm to farm, the trend on most farms was similar.

While in many parts of the country farmers met falling cereal prices by growing potatoes and vegetables, few farmers in the Chilterns adopted these crops. Market gardening spread westward along the Thames terraces in south Buckinghamshire, and southward from the mid-Bedfordshire market-gardening area towards the foot of the Chilterns. But on the Chilterns and in the clay vales soils were either too poor or too heavy to encourage vegetable growing, while much of the area was too inaccessible; even Barton-

[1] Royal Commission on Labour, *loc. cit.*, p. 17, and J. Caird, *English Agriculture in 1850–1*, London, 1852, p. 436.
[2] Pringle, *loc. cit.*, p. 40.

in-the-Clay, little more than three miles from the nearest station, was held to be too far away for it to be suitable for market gardening.[1] The stony soils of the Chilterns were also unsuited to potato growing, which increased mainly in the Vale of St Albans and the Hitchin Gap (Figure VIb). Three causes promoted this expansion: the lighter soils, the immigration of Scottish farmers, who brought not only dairying but potato growing and ley farming, and the abundant supplies of manure which London provided. It was this last consideration which restricted potato growing to a narrow belt near the railway lines; manure cost only 4s. 6d. a ton at the station, but its price was more than doubled five miles away by transport charges.[2] Figure VIb shows how highly localized this expansion was, though the parish returns, which include more distant farms which did not grow potatoes, minimize the size of the increase. On the 340 acres of Digswell Lodge Farm an average of 43 acres of potatoes was grown in 1882–9 by a new Scottish tenant, whereas none had been grown in 1873–9 by the former tenant, a local farmer whose family had occupied the farm for six generations.[3]

There were other minor changes. Although fruit-growing never became a major activity in the Chilterns, additional orchards were planted, often by smallholders, along the foot of the escarpment, particularly between Totternhoe and Ivinghoe, and in places such as Holmer Green on the plateau. Poorer soils were sometimes taken out of cultivation altogether and planted with trees, usually conifers; many small parcels of arable were planted in the western Chilterns and are usually distinguished from the surrounding beechwoods by their conifers, their straight boundaries, and their names, e.g. Jubilee Plantation (Hambleden).

It is clear that the regional pattern of agricultural change was determined mainly by the nature of the soil and by accessibility. Where land was easy to cultivate and moderately fertile it remained in arable, often with little modification in its cropping; where soils were heavy arable fields were laid down to grass and pastoral farming was widely adopted; and where soils provided poor arable but were also unsuited to grass, pastoral farming was adopted almost involuntarily by leaving temporary grass unploughed. On the flatter terrain and somewhat better soils of the Hertfordshire Chilterns changes were less marked than further west, and the differences were accentuated by the relative ease with which manure could be got. While the importance of the supply of manure is probably exaggerated by the farmer who said that

[1] Bedfordshire County Council, Smallholdings File, Bedfordshire County Record Office.
[2] Minutes of Evidence, Select Committee of the House of Commons on Railway Bills, Ques. 9223, 1881, BTC 899, in British Transport Commission Archives.
[3] Panshanger Papers.

without the abundant supplies of dung he would not have the land as a gift,[1] Spencer in his report on Hertfordshire did not see how the poorer land could have remained in cultivation without the advantages conferred by the railways.[2] The closer network of lines in Hertfordshire (Figure I) reinforced the advantages of greater nearness to London and better soils which the county enjoyed over Buckinghamshire and Oxfordshire. Railways facilitated the adoption of dairying and potato growing, and their importance was generally recognized in higher rents near railway lines, away from which, said one farmer, was "agricultural death."[3]

The effects of other factors are more difficult to estimate and their incidence was probably more localized. Wages fell little, but there was continued emigration to the towns and many complaints of the quality of the remaining labour. How far the adjustments in farming were caused by labour shortage or by high labour bills is uncertain; but it seems probable that the need for economy was more important than the shortage of labour.[4] The presence of immigrant farmers, introducing new ideas, also affected the local pattern of change; they were among those most successful in riding the depression, partly because their farming suited the new conditions, partly because they were less conservative than the local farmers, and partly because they worked hard and lived hard. Adjustments also depended on landlords; wealthy landowners might retain tenants by temporary remissions of rent and facilitate change by providing necessary buildings, while tenants of poorer landowners would have been left to fend for themselves. But this consideration, while it undoubtedly modified local details, can hardly have determined the broad regional pattern of change.

The main effect of the events of this twenty-five year period was to emphasize differences which had only been latent before, and to diversify further the pattern of farming. The agriculture of 1875 could still be recognized in the hay-making on the London Clay, the corn and sheep farming on the Chilterns, and the pastoral farming in the clay vales; but these differences were becoming muted, and other differences were arising in their place. The contrast between the arable Chilterns and the grasslands to the north and south became less marked, but that between the eastern and western Chilterns and between valley and hilltop farm increased. A further thirty years were required to complete the process; but the foundations of change were clearly laid in this period.

[1] Rider Haggard, *op. cit.*, I, p. 542.   [2] Spencer, *loc. cit.*, p. 22.
[3] Rider Haggard, *op. cit.*, I, p. 511.
[4] H. Rew, *Report on the Decline of the Agricultural Population of Great Britain*, Parliamentary Papers, XCVI, 1906, p. 37.

Supplementary Note

I can see no reason to amend any of the views expressed in this article. It is true it ignores the point, cogently argued by Mr T.W. Fletcher, that low cereal prices were advantageous to the livestock farmer and takes no account of the extent to which livestock feeding-stuffs were purchased,[1] but none of the sources on which it was based provided the material for any general statement on this point, let alone for the study of regional differences within the Chiltern area. I accept Mr Fletcher's point and it may be that if I had sought evidence I should have found it (although I do not recall any among the large quantity of material I sifted in my search for data on regional change). Knowing something about the great range of variation from farm to farm that characterises most parts of England, I am chary of accounts that rely on a few farm records and on the general impressions of observers who see only part of an area, even if the result is very much more readable than a statistical account. Farm records alone can provide on a regional basis the kind of data needed to establish Mr Fletcher's point. I accept that they are also important, not only for the insight they provide on change, but also because they provide some qualification of the generalisations of conditions on tens, hundreds or thousands of farms which any statistically-based account must be; but I still believe that, in the absence of any large body of farm records, some framework must be erected into which such 'hand specimens' must be fitted and that the parish summaries of the agricultural returns fulfil this role admirably and certainly better than any other source that I know since the Tithe Surveys. It is perfectly true that they have many imperfections and must be used with care, and that the parish is a very unsatisfactory unit of study; but the information is collected on a fairly uniform basis and has not been consciously manipulated to advance particular views. I find myself less sympathetic to the criticism made by Dr E.L. Jones that 'the acreage statistics seem to have diverted attention from changes in production which took place without correspondingly large changes in land use';[2] for the parish summaries provide information not only on acreages, but also on livestock, and these, in fact, preceded the collection of acreages. Apart from poultry farming, no changes in numbers of livestock need be ignored, whether they were accompanied by changes in land use or not. As for the criticism that the statistics reveal nothing about the profitability of different enterprises, the disposal of crops and livestock, or (at least until 1884) the yields of crops, there is no source other than field enquiry that can be used even today to provide such information on a regional basis. In my view, the acreage returns must play a major part in regional studies of agricultural change in Great Britain in the period since 1866, and I do not see how any student of agricultural change can ignore them.

1   Fletcher, T.W. 'The great depression of English agriculture 1873-96', *The Economic History Review*, 2nd Series XIII, (1961) pp 417-32

2   Jones, E.L. 'The changing basis of agricultural prosperity 1853-73' *The Agricultural History Review, X* (1962) pp 102-19

T.J. COPPOCK

August 1969

Moated Settlements in England

F. V. Emery

Reprinted from *Geography*, 47 (1962), 378-88

Moated Settlements in England

F. V. EMERY

A CURIOUS FEATURE of many Ordnance Survey one-inch maps is the appearance in swarms of the word "Moat", printed in the German lettering used for antiquities of post-Roman date. The Lowestoft sheet of the New Popular edition (sheet 137), for instance, carries no fewer than 190 "Moats". A section of this map, taken from its "New Series" edition, 1899, appears in Plate 1. The Bury St. Edmunds sheet (New Popular edition, sheet 136) has 162, and the Birmingham sheet (131) yields exactly 100, many of them hidden among spoil-heaps and canals. At the other extreme, the Swindon sheet (157) has only 10, while the Solent sheet (180), including the core of the Hampshire Basin and the Isle of Wight, is entirely devoid of "Moats". Their erratic distribution calls for investigation because most of them were designed to enclose settlements, and they are so abundant *en masse* as to constitute a little-known sector of our settlement geography: between 3000 and 4000 moated settlements are on record, from cartographic and other sources, in the English counties (see Table I).

The usual idea of a moat is a broad, water-filled ditch running as a protection below the curtain-wall of a castle, and, admittedly, such moats appeared in the design of strong-points and great houses from the Norman Conquest to the sixteenth century. But the vast majority of moated settlements belonged to the smaller feudal landowners. They figured as working units in the land-use pattern of their time, and to-day many of them survive as farms. For over 50 years, in fact, they have been known as "Moated Homesteads"; "farmsteads" might be more informative, but the title of this paper avoids both in favour of the broader "settlements" because it regards them as only one, although certainly the most usual, form of several kinds of moated site—motte-and-bailey castles, large and small farmsteads, monastic granges, hunting lodges, churches, windmills and even whole villages. The present survey, nevertheless, is concerned primarily with these "Moated Homesteads", whose defences were simply a moat and, rarely, slight earthworks.[1] They did not have, for example, the artificial "mounts" of motte-and-bailey castles.[2] A typical moated settlement is shown in Plate II, although the nature of the original settlement is more likely to be revealed by excavation at sites which are devoid of houses at the present time. Thus, at Harlington in Bedfordshire, there are three moated enclosures in close proximity, and recent excavation has uncovered buildings within two of them. One moat surrounded a house, or hall, a detached kitchen, and two other, as yet unidentified, structures; a second moat enclosed a stable, a pen for cattle or sheep, and a small pond. Pottery indicated that the site was occupied from the late thirteenth century to the end of the fifteenth century. Again, Hamble-ton Moat at Screadington in Lincolnshire, before it was erased by bull-dozer, was roughly square in plan, with sides 190 feet long and a breadth of 30 feet. The island within it showed a clay platform raised 3 feet above the original ground level, with a complex of domestic buildings occupying its southern edge. There was a hall, flanked by a kitchen (with two hearths) and a smaller room. This range was extended by another building, containing two rooms; two ovens lay outside it, and a barn. The north-eastern quadrant of the moated platform was walled off as a stockyard, with rubbish pits. Here, also, datable pottery was of the thirteenth and fourteenth centuries.[3]

Besides the majority of secular sites, many monastic houses enclosed their churches and domestic buildings within large moats, as, for instance, those in the Marshland region of Lincolnshire.[4] The more complete documentation that exists of the origins of these sites and of their role in medieval colonization of the waste can throw light on the chronology of and the motives for the general practice of digging moats.

DISTRIBUTION

Ordnance Survey maps are an obvious starting-point when trying to locate and enumerate moated settlements. The one-inch maps are obliged to be selective, and give only a generalized, partial distribution, especially where moats are clustered closely together. Some are omitted, others are shown as moats but not cited as antiquities, and others are simply called "Moat Farm". Ideally, when beginning with the map evidence of moated sites in any locality, each successive edition of the one-inch maps should be examined, because of the likelihood of variation in the number of moats shown. The New Popular maps are best for use when searching for moats, as their German lettering is more emphatic than on the Seventh Series, on which sites are easily over-looked if they lie close to built-up areas; in any case fewer moats are named on sheets in this series. A more realistic, though not complete, distribution is given by the 1 : 25,000 and 6 inches to a mile maps, which are essential for appreciating site-features and the form of settlements. Air photographs at 1 : 10,000, used in conjunction with the plans, add substantially to their value by revealing the relationship between moated sites and, for instance, the ground pattern of medieval ridge-and-furrow. They have also been used to find hitherto unknown sites. The 25-inch plans are important because their archaeology is being revised, at least in the most populous of the six regions recognized by the Ordnance Survey for archaeological purposes. These revisions are likely to correct the mistaken uses of "Moat" for the tumbled earth-works of an entire deserted village (which nevertheless often had a moated settlement), or for a system of medieval fishponds.[5]

Map sources earlier than the Ordnance Survey should not be neglected. Many moated sites appear on estate, Enclosure and Tithe plans, as well as on the large-scale county maps published by private cartographers. Their value is increased because the filling in of moats was widespread as "new farming" became established during the nineteenth century. The relative worth of different kinds of map evidence is illustrated by a study of some 160 square miles centred on the Blackwater estuary in Essex, including the whole of the Dengie peninsula,[6] where it is possible to identify with certainty a total of 39 moated settlements. Of these only 21 are marked as "Moats" on the Ordnance Survey maps and plans; the remainder are simply shown, without the distinctive "Moat" and in varying degrees of completeness, on the six-inch, Tithe or estate plans.

Among the written sources, two are outstanding, although neither is complete on the national scale. Almost all the *Victoria County Histories* included "Homestead Moats" in their discussion of earthworks, with distribution maps; the best of them, for example, Cambridge, Huntingdon and Worcester, give descriptive lists of sites. Secondly, there are the nine county *Reports and Inventories* compiled under the Royal Commission on Historical and Ancient Monuments, where moated settlements are again listed and mapped.[7] It is thus possible to estimate the number of sites on record in the English counties. It can be nothing more than an estimated figure at present, because some of the *V.C.H.* tables were derived solely from Ordnance Survey maps, notably the early editions of 6-inch plans.

Table I

MOATED HOMESTEADS IN THE ENGLISH COUNTIES

(estimated numbers)

Essex	548*	Cheshire	55
Suffolk	505	Kent	52
Yorkshire	256	Berkshire	44
Lincoln	*205*	Oxford	40
Warwick	200	Middlesex	39
Cambridge	168	Nottingham	37
Hertford	148	Somerset	37
Bedford	*120*	Northampton	35
Worcester	111	Wiltshire	*30*
Stafford	108	Derby	25
Norfolk	*100*	Durham	14
Buckingham	96	Hampshire	*12*
Huntingdon	91*	Devon	11
Hereford	76*	Northumberland	10
Shropshire	72	West Dorset	8*
Lancashire	70	Rutland	7
Surrey	61	East Dorset	*5*
Leicester	58	Cumberland	*5*
Sussex	57	Westmorland	3*
Gloucester	55	Cornwall	0

Total 3,574

* *Inventories* of the Royal Commission on Historical Monuments. Italic numerals indicate conservative estimates, based on the *Victoria County Histories*; otherwise, totals are from the *V.C.H.* lists of Class F Earthworks, "Simple Moated Enclosures". See also references 4 and 9

441

A complete distribution map of the English sites is being prepared by the author at a scale of 1:625,000, but as a preliminary measure the county totals are mapped in Fig. 1. Moated settlements are thickest on the ground in the eastern counties, especially Essex (15·4 per cent of this total) and Suffolk (14·2 per cent), but they are widespread in the Midlands, Lancashire and Yorkshire; they are fewer in the far north, in the southern counties and the West Country. High densities have also been expressed by saying that "nearly every parish contains a site of a moated homestead. In eastern England there may be several within one parish."[8] Taking the number of ecclesiastical parishes and

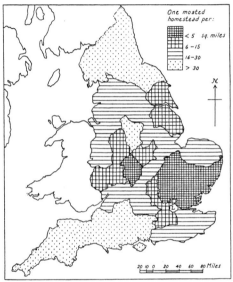

Fig. 1.—The distribution of moated homesteads in the English counties. Yorkshire is divided into its Ridings and Lincolnshire into its Parts; Lancashire North-of-the-Sands is grouped with the Cumbrian counties.

parochial chapelries in each county in 1831 (since they ante-date most of the legislation that changed the parish geography of England, and accordingly are a closer reflection of the density of land settlement in earlier times), we find the average equation of one moated site to one parish in the three counties, Essex, Hertfordshire and Lancashire; and one to every two parishes in Suffolk, Bedfordshire, Huntingdonshire and Cambridgeshire, and again in Worcestershire, Warwickshire and Cheshire. More important, there is also a marked degree of localization within counties. In Lincolnshire, numbers of sites increase in the Marshlands, along the eastern fringes of the limestone Edge, and on the clays between Ancholme and the river Witham. In Hertfordshire, they are most abundant in the eastern part of the county, in Lancashire on the plain enclosed by Preston, Widnes and Manchester. Warwickshire is divided into four hundreds not greatly dissimilar in area, but moated homesteads are distributed very unequally between them:[9]

Hemlingford Hundred, 116 (58 per cent of the county total of 200)
Darlichway Hundred, 40 (20 per cent)
Knightlow Hundred, 35 (17·5 per cent)
Kineton Hundred 9 (4·5 per cent).

Likewise in Yorkshire, where the East Riding has 114 moated homesteads, the West Riding 90, and the North Riding 52, these figures represent an average of one site per 9·6, 30·1 and 40·9 square miles respectively. Even so, it is not enough to say that such sites are abundant "especially in lowland areas and in clayey country".[10] There are striking local densities in high, dissected regions, as along the Welsh border or the Pennine margins. Moreover, why is it that only certain lowland, clayey countrysides had moated settlements whereas other, similar tracts, such as the West Country vales, appear to have supported so few?

There may be differences of distribution, also, in the various forms of moated homestead. Sites vary in plan and area. Besides the usual square or rectangular moats, there are oval, circular, triangular, pentagonal and irregular forms, as well as "double" forms, where a smaller moat appears within a large enclosure. Common sizes are the moats with sides 250 feet by 200 feet long (enclosing just over one acre), or 200 feet by 150 feet. Such dimensions occur frequently in Huntingdonshire, for instance, where the extremes range from great enclosures measuring 1200 feet by 750 feet to small circular moats having a diameter of only 70 feet, which probably protected windmills. Then the assertion that "most of these moated sites are now deserted" is true of some regions but not of others. In the Blackwater area of Essex, referred to earlier, only 1 of the 39 moats no longer has a house within or immediately adjacent to the enclosure; 24 are "Halls" standing on their own, only 1 being situated in a village. Here, also, their siting can be classified in relation to local terrain, for in this rather difficult habitat the best sites had to combine or reconcile two opposed conditions. First, they needed to avoid the unhealthy, water-logged lower levels of marsh and clayland. Thus the moated homesteads have a median height of 65 feet above sea level, occupying dry-point sites on valley-sides (17), spurs (12), and on terrace gravels within valleys (10). Their second need was a reliable supply of domestic water, which was restricted, certainly in recent times, by a low rainfall and the indifferent value of London Clay as an aquifer. Patches of glacial drift on the Clay, however, throw out springs at their margins, and yield limited supplies from shallow wells. Fifteen moats lie at this junction of clay and drift, while 8 are sited centrally on drift. Only 12 had a spring or well close at hand, and the majority clearly relied on their moats, whether stagnant or not, for both water supply and drainage. In "lowland" Suffolk,

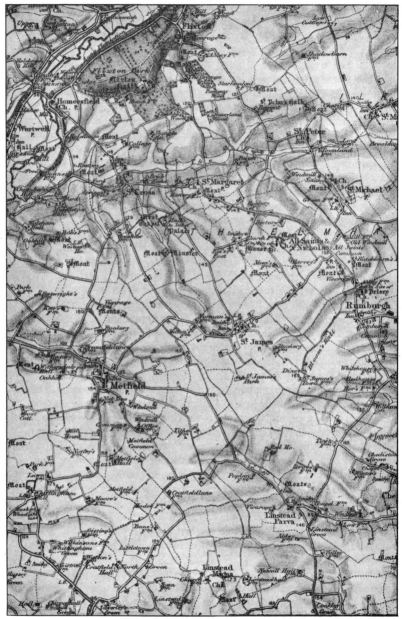

Plate I.—Part of the Lowestoft sheet (no. 176) of the Ordnance Survey One-inch map, "New Series", revised edition 1899. It covers about 30 square miles and 22 "Moats" are named.

(*Reproduced from the Ordnance Survey map of* 1899.)

Plate II.—Crows Hall, near Debenham, East Suffolk (G.R. 193628), viewed from the northwest. A square moat, with sides 300 feet long, surrounds the house; farm buildings have been built outside it.

(Photograph by J. K. St. Joseph. Crown Copyright reserved.)

of land settlement in any locality where they occur, as should the recognition of different forms of moated homestead. Secondly, there is the geographical distribution of such settlements. A proper understanding of their incidence will demand the reconstruction of all their "topographical facts", together with the structure and density of population in their period. As might be expected on geographical grounds, there is scope for comparative study between moated settlements in England and those in other European countries. For example, in Belgian Flanders the 1:50,000 maps reveal them in great abundance between Ypres and Dixmude, and spreading westwards into the polders. One tract of 8 square miles north of Ypres had 30 moated farms, although not all of them survived the holocaust of trench warfare between 1914 and 1918.[23] Many English farms, in fact, have lost their moats. The construction of large new buildings, in the course of replanning farms during the last century, has led to the infilling of moats wherever they became inconvenient. Now there is also the obscuring effect of housing and industrial developments, as they spread outwards from conurbations, cities and towns. In Warwickshire alone at least 15 moated sites were thus engulfed in recent years. They were not always completely obliterated: at Perry Hall, Handsworth, the moat survives as a children's paddling pool in the public park, while its island has become a bowling green. The threat of disappearance is sufficiently real, however, to prompt a recording of the fullest possible distribution of moated settlements, and a detailed assessment of vulnerable sites.

REFERENCES

[1] *Field Archaeology* (Ordnance Survey, Professional Papers, no. 13), H.M.S.O., 1959, p. 53.
[2] D. F. Renn, "Mottes: a classification", *Antiquity*, vol. xxxiii, 1959, pp. 106–12, with a distribution map of motte-and-bailey earthworks in England and Wales. For the distinction between simple and complex moated enclosures, see *The Victoria County History of Leicestershire*, vol. 1, London, 1907, p. 243. There are moated churches (*V.C.H. Suffolk*, vol. 1, 1911, gives three examples), and moated villages (*V.C.H. Kent*, vol. 1, 1908, records six).
[3] For another illustration see M. W. Beresford and J. K. St. Joseph, *Medieval England: an Aerial Survey*, Cambridge, 1958, fig. 18, p. 55; for examples of different kinds of moated sites, see figs. 19, 20 and 87. The excavations at Harlington and Scredington are reported in *Medieval Archaeology*, vol. iii, 1959, pp. 314–15, and vol. iv, 1960, pp. 153–4. From time to time, the larger sort of moated settlement is well illustrated in *Country Life*; e.g., 22nd October, 1959, pp. 596–600, Salisbury Hall, Shenley, Hertfordshire, pp. 654–6, Old Surrey Hall, Dormansland, Surrey.
[4] M. W. Barley, *Lincolnshire and the Fens*, 1952, London, p. 73. Illustrations of moated monastic settlements may be found in D. Knowles and J. K. St. Joseph, *Monastic Sites from the Air*, Cambridge, 1952, e.g. plate 63, p. 141 (Stanley, Wilts.), plate 105, p. 229 (Michelham, Sussex). Mr. Barley's "one hundred and twenty or more moated sites in Lincolnshire and the Fens" (*op. cit.*, p. 79) is well wide of the mark. In their first edition (1885–8), the Ordnance Survey 6-inch plans recognized with "Moats" no fewer than 139 moated homesteads and granges in the Parts of Lindsey alone. The Parts of Kesteven and Holland, comprising the rest of Lincolnshire, had 42 and 24 sites respectively, giving a county total of 205.
[5] Some of the new surveying and re-interpretation has already been used, e.g., W. G. Hoskins, "Seven deserted village sites in Leicestershire", *Trans. Leics. Arch. and Hist. Soc.*, vol. xxxii, 1956, pp. 36–51.
[6] I am indebted to Miss Paula J. Cook, St. Hugh's College, Oxford, for access to her unpublished study of this area, entitled "Moated settlements in the Blackwater region".
[7] The county *Inventories* are Hertford (1910), Buckingham (2 vols., 1912–13), Essex (4 vols., 1916–23), Huntingdon (1926), London (5 vols., 1924–30), Hereford (3 vols., 1931–4), Westmorland (1936), Middlesex (1937), West Dorset (1952).
[8] W. G. Hoskins, *Local History in England*, 1959, London, p. 112.

9 The Warwickshire total of 200 sites given in Table I, and their divisions between the hundreds, are taken from "The 'homestead' moats of Warwickshire", by Mrs. F. Lloyd Lewis (née Darby). This was a B.A. thesis submitted at the University College of South Wales and Monmouthshire, Cardiff, in 1958, and I am grateful to Mrs. Lloyd Lewis for her help, also to Mr. Leslie Alcock for bringing this work to my notice.

10 W. G. Hoskins, *op. cit.*, p. 112.

11 H. Allcroft, *Earthworks of England*, London, 1908, chap. 12, pp. 378–99, "Saxon and Danish Earthworks", chap. 14, pp. 453–93, "The Moated Homestead". Early papers include F. A. Paley, "Notes on some remains of moats and moated halls at Coton, etc.", *Cambridge Antiq. Soc. Papers (C.A.S.)*, vol. iii, 1873, pp. 287–94; R. T. Andrews, "Moats and moated sites in the parish of Reed", *Trans. East Herts. Arch. Soc.*, vol. ii, 1904, pp. 265–72; A. C. Yorke, "The round moat at Fowlmere", *C.A.S.*, vol. xii, 1908, pp. 114–19; J. G. N. Clift, "Leckhampton Moat", *Trans. Bristol and Glos. Arch. Soc.*, vol. iv, 1933, pp. 235–48.

12 Among recent studies are J. P. C. Kent, "Pancake Hall, Welham Green: excavation of homestead moat", *Trans. East Herts. Arch. Soc.*, vol. xiii, 1950–1, pp. 33–42; and M. W. Thompson, "Excavation of two moated sites at Cherry Holt near Grantham, and at Epperstone near Nottingham", *Lincs. Archit. and Arch. Soc., Reports and Papers*, vol. vi, 1952, pp. 72–82 (where it is thought they were used for watering stock and seasonal dairying when the cattle were on summer pastures). The brief examination of a West Midland site is described by P. A. Barker and J. A. Pagett, "Moated enclosure at Watling Street Grange, Oakengates: emergency excavations, 1958", *Trans. Shropshire Arch. Soc.*, vol. lvi, 1957–8, pp. 21–5. Summaries of recent or current excavations at sites in Essex, Hampshire, Kent, Middlesex, and Nottinghamshire are given by D. M. Wilson and J. G. Hurst, "Medieval Britain in 1956" (post-Conquest manors and moats), *Medieval Archaeology*, vol. i, 1957, p. 160 *et seq.*; vol. iii, 1959, pp. 314–18, including sites in Bedfordshire, Herefordshire, Shropshire, Leicestershire, Warwickshire, Worcestershire and Norfolk; vol. iv, 1960, pp. 153–6, with sites in Hertfordshire, Lincolnshire, and Staffordshire. See two other reports, M. W. Thompson, "Excavation of a medieval moat at Moat Hill, Anlaby, near Hull", *Yorks. Arch. Journ.*, vol. xxxix, 1956, pp. 67–85, and M. Biddle, L. Barfield, A. Millard, "The excavation of the manor of the More, Rickmansworth, Hertfordshire", *Arch. Journ.*, vol. cxvi, 1959, pp. 136–99. See also references 13, 19, 21, below.

13 G. J. Copley, *An Archaeology of Southeast England*, London, 1958, p. 173, cf. p. 184. See also T. C. Lethbridge and C. F. Tebbutt, "Preliminary investigations of an early medieval moated site at Manor Farm, Southoe, Hunts.", *C.A.S.* vol. xxxviii, 1936–7, p. 158; cf. notes on Flambard's Manor, Meldreth, *C.A.S.*, vol. xxxv, 1933–4, p. xxviii, and on "The Temple, Isleham", *C.A.S.*, vol. xxxviii, 1935–6, p. xiii; also F. G. Walker, "Report on the excavations at Barton Moats", *C.A.S.*, vol. xii, 1908, pp. 296–313, where construction of the moat was assigned to the period 800–1000, and A. R. Solley, "Moated site at Mundon", *Essex Review*, January 1947, p. 9.

14 See reviews by B. Hope-Taylor in *Antiquity*, vol. xxxv, 1960, pp. 227–30, and L. Alcock in *Medieval Archaeology*, vol. iii, 1959, pp. 332–4.

15 D. Justin Schove and A. W. G. Lowther, "Tree-rings and medieval archaeology", *Medieval Archaeology*, vol. i, 1957, pp. 78–95; thirteenth-century climate is discussed on pp. 84–8.

16 J. Titow, "Evidence of weather in the Account Rolls of the Bishopric of Winchester, 1209–1350", *Economic History Review*, vol. xii, 3rd April 1960, pp. 360–407.

17 Rupert Coles, "The past history of the Forest of Essex", *Essex Naturalist*, vol. xxiv, 1935, pp. 115–33. Fig. 1, p. 118, is a map of "Vegetational Regions", distinguishing four "degrees" of forest on the basis of soils and rainfall, and fig. 6, p. 130, "Extent of the Forest *c.* 1400 A.D." shows moated and unmoated medieval houses; the density of moated settlements on the northwestern "Forest Lands" of wet boulder clay is associated with active clearance, especially between 1225 and 1301.

18 E.g. at Scredington, Lincs. (M. W. Barley, *op. cit.*, p. 98); Wyboston, Keysoe, Harrowden, and Holme, in *V.C.H. Bedfords.*, vol. i, 1904, p. 308.

19 A. W. G. Lowther, "The Mounts, Pachesham: interim report on excavations", *Proc. Leatherhead and District Local History Soc.*, vol. i, 1947, pp. 6–11; 1948, pp. 5–10. Trial excavations were also made at the moated settlement of Effingham-la-Leigh, Surrey, showing a complex history from *c.* 1100–1300. Mr. Brian Hope-Taylor has investigated (for the Ministry of Works) the Preston Hawe site, at Burgh Heath near Banstead, Surrey: see Copley, *op. cit.*, pp. 184–5.

20 T. F. Tout, *The History of England*, vol. iii (from 1216 to 1377), Oxford, 1905, pp. 153–4, 173–4.

21 A. Williams, "A homestead moat at Nuthampstead, Herts.", *Antiquaries Journal*, vol. xxvi, 1946, pp. 138–46.

22 Personal communication to the writer, from Nursling, Southampton, dated 30th July, 1957.

23 Sheets 20 (Roulers) and 28 (Ypres) at 1 : 50,000, published 1939, last revision 1911; cf. the same sheets published in 1953 (Type R), Institut Géographique Militaire, Brussels, revised from air photographs and rapid field survey, 1952–3. Comparison of sheet 28 in each edition shows that since 1914–18 ten farms immediately west of St. Julien have lost their moats.

367, 369, 371, 373, 376, 420n, 421n, 424n, 425n, 426n, 427n, 428n, 430n, 432n, 434n; British Transport Commission Archives, 433; Census Enumerators' Books, 383, 389, 393, 414-15; Census of Population, 18, 273, 277, 361, 377, 381-414; Census of Distribution and other services (1951), 279, 285n; County Rate Books, 227-9, 287n; Customs Accounts, 76, 78, 198; diaries, 110; Domesday Book, 29-51, 55-9, 113, 449; Enclosure Award maps, 441; estate papers, 173-91, 420n, 422n, 423n, 424n, 426n, 427n, 430n, 433n, 435, 441; Factory Inspectors' Returns, 337-56; Guild Rolls, 105, 108, 110, 113; Hearth Tax, 207; Hop Excise (1807-61), 244-51, 263n; Hundred Rolls (1279), 55, 59-67; Land Tax Returns, 23n, 206-7, 227-30; Lay Subsidy, 64n, 71-81; Local Reports to the General Board of Health (c 1850), 338, 355n manorial records, 17, 23n, 113, 129, 137, 445; Ministry of Agriculture Survey of farm holdings (1942), 331; newspapers, 422n, 423n; Nonarum Inquisitiones, 85-100; Ordnance Survey Maps, 313, 318, 439-41, 444, 446, 448, 450n; Parish Registers, 23n, 141-2; Probate Inventories, 117-37; Property Tax (1799-1816), 227-8; Reports and Inventories of the Royal Commission on Historical and Ancient Monuments, 441, 450; Report of the Boroughs and Corporate Towns Commission (1837), 291-312; River Pollution Commissioners, First Report (1870), 338, 355n; *The Royal Commission ↑ on the Housing of the Working Classes* (1885) 321n; Schedule A of Income Tax (1842-3 and 1859-60), 227, 229-30; Stanway's survey of the cotton industry (1833), 338, 347, 350, 355n; Surveys and terriers, 119, 123-4, 126-7; Taxation of Pope Nicholas ,IV (1291), 85; Tithe awards, 255, 259, 317-18, 331, 435, 441; toll list, 78; topographies, 195-207, 275, 284n, 285n, 313, 255n, 381, 426n, 431n, 434n; trade directories, 18, 270, 272, 285, 287n, 389; tradesmen's account books, 103; Victoria County Histories, 441, 450n, 451n; *see also* Archaeological evidence; Place-name evidence; Problems of interpretation

Statistical methods, 18-19, 23n, 113; age-specific marital fertility rates, 147-51; association analysis, 23n, 286; correlation analysis, 250, 255, 265; crop combinations, 18, 118-37, 214-24; factor analysis, 18, 285; family reconstitution, 141-2, 145, 164, 169-70; frequency distribution analysis, 152-6, 158; mean, median and modal ages of first marriage, 145-7; non-parametric, 19; numerical taxonomy, 18, 24n, 415n; principal component analysis, 285; regression analysis, 18, 19, 251, 255, 256, 265; sampling, 383-4, 389, 414; simulation, 24n, 285; significance tests, 18, 150, 152, 157; town ranking, 285-6; variance analysis, 18, 150

Systems theory, 19, 285

Theoretical analysis, 13, 14, 19-22, 25n, 170, 185, 260-2, 265, 285-6, 332, 377-8, 414; *see also* Models
Trade, 65, 182, 183-8, 196-204, 258, 261, 296, 297, 307, 310, 335-7
Transport, 105, 109-10, 183, 185, 185n, 199-207, 238, 253, 254, 258, 274, 278-9, 281, 282, 295, 296, 297, 299, 305, 307-8, 310, 322, 342, 345, 370, 430, 431, 433, 434;↑

Urban administration, 291-312; administrative functions, 110, 271, 272-5, 277, 279, 281, 286, 294; central business districts, 302, 332, 389-90; centrality, 277-81, 283, 284, 285-6, 287n; commercial functions, 270, 272-4, 276, 278, 279, 281-6, 302, 305, 310; competition, 277-9, 281, 282; ecclesiastical functions, 276, 305; educational functions, 270, 272, 275, 277, 307; functional index, 286; growth, 269, 277, 278-80, 282, 283, 291-311, 313, 322, 332-3, 419; hierarchy, 113, 269-84; 'improvement', 292-3, 299, 301, 302, 305,

307, 308, 309, 311, 312; industrial functions, 65n, 103, 188, 272-3, 277, 279, 282, 283, 296-7, 301, 305-6, 310-11, 318, 319n, 340-54; market functions, 103-12, 272-84, 291, 301, 305, 307, 310, 311; military functions, 274, 276, 277, 282, 294-5, 304; morphology, 292, 294-312, 317-33, 381-414; labour supply, 346, 361-2, 365, 367, 369; occupational structure, 350, 385, 388-92, 404-14; origins, 274-5, 276, 281, 297; population zones, 404-14; port functions, 296-7, 301, 307-8, 310, 391-2; ranking schemes, 269-84, 286-7; regions, *see* Regions, urban; rents, 317, 322n, 326; resort functions, 282, 283-4, 299, 301; spheres of influence, 25n, 103-13, 303-4, 269-70, 271, 273, 274, 276, 279-80,

282, 283, 287n, 291, 368, 370; *see also* Boroughs

Villages, deserted, 50-1, 87, 440, 450n, industrial, 118, 311, 367, 369; mining, 283, 310-11; as nuclei of suburbs, 317, 318, 324, 327, 391-2; shrunken, 91-2, 95

Wages, *see* Agricultural wages; industrial wages

Waste, 35-6, 47, 50, 59, 61, 65, 86, 88, 94, 293

Wealth, distribution of lay, 24n, 71-81

Wood, for agricultural use, 46, 253; for building, 36, 46, 47; for fuel, 29, 36, 46, 182, 183, 184

Woodland, clearance, 29, 35, 40, 47, 58, 59, 448; distribution of, 29-51, 419; for pannage, 31, 35, 42, 43, 50; *see also* Forest